Congress vs. the Bureaucracy

A recipient of

The Julian J. Rothbaum Prize

whose sponsor advocated
the highest standards of scholarship
in all disciplines

CONGRESS VS. THE BUREAUCRACY
Muzzling Agency Public Relations

MORDECAI LEE

UNIVERSITY OF OKLAHOMA PRESS : NORMAN

Also by Mordecai Lee

The First Presidential Communications Agency: FDR's Office of Government Reports (Albany, N.Y., 2005)

Institutionalizing Congress and the Presidency: The U.S. Bureau of Efficiency, 1916–1933 (College Station, Texas, 2006)

Bureaus of Efficiency: Reforming Local Government in the Progressive Era (Milwaukee, 2008)

Nixon's Super-Secretaries: The Last Grand Presidential Reorganization Effort (College Station, Texas, 2010)

Library of Congress Cataloging-in-Publication Data

Lee, Mordecai, 1948–
    Congress vs. the bureaucracy : muzzling agency public relations / Mordecai Lee.
      p. cm.
    Includes bibliographical references and index.
    ISBN 978-0-8061-4203-6 (hardcover : alk. paper)
    1. Legislative oversight—United States—History. 2. Executive-legislative relations—United States—History. 3. Government publicity—United States—History. I. Title.
    JK585.L42 2011
    328.73'07452—dc22

                                                                    2011003720

1 2 3 4 5 6 7 8 9 10

For Armon and Barbara Kamesar and Bernard and Jean Levy, my uncles and aunts. At important times in my life, they were my de facto parents and true guardian angels. I owe them much.

So the real issue became whether bureaucracy was more powerful than the representatives of the people, whether they could compel the Congress, through pressure and propaganda, to appropriate unnecessary funds, or whether the representatives of the people themselves should judge as to how the public's money was to be spent.

—Congressman Clarence Brown (R-Ohio), March 30, 1950, at a public hearing on "The Role of Lobbying in Representative Self-Government." U.S. House, Select Committee on Lobbying Activities, 81st Congress, 2nd session, 149.

CONTENTS

TABLES

Preface and Acknowledgments

In life, one does not get many, if any, chances for a do-over. As a doctoral candidate at Syracuse University, I had submitted a dissertation proposal in 1972 that entailed a comprehensive history of congressional efforts to control the public relations in the executive branch. Like many students at that stage of their education, my eyes were bigger than my stomach. Once I started the field research as a Guest Scholar at the Brookings Institution in Washington, D.C., I gradually realized that the topic was too sprawling. I was overwhelmed. After a few painful reality checks and several stops and starts, in desperation I turned to my dissertation supervisor, Dwight Waldo, for help. His advice was empathetic and pragmatic: I should do what most dissertation writers eventually do at that stage—scale back and *just finish.* Expediency and pragmatism trumped ambition and overreach. A magnum opus would have to wait. It was the best advice I ever got.

By then, I was a legislative assistant to Milwaukee congressman Henry Reuss. In June 1975, when Congress adjourned for the summer (hard to conceive in current times), he granted me a leave of absence for two months, cutting my salary to a de minimis level, just enough to maintain my status as a congressional employee and retain my eligibility for health insurance. Reuss was about to go home and spend the summer back in

Wisconsin. He knew that things would be slow on the Hill for the duration and was delighted to save money in his staff salary account. We agreed that I would be permitted to work on my dissertation at my desk in his office suite. For me, the advantages were obvious, including the latest IBM Selectric typewriter, access to unlimited copying, and proximity to the Library of Congress. For him, it meant I was available to handle any sensitive and important matters that might come up. Indeed, that happened a few times over the summer.

By now *obsessed* with finishing (another widely shared experience of dissertation writers), I threw myself into it. I remember even going to work at the Rayburn House Office Building on the Fourth of July, 1975. Based on the sign-in and sign-out sheet, I was, literally, the only (non-security) person working in the building that day. The Capitol Police seemed startled when I walked in the front door. That was also the only day I ever was able to park in the "horseshoe" driveway on the east side of the building—absolutely the best parking spot in the House. Still working at sunset, I could hear the fireworks crackling away while I feverishly tried to get this millstone off my neck. It was a memorable day, emblematic of the dissertation experience. Following Professor Waldo's advice, my dissertation ended up exploring only one congressional effort to limit public relations—cuts in the publicity budgets of the military during the 1960s and early '70s.

Thirty-five years later, this book is my do-over, the dissertation I had wanted to write but was not capable of at that stage of my career. I am extremely thankful that life presented me with this second chance. I would like to think that during the intervening time I gained in perspective and insight so that the final result is better than anything my earlier failed foray could ever have been.

What intrigued me then as now is that for over a century Congress has struggled to come to terms with the rise of the bureaucratic state. In large part, that struggle has been an attempt to protect its own centrality and prevent the bureaucracy from dominating, even marginalizing, the role of the legislative branch. One of the central thrusts of this power struggle has been Congress's effort to muffle the bureaucracy by limiting its public voice, whether that voice is aimed toward the media, the public at large, or Congress itself. An assistant attorney general in 1977 tried to capture the consistent premise of several different congressional enactments related to external communication:

> Since the turn of the [twentieth] century Congress has attempted in various ways to control perceived excesses that have arisen as the Executive branch has evolved. No longer merely providing necessary support for the Presidency, the Executive branch has become a force in its own right, achieving the status of an independent institutional bureaucracy. The . . . laws are merely variations on this simpler theme, particular examples of a continuing effort by Congress to check the expanding activities of the federal bureaucracy not directly related to any statutory program or mission (Memorandum to Robert J. Lipshutz, Counsel to the President, from John M. Harmon, Assistant Attorney General, Re: Statutory Restraints on Lobbying Activity by Federal Officials, November 29, 1977, 2).

This inquiry seeks to bring together, for the first time, a comprehensive history and analysis of congressional efforts to curb the voice of the federal bureaucracy.

In an earlier book, *The First Presidential Communications Agency,* I explored one of the most prominent (and unsuccessful) examples of government public relations. In 1939, President Franklin Roosevelt had created and then fended off threats to the existence of the Office of Government Reports (OGR), an agency he had placed in the Executive Office of the President. However, congressional hostility (motivated by a mix of partisan, ideological, and institutional concerns) overwhelmed him in the spring of 1942, and he was compelled to "hide" the OGR for the duration of World War II in the Office of War Information. When President Truman tried to revive the OGR after the war, as Roosevelt had planned to do, the Republican 80th Congress refused to appropriate funding for it. The OGR closed its doors in 1948.

At the conclusion of that story, I analyzed the causes of the ferocity of the fight over the OGR. It seemed that its fate epitomized a larger topic, of Congress seeking to adapt to the rise of the administrative state in the twentieth century with an institutional desire to control the emerging bureaucracy. The tale of the OGR represented a specific legislative effort to deny the president an institutional (as opposed to personal) voice, the capability of communicating directly with the public. But what happens between presidents and Congress can sometimes obscure the more prosaic power struggle that Congress may have with garden-variety executive branch departments and agencies, where so much of federal business is conducted. This inquiry seeks to complement my previous work about the presidential OGR by focusing on Congress versus public relations in public administration.

From my "real world" political experiences as a legislative assistant on Capitol Hill in Washington and then as a state senator in Wisconsin, as well as from my academic work, I was familiar with the wide gamut of legislative techniques intended to assert power over the bureaucracy. I was seeking a more nuanced perspective that might create a larger picture from some of the case studies I had already explored, as well as other instances that I vaguely knew existed. But I was having trouble defining precisely *what* the subject was.

Professors like to claim—often to very skeptical listeners—that we work all the time, even when it does not look like it. The specific idea for this book's central theme occurred to me late one lazy summer evening, when I was watching TV. While waiting for the ten o'clock news, I was idly watching, for the umpteenth time, a rerun of the 1999 movie *Austin Powers: The Spy Who Shagged Me*. One scene spoofed the typical and irresolvable argument between a parent and a teenager, in this case Dr. Evil and his equally evil son, Scott:

Dr. Evil: What do you think, Scott?
Scott (sarcastically): Yeah, Codename: Thompson Twins was really impressive.
Dr. Evil: Shhhh!
Scott: I'm nineteen, I don't—
Dr. Evil (interrupting): Shh! Shh-Shh. Shh-Shhhhh-Shh. Shh-shh! It's Morse code. (Reading imaginary paper) Let me decipher . . . it says "shhhhh!"
Scott: You are so lame.
Dr. Evil (like Electric Company): Sssssss . . . huuuuuh . . . Shhhhh!

Even though I had already seen that exchange many times before, I laughed out loud all over again about the eternal power struggle between parents and children. By silencing his son regardless of the merits of the situation, Dr. Evil was seeking the upper hand, the power position. Hey, wait a minute, I thought. That is similar to what happens between Congress and the bureaucracy. I was off to the races. The working title and theme of my project became "Shushing the Bureaucracy." My thanks to Mike Myers, academic muse.

The research question that emerged from "working" that night was, How consistent and persistent have been congressional initiatives to mute the bureaucracy? Was there a systematic pattern of authoritative legislative behavior in denying agencies use of public relations to make their case to the public at large? If so, then could one reasonably identify an underlying rationale and theme for these related actions? If one views authoritative congressional decisions as reflecting a majority consensus within an institution, what was that picture? Had Congress realized that a silenced bureaucracy, unable to appeal for external support, would be less autonomous and more easily dominated by legislators? And, ultimately, did it *work*? Answering those questions is the goal of this inquiry.

As all researchers know, our success is almost always due to the help of information professionals. That is particularly the case for historians and especially so for those interested in government history. The maze of published and unpublished congressional documents is difficult to traverse, let alone find the way to one's destination. I am indebted to so many librarians and archivists who guided me that I regret I cannot name them all individually. Instead, to give credit where credit is due, I thank them by their institutional affiliations. Sources of assistance in my home state included the government documents and interlibrary loan departments of the University of Wisconsin–Milwaukee's Golda Meir Library, Milwaukee Public Library's downtown central branch, Marquette University's Raynor Library and Law Library, the University of Wisconsin–Madison's Memorial Library and Law Library, and the Wisconsin Historical Society library and archives. At the library of Waukesha North High School, I was able to access several newspapers on the ProQuest historical newspapers database that my home institution did not subscribe to. I received some startled glances from the high school students sitting on either side of me in the long row of PC stations. They must have been wondering, who *is* that old guy?

In the capital, I was greatly helped by the U.S. Senate Library, Center for Legislative Archives (maintained for Congress by the National Archives— an executive branch agency), Library of Congress Research Room, Smithsonian Institution Archives, Document Distribution Center of the Government Accountability Office, Office of Legal Counsel of the Department of Justice, the Washingtoniana collection at the Martin Luther King Jr. Memorial Library of the District of Columbia Public Library, and the inspector general of the Defense Department. Other very helpful sources outside Washington included the Idaho Historical Society, the University of Idaho library, the University of Southern California library, and the National Archives' presidential libraries of Franklin Roosevelt and Richard Nixon. Three elected officials who had been colleagues of mine in the Wisconsin State Legislature provided indispensable assistance. My congressman, F. James Sensenbrenner, obtained reports from the Congressional Research Service and copies of several bills; Milwaukee mayor (and former congressman) Tom Barrett helped interpret some confusing congressional documents and actions; and U.S. Senator Russ Feingold helped procure the cooperation of the State Department's Office of the Historian. The website *Biographical Directory of the United State Congress, 1774 to Present* was an essential source of biographical information about the many legislators mentioned in this study; unless I note otherwise, all background information on U.S. senators and representatives came from this source.

Andrea Zweifel, my program associate, proved again her incredible proofreading knack by repeatedly catching typographical errors that had eluded me. A salute to Library of Congress scholar Kevin Kosar, who helped refine my thinking and cheered me on, especially during the last laps of a marathon that is called book writing. With the subtitle of his own excellent article he captured the subject matter with what I think is absolutely the most concise and descriptive phrase: "The Limits of Legal Restrictions." I had to go with second-best. Finally, special thanks to Jay R. Dew, acquisitions editor of University of Oklahoma Press, who believed in this project. Through constant encouragement and support he made this book possible despite a pair of back-to-back, one-in-a-million publishing obstacles caused by outside readers. He was the kind of editor that authors dream of.

Whatever mistakes managed to make it through to publication despite the help of so many people are my responsibility alone.

CONGRESS VS. THE BUREAUCRACY

INTRODUCTION

In 1905, Congress reacted negatively to the news that the Panama Canal Commission had hired a full-time press agent. It was on the verge of enacting legislation to ban the Commission from doing so when President Theodore Roosevelt beat a hasty tactical retreat. When he promised the congressional leadership that the Commission would not do that, the issue became moot and no appropriation rider or other legal prohibition was necessary.[1] Exactly a century later, in 2005, during the presidency of George W. Bush, Congress was *still* reacting negatively to agency public relations activities and *still* trying to define what was acceptable and what not. That year Congress included in an appropriation bill a ban on federal agencies using video news releases "unless the story includes a clear notification within the text or audio of the prepackaged news story that the prepackaged news story was prepared or funded by that executive branch agency."[2] Agencies were free to continue to distribute such video releases, as long as the sourcing was clear.

These two events are separated by one hundred years of enormous change in U.S. society, economy, technology, government, public administration, and politics. Yet they are nearly identical. The similarity of the two events captures both the consistent direction of the congressional reaction to agency publicity as well as the difficulty of limiting it. In both cases, Congress was reacting authoritatively to the practice of public relations by federal departments and agencies, expressing a disagreement with particular external communications activities by the bureaucracy, and indicating a preference for a more silent executive branch. So, after a century of legislating restrictions on agency publicity, the "problem" from Capitol Hill's perspective had *still* not been fixed definitively, and additional legislation continued to be enacted. This inquiry seeks to document the historical arc of congressional efforts in the twentieth century to control the public relations activities of federal agencies and the effect—or lack of—resulting from those efforts.

The theme of the book is that when Congress has tried to exert its statutory and financial powers to threaten bureaucratic autonomy by limiting agency public relations, the bureaucracy has almost always succeeded in negating Congress's will and protecting its ability to communicate externally. After recounting the historical evidence for such a conclusion, I argue that this is not necessarily a threat to democracy. Members of Congress are generally oriented to short-term rewards of reelection and election to higher office. On the other hand, the bureaucracy can be seen as a countervailing institution that focuses on long-term goals of survival, balance, and growth. Congressional efforts to choke off the bureaucracy's public voice could threaten any agency's ability to survive. Public administration's apparent ability to veto this element of legislative power contributes to stasis and balance in the relationship between Congress and the bureaucracy. More generally, the bureaucratic veto over congressional efforts to control public relations is an element in the overall balance and viability of the federal system of governance in the modern era.

ANALYTICAL FRAMEWORK OF THE STUDY

Autonomy as a Bureaucratic Goal

In 1950, Emmerich wrote about the built-in desire of government bureaucracies for autonomy. That same year, Simon, Smithburg, and Thompson described government agencies as engaging in an ongoing "struggle for existence." At the end of that decade, Fenno observed this struggle in the context of the structure and operations of cabinet departments. More than half a century later, in 2008, Roberts noted the continuing vitality of the bureaucratic imperative for autonomy in the U.S. federal government.[3]

In his pioneering study of the origins of the U.S. administrative state between 1862 and 1928, Carpenter documented a theory of political development that focused on federal agencies as potential independent actors in the political system. Some emerged to become strong and independent bureaus, others not. Carpenter theorized, based on historical documentation, that the central dynamic occurring at the time was of a bureaucratic desire for autonomy. Rather than being buffeted by the dictates of Congress (and to a lesser extent, in those days, by presidents), federal agencies could direct their own destinies by autonomizing. Autonomy meant the ability to survive, grow, and guide the policymaking process (i.e., by Congress), dominate its niche, and determine its own agenda and programs. In Carpenter's historical interpretation, the autonomy imperative provides a theory that explains the different fates of federal agencies in the late nineteenth and early twentieth centuries. Carpenter identified the components that contribute to becoming an autonomous agency: "When agencies—by virtue of their recognized legitimacy in a policy area, by virtue of their superior ties to voters or their superior publicity, by virtue of their established reputations for impartiality or pursuit of the national good—can make it politically costly to oppose or restrain their innovations or deny them leeway, they have achieved a form of autonomy."[4]

Hence, Carpenter identified five levers of power that contribute to agency autonomy: (1) developing legitimacy, (2) ties to voters, (3) publicity, (4) reputation for impartiality, and (5) reputation for pursuit of the public interest. If an agency attained such autonomy, it largely freed itself from congressional control that it disagreed with. For example, despite the strenuous opposition of House Speaker Joe Cannon, "arguably the nation's most powerful politician," in 1905 Congress passed a major grant of power to the U.S. Forest Service and its head, Gifford Pinchot. The Forest Service had achieved that powerful position by autonomistic behavior and policies. This made Congress a virtual bystander in the legislative process. According to Carpenter, "Congress could do little but stand by and watch."[5] To maintain its power over executive branch agencies some power centers in Congress could try to thwart bureaucratic autonomy by preventing agencies from pursuing the five pathways to autonomy. This would create an action-reaction dynamic between federal agencies and their opponents in Congress—with the former seeking autonomy, the latter *institutionally* desiring to prevent it.

Carpenter's theory of bureaucratic autonomy was built partially on Arnold's preceding theory of congressional action. Arnold posited that public opinion is a key factor for a legislator. For issues lacking a significant and salient public opinion, a politician is largely a free agent; there are no major negative consequences when he or she faces the voters the next time. Conversely, when citizen preferences appear to be discernable, based on electoral calculations, a legislator feels obligated to vote in harmony with public opinion. Such citizen preferences can be developed by effective coalitions "from both inside and outside Congress."[6] Well-organized coalitions can effectively narrow the range of options available to a pragmatic and reelection-seeking politician. Refining Arnold's theory on the basis of his own detailed review of case studies for four federal agencies, Carpenter suggested that "bureaucrats have incentives to take coalition-building strategies *directly* to the electorate."[7] Going back to the example of Forest Service legislation in 1905, Pinchot's successful publicity activities and his initiatives at coalition building created a political environment that forced Congress to approve legislation, Speaker Cannon and allies notwithstanding. Pinchot's autonomizing efforts had worked.

Carpenter's and Arnold's theories identify successful agency public relations as one of the key factors in determining whether the legislature or the bureaucracy holds the dominant power position. The purpose of this study is to examine in depth this historical action-reaction relationship between the federal bureaucracy and Congress over agency publicity and the attendant public support it can generate. The central focus is on congressional reactions triggered by agency public relations activities in the twentieth century as an example of what Schick called congressional intervention in the "details" of administration.[8] I examine congressional-agency battles over public relations in depth. Carpenter's and Arnold's approaches are historical examinations of a handful of agencies over a limited time period. My approach broadens the perspective to the entire federal executive branch and over a longer historical era, but with a focus limited to agency public relations. The goal is to present a textured picture of agencies making use of a developing form of public relations expertise to autonomize and of members of Congress trying to learn how to manage that phenomenon.

Agency Public Relations as Autonomistic

In seeking common themes within the case studies of federal agencies that had become autonomous, Carpenter noted the frequency with which successful external communications were associated with those bureaucracies. Referring to several bureaus of the U.S. Department of Agriculture (USDA) and to the Post Office Department, he observed that "perhaps the most important venue of bureaucratic reputation lay in the rapidly expanding media. . . . both agencies were treated with favor by urban and rural presses."[9]

In his 1922 trailblazing study of public opinion, thus at about the midpoint of Carpenter's focus, Lippmann had identified the power of the "press agent" or "publicity man" to organizations (whether public, private, or nonprofit) in the United States at that time: "Were reporting the simple recovery of obvious facts, the press agent would be little more than a clerk. But since, in respect to most of the big topics of news, the facts are not simple, and not at all obvious, but subject to choice and opinion, it is natural that everyone should wish to make his own choice of the facts for the newspapers to print. The publicity man does that."[10]

This new profession influenced reporting, which in turn influenced public opinion—a source that politicians were acutely tuned into. In the conclusion of his book, Carpenter observed that the importance of publicity to autonomizing agencies has been noted in the academic political science literature as early as 1934. He highlighted an observation of E. Pendleton Herring that "a bureau . . . can coerce the legislators through its powers of propaganda. The procurement of apparent popular support through skillfully conducted publicity may so fortify its position that Congress would hesitate to abolish the bureau or reduce its appropriation."[11]

Herring's early insight about bureaucratic autonomy at the beginning of the New Deal provided independent support from a leading academic theoretician of Carpenter's identification of the importance of public relations. Although not cited further by Carpenter, Herring went on to develop this theme over the next few years. In 1935, he concluded that "skillful and effective use of publicity is one of the essential devices of successful administration," and one effect of agency public relations is to "create opinion which it uses to secure increased appropriations from Congress, a larger staff, or more authority." When an agency is successful at creating a supportive public opinion, Congress is "left sputtering and protesting in the dust."[12] Here Herring was also presciently confirming one element of Arnold's later theory of congressional action, namely, that public opinion limits Congress's freedom of action. The next year, while continuing his endorsement of the legitimacy and potential impacts of agency public relations, Herring also called on politicians on Capitol Hill, who were being circumscribed when public opinion supported administrative agencies, to "be an active opposition" to those publicity activities, if only in congressional counter-publicity efforts.[13]

Subsequent to Herring (and preceding Carpenter and Arnold), public administration literature explored in more detail the *purposes* of agency public relations and the potential *effects* of such activities on Congress. Purposes and effects are virtually impossible to untwine in public communications. For example, a noncontroversial public relations program intended to increase the public's care in the use of campfires can increase public support for the Forest Service, hence contributing to that agency's autonomy. Writing only a few years after Herring, McCamy in his landmark study of federal agency publicity identified several overlapping goals (i.e., purposes *and* effects) of bureaucratic public relations.[14] A typology of the techniques of government publicity described by McCamy could be categorized into three rubrics:

> *Pragmatic:* external communications activities that are directly related to accomplishing the core mission of the agency by facilitating the delivery of public sector goods and services.
> *Democratic:* communication techniques that contribute to the functioning of democracy.
> *Autonomic:* using Carpenter's nomenclature, public relations activities that have the purpose or effect of increasing agency autonomy.[15]

The first cluster of uses of public relations in public administration, based on McCamy's writings, covers those that are pragmatic in the sense of helping an agency accomplish its core missions and goals. For example, an agency could use publicity techniques to reach those members of the public at large who might qualify for the services of the agency or for a new agency program. This would have the effect of increasing the utilization of the goods and services that the agency is seeking to deliver. Also, for some agencies, the dissemination of information is central to their raison d'être. For example, some USDA programs are premised on providing the latest information on agricultural techniques to farmers as a way of increasing their productivity and incomes. Other pragmatic external communications activities include notifying the public of new laws and regulations (if you commit a gun crime, you'll get an additional penalty), public service campaigns to promote safe behavior (buckle up), promoting voluntary compliance to reduce regulatory and enforcement costs (we thought you'd like to know), and encouraging citizens to serve as the eyes and ears of the agency (such as 911 and hotline programs). The common theme of these different pragmatic external relations activities is that they all "do" something—all are oriented to the efficient delivery of goods and services.

Second, several of the purposes of agency publicity that McCamy identified can be justified by the democratic context of public administration. For example, the constitutional protections for the press in the First Amendment are premised on the press functioning as an instrument of democracy. Through a press that is totally free of government, citizens learn about the activities of elected officials and of the government as a whole. This permits the development of an informed public, the sine qua non of democracy. In this way, government and elected officials can be held accountable. Therefore, executive branch agencies should be responsive to requests for information from reporters, such as by appointing a trained public information officer to be a one-stop contact point for journalists. However, media coverage tends to be episodic, "like the beam of a search-light that moves restlessly about."[16] So along with cooperating with the press in order to support democracy, agencies also have a generalized duty to report to the public on a more systematic basis about their activities and record. At the time of McCamy's writings, direct public reporting was a major topic in public administration.[17] The common theme of these public relations techniques is that they do not "do" anything; rather, they are information for information's sake.

Some of the purposes and effects of McCamy's study of public relations in public administration can be categorized as autonomic, those that
advance the institutional and political interests of an agency by contributing
to it becoming more self-guiding and independent. Such activities include
developing and maintaining a favorable image with the public at large and
replying to attacks on the agency. Generally, according to McCamy, "in the
sense that *all* publicity has an indirect influence upon legislative decisions,
all administrative publicity offices have the objective of affecting legislation."[18] In a separate piece later that year, McCamy wrote that government
agencies often suggest new laws to Congress and, to generate support,
sometimes use public relations to turn "to the public outside of legislative
halls to get support and pressure from 'back home.'"[19]

After McCamy (but before Carpenter and Arnold), several other theorists
highlighted that public administrators work to develop external support
for agency activities. In 1950, Graham suggested that "the art of achieving
and maintaining support for sound public policies is as much a part of
public administration in a democracy as is the execution of policies."
That same year Simon, Smithburg, and Thompson described public relations as one of the survival tactics that agencies could use in the struggle
for existence. Specifically, obtaining public support makes agencies "less
subject to the influence or control of conflicting interests expressed through
legislative or executive action." A year later, Pimlott wrote that "the fear
that the executive branch may use the information services to strengthen
itself against the legislature has always been uppermost in the mind of
Congress." Seeking a more nuanced explanation of why successful agency
public relations would disempower Congress, he offered as one reason
that "government public relations threatens the member of Congress not
only in Washington but in his constituency, where he has traditionally
been the chief spokesman of the central government and the chief medium
of communication with the capital."[20]

Finally, in the 1980s, Rourke's study of bureaucratic politics provided a
cogent description of the consequences that successful agency public relations had on limiting Congress's (and the president's) power over an agency:

> Basic to any agency's political standing in the American system of
> government is the support of public opinion. If it has that, an agency

can ordinarily expect to be strong in the legislative and the executive branch as well. Because public opinion is ultimately the only legitimate sovereign in a democratic society, an agency that seeks first a high standing with the public can reasonably expect to have all other things added to it in the way of legislative and executive support. Power gives power, in administration as elsewhere, and once an agency has established a secure base with the public, it cannot easily be trifled with by political officials in either the legislative or the executive branch.[21]

Though not academic historians, Caro and Sheehan more recently restated the link between public support and political power. Caro's observation about legislators is equally applicable to public agencies: "In a democracy, the bedrock of political power is public support, so one of the most basic requirements for a public official is the ability to influence public opinion, and the journalists who mold it. None of the lower arts of politics is more essential to the politician than the ability to obtain favorable publicity." Regarding the effort by the U.S. Air Force in the 1950s to develop missiles and satellites, Sheehan highlighted "the public and congressional support that favorable publicity could provide."[22] Hence, the literature, though sparse, provides pre hoc confirmation of one aspect of Carpenter's and Arnold's more theoretical approaches, namely, that effective agency public relations have autonomistic effects, by diminishing Congress's ability to control the agency.

Examples of agency external communications that can promote autonomy include those aimed at the public at large (i.e., *public* relations), the news media (i.e., media relations, called press relations in the pre-electronic era), or directly at Congress (i.e., legislative relations and congressional liaison, aka lobbying). These forms of external communications can lead to persuasion, persuasion can lead to support, support can lead to advocacy, and advocacy from constituents narrows politicians' ability to impose their will on an agency. External relations offers a path to bureaucratic autonomous power. As stated by Carpenter, "Agencies as separate political actors can forge links with voters in their own right."[23] From the view of Capitol Hill, this would just not do.

Though the academic literature reached a consensus during the twentieth century about the ability of an agency's external communications programs to help it gain autonomy and reduce congressional leverage, this political phenomenon was apparent to a reporter as early as the late nineteenth century. In 1894, a reporter for the *New York Times* tried to explain why the U.S. Geological Survey and its chief, John Wesley Powell, were treated so generously by Congress despite enormous printing bills for maps, surveys, and annual reports. Powell, he observed, had acted with "great shrewdness." First, regarding the contents of publications, "great care is taken to avoid technical statements, so that they may be understood by those who are not geologists." That then meant those items "are bound to be popular . . . and as a result the criticisms of the enemies of the survey are more than likely to be neutralized."[24]

TOPIC OF THE STUDY: CONGRESSIONAL REACTION TO AGENCY PUBLIC RELATIONS

The rubric of congressional oversight covers the broader subject of congressional interactions with executive branch agencies, particularly legislative efforts to oversee the federal bureaucracy. Much of the literature has focused on the principal-agent relationship between Congress and the bureaucracy.[25] A recent theoretical review of agency oversight concluded that there are "structural complexities of any efforts to control the bureaucracy by electoral institutions."[26]

Here the focus is on a subset of the larger topic of congressional oversight, specifically, oversight of agency public relations. If autonomizing agencies are a threat to congressional dominance and public relations is one of the tools of autonomy, then how has Congress *reacted*? Shipan has identified such an action-reaction dynamic as factor in congressional oversight of administration.[27] Certainly, Congress is not a monolithic institution. Rather, it is a body with fluid and rapidly changing governing coalitions. Yet, ultimately, if and when Congress acts, it does so authoritatively.[28] When Congress enacts a law or appropriates funding, it is doing so, by definition, as an institution. Therefore, regardless of the shifting behind-the-scenes political coalitions over time that reflect an ever-changing governing majority, statutes and appropriations are instances when Congress has legislated. From such cases, it is reasonable to investigate historical patterns of action, and from those patterns to explore generalizations. This study chronicles a century of authoritative congressional reactions to agency public relations with a view to seeking generalizations about legislative behavior in face of autonomizing tendencies of federal agencies. Political oversight is one of the factors that differentiate the practice of public relations in the public sector from that in the private sector.[29]

In 1910, a reporter described how some congressional opponents of the Forest Service sought to strengthen their ability to control that agency's programs and policies by choking off its efforts to generate public support through publicity: "It seems that the one best hope of checking the [conservation] movement is to put an end to the 'press agent,' as the newspaper men handling publicity in the bureaus have been contemptuously called. The plan for the attack is unique, but simple, the idea being to remove the cause of public support and close the channels of publicity through which the acquirement of information by newspapers and magazines is made possible."[30]

Four decades later, confirming Carpenter's theory, the autonomizing power of agency publicity continued to be a factor on Capitol Hill. A member of Congress sought to articulate the action-reaction relationship between agencies and Congress. Who was the principal and who was the agent? During a public hearing of the House Select Committee on Lobbying Activities in 1950, Congressman Clarence Brown (R-Ohio) was grappling with this concept by asking a witness a largely rhetorical question:

Is it your opinion that the demand for new Government services should spring from the people or should spring from those who desire to render the services for the people? . . . Should not the people say, through their representatives, their elected representatives in Congress [what they want]—and I want you to bear in mind that 99.99 percent of those who want to do all these things for the people are not directly responsible to the people, are not elected by them, and cannot be reached by the people to be punished if they do something that is wrong.

A few minutes later, he continued:

So the real issue became whether bureaucracy was more powerful than the representatives of the people, whether they could compel the

Congress, through pressure and propaganda, to appropriate unnecessary funds, or whether the representatives of the people themselves
should judge as to how the public's money was to be spent.[31]

Yet, as discussed in the preceding section, the autonomizing effects of
agency publicity can be a result of external communications activities
that are inherent in the administrative process, those having explicitly
pragmatic and democratic purposes. A legislature cannot ban public
administrators from cooperating with the news media, from engaging in
public service campaigns to accomplish legislatively supported public
policy goals, from seeking publicity to notify the public of congressionally approved and funded programs and services, or from issuing annual
reports. Therefore, if banning public relations in public administration is
a beyond-the-pale goal, then how has Congress *managed* these activities
to reduce such autonomic effects? What is the exoskeleton it has tried to
construct around agency publicity to limit and channel it? Has Congress
been able to differentiate between objectionable autonomizing communications programs and those that are pragmatic and democratic? Has it
been able to draw the line between propaganda and information? This is
a historical case study to examine those instances when Congress acted
authoritatively to limit or control agency public relations.

SCOPE OF THE STUDY

The focus is on the axis between Congress and executive branch agencies.
Therefore, several partially related subjects fall beyond the scope of the
project, including counterpart efforts by some presidents to manage the
bureaucracy's contacts with Congress, or efforts by civil servants to lobby
Congress regarding salaries and other conditions of employment. Additionally, this study excludes congressional efforts to impose limitations on
the use of federal funds for external communications by third parties, such
as nonprofits receiving federal grants and businesses providing goods and
services to federal agencies, especially related to military procurement
contracts. Also, Congress from time to time has imposed limits on agency
spending for paid advertising, such as for military recruitment. This, too,
is beyond the scope of the study, in particular when paid advertising is

clearly and narrowly related to enlisting volunteers, as opposed to activities that are only indirectly related to recruitment such as image building and localized activities usually called community relations.

Similarly, my focus is on congressional efforts to control the *domestic* dissemination of information by agencies, since that would be a component of Carpenter's theory of the autonomizing tools available to an agency. Domestic audiences are the constituents of members of Congress. U.S. citizens and their opinions are integral parts of the power dynamic whereby agencies gain autonomy. Agency external communications aimed at audiences abroad, by contrast, do not help an agency obtain autonomy, and such international activities are, therefore, excluded from this study.

Though the focus is on administrative agencies, inevitably the activities of presidents, cabinet members, and other appointed officials become involved. To the extent possible, this inquiry is about congressional treatment of public administration, not of presidents and their administrations. The latter subject, of course, invokes constitutional issues of separation of powers, a subject unto itself.[32] However, academic writers long ago debunked the notion of any meaningful politics-administration dichotomy in government. Therefore, some cases that involve congressional criticisms of the external communications of a president's administration or of agency officials who are presidential appointees (directly or indirectly) are inevitably examined here. Nonetheless, I attempt to maintain a focus on the administrative side of the executive branch rather than its overtly political aspects and activities, using a commonsense approach to differentiate them.

The study also excludes federal organizations that are not line agencies. Generally, staff agencies are executive branch-wide in scope and do not "do" anything besides serve the executive branch in general. In some cases they are closely aligned with the president by being part of the Executive Office of the President. Most relevant to the scope of this study, there have been four executive branch-wide staff agencies that engaged solely in information dissemination, largely information generated by other federal agencies. Therefore, Carpenter's dynamic is not a good fit for them. This exclusion removes the Committee on Public Information (1917–19), the Office of Government Reports (1939–42, 1946–48), the Office of War Information (1942–45), and Federal Information Centers (1966–present) from the study.[33]

A way to delimit with some simplicity the subject of the study is by juxtaposing congressional and presidential efforts to control the federal executive branch with internal and external agency communications. Public communications are those that the bureaucracy seeks to circulate externally to advance its interests, sometimes triggering reactions from Capitol Hill and the White House to control these public relations activities. Conversely, an agency or department sometimes seeks to keep certain information out of the public realm because its release would be detrimental to the agency's interests. For those situations, Congress and presidents sometimes try to pry that data and obtain it for their own policymaking and political purposes.

Hence, this is a study is of congressional efforts to control, or at least manage, external communications activities of federal departments and agencies, since such activities contribute to agency autonomy from Congress. As such, it excludes congressional efforts to obtain internal agency information that the agency may wish to withhold, as well as presidential efforts to control either internal or external communications of the federal bureaucracy. A schema of this approach to identifying the topic of the inquiry looks something like table 1.

This study is also limited to *authoritative* congressional efforts to manage agency public relations—that is, to what Congress *did*, not what individuals in Congress merely *opined*. There are innumerable cases of individual members' verbal and written attacks on executive branch external communications.[34] These are what Mayhew has defined as position-taking activities by legislators.[35] Still, actions (or inaction) by a formally constituted committee of Congress signals some degree of authoritative institutional behavior. For example, I examine three committee investigations of the early twentieth century (1910–14) in some detail because they reflect the original triggering of congressional attention to agency public relations. Although these hearings and their reports did not lead to any formal *actions* by Congress, they are part of the earliest reactions by Congress to the phenomenon of agency public relations and are therefore valuable to analyze. Similarly, a few committee reports in the 1930s and '40s, though

TABLE 1
Scope of the Study

	Congressional Efforts to Control	Presidential Efforts to Control
Federal agency external communications	This inquiry	NA
Federal agency internal information	NA	NA

not leading to any overt actions, were important: the Byrd Committee report in 1937, which was largely written by the Brookings Institution; the Tydings Committee report in 1942; and the Harness Committee reports in 1947–48.[36] I discuss the latter committee investigations and reports briefly, mostly to identify the context of subsequent concrete reactions by Congress to agency public relations.

This study also treats appropriations committee reports attached to appropriation bills as reflecting authoritative congressional directives to federal agencies.[37] Federal agencies generally feel bound to follow the directives accompanying funding laws, if only because the next year they will be facing the same committee (or subcommittee), probably with little change in its membership, and the same policy areas of interest. Therefore, most executive branch departments and agencies consider appropriations committee reports as similarly reflecting the authoritative voice of Congress, even though they were not laws. Including such committee reports and actions, another way to state the research inquiry is: What, if anything, did Congress actually *do* to manage federal agencies' use of publicity to autonomize?

This issue of congressional reaction to agency uses of public relations to autonomize has not been addressed on a comprehensive basis by earlier research. In part, the reason is that this topic is at the interstices of multiple subject areas that are usually treated as distinct: legislative oversight of administration, public administration, public opinion, role of the news media, and government public relations. Therefore, this study will likely be of interest to several different academic disciplines and fields, including

U.S. history, political science (including the subfields of legislative studies, political communications, political development, and policy studies), public administration, public affairs, mass communications, journalism, and public relations.

RECONSTRUCTING CONGRESSIONAL NORMS TOWARD AGENCY PUBLICITY: THE NORMATIVE REGULATORY FRAMEWORK

In Carpenter's view, legislative conflict over federal agencies tends to be between coalitions of agency supporters and agency opponents. As he documented, in some cases autonomous agencies were largely able to marginalize independent congressional decision making. Those agencies had such broad public and legislative support that hostile legislators were reduced to an ineffective minority. Also, following Arnold's theory of congressional action, the enactment or rejection of a limitation on agency public relations is a reflection of politicians' sense of the electorate and the freedom of action (or lack of) that public opinion gives them in any particular policy area. Therefore, crucial to the difference between success (authoritative congressional reactions to agency public relations) from failed initiatives are the votes of legislators unaffiliated with any permanent camp.

Because the success of any congressional attempt to limit agency public relations is unpredictable, sponsors need to frame their arguments in ways that persuade such uncommitted legislators to support the initiative. They need to make a case that a particular public relations activity goes beyond the bounds of reasonableness, as defined by unwritten (and changing) congressional norms regarding the federal bureaucracy in general and agency publicity in particular. If the central justification for the proposed authoritative reaction is presented as nakedly partisan or ideological (in the left-right sense), then support from members of the other party or other ideology is less likely. So, the arguments need to be (at least superficially) nonpartisan, nonideological, and based on appeals to a value system held by a majority of legislators. Therefore, arguments made in support of proposals that are subsequently *enacted* or are the earliest formal committee statements can be interpreted as fairly reflecting the normative structure of congressional views of agency public relations and the subsequent legislative effort to silence, or at least muffle, the bureaucracy's public voice.

As a preview of the historical case studies to follow, I note six recurring themes that have been articulated in support of legislative limitations on agency public relations, mostly during the first two decades of the twentieth century: (1) The basic appropriateness of government public relations is questionable. (2) Agency publicity is really propaganda. (3) Agency public relations is a waste of tax dollars. (4) Agency public relations is a manifestation of a mushrooming bureaucracy. (5) Support of such criticisms from one's constituents is likely. (6) Support of such criticisms from the news media is likely. The following is a brief summary of examples of these six components, especially as reflected in the arguments for some of the earliest congressional limitations, between 1905 and 1914.

Public Relations Is Inappropriate in Public Administration

In 1905, Congressman John J. Fitzgerald (D-N.Y.) railed against the Panama Canal Commission having a press agent, saying, "It does not seem to me to be a proper use of this money." Congressman William Hepburn (R-Iowa), the bill's floor manager, responded in *agreement*, saying, "I do not believe that is a proper appropriation of this money."[38] When the bill reached the Senate, Senator Ben Tillman (D-S.C.) said, "We do not think that it is the business of any department of this Government to take public money to undertake to bamboozle us,"[39] and Senator Eugene Hale (R-Maine) echoed that, saying, "That is not the business of the Government or any bureau of the Government."[40]

Similarly, in 1906, when Senator Weldon Heyburn (R-Idaho) made his first major speech regarding U.S. Forest Service press activities, his main objection was that the purpose of the press bureau was to "break down" anyone offering criticism of Forest Service policies.[41] A government agency, he felt, should not publicly take on its critics, respond to them, or try to rebut them. Two years later, during the extended debate on the agricultural appropriation bill, Congressman Frank Mondell (R-Wyo.) said that Forest Service press releases were inappropriate because they were "placing an exaggerated value on its work" as well as attacking its Capitol Hill critics.[42]

Congressman Robert Bonynge (R-Colo.) particularly denounced as misleading and wrong the impact of a newspaper running a Forest Service press release without stating that the information came from the Forest Service.[43] Similarly, when the bill moved on to the Senate, its members asserted normatively that agency public relations was wrong. Senator Lee Overman (D-N.C.) questioned whether a federal agency even had the "right" to engage in public relations activities.[44] Senator Clarence Clark (R-Wyo.) said, "I do not believe it is a part of the business of the Government of the United States to subsidize writers"—that is, help reporters by submitting to them agency material that was presented in newspaper-friendly format.[45]

During three investigations of agency publicity activities in the early 1910s by House committees, politicians continued to hammer against the appropriateness of public relations in public administration. For example, the minority report on the Census Bureau declared that the activity was so objectionable that, if asked explicitly to approve it, Congress "would not do so if a measure for that purpose were proposed."[46] Regarding the USDA, Congressman John Nelson (R-Wyo.) called its public relations "an abuse, a manifest abuse."[47] Rules Committee chair Robert Henry (D-Tex.) said, "The very reason I do not think [a departmental press bureau] is legitimate is because I think the newspaper correspondents could get the legitimate news by going to every department and every Cabinet officer."[48]

The legislative perspective from these initial incidents, then, is that it was inappropriate for agency officials to deal with the press. This reflected a normative attitude regarding what was right and what was wrong in federal administration. The view from Capitol Hill was that entities in the executive branch were to be seen and not heard. If they indeed had anything to say, they should say it to Congress in various reports, not directly to the press or to the public. It was not the function of professional public administrators to engage in media relations.

Publicity Is Really Propaganda

One of the earliest uses of the term "propaganda" against agency external communications was during Senator Heyburn's initial public attack on Forest Service press relations in 1906. Senator Joseph Bailey (D-Tex.), sympathetic to Heyburn's complaints, interrupted him and characterized what Heyburn had been describing as "propaganda."[49] His introduction of that term to characterize Forest Service behavior added weight to Heyburn's speech. The word then recurred throughout the life of the controversy. Two years later, Senator Thomas Gore (D-Okla.) used it when asking a question during the hearing on the agriculture appropriation bill. Forest Service head Pinchot denied that what he did was propaganda. Rather, it was "to extend the knowledge of forestry."[50] Senator Lee Overman (D-N.C.) repeated the term "propaganda" during the floor debate on the bill.[51]

In the 1930s, "propaganda" still had an inflammatory meaning, partly associated with the Nazi regime that came to power in 1933 in Germany. The German government included a minister of propaganda, Joseph Goebbels. When a Republican congressman in 1939 used the word to describe the public relations activities of New Deal agencies, the Speaker of the House, "who rarely takes part in debate," felt obliged to step down from the speaker's chair and state his "objection" to applying the word to federal agencies.[52] The word was a key verbal weapon when the conservative coalition in Congress sought to limit agency public relations during the New Deal and Fair Deal.

But what, specifically, did it mean? For example, in the 1980s, during a congressional hearing on enforcing a legal ban on agency propaganda, a congressman wryly said, "Propaganda is a pejorative word. If you do not like what they are doing, it is propaganda. If you like what they are doing, it is information."[53] Despite the difficulty of defining it, in U.S. political language "propaganda" has continued to convey a sinister and negative meaning.[54] Nearly a century after its first use in this context, it is still a powerful epithet and political attack line. In 2005, Berry wrote that it is "a rather inflammatory word that suggests manipulation and dishonest communication."[55]

Supposedly the techniques of propaganda are so powerful that they cannot be resisted. One of the characteristics of the Progressive Era was the increasingly common use of the term, along with emergence of a cadre of critics who tried to expose the use of propaganda by special interest groups. When politicians invoked the term, they knew they were using a powerful weapon. Further, by combining attacks on "propaganda" and "bureaucracy," two separate but equally negative terms in our popular and political culture, legislators were inventing a double-barreled synergy of evil that was a surefire winner for decades to come.[56]

Agency Publicity Is a Waste of Tax Dollars

Almost every politician orating against the Panama Canal Commission's press agent mentioned the salary of $10,000 and that expenditures such as this were a waste of money. For example, Congressman Henry Clayton (D-Ala.) denounced the apparent attitude justifying such a job that "the money of the people may be used to some extent for unnecessary purposes,"[57] and Congressman Robert Macon (D-Ark.) echoed the "unnecessary" characterization a month later.[58] Senator Tillman termed the press agent's role and high salary as a "luxury" that should not be financed with taxpayer funds.[59] Senator Charles Culberson (D-Tex.) said that the new press agent role should not be underwritten by the "use of public funds."[60] Congressman Fitzgerald wondered why a publicity agent should be paid more than cabinet secretaries.[61]

During the fight against the press relations activities of the Forest Service, Congressman Mondell said that one of the reasons for his floor amendment was to "to prevent that kind of use of the people's money"[62] and that these activities should not occur at "public expense."[63] Senator Overman noted how fast the Forest Service's budgets had been going up. Cutting public relations would be a good first step to stopping wasteful spending and budget increases.[64] Senator Thomas Carter (R-Mont.) denounced Forest Service administrative and overhead expenses, "including the payment of lectures, the payment of editorial writers and reporters, [and] the maintenance of a bureau of publicity."[65]

Most criticisms of Census Bureau and USDA public relations during the three House committee investigations included the accusation that such activities were a waste of money. Congressman Nelson opposed the activities not only for their overt costs but because of the precedent they set. He feared that "if this press activity is to continue [in the USDA], other bureaus and departments will want press agents, if they have them not already, and it will soon amount to an expenditure of hundreds of thousands dollars."[66]

Public funds were scarce and needed to be husbanded carefully. They should be appropriated for activities that were important and denied to those that were unimportant. Public relations belonged in the latter category. There was, apparently, no possible justification for spending money on such efforts.

Agency Publicity Is a Manifestation of Bureaucracy

Congressman Clayton said that the lack of detailed information provided Congress about the new press job at the Canal Commission was an indication of a larger problem—"a want of business methods" by the Commission.[67] Here was a government agency that was (supposedly) inherently less efficient than the private sector. When Senator Carter introduced his amendment to ban agency lobbying of Congress, he launched a classic attack on the power of the emerging administrative state and its potential threat to Congress: "We have grown to be the victims of a vicious system, under which the men on the pay roll of the country, using the time of the public, likewise begin to importune Congress for a change of law, for an increase of appropriations, and for an additional loot on the Public Treasury."[68] This was a phenomenon which, he said, he wanted to "forestall." Similarly, Congressman Mondell justified his original floor amendment against the Forest Service because of the bureaucratic tendency to issue press releases that "contain a large puff of its work and accomplishment."[69] By stopping the public relations machine of the bureaucracy, Congress could weaken the power of the bureaucracy and its influence on Congress itself.

These were early expressions of what was to become a nearly universal value judgment in U.S. political culture, namely, that government agencies were, by definition, less efficient than those in the private sector, and that this inefficiency was a primary rationale to oppose the growth of the federal bureaucracy. Cutting the size of government was, from this perspective, always a good thing. With every reduction in the bureaucracy, so occurred reductions in government inefficiency. What was needed was more business and less government.

In this case, agency public relations was merely one element of bureaucracy itself. Congressional politicians were already intuitively feeling not only that the emergence of the administrative state was a threat to their institutional power but also that attacking the bureaucracy would become

a winning political theme. Criticizing the external communications programs of government agencies was one part of being against bureaucracy
itself, an almost reflexive legislative attitude.

Support for Criticizing Agency Publicity from Constituents

When Congressman Macon introduced an amendment in January 1906
against having a press agent at the Panama Canal Commission, one of his
justifications was that, "if we can not do anything else, we can call the
attention of the people" to it.[70] Congressman John Sharp Williams (D-Miss.)
said he was sure that "all right-thinking men" would agree with his opposition to the new position.[71] Members of Congress were intuitively identifying a voter applause line. Constituents would almost universally support
their legislator's efforts to cut agency public relations. Here was a political
issue that seemed to draw endorsement from a wide spectrum of voters. A
politician did not have to be "moderate" about this and could count on
voter agreement with all-out efforts regarding this topic.

Several times in his comments on the floor of the House, Congressman
Mondell explicitly argued that the public relations activities of the Forest
Service needed to be brought to the attention of the public at large. He
was confident that the voters would disapprove of such activities. In one
case, he referred to an already existing negative public opinion when he
said that it was "popularly believed" that government money was being
spent on public relations.[72] A few minutes later he bemoaned the difficulty of disseminating information about the results of congressional
investigations of such activities. He was sure that public opinion would
then be strongly against agency public relations.[73]

Complaints about agency external communications were often couched
in terms that would strengthen their appeal to rank-and-file voters.
Politicians were sure that public opinion would oppose such self-serving
and wasteful programs. For example, Congressman Nelson said that one
of his motivations in criticizing USDA publicity was that he "wanted
this practice called to the notice . . . of the country."[74] Agriculture Committee chairman Asbury Lever (D-S.C.) was aware of the popularity and
appeal of these criticisms. He sought to protect the department even
though the normal politician's instincts would be the opposite. Bashing

bureaucratic propaganda was practically an irresistible situation. For Lever's behavior in such circumstances, USDA secretary Houston praised him for being "unwilling to play the demagogue."[75]

Support for Criticizing Agency Publicity from the News Media

The press coverage of the debate over the Panama Canal bill was dominated by references to the controversy over its press agent. When the bill was being debated in Congress, at least sixteen articles about it were published in the *New York Times, Washington Post,* and *Chicago Tribune.* Of those, twelve referred to the controversy over the Commission's press agent in a headline or subheadline. Reporters and editors were signaling how newsworthy they found attacks on the press agent function in a government agency. This contributed to a sort of closed loop: the more the press coverage mentioned those attacks, the more politicians chose to continue attacking the position. Similarly, about a dozen articles from the *Washington Post* and *New York Times* referred to the 1908 controversy over publicity activities at the Forest Service. On a relatively consistent basis, press coverage of the progress of the agricultural appropriation bill and of Senator Heyburn's diatribes against the Forest Service highlighted, or at least mentioned, the issue of bureau press relations. The topic was good copy.

The three House committee investigations between 1910 and 1914 attracted some press attention, something not always true about legislative issues and hearings. The most striking aspect of these incidents was the unusual case of three reporters testifying against USDA external communications at the public hearing on the meat inspection issue. Such professional condemnations of departmental press relations confirmed the already set antagonism that most reporters would express to agency flacks, whether those staffers helped the journalists do their jobs or not. It was simply hate at first sight. Reporter Hunt went so far as to say that "nine-tenths of these press agents are properly called suppression agents"— in other words, they try to prevent reporters from writing stories rather than help them obtain facts and figures. Picking up the negative attitude of the reporters, Congressman Nelson generalized that "the departmental press bureau is unfair to the Washington correspondents."[76] In a 1918 editorial, the *Atlanta Constitution* complained about the amount of mail it received from "bureau publicity agents" of federal agencies. It claimed that "the mails are clogged, newspaper offices are cluttered—so much so that undoubtedly considerable really valuable matter is lost—and the government is burdened with a heavy and an altogether needless expense."[77]

For politicians, complaining about agency public relations often led to good press. Here were the early indications of the professional antagonism that reporters had toward press relations staff in administrative agencies, which would emerge as another permanent element of the congressional anti-agency template.[78] Even if reporters needed such agency specialists to help them do their job, they still had a professional hostility to the function. Therefore, legislators could usually expect positive coverage when they attacked agency public communications. The expectation of coverage of criticizing government press officers was like oxygen for politicians.[79]

THEME AND STRUCTURE OF THE STUDY

The six components of the congressional reaction to agency publicity are drawn from some of its earliest manifestations at the beginning of the twentieth century They regularly reappear during the other successful and authoritative congressional actions through to the beginning of the twenty-first century. What differentiated successful from unsuccessful attempts to enact congressional controls over agency public relations? The ones that passed were those that successfully created majorities based on a shared legislative culture defining appropriate versus inappropriate agency publicity. In turn, that legislative culture was partly tied (per Arnold) to interpretations of the electorate's preferences for the next elections. Generally, the tipping point can be operationalized as between the electorate's positive views of an agency (especially in the case of an autonomous agency) and the electorate's perceived anti-bureaucracy and anti-propaganda views. Hence, a majority in Congress would represent on an ad hoc basis whether the agency was popular or was susceptible to accusations of propaganda against it.

Even supporters of popular and autonomous agencies would want to avoid recorded roll call votes on "are you for bureaucratic propaganda?"—whereas opponents sought precisely such parliamentary opportunities. Both sides knew that most legislators did not want an opponent in the next election to claim that the incumbent supported wasteful and self-serving bureaucratic propaganda. So, finally, the descriptive theory predicts that majorities supporting congressional limitations on agency publicity were more likely when a *recorded* vote loomed.

It is the argument of this book that the autonomizing imperative of the bureaucracy has tended to trump the legislative power of Congress. The case studies in the chapters to follow present different strategies and tactics by Congress to control the various public relations activities of executive branch departments and agencies. They also show how these control efforts were subtly corroded by the bureaucracy to the point of having little to no real-world impact. The resistance to congressional control initiatives was rarely overt or confrontational. Rather, the long-term institutional interests of the bureaucracy were able to prevail over the usually short attention span on Capitol Hill, even when the legislative branch persisted for several years with a particular control effort.

In this book I explore how, event by event and year by year, Congress tried to muffle the voice of the bureaucracy. These were a series of ad hoc legislative reactions during the twentieth century to agency publicity and the autonomy that such publicity helped an agency achieve. Each chapter is based on a key decision that Congress made about agency public communications. The chapters are presented in chronological order of when those authoritative decisions *started*. The only exception to the focus on final legislative decisions is chapter 3, which describes three House committee inquiries; although none resulted in authoritative decisions, these committee investigations and their subsequent formal reports were significant because they reflected initial congressional reactions to agency publicity activities, when such activities were novel and, to some extent, a surprise to legislators. All other chapters focus on authoritative congressional reactions. In some cases, these were in response to specific activities in individual agencies (chapters 1–3, 7). Others are about legislative reactions that applied across the board to the entire executive branch (chapters 4–6, 8–10). The sequence of chapters is designed to convey a sense of the arc of the larger story of what happened, when it happened, and these events unfolding chronologically one after another.

Congressional reactions to agency publicity have sometimes over-lapped and intertwined, so these efforts have at times been treated by practitioners and academics as a nearly indivisible passel. However, each authoritative legislative action has a distinct history, application, later life, and impact. Therefore, the structure of the book reflects my attempt to untwine the tightly bound rope that Congress has gradually woven to rein in the bureaucracy's ability to act autonomously. Most chapters focus on one strand of the rope, usually a specific law. Each chapter about an authoritative congressional reaction is presented as the complete life of that law through to termination, if applicable. For biographies of laws still in force at the time of writing, the chapters end with the most recent authoritative developments. In an effort to indicate the interactions between different authoritative congressional decisions, I flag these connections with a cross-reference to related developments in other chapters.

Finally, a note on terminology. This inquiry focuses on efforts by Congress to manage the bureaucracy's ability to speak to external audiences, whether through press relations, publications, websites, communications with the public at large, or direct or indirect lobbying of Congress itself. In search of overall terms to convey this broad panoply of agency activities, I sometimes use "external communications," "publicity," "external relations," and "public relations" interchangeably, if only for some variety in the text. In American usage, "public relations" generally has a vaguely sinister meaning, suggesting manipulation, insincerity, and false presentation. I have tried to strip away those connotations and use the concept conveying the original and plain meaning of the two words in the term, namely, that "public relations" refers to those relationships that an organization has when interacting with the citizenry as a whole and other general public audiences.

PROLOGUE

Beginnings of Agency Public Relations, Beginnings of the Congressional Reaction

Where to start? History is messy. It rarely presents a bright red line marked "Start" or a finish line. Although the focus of this study is on the twentieth century, events at the beginning of that century were not ex nihilo. As a generic activity, public relations in public administration is as old as government itself. From the beginnings of the federal bureaucracy, cabinet secretaries and agency heads used what would neologistically be called public relations to promote their agencies (and, sometimes, themselves). For example, annual reports that were ostensibly addressed to Congress or the president were sometimes used as vehicles for broader public dissemination and, as hoped by their authors, greater public support. From 1823 to 1829, John McLean served as postmaster general. Given the role of the Post Office at that time as the nearly exclusive medium for dissemination of government information, his office was considered by the public as a very important position. He began the tradition in the Post Office of annual reports, ostensibly to the president but also intended for broad readership. His annual reports were "widely reprinted in newspapers from Maine to Missouri. . . . McLean took care to prepare them in a spare, lean style that contrasted markedly with the florid prose of the public oratory of the day and to include a variety of interesting statistics documenting the scale of the enterprise over which he presided."[1]

Similarly, it is folly to try to identify definitively the first full-time de facto professional public relations specialist (regardless of official title) in the federal bureaucracy. After all, congressional reaction to agency publicity requires, as a prerequisite, that such activities occurred in the first place to trigger such attention. A likely candidate for this "first" moniker is William A. Croffut, who edited the publications of the U.S. Geological Survey (USGS) from 1888 to 1895.[2] Previously, Croffut had been a prominent reporter, author, and Republican political activist. For example, in 1886 he wrote the first popular biography of tycoon Cornelius Vanderbilt.[3]

At the time, the USGS was headed by famed explorer John Wesley Powell. He was one of the first public administrators to understand what politicians on Capitol Hill had been gradually learning since the Civil War, namely, the power of publicity and its subsequent influence on decision making.[4] Powell originally hired Croffut to professionalize the editing of USGS scientific publications. The two gradually expanded the focus of these publications from a narrow readership of scientists "to influential persons devoted to social problems; and to newspapers."[5] Testifying at a congressional committee hearing, Powell justified his publication and publicity policies: "The knowledge acquired by research in this field is rapidly disseminated among the people through *the daily press, the magazines,* and especially through schoolbooks, and the demand for the Survey reports from institutions of learning is great and pressing. A steady flow of knowledge *goes out to the people* in this manner."[6]

Croffut wanted to maximize the "appeal and publicity" of USGS publications.[7] This included increasing press coverage of those publications because, in those days, the work of journalists largely focused on summarizing official reports issued by the government.[8] According to one reporter writing in 1894, "the geological survey tells the country from time to time all about its production of gold . . . and dozens of other things which would be considered 'good news' in many newspaper offices."[9] In general, Croffut was a "popularizer of geological survey reports."[10] This suggests that he was an early federal public relations professional, if not the first.

Croffut and Powell left government service in 1895. But they had triggered congressional concerns about the cost and political impact of federal publications, whether disseminated to an agency's narrow constituency or to the public at large. Congress passed a major revision of federal printing laws, which it had struggled to do for nearly a decade.[11] One of its purposes was to reassert control over the volume and costs of agency publications. Congressional efforts to control public relations had begun.

CHAPTER 1

TERMINATING THE PANAMA CANAL COMMISSION'S PRESS AGENT, 1905

> *"No part of the money hereby appropriated shall be used to pay the expenses of a literary bureau connected with the Isthmian Canal Commission, or pay the salary, compensation, or allowance, by whatever name called, of any person who may be engaged in such work for or in behalf of said Commission."*
>
> CR 40:1 (December 15, 1905): 449

T he long and convoluted building of the Panama Canal is also the event that kicked off Congress's reaction to agency publicity in the twentieth century. It began with a brief comment on the floor of the House of Representatives on December 6, 1905, and then mushroomed into a major political issue. In retrospect, although President Roosevelt's political maneuvering obviated the eventual need for formal legislation, the circumstances, content, and context of the incident can be seen as the first overt congressional reaction to agency public relations in the modern era.

PUBLICITY AS POLITICS, POLITICS AS PUBLICITY

The turn of the century signified a gradual change in U.S. politics and its relationship with the mass media. With the rise of the penny press, the antecedent of the modern news media, the ebbs and flows of public opinion between elections became more and more important. Politics was being played out on a larger stage. Appealing to public opinion became an integral part of the new twentieth-century politics. When a politician was "popular," he (they all were men then) possessed, however fleetingly, power to advance his causes and goals. Popularity was a new coin of the realm. Theodore Roosevelt is usually identified as the first modern president to focus on using White House press relations as a way of accomplishing his political goals. He cultivated the press, created news to fit his political needs, gave reporters a room in the White House, and followed news coverage carefully.[1] The Speaker of the House, Congressman Joseph Cannon (R-Ill.), called Roosevelt "the greatest press agent that ever lived."[2]

For example, Roosevelt liked to claim he had "discovered" Sundays. He meant that he realized how easy it was to dominate the headlines of the Monday morning newspapers by doing or saying something newsworthy on Sunday. After all, in normal circumstances, Sunday was a day when little news was "made" because most sources of news were closed, such as businesses, government agencies, and—especially, from Roosevelt's perspective—Congress. So, by planning to do such things as give a speech, release a letter publicly, or talk to reporters on Sunday, Roosevelt could dominate the news at the beginning of the week, possibly even influencing the spin of coverage for the rest of the week.[3]

Along with his innovative approach to media relations, Roosevelt helped change the conception of his office and the role of the federal government in other important ways. He was an aggressive president in terms of the exercise of his power and advanced an expansionist foreign policy that differed greatly from the nation's isolationist past. The failure of the French to build the Panama Canal presented him with an irresistible opportunity to accomplish what no one else had been able to do, to transform the United States into an imperialist and colonialist power, to expand the global reach of the U.S. military, and to facilitate the dominance of his nation's advantages in international trade. The fact that the construction of the canal was an unprecedented undertaking in scope and venue for the federal government was no deterrent for Roosevelt. Also, the quite illegal creation of the Republic of Panama out of Columbian territory was not a problem for him.[4] Roosevelt thought big and acted big, with little concern for legalities, niceties, or even advance approval from Congress at times.[5]

After much controversy and several false starts in terms of the construction and governance of the project, things finally seemed to be falling in place in mid-1905. A newly reconstituted five-member board, now called the Panama Canal Commission, was given the full power to manage the construction of the canal and exercise de facto civil governance in the canal construction area. Roosevelt, who was intimately involved in all details regarding the canal, wanted to be sure to have a direct and trustworthy link within the commission to get frank and honest reports on the status of the project. He decided to arrange behind the scenes for the commissioners to appoint Joseph B. Bishop as the commission's secretary. Bishop was an old and trusted acquaintance of the president as well as a political supporter.[6] He was a longtime reporter and editorial writer in New York City, and the two of them initially became acquainted through the loosely knit network of good-government reformers in the city, as well as the somewhat overlapping group of relatively well educated, upper-class citizens. McCullough described him as "undersized and grouchy-looking, with a little, pointed gray beard and a shiny bald head."[7] Roosevelt wanted Bishop to be his eyes and ears for the project. Bishop would be expected to keep the president informed through direct communications of the goings-on at the commission and the status of construction.

A trial balloon of the president's desire for Bishop to serve as the commission's secretary was shot down in mid-1904 by Senator Orville Platt (R-Conn.), a Republican regular who looked askance at reformers like Bishop and, for that matter, the president himself. Platt explained matter-of-factly that, "as Mr. Bishop has been in no way identified with the organization [i.e., party machine], his appointment would add nothing to its strength."[8] Given that Roosevelt was in the midst of running that year for election to a full term, he decided to let the matter drop.[9]

Meanwhile, the Panama Canal project continued to be controversial with vested interests that would be harmed by it. The major national railroads, then possessing enormous political power and influence, feared the competition that the canal would create and worked to turn public opinion against the project—while trying to stay as much as possible in the background. Other interests favored alternate routes and joined the fight against the Panama location. For example, New Orleans pushed for a canal route through Nicaragua, which would be expected to favor trans-shipping through its port.

Since the beginning of 1905, the railroads were already in a major publicity-oriented fight with Roosevelt. As part of his trust-busting campaign, he wanted to impose more effective regulation of the railroads and the rates they charged by strengthening the powers of the Interstate Commerce Commission. The railroads decided in February to initiate a major fight for public opinion or, in the more common term then used, sentiment.[10] This was a grafting "of new-style publicity practices to traditional democratic life."[11] They hired the first publicity agency in the country, sometimes called the Publicity Bureau, or Michaelis & Ellsworth.[12] The campaign included mailing dozens of press releases, sending employees to visit newspaper editors throughout the country, maintaining a clippings file of coverage, disseminating millions of copies of brochures and flyers to opinion leaders and the public at large, and seeking supportive resolutions from friendly special interest groups and politicians. The effort was so extensive, aggressive, and unprecedented that it triggered accusations by editors of pressure tactics and even bribery.[13] Nevertheless, by November 1905 the railroads could see that their efforts were not working and decided to terminate them.[14] Congress eventually passed legislation, known as the Hepburn Act.

At the same time as the railroads' publicity campaign against increased regulation, another campaign by the railroads and other interests against the Panama Canal was in the offing. In a 1905 speech, Secretary of War William Howard Taft described the opposition:[15]

> One of the great obstacles to success in building the canal is the opposition of powerful persons and interests to its construction. . . . it takes different forms. It is found in the misrepresentations of conditions on the Isthmus, in unfounded reports concerning friction between those having authority in the canal work, in intimations of irregularities and frauds and favoritism in contracts without any evidence whatsoever to justify suspicion, and generally in the constant suggestion of a presumption that the expenditure of millions in building the canal must involve what is called "graft."
> . . . if they are to be permitted to delay the work on the canal and to paralyze the energy of those upon whom the burden of pushing the

work must fall, then they will be productive of evil and will become exactly what many private interests would be glad to have them become—the grave of all the high hopes for a trans-isthmian canal.[16]

Bishop later said that around this time he had been offered a well-paying job to run "a publication bureau" for the combination of interests opposed to the Panama Canal. His role would have been "to put out arguments against" the canal, to influence press coverage and sway public opinion in order to impact congressional decision making. The goal of the project would be, at least, to delay the canal's construction. Even though he declined the job, the project went forward. Negative, even false, information about the canal project was circulated to, and sometimes printed by, newspapers around the country.[17]

HIRING A PRESS OFFICER FOR A LITERARY BUREAU

These efforts to influence public opinion against the canal prompted Roosevelt, ever sensitive to public relations, to feel that someone needed to work on a regular basis to counter such continuing negative publicity. A year after his failed trial balloon regarding hiring Bishop, Roosevelt decided to revive it, but with a twist. Bishop would be not only his eyes and ears on the commission but also a government public relations professional. His job would be to counter the harmful publicity by responding to every allegation and negative article with "facts," generating positive publicity about the canal work and, generally, helping turn the spin of press coverage and public opinion toward a positive stance regarding the canal construction. Bishop would be the first openly acknowledged and formal press officer in a federal agency and, concomitantly, the first to trigger major congressional opposition.

Later, testifying before a congressional committee, Secretary Taft explained the role of, and need for, a press officer at the Canal Commission:

Taft: The attacks on the canal, its construction, and the preposterous misrepresentations concerning everything, both on the Isthmus and here, had gotten to such a point that it seemed necessary for the Commission to protect itself in some way.
Senator Tillman (D-SC): So he is the press agent . . .?

Taft: You can call him a press agent if you choose to. . . . it is the duty
of the Commission to correct impressions that are circulated mali-
ciously for the purpose of interfering with its work.[18]

In September 1905, Canal Commission chairman Theodore Shonts
announced that Bishop had just been hired as the commission's secretary,
a new office, with special responsibilities for "the publicity and literary
branch of the commission's work." He described the new position as "an
innovation" and explained that Bishop would "furnish all proper information to the press and the public."[19] He would be the canal's "press
agent." According to one of the articles covering the announcement, Shonts
explained the benefits of a federal agency having a press officer like this:
"Hitherto Mr. Shonts and Assistant Chief Pepperman, of the offices of
administration, have been the sources of news concerning the doings of
the Canal Commission here and on the isthmus. Hereafter, those who
wish to know if anyone has died of yellow fever in Panama, or if any one
has resigned, or how much a Chinese laborer will earn, and how much it
costs to subsist in Panama, he will be directed to Mr. Bishop. Mr. Shonts
and Mr. Pepperman, as dispensers of news, now cease to exist."[20] Besides
fulfilling these literary and publicity responsibilities, the statement added,
Bishop would also serve as the official historian of the canal project.[21]

Bishop quickly assumed office and began working with the press.
Reporters frequently stopped by the offices of this first openly acknowledged federal press officer. He said they "congregated in my office" on a
routine basis, with questions, asking for news or confirming information
they had received elsewhere.[22] As a former reporter, Bishop insisted that
he was not a flack for the commission and that his credibility was key to
doing his job, even if it meant releasing information that was unflattering
to his agency: "I give out the situation as it is."[23]

In a relatively ad hoc manner, Bishop was inventing public relations
in public administration, establishing standard operating procedures that
later were viewed as routine for practitioners. In terms of media relations,
he served as the authoritative spokesperson for the agency. His functions
included issuing to the press formal announcements of commission decisions[24] and authoritative statements on commission policies,[25] releasing to
the public internal agency reports,[26] and providing background information

requested by newspapers and magazines for features.[27] Bishop's news relations doctrine included releasing bad news as well as good news,[28] issuing
reaction statements to other news coverage,[29] and sometimes opting not to
issue responses to false stories so as not to give them further credence.[30]

At the same time, Bishop saw his public relations duties as extending to
other constituencies besides reporters. He made sure to submit all official
agency reports to Congress.[31] To the public at large, he regularly issued
the widely disseminated *Bulletin* summarizing major developments and
responded to individual requests for information from individual citizens and from organizations.[32] Within the agency, he kept senior officials
informed of trends in public opinion, helped them prepare for speeches
and interviews, and maintained a file of press clippings to track earlier
coverage.[33] These public relations functions became the templates of public
information work in federal agencies and have changed little over a century
except in the technologies used to perform them.

After a few months on the job, Shonts expressed satisfaction with the
impact of Bishop's work:

> Shonts: He was instrumental to a remarkable degree in stating the
> facts as to conditions on the Isthmus and rectifying errors that were
> published everywhere during last summer.
> Senator Eugene Hale (R-Maine): Through the press?
> Shonts: Through the press; yes.
> Senator William Allison (R-Iowa; committee chair): Of what practical
> benefit is he to the construction of this work?
> Shonts: [Bishop's job is] to give out truthful and accurate information in
> a way that would give the facts, the absolute truth to the people. . . . I
> think the result of his efforts saved us vast sums of money by helping
> create a healthy sentiment, and have had such a result in a very
> few months.[34]

It did not take long for the press to begin complaining about Bishop's
work. One reporter termed a statement released by the Canal Commission
as "purported to be" its official position, insinuating something vaguely
improper, even misleading, about it.[35] A *New York Times* editorial sneered
at Bishop's seeming Pollyanna pronouncements and flatly accused him

of "withholding the truth." Regarding major disagreements between the commission and Secretary of War Taft, "of these things the newspaper men heard nothing from the appointed Secretary and Historian. He was always an optimist. The picture he painted was in colors of the rose."[36] Similarly, the *New York Evening Post* complained about the secrecy surrounding the commission's work. The citizenry, the *Post* said, "are not to be satisfied with official typewritten bulletins that all is well. The evasions and suppressions that have been practiced have become tiresome to persons who are interested in getting a full, free, and true account of what is being done. The attempt to say what shall and what shall not be published about canal affairs is as futile as it is stupid."[37] The *New York Herald* published a column titled "The Kind of Man Bishop Is," which attributed to him extremely unflattering and derogatory comments about sitting senators and House members. The story, of course, created great ill will toward him on Capitol Hill. Bishop said the wholly fictional story had been ordered up by the paper's owner, James Gordon Bennett, a political opponent of President Roosevelt.[38] A reporter for the *Boston Globe* simply could not understand "why the Panama Canal Commission needs a press agent any more than the war department or the state department."[39] These examples of press hostility to a federal agency's information officer also set the tone for the century, a built-in and permanent professional hostility to the public relations counterparts reporters had to deal with.

Hence, the initial three months Bishop functioned as the press officer at the Panama Canal Commission brought what were to be long-lived, even permanent, templates regarding the work of public information officers and their treatment by the media.

CONGRESS REACTS

Although federal agencies had previously engaged in activities such as disseminating reports and publications that could be viewed as early public relations activities, it was indeed an innovation for senior federal officials to acknowledge the formal employment of someone to perform press relations and publicity functions. Here was a federal agency openly employing a public relations specialist, with responsibility for dealing with reporters and newspapers. This was a major step in the evolution of public relations in government. Just as the public acknowledgment of Bishop's work essentially formalized press relations in public administration (action), politicians on Capitol Hill similarly innovated by responding with attacks on such activities (reaction). So began Congress's reaction to external communications in public administration. One institution sought to voice its views, the other to stifle that voice. The political response came at the first legislative opportunity about three months after Bishop began performing his press agent activities.

During the initial press coverage of Bishop's appointment as press agent at the Canal Commission, Congress had not been in session. About three months later, the 59th Congress began its first session, on December 4, 1905.[40] That day, President Roosevelt's request for a supplemental appropriation of $16.5 million for additional canal construction expenses was introduced.[41] It was referred to a committee, but the committee held no hearings on the bill and did not convene in executive session to vote on it. Instead, two days after that, the bill was back on the floor of the House without any committee recommendation. The floor debate would be the first opportunity for those on Capitol Hill to comment, formally, about Bishop's appointment.

Congressman William Hepburn (R-Iowa), the floor manager of the bill, was barely into his initial summary of the contents of the bill when he was interrupted by John Fitzgerald (D-N.Y.), who complained about the lack of detailed background information from the Canal Commission about the bill:

Fitzgerald: It is impossible to tell for what purpose any amount stated here has been expended, except as stated under a general head. It is reported quite commonly, I understand, that this commission to-day is employing a so-called "press agent," located in this city, at a salary of $10,000 a year. It may be a very necessary position, but how could Congress ascertain if a thing like that was so; and if it be a fact and it was deemed improper, how could Congress prevent it?

. . . I now ask the gentleman if he knows whether it is a fact that this Commission has employed in this city a so-called "press agent" at a salary of $10,000 a year?

Hepburn: I do not.

Fitzgerald: Could the gentleman think that that was a necessary and proper expenditure by this Commission?

Hepburn: Well, I would not think that a personage of that kind would equal in usefulness an Irishman who could well wield a shovel.[42]

A few minutes later, Fitzgerald dropped the pretense of a fair-minded seeker of facts and stated flatly on behalf of the minority party that the employment of a press agent by a federal agency "does not seem to me to be a proper use of this money." Republican Hepburn did not hesitate to agree with Democrat Fitzgerald. He said, "I will go just as far as the gentleman in reprobation if such a condition exists. I do not believe that is a proper appropriation of this money if it has been made. I am not a friend of that kind of expenditure."[43]

Bishop's press responsibilities and relatively high salary became a running item throughout the floor debate that day and the next.[44] Some of the comments included an assertion that press work by a federal employee was a misappropriation of public funds, a sarcastic reference to the commission's "publicity department" as an effort to make Bishop's press work sound "a little sweeter," and a complaint "that he does not distribute enough" information to Congress.[45] One congressman asked the rhetorical question, "What was the necessity of employing a press agent," and a member asserted that it was an expenditure "for unnecessary purposes."[46] Another member denounced the commission for "experimenting" by hiring a press agent.[47] But despite the unanimity of opposition to a government press agent, the House passed the bill the next day without any amendments related to Bishop's role.

Even though the lower house took no concrete action against it, Bishop's job was still a development that was unheard of, and the press coverage reflected it.[48] According to the *Washington Post*, Bishop's job dominated the debate, and the *New York Times* emphasized that the idea of the commission having a press agent "was especially condemned" by both Democrats (as would be expected of the opposition party) and Republicans (the majority party and the party of the president).[49] This relatively modest but encouraging coverage (from a politician's perspective) pales in retrospect. Fitzgerald had struck the mother lode. With a brilliant intuition that so many politicians possess, he and then some of his colleagues quickly realized that Bishop's unprecedented publicity activities might be a political Achilles' heel that could be exploited. Here was the beginning Congress's extended reaction on federal public relations, the effort to muffle the public voice of executive branch agencies.

Now it was the Senate's turn. Minority Democrats quickly announced that they would probably oppose the bill. The Republican Senate leadership would not make the same mistake the House had made. The bill was sent to the Appropriations Committee for an in-depth review. The committee chair quickly scheduled a public hearing for Tuesday, December 12. Bishop, of course, was invited to testify. First, Secretary of War Taft and then Shonts led off with a vigorous defense of the need for a press agent on the Canal Commission staff (quoted above), besides commenting on other (unrelated) issues raised in the House floor debate. While Taft and Shonts were testifying, some senators on the committee could barely wait to jump in with their criticisms. Tillman said that Bishop's was "a bureau of misinformation," and that he "was trying to get back to headquarters [for information] and not go through Mr. Bishop, because [he] did not like to bother with that filter." Hale condemned Bishop for "taking upon himself the charge of manufacturing public sentiment through the press."[50]

Then it was Bishop's turn to testify. He plainly described the press and public relations activities he had been engaging in. According to the *Washington Post*, he faced "sharp questioning."[51] One senator grumbled that Bishop's answers were evasive ("If there is anything more, we do not seem likely to get it") but another contradicted that, saying that Bishop "did not in any way hesitate or qualify or give any intention of a desire to conceal his relations to the Commission."[52] Sometimes Bishop came across as guileless, beginning his answers with "Oh, yes" or "Oh, no." Although he was deferential ("Yes, sir"; "No, sir"), he stood up to politicians' usual tricks. When one tried to put words in his mouth, he answered, "I have not made the slightest intimation of that kind." A few minutes later, when he was repeatedly interrupted by a hectoring senator, he asked, "May I be allowed to finish my statement?" In general, he presented a factual summary of his work as a press agent, without evasion. Pretty soon the senators ran out of questions.[53]

For lack of anything else to do regarding this new activity in federal administration, the chair adjourned the hearing. In general, the members of the committee had been looking for a scandal to express outrage about but were surprised and a little disappointed that in Bishop's testimony they could find only a little to declaim against. One senator kept making the point that Bishop's role was an "innovation," but beyond documenting that assertion he did not seem quite sure what to do with the revelation. Still, the legislators felt they were onto something that was not good and deserved to be criticized. However, as on the House floor, when the Senate committee acted on the bill it recommended no amendments related to Bishop's role.[54]

The Senate took up the bill two days after the hearing. Bishop was not mentioned that first day but largely dominated the floor debate the next, December 15.[55] Senators Tillman and Hale led the attack. They articulated several different arguments why, as legislators, they opposed the innovation of a federal agency having a public relations officer. Among Tillman's arguments were these:

> A federal agency should not need to hire someone "to exploit its work and to defend it through the press."
>
> The role of a public relations officer would be that of "hypnotizing public opinion or of misinforming the people."
>
> "People who were entirely innocent and who need no defense would not take the trouble to be worried and put a $10,000 man at work upon the duty of defending them."
>
> "I can not for the life of me see what justification there is for the public money to be spent in that way. The press representatives in Washington . . . [are not] disposed to lie or misrepresent."
>
> "The newspapers of this country would be glad to publish the truth" and do not need a government press agent to do that.
>
> "We do not think that it is the business of any department of this Government to take public money to undertake to bamboozle us or the people either, or to defend themselves, whether they are accused justly or unjustly. They must rely upon the integrity of their motives and the purity of their administration to get the confidence of Congress and the good will of the people."[56]

Hale added to Tillman's arguments that, "if the Government or any part of the Government establishes as a part of its duties a press agency to create public sentiment through disseminating their statements and their reports to the press, you have got first a prejudiced press; you have got a selected press. The newspapers are selected to disseminate this intelligence and make this public sentiment, and at last, if you have an unscrupulous Administration, you have a hireling press."[57]

No one tried to defend Bishop's role as a government press agent. At the end of this one-sided onslaught, Senator Charles Culberson (D-Tex.) introduced an amendment that would ban spending any money from the bill on "a literary bureau" at the commission.[58] By now, it was late in the day. The Senate adjourned, planning to continue the debate the next day. The newspaper coverage of the debate the next morning included the attacks on Bishop's job. The newsworthiness of the subject is indicated by the fact that the subheadlines of the stories in two of the papers focused on Bishop, with the *Chicago Tribune* blaring "Denounces the Press Agent's Work" and the front-page story of the *Washington Post* stating "That $10,000 Canal Press Agent Criticized Again."[59]

The issue would be joined on the sixteenth, when Culberson's amendment inevitably came up for a vote. Culberson began with an attack on the basic concept of Bishop's job. It was a "gross abuse" and an "impropriety . . . to create or to control or to direct public opinion."[60] But then Senator Hale asked Culberson for permission to interrupt to make an announcement. He had just been assured by the administration that the Canal Commission would delete Bishop's press responsibilities from his job description. With that public commitment, Culberson agreed that his amendment was no longer needed. The administration had folded. It could see that the Culberson amendment would pass if voted on, with bipartisan support and by a wide margin. Such a public repudiation would hurt the administration politically. Therefore, being pragmatic, it would be better to "volunteer" to accomplish the result by internal management decisions rather than by enshrining the prohibition in federal law and taking a public defeat. But the results were the same. In this first extensive floor debate about a formal press relations function in public administration, the legislative branch was united in opposition. Though never enacted de jure, Congress had acted authoritatively on a de facto basis to manage agency public relations.

Hale seemed somewhat relieved because, he said, of the "difficulty in dealing with this situation by any legislative provision. The Senator [Culberson] has found that difficulty in framing any legislation or language that will meet the real evil . . . the difficulty of putting [it] into words."[61] For example, Culberson's amendment had proposed to ban "a literary bureau." Had it been enacted, the Canal Commission could have gotten around such a prohibition by simply changing the title of Bishop's literary and publicity duties without changing the duties themselves.

Even though the issue was now moot, one more senator felt the need to speak on the subject. Senator William Stone (D-Mo.) denounced "the work of that ornamental, Argus-eyed purveyor and dispenser of canal literature known as the 'historian,' who has been employed at an annual salary of $10,000 to guard the Commission against the machinations of the wicked world outside."[62] Again the newspaper coverage of the Senate debate focused in part on Bishop. The main headline of the front-page story in the *Washington Post* was "Bishop Called Off." The second subheadline of the front-page *New York Times* story was "To Abolish Press Bureau."[63]

SUBSEQUENT DEVELOPMENTS

Although the administration had backed down, the issue was not dead. The next month, January 1906, when the House was considering another Panama Canal appropriation, Congressman Robert Macon (D-Ark.) introduced an amendment to ban the use of funds for "press agents or other sentiment-promoting" staff. Macon explained that, although Bishop's specific press duties had been dropped, this amendment was needed to prevent the Canal Commission from hiring someone else to do the same kind of work. Furthermore, by approving the amendment, they could "call attention of the country to the existence of such an evil."[64] In other words, he was trying to score a partisan point, seeking to embarrass the Republican administration publicly by revisiting the December controversy. Between not wanting to beat a dead horse and not wanting to give the Democrats a partisan victory, the House members rejected the amendment. Still, the subject refused to die, with legislators occasionally referring to it in floor speeches, committee meetings, and public statements.

They had found an effective attack line; it was too good to let go of, even after winning.

After the administration agreed to drop Bishop's press duties from his work as secretary, some legislators and reporters misunderstood what had been agreed to. One of the causes of the confusion was that Senator Hale had announced the commitment by the administration, but there had been no formal announcement or written statement from the executive branch. Many legislators thought that Bishop's job as commission secretary (with attendant press duties) was to be abolished or, at least, that Bishop would leave his job as secretary since he could no longer perform press duties.[65] When neither happened, it caused much harrumphing on Capitol Hill and in the press. Roosevelt simply had a much narrower view of what he had committed to. As far as he was concerned, his only promise was that Bishop would cease functioning as the press spokesman for the commission. Otherwise, nothing had to change. Bishop could continue as the commission's secretary and he could continue at his $10,000 salary.

Roosevelt's original motivation in naming Bishop to the post, it will be recalled, had been to serve as Roosevelt's eyes and ears for the canal project. So, despite the elimination of Bishop's press duties, this original purpose remained in force. To quell the press agent controversy, at the end of 1905 Roosevelt nominated Bishop to be a *member* of the Canal Commission itself.[66] But that move only poisoned the political waters even more. Senators acted as though the president had been devious and was seeking to outmaneuver them or, at least, was disregarding them. The whole episode left them in a sour mood.[67] Therefore, the Senate refused to confirm Bishop's appointment.[68] Eventually Bishop simply stayed in his position as secretary and served in that position for nine years.[69] He also fulfilled one of his original roles when first hired as secretary: to serve as official historian of the canal (different from his press and literary bureau activities). He wrote a history of the building of the canal and coauthored an admiring biography of George W. Goethals, its chief engineer.[70]

Ironically, Bishop also continued with some public relations activities after the 1905 congressional debate, though not so naming them as such. For example, after he moved his office from Washington to the Canal Zone, he initiated the official weekly newspaper *Canal Record*.[71] This was not press relations in any formal sense—more like an employee and stake-holder newsletter. The paper was very informative about the progress of the project and widely distributed and read by its primary and ostensible audience, but also by members of Congress and the stateside press. It became very popular. Many newspaper articles about the progress of the canal work were based on information in the *Canal Record*.[72] In May 1908, a senator claimed that "in to-day's mail" he had received press-oriented material from the Canal Commission, but it was unclear what he was referring to.[73] It is unlikely that it was a press release; more likely it was an issue of the *Canal Record*. Bishop was being careful not to engage in press relations overtly but, rather, did so indirectly.

Eventually the *Canal Record* became so popular that a congressman wanted to be sure to shield it from further anti-publicity legislation passed by Congress. In 1913, the House was debating a ban on employing publicity experts in the federal government (see chapter 4). One of the members raised concerns about the amendment, wondering if it might "in any wise affect the publication of the Panama Canal Record?" Con-gressman Fitzgerald, the first to complain about Bishop's press agent work during the House floor debate in 1905, soothingly responded that the "Record is published by the Panama Canal Commission and not by a publicity expert" and therefore would not be affected by the proposed amendment.[74] Fitzgerald's contorted differentiation between the publicity activities he had vociferously objected to in 1905 and the news publica-tion from the same person was a distinction without a difference, an early example of the hypocrisy that politicians (and bureaucrats) could display about agency publicity. For no reason that could be stated in clear statutory language, in some cases it was acceptable and in others not.

• • •

Although it was a minor political issue that came and went in a few months, the fight over the Panama Canal Commission having a press agent was the tripwire for a permanent theme that was to emerge in U.S. politics: legislative hostility to public relations in public administration and, consequently, legislative efforts to stifle these activities. A silenced bureaucracy was a servile one. Although Congress did not enact any formal legislation, by forcing a political commitment from the administration it had prevented Bishop from openly functioning as a press relations officer. Significantly, though, he figured out a way to do this work indirectly, by distributing copies of the *Canal Record* to newspapers. This was the beginning of the template of a pas de deux: Congress trying to control agency publicity and the agency finding a way around it.

CHAPTER 2

BANNING FOREST SERVICE PRESS ACTIVITIES, 1908

"No part of this appropriation shall be paid or used for the purpose of paying for in whole or in part the preparation or publication of any newspaper or magazine article, but this shall not prevent the giving out to all persons without discrimination, including newspaper and magazine writers and publishers, of any facts or official information of value to the public."

35 Stat. 259

Newspaper ink was barely dry from the fight over the press agent at the Panama Canal Commission when the next congressional reaction to agency publicity occurred. It started quietly, behind closed doors, and then mushroomed into a fight between the House and Senate regarding the appropriate degree of legislative control over agency public relations.[1]

GIFFORD PINCHOT'S PUBLICITY PROGRAM

Senator Weldon Heyburn (R-Idaho), though a fellow Republican of President Theodore Roosevelt, had gradually been getting more and more hostile to the administration's conservation policies, particularly the president's designation of federal lands as forest reserves.[2] The effect of these executive actions was to exclude these lands from development, mining, and settlement. Heyburn came from the more traditional wing of the Republican Party that felt the business of the nation was business. Their political ideology was that virtually any economic development was a good thing and that the federal government's land policy should solely focus on facilitating business exploitation of publicly owned lands and expediting their privatization. Roosevelt's string of executive orders withdrawing more and more federally owned lands from development and placing them in forest reserves hampered the kinds of policies that politicians like Heyburn would traditionally support.[3]

In 1904, Heyburn requested that the Senate's Public Lands Committee investigate the administration's forest reserve policy.[4] In response, the committee convened a series of three public hearings in early 1904 to hear his charges and receive testimony from businessmen.[5] Afterward, the committee made no recommendations for action. Heyburn had been given an outlet for his views, but little more. Over the next two years, he gradually intensified his public criticisms of the administration's forestry policy.[6] He fundamentally disagreed with the doctrine of conservation that had been coined by Gifford Pinchot, head of the U.S. Forest Service and adopted enthusiastically by Roosevelt. Pinchot was a master bureaucrat, a successful bureaucratic entrepreneur, and a leader most responsible for the Forest Service's large degree of autonomy from Congress.[7]

Roosevelt prided himself as an outdoorsman and hunter. For him, conserving the nation's forests fit into his efforts to create a national park system as well as his economic reforms, such as trust busting. He liked Pinchot's focus on ending the various "insider" privileges, concessions, and access rights to federal lands that had been granted to special interests and corporations, often after corrupt lobbying and bribery. These special interests and large corporations essentially extracted one-time wealth from those lands, with the federal government being compensated little, if at all. Pinchot wanted to "conserve" these natural resources, shifting from such irrevocable uses to sustainable ones that could be renewed and then reused, such as forestry and grazing. He also wanted to shift from single uses of these lands to multiple uses. So, for example, Pinchot conceptualized selective wood cutting followed by reforesting or careful grazing followed by regeneration of grasslands as exemplifying conservation. Whenever the political status quo is changed, those stripped of benefits and privileges can be predicted to fight vociferously to prevent their diminished status. Hence, Roosevelt's and Pinchot's conservation program was controversial politically, with corporations and special interests and their political allies resisting these changes, like Heyburn.[8] But Pinchot's success at pursuing agency autonomy had, for the time being, marginalized these critics.

As with his other causes, Roosevelt used the media to promote his views on conservation and denounce his opponents as working against the public interest. This put him on a collision course with Heyburn. After Roosevelt was elected to a full term as president in 1904, Heyburn tried to influence the president's actions on forest reserves in Idaho behind the scenes. Roosevelt summarily rejected those overtures in one-on-one meetings at the White House as well in a private exchange of letters. Then, in mid-1905, Roosevelt forwarded the letters to Pinchot with a note: "You can have my letter and Heyburn's response to it made public any way you see fit."[9] Pinchot promptly arranged for the letters to be printed as a Forest Service pamphlet and distributed it widely. The press, as intended, picked up the story and ran it with the slant desired by Roosevelt and Pinchot. They depicted a president and his forestry chief bravely protecting the nation's precious lands and forests from the depredations of a parochial politician trying to exploit those natural resources for narrow and selfish interest groups.[10] Heyburn, of course, was outraged and began scouting for ways to get his revenge.

Like Roosevelt, Pinchot was a master publicist.[11] He realized that he needed to win public opinion to succeed in pushing his conservation and forestry program. At first he pursued mostly an aggressive *publication* program, essentially an enhancement of traditional print-oriented efforts to disseminate information that had been the mainstay of federal agencies throughout the nineteenth century. In part, this print focus was driven by technology and the available channels for external communication. The reliance of federal agencies on disseminating publications was the phenomenon that had prompted Congress to seek to control printing activities and costs in the late nineteenth century (see Prologue). Testifying at a congressional hearing, Pinchot explained the rationale for that approach: "We have done our best to reach a sufficient number of people to influence public opinion generally through our own publications. . . . We have printed and distributed something over 4,000,000 this year of these little cheap leaflets."[12]

Pinchot recognized, however, that even such a massive publication program had its limitations. No matter how inexpensively he was able to produce these publications, he could not reach most of the attentive citizenry that way and stay within budgetary realities. Instead, he realized that the cheapest route to that large an audience was through free press coverage. At the same congressional hearing, he elaborated on why he turned to this approach over the traditional publication program. First, "we prepare the news—the valuable information that is news—in such shape that the newspapers will take it, not in any sense of puffing our work; simply a definite statement of facts. The newspaper men come around and get that and print it. In that way we are getting before the people, with an utterly insignificant cost—two men do all this work." Second, "we would put the same matter in different ways, so that the information would go out again and again."[13] In his memoirs, he presented the two alternatives bluntly. Newspapers carrying Forest Service press releases "printed hundreds of millions of copies in a year, and their items about our work reached a thousand readers to our bulletins' one."[14]

Pinchot could not understand why other senior public administrators generally avoided press coverage or dealt with reporters only on a reactive basis. He saw the press as an easy means for reaching public opinion. Pinchot had discovered that the emerging concept of free publicity not only related to politicians but also could be adapted to the needs of public administration. He bluntly directed his staff: "Use the press first, last, and all the time if you want to reach the public."[15] This was a major step in the evolution of the administrative state, and it was Pinchot who had invented it.[16] According to Ponder, he was "unique" in his understanding of media relations, the first to use them on such a broad, proactive, and systematic basis.[17] Bishop's work with the Panama Canal Commission was essentially reactive and sought to neutralize efforts to sway public opinion by canal opponents; Pinchot went a step further by initiating press coverage in order to persuade public opinion to be supportive of his programs and policies. The chairman of the House Agriculture Committee confirmed the novelty when he said, approvingly, during a floor debate that Pinchot had "devised" this new approach to reaching the public through dissemination of materials to the press.[18] Similarly, the secretary of agriculture called this activity an "experiment."[19]

During these years in the early 1900s, Pinchot gradually developed a sophisticated multidimensional campaign for conservation. He wrote speeches and congressional messages for Roosevelt and encouraged the president to travel around the country talking about conservation. He helped convene several conferences and establish organizations with forestry as a focal point. Then he arranged for press coverage of those events and sent Forest Service personnel to attend and influence decisions made by those conferences and associations. Pinchot widely distributed copies of his annual report to Congress and issued dozens of pamphlets and brochures, which he sent to a mailing list of thousands of reporters and newspapers. These proto–press releases were new to editors and reporters. Many welcomed receiving them and ran stories on the topics of the releases, sometimes verbatim.[20] Pinchot also organized a systematic clippings file. Newspapers were encouraged to send to the Forest Service copies of articles based on information contained in their press materials.[21] By this feedback loop, he could see which stories interested the press, how widely a release was picked up, and what the spin of the coverage was.

Pinchot's vision was not limited to the narrow scope of "publicity," that is, the dissemination of agency publications and push for press coverage. He also had an expansive and original perspective on the full breadth and potential of public relations in public administration. He urged his staff to accept speaking invitations from local groups whenever possible and to use those opportunities to explain the Forest Service's conservation program. Similarly, he encouraged his employees to take the initiative to attend meetings, conventions, and conferences of organizations with any possible interest in Forest Service policies. At those events, the staff were to take advantage of any platform and opportunity to explain the agency's policies and to encourage the organizations to pass resolutions endorsing these policies.

For Heyburn, attacking the publicity activities of the Forest Service would be an extension of his overall criticism of the agency. But he needed a forum. In contrast to some other congressional committees (and the more common practice in contemporary times), the Committee on Public Lands did not hold frequent public hearings. It often reported out bills without even holding public hearings on them.[22] Aside from the three hearings on Heyburn's complaint in 1904, this committee held only one other hearing that year (not on the forest reserves issue) and then none in 1905.[23] Heyburn's criticisms of the administration's forest policy were growing, yet there were no committee hearings from him to use as a platform for his views.

FIRST CRITICISM

By early 1906, Heyburn was eagerly seeking an outlet for his open war with the administration over forestry policy and especially to unveil a new attack. When the committee met on January 17, 1906, Heyburn asked to address it "briefly."[24] His comments were wide ranging, criticizing many aspects of President Roosevelt's conservation program and Forest Service policies. At the end of his comments, he added his new line of attack: Heyburn "charged that Chief Pinchot maintained a press bureau to praise the work of the forestry chief."[25] The press took notice.

Heyburn next let it fly on the floor of the Senate, on January 29, 1906. Most of his comments were a restatement of his general criticism of the administration's forest reserve policy. These comments, repeated so many times by him previously, were neither new nor news. But twice during his speech he alluded to the Forest Service's press activities.

Heyburn: I have been criticized in some of the articles that have been inspired in this case. . . . it was only part of a plan to attack the opposition to their plans by degrading it, by discrediting it, and bringing it into contempt. Throughout the county the press was fed with such statements, and I have one here, to which I desire to call the attention of the Senate: "The President's rebuke." This comes from the Pittsburgh Dispatch of September 28, 1905, and it is a sample of the work of the press bureau that has undertaken to break down an honest and fair criticism of the manner of the execution of this law.

Senator Benjamin Tillman (D-S.C.): The Senator used the word "press bureau" rather emphatically. Do I understand him to say that there is any evidence that the Bureau of Forestry has a press agent or something in the line of Mr. Bishop?

Heyburn: I will read the answer to that from a document, and then I will leave it to the Senator's own judgment.[26]

He next read into the record the text of some articles on the subject of President Roosevelt criticizing Heyburn for the latter's position on forest reserves, then returned to his basic line of attack: "I do not care for this combination press bureau that has been organized for the purpose of blackening my character. . . . I propose that this body and I propose that the country shall know exactly what they have done and the relation that I bear toward them. You can not possibly get at this from the right point of view without knowing something of the source from and the spirit in which these attacks emanate."[27]

Heyburn claimed that the Forest Service press bureau had three full-time employees who were engaging in swaying public opinion to support Pinchot's forestry policies and to oppose efforts by people like Heyburn to stop those policies. Senator Joseph Bailey (D-Tex.) reacted to Heyburn's speech sympathetically by denouncing the "propaganda" being spread and demanding that the three employees be fired.[28] Heyburn was, however, merely giving a speech. He did not propose any action or introduce any legislation.

In terms of the instant reviews as measured by press coverage, Heyburn's attack on agency press relations was a success. The next day, both the *New York Times* and the *Washington Post* carried stories covering his speech. Though his repetition of old arguments against the Forest Service was not new and did not deserve coverage, his criticism of its press agents was and justified coverage. The lead in the *Times* was "Charges that a press agency is maintained at Government expense in the Forestry Bureau were made in the Senate to-day by Mr. Heyburn of Idaho."[29] Clearly the novelty of a government agency engaging in press relations had not worn

off from the previous month's coverage of Bishop's work at the Panama
Canal Commission. It still was considered a newsworthy item.

Being newsworthy was one thing, but did it have political "legs"? Could
Heyburn utilize the moment to weaken the Forest Service by pushing
through any tangible action against its press bureau? He seemed unsure
quite what, if anything, to do next.

About a year later, a House committee was conducting a broad-based
investigation into the USDA, including the Forest Service. The committee's
report concluded that "the administration of the Forest Service does not on
the facts deserve adverse criticism, but upon the contrary the Forest Service
has been administered honestly and with great administrative, executive,
and business ability."[30] Here was a demonstration of the coalition that
Pinchot had successful developed within Congress in support of his
policies. The committee report was a flat repudiation of Heyburn's verbal
onslaught against the Forest Service, including its public relations activities.

Nonetheless, the genie was out of the bottle. Heyburn was benefiting
from the "if there's smoke, there's fire" aspect of politics. As long as he
kept publicly complaining about Forest Service public relations, he was
bound to raise ongoing concerns with other legislators. Every year he
gave a major speech on the floor of the Senate attacking the Forest Service, including its press activities,[31] though he never initiated any related
concrete proposal for legislative action. Still, as exhibited in the Panama
Canal case, the press was a willing participant. For example, in August
1907, a few months after the House committee report, the *Washington
Post* ran a story with the headline "Pinchot Likes Puffs," which claimed
that the Forest Service was violating the postal laws by using its franking
privileges (free use of the mails) to facilitate receiving back from newspapers copies of issues that had utilized its press releases. According to
the article, unnamed "legal officers of the government" were looking
into the practice.[32]

CONGRESS REACTS

Congressional attention to Forest Service public relations coalesced in the
spring of 1908 as part of the FY 1909 appropriations process. As usual, the
process began in the House.[33] During a routine hearing by the Agriculture

Committee on the Forest Service's budget in January 1908, committee member Ernest Pollard (R-Neb.) asked Pinchot if the Forest Service had a "press bureau"? No, Pinchot answered; he did have two staffers who released information to the newspapers, but he did consider that a press bureau.[34] Pinchot was apparently interpreting the term used by Congressman Pollard strictly. The Forest Service did not have a unit with the formal name "Press Bureau." Yes, it had a Division of Publications and within it an Articles Section, but no Press Bureau. As used in those times, "press bureau" often referred to offices of political parties, campaign organizations, or special interest lobbies that pumped out highly slanted advocacy material for that party or campaign for free publicity in sympathetic newspapers. From Pinchot's perspective, the Forest Service did not have a press bureau because what it did have provided only factual information aimed at educating public opinion. Then Congressman William Cocks (R-N.Y.) asked him if the Forest Service ever paid newspapers to run its press releases? Again, Pinchot answered no; the materials his agency provided newspapers were run for free. Committee chairman Charles Scott (R-Kans.) helpfully asked if the material released to newspapers was simply a repackaging of information that was already published by the Forest Service in its own publications and bulletins. Yes, said Pinchot.[35]

The agricultural appropriation bill was debated on the floor of the House on March 30, 1908. Congressman Franklin Mondell (R-Wyo.), a sometime ally of the western timber interests that were being thwarted by Pinchot, offered an amendment that banned using any of the funds contained in the bill for "paying in whole or in part the preparation of any newspaper or magazine articles."[36] Mondell explained that he fully supported the broad dissemination of information "to give the public knowledge of what the Department is doing." But he thought Pinchot's bureau went beyond that, by "paying for the preparation of newspaper and magazine articles placing an exaggerated value on its work, and particularly in encouraging people who see it to impugn the motives or criticise Members of Congress and Senators and other men in public life who do not agree with some of the policies and some of the acts of the Bureau."[37]

This was a serious charge that got to the heart of legislative sensitivity about agency public relations. It suggested that agencies were not to be considered independent players in the political process. Rather, they were to be passive recipients of legislative (and presidential) direction. From the perspective of Capitol Hill, legislators should be immune from any *public* response by an agency to legislative criticism, no matter how unfair or uninformed. In other words, criticism was a one-way street. It was acceptable for members of Congress to attack a federal agency, but it was inappropriate for an agency to respond, with either a defense or a counterattack. This attitude reflected a legislato-centric culture that viewed agencies as army privates expected to take orders unquestioningly from higher-ranking officers, certainly not to argue back.[38]

On the House floor, Chairman Scott leapt to the defense of the Forest Service. The information it was releasing was simply a re-presentation of material published in its own brochures and pamphlets; some of the press releases did not even mention the agency; it did not pay any newspapers or magazines to run the material; and the information was useful to the public. Mondell clarified that he particularly objected to newspaper articles being published that did not explicitly state that the Forest Service was the author and source of the article. The debate was relatively brief. When it was over, Mondell's amendment passed 51–27, nearly a two-to-one margin. In politics, that was a landslide. The *Washington Post* coverage of the debate about the entire bill highlighted the attacks on Forest Service press relations.[39]

Attention now moved to the Senate. At a public hearing on the House-passed version of the appropriation bill, Pinchot testified that he had only "two items, or three," that he was asking the Senate to change in its version of the bill. One was the Mondell amendment. Pinchot shrewdly emphasized that he in fact supported the purpose of the Mondell amendment, *as he understood it,* to ban payments *to* newspapers for the publication of press releases. But he should be permitted to expend funds to *prepare* material for release to the media. Pinchot appealed to the penny-pinching nature of legislators by contrasting the costs of printing and distributing agency bulletins and other publications with press releases that were picked up by newspapers: "This method is vastly cheaper. We get a very large publication at practically no cost. If you figure out what it would cost to make public this same valuable information under the newspaper plan it is not more than 1 per cent of what it would cost under the bulletin plan."[40]

The Senate committee ended up recommending an amendment dealing with this issue and the complaints about Forest Service personnel attending conferences of forestry-related organizations that was supportive of Pinchot: "That no part of the money herein appropriated shall be used to pay the transportation or traveling expenses of any forest officer or agent except he be traveling on business directly connected with the Forest Service and in furtherance of the works, aims, and objects specified and authorized in and by this appropriation; Provided further, That no part of this appropriation shall be paid or used for the purpose of paying for, in whole or in part, the publications of any newspaper or magazine article."[41] Clearly, this wording had been carefully drafted. It would not affect Pinchot's current practices regarding staff travel to conferences or his press bureau. Whenever he sent staff to conferences, he fully justified it as based on the mandate of the Forest Service. Similarly, he never paid newspapers or magazines to publish his press releases. The amendment provided the appearance of action rather than action itself.

When the agriculture appropriation bill for FY 1909 got to the Senate floor, Heyburn and others were waiting. In the meantime, Heyburn had taken the first tangible (if modest) legislative step against Forest Service public relations. He persuaded the Senate to enact a resolution requiring the agency to submit a detailed report on staff travel to conferences.[42] He was hoping this would prove his allegations about agency staff attending conferences to lobby for public support for current forestry policies. No senator opposed his request since it was merely a requirement for a report rather than concrete statutory action. However, other than a generalized response from the secretary of agriculture, the detailed report was not submitted until May 16, after the submission of the conference committee report on the annual agricultural appropriation bill and therefore too late for any new amendments to it.[43] Given Pinchot's political skills, that careful timing was most likely intentional. Heyburn was not going to be given any new ammunition to use against the Forest Service until its annual funding had been put to bed.

Even without the information from the requested report, when the bill reached the Senate floor, Heyburn went on a full-scale attack. He kicked off a debate that "spread over a week, including a night session."[44] One of his topics was the Forest Service's aggressive public relations program, especially the attendance of its staffers at conferences and conventions of other organizations. He brandished a letter from an Idaho-based reporter claiming that he had witnessed Forest Service employees falsely charging such expenses to other budget categories. Senator Reed Smoot (R-Utah), a friend of the agency, flatly denied the charge and offered to submit paperwork that would document that the costs of the trips in question were indeed charged to the accurate budget category. Heyburn declined the offer.[45] Attacks by other senators on Forest Service press relations and conference travel came up again and again during the floor debate on the bill.[46]

At first, the committee's amendment was adopted.[47] But some senators, hostile to the Forest Service, succeeded in reopening the question. Clarence Clark (R-Wyo.) proposed reconsidering the amendment and rejecting its section on publications, so that the wording of Mondell's House amendment would be restored. It was adopted.[48] Seeking to circumscribe the agency further, senators proposed two more amendments. Senator Thomas Carter (R-Mont.) introduced an amendment to ban all federal agencies from the preparation or publication of articles "directly or indirectly, advocating legislation or an increase of an appropriation by Congress."[49] This was an early insight into the connection between agency press relations and agency lobbying (see chapters 5, 9). Carter's amendment was, however, ruled out of order, since it went beyond the scope of a bill appropriating money solely to the USDA—and Carter's perceptiveness passed without much attention. Then Senator Jacob Gallinger (R-N.H.) suggested adding language banning the use of an agency's franking privilege to receive back issues of newspapers containing articles that were based on agency press releases.[50] This issue had first been first raised publicly in an article in the *Washington Post* the previous summer.[51] Again, based on a point of order, this time claiming that the amendment was "general legislation" and thus not permitted as part of an appropriation bill, the amendment was ruled out of order.

The parliamentary situation was back to square one. The Senate had rejected the committee amendment shifting the ban from payment for preparation to payment for publication. The original Mondell House amendment, banning payment for preparation, was back again as the pending language. Now, on behalf of the committee, Senator Francis

Warren (R-Wyo.) introduced an amendment that used a different wording to try to move closer to the committee's position, notwithstanding the success of the anti-Pinchot senators defending the Mondell language so far. Warren's suggested amendment maintained the ban on spending money for the preparation of press releases (Mondell's approach) but watered it down with a caveat: "but this shall not prevent the giving out to all persons without discrimination, including newspapers, magazine writers, and publishers, of any facts or official information of value to the public." The wording seemingly negated the Mondell prohibition. But since Warren's amendment kept the original Mondell language, it maintained its appeal to the anti-Pinchot senators. His amendment passed,[52] and it became the final language contained in the Senate's version of the bill. According to the *Washington Post*, that amendment was the "only one small victory" that anti-Pinchot senators had in all their attacks on the entire bill, surely an indication that attacks on agency publicity activities were able to attract broader support than substance-based votes supporting or opposing an agency.[53] Again, press coverage focused on the criticisms and amendments against Pinchot's publicity activities as a key element of the debate over the entire bill.[54]

Since the two houses had passed different versions of a bill, this issue was one (of many) that had to be resolved by a conference committee. As with all other issues, the conferees from both houses sought ways to either split the difference between the two versions or, using twenty-first-century lingo, find a win-win solution. As one of the three senators on the conference committee, Warren could emphasize that the Senate had approved Mondell's House amendment and then added some additional clarifying language of its own. Therefore, he could argue disingenuously, the House should have no problem since its version was enacted intact. Since the Senate had accepted the House language, a fair compromise would be for the House to reciprocate and accept the Senate's add-on wording. His argument carried the day.[55] Both houses accepted the conference committee recommendation, and President Roosevelt signed it into law on May 23, 1908.[56]

The fight over Forest Service publicity activities had ended with a formal law stating Congress's desire to hamper the public relations programs of a federal agency. This was, most likely, the first time that Congress formally and authoritatively acted to reduce agency publicity. However, because of his high standing with a majority coalition in Congress, Pinchot had successfully modified the wording of the new law so that it would have negligible impact on the public relations of the Forest Service.

SUBSEQUENT DEVELOPMENTS AND IMPACT OF THE LAW

The 1908 provision in the agriculture appropriation bill was renewed without serious debate for FY 1910.[57] But during the House debate in 1910 on the FY 1911 bill, several members sought to reopen the issue and push for more legal restrictions on Forest Service press activities. Congressmen Mondell and Fitzgerald (who had first raised objections to the press agent of the Panama Canal Commission; chapter 1) reraised their complaints about the press bureau at the Forest Service.[58] As part of that debate, Congressman James Tawney (R-Minn.) introduced an amendment to delete from the law Senator Warren's 1908 add-on language to Mondell's original amendment. He explained that Warren's language essentially gutted the restrictions contained in Mondell's original amendment. After a quick but sharp debate in which both sides repeated the positions they had expressed two years earlier, his motion was defeated on a voice vote.[59]

In March 1910, a few weeks after the agricultural appropriation bill had passed, the House was debating the annual legislative, executive, and judicial appropriations bill.[60] Tawney resumed his attack on the Forest Service (even though it was not funded by this bill) by focusing on the amount of money it spent for travel to conferences and for giving talks. Some congressmen rose to justify the lectures and trips.[61] In the run-up to the debate on the broad-scoped bill, some on Capitol Hill were talking about an omnibus anti-publicity appropriations amendment. According to a front page story in the *New York Times,* an early draft stated that "no part of the appropriation in the bill shall be available for the services of press agents" in federal departments and agencies.[62] But nothing came of the idea; the amendment was never introduced as the bill was working its way through the House and Senate.[63]

After the failure in 1910 to strengthen the 1908 ban on Forest Service publicity, the provision was then routinely renewed every year by Congress without any serious debate. Finally, in 1922, Congress shifted the provision from the annual agriculture appropriation bill to permanent law, where it remained, essentially unchanged, through to the end of the twentieth century (and beyond).[64] Despite its limited impact, this first authoritative congressional action regarding agency public relations could be seen as an indication that "slowly Congress was resuming control" over the Forest Service and its public relations.[65]

• • •

In the short term, given Pinchot's political nimbleness and the help of his supporters in the Senate, the impact of the legal prohibition had the weight of a feather. McGeary concluded that "the prohibition was singularly ineffective."[66] According to Ponder, "none" of the congressional efforts to control agency publicity activities during Theodore Roosevelt's presidency were effective.[67] The same was true after Pinchot had left the bureau.[68] For example, two summaries in 1930 of Forest Service information activities— long after the enactment of the 1908 limitations—described a public relations program as extensive as when Pinchot had invented it.[69] A decade later, a syllabus for an in-house training session on public relations equally reflected the extensive scope of activities constructed by Pinchot.[70] Finally, Kaufman's 1960 study of the Forest Service indicated a continued emphasis in the organization's culture on public relations, by both the Washington headquarters and rangers in the field.[71]

CHAPTER 3

INVESTIGATING PRESS OFFICES IN
TWO AGENCIES, 1910–1914

Census Bureau, 1910: *A House Committee should determine if the Census Bureau "maintains a press bureau, or retains any person whose duty it is to write articles for, or disseminate news to, newspapers, magazines, or periodicals."*

H. Res. 236, 61st Congress (U.S. House,
Committee on the Census, *Press Bureau*, 23)

Department of Agriculture, 1912: *A House investigative committee should be appointed "to obtain full and complete information of the expenditure of public moneys for press bureaus."*

H. Res. 545, 62nd Congress (U.S. House, Committee
on Rules, *Department Press Agents*, 4)

Department of Agriculture, 1914: *"Is there under the administration of the Department of Agriculture a press agency, or bureau of any kind or character, that is run for the purpose of preparing and giving out information for publication?"*

H. Res. 573, 63rd Congress (*CR* 51:14 [August 17, 1914]: 13860)

W ithout passing formal legislation, in 1905 Congress had prevented the Panama Canal Commission from employing a press agent, but the agency found ways around that political understanding. Similarly, in 1908 Congress had authoritatively enacted a legal restriction on Forest Service press activities, but the wording of the law made the statute ineffective. These were part of the initial reaction by Congress to the relatively new phenomenon of agency public relations. Also part of this initial reaction were three formal committee investigations between 1910 and 1914. These reports did not recommend any statutory action by Congress, but they are important demonstrations of Congress grappling with the subject. They were initiated by members of Congress who thought that publicity activities were a threat to Congress's institutional interests, but other members of Congress were agency supporters who defended the use of public relations in public administration. In general, these events mark Congress's growing recognition of public relations as an element of modern management and its struggle to delimit precisely which, if any, of these communication activities were improper and a threat to its own power

REGULARIZING FEDERAL AGENCY PUBLICITY ACTIVITIES

In March 1909, Theodore Roosevelt left the White House and was replaced by William Howard Taft, Roosevelt's hand-picked successor.[1] Three months later, the U.S. Department of Agriculture (USDA) asked if Taft would be willing to sign an executive order superseding civil service regulations to permit it to employ a "publicity agent." Since 1908, the department's Bureau of Soils had been employing John R. Bowie as a publicity agent, but formally in the position of special agent and therefore not requiring any formal Civil Service Commission (CSC) recruitment and selection process.[2] During that year, Bowie had performed to the satisfaction of the bureau and department. In the formal and somewhat dry words of a government document, his duties as a press agent were explicitly defined as comprising three activities: "the selection and synthesizing of the most valuable matter for public use from among all the researches and operations of the Bureau of Soils and preparing the result of such work in the most useful and attractive form, and securing its publication in the best organs for dissemination of the information to the farming classes, which are the ones to be benefited."[3] This is an effective summary of the work of press release writers and continues to be valid to this day.

Because of his success, the bureau and department were eager to hire him to the job on a permanent basis, but they were blocked by CSC rules. A position in the classified service could be filled only through the regular recruiting, testing, and appointment process. But the agency feared that "the duties of the place are of such an exceptional nature that an examination by the Commission would not necessarily disclose the best qualified applicant."[4] Therefore, President Taft was jointly petitioned by the USDA and CSC to exercise his statutory powers and suspend the requirements of the civil service law by signing an executive order exempting the position from those requirements. Taft agreed and signed Executive Order 1101 on June 29, 1909. In it he permitted the appointment, without going through a CSC process, of Bowie "as a publicity agent in the Bureau of Soils in the Department of Agriculture." The term "publicity agent" was used twice in the text of the executive order.[5]

This executive order can be seen as an important signal of the emergence of public relations in public administration. It was being regularized, to the point of having a civil service job description and a standard definition of the position's responsibilities and skills. Despite the highly publicized attacks on the Panama Canal Commission and the Forest Service (chapters 1 and 2), external communications was nonetheless continuing to be institutionalized as part of the day-to-day work of the bureaucracy. Notwithstanding the congressional attacks, agencies were becoming explicitly aware of the integral role that public relations could play. For example, the U.S. Marine Corps had established a de facto publicity bureau in its recruiting office in Buffalo, New York, as early as 1905—the same year Congress had ferociously attacked the press agent at the Panama Canal Commission.[6] In 1907, the Corps created a formal "Publicity Bureau" in its recruiting office for the Chicago area.[7] For its time, that office ran a sophisticated and comprehensive public relations effort to publicize the Corps, attract recruits, and keep local newspapers informed of the subsequent careers of recruits from their area. Success bred further expansion of the office's activities. Naturally, other Marine recruiting offices were eager to copy that model in their own areas. For example, by 1913, the Corps' recruiting service had a large publicity bureau in New York City.[8] Within only a few years, it became unimaginable to run a Marine recruiting effort without the use of publicity techniques.[9]

This process of regularizing external communications activities in the federal bureaucracy accelerated during the Taft administration (1909–13). According to Ponder, "despite, or perhaps because of, Taft's seeming indifference to departmental publicity, practices such as hiring publicists and issuing 'handouts' to stimulate news coverage had been adopted by numerous executive agencies."[10] In fact, it was becoming so commonplace that press releases were no longer as likely to be published verbatim as when Pinchot pioneered the practice. By the beginning of the Wilson administration (1913), almost every cabinet department had at least one press relations specialist, often serving as a special assistant to the secretary.[11] The growth in the practice of federal public relations was happening simply because its value to an agency was apparent. It was too good to ignore, notwithstanding the risk of congressional attacks.

Certainly there was a mix of the self-serving and the practical in the inexorable growth and nurturing of a publicity office in federal agencies. In some cases there was a tangible need for someone to deal with reporters who came by looking for stories or seeking to confirm information they already possessed. In other cases publicity was an inexpensive and fast shortcut to disseminating information to large and widely dispersed audiences. Finally, public relations was a way to promote the interests of the agency and garner the support of public opinion for its policies and activities. Regardless of motive, having a publicity office was becoming a necessity.

To those advocating institutionalizing public relations in public administration, congressional hostility was emerging as more than ad hoc and agency specific; rather, it began to reflect a consistent and generic pattern. Besides the controversies on Capitol Hill over the press activities of the Panama Canal Commission and the Forest Service, beginning around this time and through to 1912 some legislators were considering (but never implemented) the idea of amending federal appropriations law to ban all federal funding for all departmental "press agents."[12] The signing of the presidential executive order in 1909 permitting the USDA to employ a publicity agent notwithstanding CSC regulations was the tip of the iceberg of public relations normalizing its status in federal public administration.

Still, after the significant public controversies regarding the press bureau of the Panama Canal Commission (which Taft had personally played a role in) in 1905 and the Forest Service press bureau in 1908, it seems somewhat surprising that a president would agree to touch such a potentially political hot potato by signing this executive order. It is possible that Taft thought that the *publicity* work of the USDA to help farmers was much less controversial and more politically safe than the *press* work of bureaus facing major congressional challenges to their raison d'être. It is also possible that because of Taft's lack of political finesse he did not realize that the executive order could be made controversial by a congressional opponent. He went ahead and signed it, and no hullabaloo ensued. That is itself significant, indicating the ad hoc nature of the efforts by Congress to silence the bureaucracy and the haphazard nature of the selection of issues to confront. There would need to be at least one person on Capitol Hill willing to take the time and effort to lead the fight on a public relations issue and, just as important, somebody who knew about it. The signing of the executive order and the subsequent lack of controversy indicate the absence of knowledge about it at Washington's political levels, the absence of a politician willing to lead the charge against it, or both.

A PRESS AGENT AT THE CENSUS BUREAU, 1910

About half a year after President Taft had signed the executive order approving the appointment of a publicity agent and two years after the controversy over Gifford Pinchot's press bureau, Congressman Joseph Robinson (D-Ark.) challenged the existence of a press agent at the U.S. Census Bureau.[13] Robinson must have thought he had landed a trifecta: an issue that Congress institutionally had shown itself to be hostile to, a partisan issue to embarrass the majority Republicans in the House as well as in the White House, and a racial issue to stir up racist white southern solidarity.[14]

In 1909 and early 1910, the Census Bureau (a unit within the Department of Commerce and Labor) was gearing up to launch the decennial census. Its pressing needs were to hire a temporary staff of enumerators and then to conduct a census with the maximum voluntary cooperation of the citizenry. Federal law gave Census Bureau director E. Dana Durand the discretion to appoint from outside the civil service system twenty "special agents" to handle unusual assignments. The only prohibition in the law was that they could not be employed in "clerical work." In August 1909, Durand appointed Whitman Osgood as a special agent with the informal assignment of serving full-time as a press agent for the bureau. Osgood had briefly worked in the Census Bureau during the 1900 census as a statistician. He then entered journalism, working for several Washington-based newspapers as a reporter and then as editor of news stories telegraphed to newspapers outside the capital.[15] Now, after nine years in the newspaper business, Osgood's assignment was to write news releases about the upcoming census. His goal was to inform the public about the rationale and need for a census, about the confidentiality of census information, and about the importance of voluntary cooperation with census enumerators.

Durand thought that extensive free press coverage leading up to the census could be used to reduce costs, staffing, and time needed for a national census. In his view, it was "absolutely necessary in order to prepare the minds of the people for the census, so that there will be no prejudice against it, and no misunderstanding of it, but rather a willingness to answer the questions and a preparedness to answer them, in consequence of the people having thought over in advance the nature of the inquiries, and formulated the answers to the questions more or less in their minds. That applies particularly to agricultural sections."[16]

Osgood began churning out two major kinds of press releases about the census. Some were considered "news" and therefore released with embargo dates on them, with newspapers prohibited from using the information before the day and time the embargo ended. His other major product was feature stories that were not time sensitive and were not embargoed. Both categories of releases were distributed to daily newspapers, weekly and rural papers, magazines, foreign-language papers, and press associations. The Census Bureau maintained a mailing list of nearly 30,000 recipients. Besides creating these two kinds of news releases, Osgood's responsibilities included releasing human interest stories about the Census Bureau and its staff; responding to individual in-person inquiries from Washington-based reporters; sending information about the census to civic groups, religious organizations, and schools; and distributing publicity materials to encourage citizens to apply for enumerator jobs.[17] In general, the overall purpose of his job, based on the goals set by Durand, was to disseminate information that would educate the public about the census and its importance, prepare them for a visit by an enumerator, and encourage maximum voluntary cooperation. This was, for the times, a sophisticated and insightful utilization of the tools of public relations to contribute to the goals of public administration.

On January 15, 1910, Congressman Robinson introduced a House resolution directing the secretary of commerce and labor to submit a comprehensive report about the press bureau at the Census Bureau.[18] His action triggered some press coverage, indicating that the topic, as usual, had risen above the normal political din.[19] The Census Committee, to which the resolution had been referred, decided to hold a hearing on the resolution before voting on whether to recommend to the House its enactment or rejection.

Acting quickly, the House committee held the hearing on January 20 and had only one witness, Census director Durand. In a felicitous phrase, Catton described the demeanor of the committee members during the hearing: "The congressmen were disturbed, but they did not quite know what they were disturbed about."[20] But Catton's characterization seems to be based only on the plain meaning of the language of the hearing transcript, ignoring the legislative culture in which public hearings are embedded. Ostensibly, public hearings are intended as fact-finding fora by which a legislative body develops a knowledge base for subsequent decisions; congressional ethos restricts the purpose of questions to elucidate information.[21] So, although the questions posed by Robinson and his minority party colleagues were, formally, fact-finding ones reflecting open-mindedness, they were in effect attacks in disguise, a predetermined effort to build a record justifying their opposition to the Census Bureau press agent. Their questions were more in the nature of argumentative challenges, simply wrapped in the elaborate language of congressional courtesy of the times. In that context, both the majority and minority party members—contrary to Catton—knew exactly what they had found and intended by their questions to create a record demonstrating that the Census Bureau's press agent was either a benign phenomenon or a malevolent one.

Most of the questioning by Democratic members of the committee was hostile, pointed, and sharp, almost like a badgering cross-examination by a prosecutor at a criminal trial:

Courtney Hamlin (D-Mo.): Is it not a fact that this same man sends out political matter that does not pass under your supervision at all?

Robinson (after an exchange with Durand declining to answer Hamlin's question with a yes or a no): I understood you to answer the question in the affirmative.

Hamlin: And have not these requests [to congressmen for mailing lists of newspapers] gone exclusively and entirely to the Republican Members of Congress?

Durand: Not to my knowledge. I do not think any of those statements are true; certainly not to my knowledge. It is entirely unnecessary.

Robinson (citing an article based on a Census Bureau release describing Durand's appointment of district supervisors): Of what benefit and what assistance could this article be in the taking of the census or in the educating of people who are ignorant as to the purposes and methods of the census?

Durand: I should say that was of very great value.

Robinson: Do you not know . . . ?

Durand: I do not know it.

Conversely, most of the questions from Republican members of the committee were softballs or simply statements supportive of Durand's testimony:

Edgar Crumpacker (R-Ind.), chairman: Is it your idea that by this means [Osgood's work] the enumerators will be able to secure more reliable data and will be able to do the work in much less time?

Durand: It is my idea that it will result in great economy in money, and also in a great improvement in the character and the quality of the statistics.

Crumpacker: Do you know whether enumerators have any difficulty in securing information from citizens through the fear that the information may be used for the purpose of taxation or something of that sort?

Durand: That fear is encountered almost constantly . . .

Crumpacker: And that assurance is given in these news articles?

Durand: That is one of the most conspicuous things that stand out in those articles.

James Hughes (R-W.Va.): From the number of inquiries that I get with regard to the census, I do not think that too many letters [i.e., press releases] could be sent out explaining how it is done. I think that it is a very good thing to do.

Otto Foelker (R-N.Y.): Would not your department also be charged with favoritism if you did not follow that rule [of dropping newspapers from the mailing list if they violated an embargo]?

Durand: I do not think that we could get a newspaper man to publish anything . . . unless we insisted on a release date.

Campbell Slemp (R-Va.): If this were paid advertising it would cost a great amount of money?

Durand: Yes.

Hannibal Godwin (D-N.C.): Do you pay for the articles?

Durand: We do not pay for publishing them.[22]

At one point, the partisan sniping became so intense that Durand briefly disappears from the hearing transcript. Republican and Democrats got into a tit-for-tat mode of directly debating each other that extended for twenty-three consecutive comments between Durand's last statement and his next one.[23]

Throughout the hearing, Robinson and his allies tried to build a case through charges, insinuation, and assumptions that (1) Durand was violating his statutory authority by hiring a special agent to do clerical work (assuming that press release writing was clerical in nature); (2) Durand did not have explicit statutory power to hire a press agent at the Census

Bureau; (3) Durand and Osgood were tilting their work to favor Republican newspapers; (4) daily newspapers were being advantaged by Osgood's release schedules over weekly papers; and (5) embargoed press releases were somehow inappropriate.

However, Robinson's most explosive charge was racial. He claimed that Osgood (who was white) and his assistant, Thomas Jones (also white), were covertly trying to reach the African American population and encourage a disproportionate number to apply for jobs as enumerators at the expense of hiring more white enumerators:

> Robinson: So that a part of the duties of Mr. Osgood, and Mr. Jones in assisting him, is to educate the negroes as to how to get jobs as enumerators, as well as to educate the people to report to them? . . . In answer to my question I understood you to say that Mr. Osgood and Mr. Jones have been sending out to lodges, churches, and other organizations for colored people information as to how to make application and secure appointments as enumerators. . . . You have not sent anything of that sort to any white lodges and schoolhouses, have you?
>
> Durand: But it goes more or less without saying that in the South the [white] supervisors will not use any means, in most cases, to induce colored persons who are competent to apply. In fact, they would rather that they would not apply.

This Democratic accusation, of course, was a cynical and demagogic attack deliberately aimed at converting the conservative Republican members of the committee (and the whole House) to Robinson's side.[24]

Four days after the hearing, the committee issued its report. By majority vote, it recommended that the House not approve the resolution Robinson had introduced a few weeks earlier compelling the secretary of commerce and labor to submit a report about the press agent at the Census Bureau. One of the reasons for the committee's position was that "all the facts that could be gotten by adopting the resolution" had been obtained at the hearing. "Census Director Upheld by Board," read a newspaper headline.[25]

Robinson and four of the other five Democratic members filed a minority report that asserted a few of the arguments they had been insinuating through their questions in the hearing. In particular, they contended that press work was primarily clerical and that, as a special agent, Osgood was prohibited by law from doing any clerical work. Then, shifting from a legalistic argument to a substantive one, they declared flatly, "We do not believe that the Congress, in the passage of the census act above referred to, intended to provide for such a service or authorize it."[26] In other words, press relations work was illegal unless Congress specifically and explicitly permitted it.

Still, this was a minority report from the minority party. The majority party was not about to let the minority party assume control of the decisions that were their own prerogative to make. So when the committee report came up on the floor of the House on January 24, it was accepted and no further action was taken on it.[27] Robinson's resolution had been shelved. At the end of the week, Robinson totally dropped his pretense of wanting a fact-finding report. He introduced a bill "forbidding the maintenance of a press agent or press bureau by the Census Bureau."[28] It was referred to the Census Committee and, predictably, never heard from again.[29]

A PRESS BUREAU AT THE
DEPARTMENT OF AGRICULTURE, 1912

Two years later, the issue came up again in the House. This time, however, the Democrats were the majority party, the opposite of the power situation during the 1910 hearing about the Census Bureau. The issue that triggered congressional attention was fallout from a controversy over federal meat inspection. In 1906, Upton Sinclair had published his novel *The Jungle*, which described the unsanitary conditions in slaughterhouses. Before the year was out, Congress passed and President Theodore Roosevelt signed the Pure Food and Drug Act. Case closed and a happy ending. Actually, not. Even after the new law was signed, significant battles still took place about the stringency of USDA inspections, whether the department had been co-opted by the industry, and whether the public interest was being protected.[30]

In 1912, six years after the enactment of the new law, Congressman John Nelson (R-Wis.) charged that the USDA and the meat industry were in league to weaken surreptitiously the inspections and regulations the new law imposed to protect consumers.[31] His charges provoked a major investigation by the House Committee on Expenditures in the Department of Agriculture. The department decided to protest the charges vigorously and defend itself aggressively. According to the *New York Times,* on the eve of the hearing the USDA's "Publicity Bureau" distributed by messenger to key reporters a statement "ridiculing the charges."[32]

During those hearings, the committee chair permitted the USDA's top lawyer, George P. McCabe, to sit at the committee table and ask questions of witnesses. He assumed an active and adversarial role regarding testimony that criticized the department. At one point, Nelson and McCabe practically got into a physical altercation.[33]

While the USDA was pressing an aggressive posture at the hearings, its press office was engaging in a parallel effort to promote the department's perspective. Every day after the hearing ended, it disseminated press releases to reporters covering the hearings with defenses of the charges made against the department that day and preemptory attacks on what witnesses were expected to say the next day. Many of the press releases were "in such shape they can be used just as they are sent out." This meant that lazy journalists or those seeking a new angle beyond what had already occurred at that day's hearing could file the department's release without any editing and make it appear as though it contained their own reporting.[34] One variation contained phrases like "Secretary Wilson said to me" in a supposed interview. The mock interviews contained the department's rebuttal to witnesses. The subheadline of another release, regarding the testimony of a critic of the department, read "Mrs. Crane fails to make good" and then argued that a key detractor had failed to substantiate her charges. At other times the department's main press agent, John R. Bowie, handed reporters information impugning the credibility of some witnesses and containing other derogatory information that strengthened the department's contentions at the hearing.[35] Overall, this was an extremely aggressive, probably unprecedented, use of press relations tactics by a government agency facing charges before Congress.

Eventually, Nelson announced that he would submit a separate resolution calling for an investigation of the department's press relations.[36] Unusual even for the journalistic standards of the day, a reporter for the *New York Times* inserted himself into the story by confirming Nelson's charges even before Nelson's resolution had been formally introduced. Instead of limiting himself to the traditional detached journalistic formula of quoting news makers, the reporter described the activities of the department as "a scandal with which every newspaper correspondent in Washington is familiar" and noted that "the truth of his [Nelson's] charges is known to every correspondent in Washington."[37] Even the *Chicago Tribune,* which sided with the hometown meat industry, called the USDA's aggressive press activities "an unusual proceeding."[38]

Nelson's resolution was officially introduced on May 20, 1912, and referred to the powerful House Rules Committee.[39] The resolution called for the creation of a special House committee "to obtain full and complete information of the expenditure of public moneys for press bureaus . . . by the Department of Agriculture and by other departments" and for the committee to recommend "what steps are necessary to protect public funds from newspaper exploitation without warrant of law."[40]

Acting quickly, the committee held a hearing on the request the next day. Nelson was the lead-off witness. He described the forceful public relations tactics that the USDA was engaging in during the meat inspection hearings, introduced some examples of the department's releases, and elaborated on his objections to these practices. For example, he contended that the department was violating the law by misusing its franking privileges when it sent out materials challenging the integrity of witnesses, since those attacks had nothing to do with the department's mandate, programs, and activities. Nelson pointed out the 1908 legislation limiting the press activities of the USDA's Forest Bureau (since expanded to cover the entire department) and implied that the department was violating this law. He called for Congress "to put a stop to this press-bureau business. It is an abuse, a great abuse, which will grow intensely and ramify throughout all the departments of the Government, and unless it shall be speedily checked it surely will handicap good legislation and may greatly harm the public service." Committee members had only a few questions. Finis Garrett (D-Tenn.) agreed that the daily summaries from the department about the public hearings had "nothing whatever to do with any work of the Department of Agriculture." Chairman Robert Henry (D-Tex.) inquired if Nelson had formally submitted a complaint to the postmaster general about the alleged misuse of the frank? No, he replied.[41]

Nelson had arranged for three reporters to testify. This would probably strike a twenty-first-century reader as highly unusual, given the insistence of reporters that they are merely observers and not participants. These reporters were, however, willing to share their negative experiences from the meat inspection controversy. The three reporters were Charles P. Hunt of the *Arizona Republican,* Isaac Gregg of the *New York World,* and Charles Willis Thompson of the *New York Times.*[42] All three described the kinds of materials that they had been receiving from the USDA during the meat inspection hearings, sometimes by messenger and sometimes through the mail. They also described Bowie offering them documents that supposedly impugned the character of witnesses or undercut their credibility. All three condemned these particular press bureau activities. Thompson was more nuanced in his comments, adding that generally the press bureau work of the departments was helpful, "legitimate," and "pretty straight stuff." But, he said, USDA press relations during the hearings were "about as wide an extension of the press-agent business as I have ever seen."[43]

At the conclusion of the hearing, Nelson was asked if the press agent practices aired at the hearing were continuing? He said that as a result of his own publicity efforts to expose the press relations of the department it looked to him like they had sharply lessened, "so that the publicity cure is working now."[44] Indeed, the hearing itself garnered substantial publicity.[45] In other words, based on how Nelson crystallized the lesson of these events, publicity by legislators attacking publicity by departments was an effective tactic.

The committee never acted on the resolution or submitted a report explaining its decision not to recommend adoption of Nelson's resolution. The explanation came from the chairman's comment during the hearing. Referring to the nine House committees with jurisdiction to investigate expenditures in each of the cabinet departments, he said to Nelson and the three reporters regarding departmental press agents, "That is a good field in which to do patriotic work, to go before these nine committees and get them busy on these things."[46] Similarly, Henry was quoted in a newspaper as saying that "we have established definitely that there is something to investigate in the press agent activities of government departments."[47] But he left that investigation to other committees to decide if they wanted to pursue the matter. The lack of action by the Rules Committee could be related to Nelson's concluding comment at the hearing about the apparent diminution of the USDA press activities as soon as he began complaining about them publicly and with the scheduling of the Rules Committee hearing. Committee members may have interpreted that as indicating that the problem had largely taken care of itself.

The committee's inaction also made sense politically. The month after the hearing, the two parties held their presidential nominating conventions, and then the country's attention was consumed by the three-way presidential election between Taft, Roosevelt, and Wilson. The House Democrats may have been perfectly comfortable letting the charges against one of the departments of the administration hang in the air unresolved throughout the fall campaign. It was one minor way to promote the chances of their party's candidate as a reformer. Also, the legislative outcome may have been tied to the partisan alignment during this controversy, which was the mirror image of the 1910 hullabaloo over the press agent in the Census Bureau. In this case, Republican Nelson was asking for a special committee of inquiry to be set up. Majority Democrats would not be interested in giving a "win" to a member of the minority party or letting the Republicans set the legislative and political agenda of the House. They had given him a public hearing, which was an opportunity to release embarrassing information about the tactics of a cabinet department in a Republican administration. But that was as far as the majority party was willing to go in terms of granting a request from a member of the minority party. They were in charge, and this kind of decision was to be made only to help their own kind.

A PRESS AGENCY AT THE
DEPARTMENT OF AGRICULTURE, 1914

Even though Congress took no tangible action as a result of the hearing on the Nelson resolution, those events had an impact on the USDA. The department had conducted an extremely aggressive publicity strategy to promote its position on the meat inspection controversy. Those tactics had led to a public hearing and investigation, to three reporters condemning the tactics when they testified at the public hearing, and to widespread press coverage of the department's publicity activities. Such negative publicity would have had an effect inside the department. Public relations professionals like Bowie would have understood that the net impact of the controversy was negative. The department had lost goodwill, alienated the press corps, and looked bad on Capitol Hill; its good-guy image of "we help farmers" had been degraded. The department now looked mean and vicious. Its subsequent actions demonstrate that an internal reappraisal occurred, lessons were learned, and decisions were made about the future.

The Nelson hearing had taken place in mid-1912 during the last full year of Taft's presidency. Subsequently, Taft lost reelection and Woodrow Wilson became the next president in March 1913. He named David F. Houston as his secretary of agriculture. One of Houston's early priorities for the department was "to place the information activities on a new footing." He invited the administration's newly appointed ambassador to Great Britain, Walter Page, to review the department's publicity. Page was a former reporter and publisher and looked at government external relations from that perspective.[48] He urged that USDA publications be made more "popular," that is, more appropriate for consumption by the public at large. He suggested that information the USDA distributed needed to be improved—written the way reporters wrote: easy to read, easy to understand, appealing, and attractive. Houston agreed and established the Office of Information within the secretary's office. His charge to the new unit was "to supervise the preparation of printed matter and particularly to facilitate the securing of news items."[49]

Even though Houston had not headed the department during the meat inspection publicity hearings, he understood the political terrain and proceeded cautiously. First, he kept the Office of Information's profile low. Even though every key unit in the department would contribute a chapter to its annual report to Congress (including such a relatively minor entity as the library), there was no chapter from the Office of Information.[50] Second, Houston was careful to reassure the press corps that the existence of the new office would not affect reporters' direct access to bureau chiefs.[51] Third, he hired a reporter to run the office, signaling that the needs and perspective of reporters covering the department would be understood and respected.[52] Fourth, the positions in the office were in the classified civil service (including its chief and assistant chief) as a way of demonstrating that its information programs would be nonpartisan and nonpolitical.[53] Fifth, the department's assistant secretary preemptively explained the secretary's action to the House Agriculture Committee to help prevent opposition on Capitol Hill.[54] Finally, when explaining the work of the new Office of Information, Houston emphasized his desire to get useful information to farmers. To make that point, in his first annual report to Congress since becoming secretary he wrote that the contents of Office of Information releases were "limited entirely to making known the facts of discovery and the official rulings of the department"[55] According to the *New York Times,* this was an effort at the "popularization" of the department's knowledge.[56] Clearly, the new Office of Information was a sharp break from the USDA's 1912 meat inspection publicity bureau.

Still, politicians in Congress were wary. On June 20, 1914, about a year after the Information Office had been created, Congressman William Humphrey (R-Wash.) introduced a resolution calling for the secretary of agriculture to submit a report on the operations of his press agency.[57] It was referred to the House Agriculture Committee. As during the first controversy over the USDA's public relations activities, the Democratic Party held the majority in the House. But at the other end of Pennsylvania Avenue, the White House was now occupied by a Democrat. This would have an effect on the political dynamics of the issue.

Without even bothering to hold a public hearing on it, the committee endorsed the request and recommended that the full House pass it.[58] Unlike what had happened in the 1910 controversy over the Census Bureau's press agency, when a different committee filed its recommendations, this report did not have a minority report. It was adopted unanimously.[59] The recommendation came up for floor debate on August 17, 1914. Committee chairman Asbury Lever (D-S.C.) briefly described the Humphrey resolution and noted the committee's unanimous support for its passage. Yet his endorsement was lukewarm: "The committee does not believe that the Department of Agriculture has any facts which it desires to conceal."[60] Or, in the political logic he would have been thinking, "We'll go along with a request for a report. We have nothing to be defensive about. But I'm a strong supporter of the department and also a fellow Democrat of the president and his appointee, the secretary of the department." Besides the partisan angle, Lever was also hinting at two different, emerging perspectives on agency publicity. For Humphrey, it was self-serving propaganda that should be stopped. But for legislators like Lever, USDA publicity and publication programs were part of the department's mission to disseminate helpful information to farmers. Two legislators, looking at the same publicity program, could view it differently. This was an example of the political maxim "Where you stand depends on where you sit." The elusive boundary between bad and good public relations was a political Gordian knot that would bedevil future legislators.

On the floor, Humphrey first described a USDA press release regarding a national bird census that included some quotes from USDA experts on the subject. He then gave a detailed explanation of his objections to such press releases and what he hoped to accomplish with the resolution. In particular, he articulated a legislative perspective on why such publicity offices should be opposed. It was a cogent and explicit rationale that deserves to be quoted at some length:

> The trouble about this publicity proposition is that they only publish one side, the side furnished by these great experts, and then the people believe that the Members of this House are not performing their public duty when they refuse to make appropriations to pay these experts. The experts get publicity only on one side, and that is the favorable side. The Members of the House have publicity, but it comes from both directions. They are both criticized and praised. As a result, the impression is gradually gaining ground throughout this country today that the ability and honesty of this country rest in its bureaus, and that whenever we refuse to make appropriations here we are failing in our duty. . . . This impression in regard to the bureau expert and of Congress is largely brought about by this constant publicity sent out by the departments. It is not fair to the people of this country. Through this advertisement the people have come largely to believe that the bureau chief is always a wise man, a great man, and a patriot, and that the Congressman that refuses to vote for any appropriation he asks is a petty politician.[61]

Humphrey's description zeroed in on the heart of legislative objections to agency publicity. Through effective external communications, agencies could develop a positive public image and obtain citizen support. Such public opinion would impact congressional decision making, limiting the options available to legislators. Thus, public relations was a key lever for government agencies to obtain autonomy and power. Conversely, a legislative effort to gag the bureaucracy was a counterstrategy to prevent it from happening. For Humphrey, this was a raw struggle for power and preeminence.

The floor debate was brief. Congressman Hiram Fowler (D-Ill.) proposed an amendment to the resolution that would also require the USDA to provide information if its press bureau was helping "private interests, either directly or indirectly." Apparently, based on a tangential comment during the floor debate, he wanted to find out if the department's press office was essentially a free source of information for press syndicates and wire services that distributed packaged articles for profit. Fowler's amendment was adopted without debate, as was the amended resolution.

The report from the USDA secretary, as required by the adopted Humphrey resolution, was sent to Congress four days later.[62] In his report, Secretary Houston responded to the five questions that were posed in the adopted resolution. He stated that the USDA did not have a press agency (using the then-common meaning of the term) and did not employ a publicity expert as banned by Congress in 1913 (see chapter 4). Rather, it had an Office of Information, which was strictly limited to the dissemination of useful information to farmers that was at the heart of the mission of the department. Sometimes such information could be disseminated faster and more cheaply through the press than through agency publications. Furthermore, press stories mentioning information contained in USDA publications were one way to prompt farmers' requests for those publications.[63]

He provided details on the composition of the Office of Information. It had a staff of twelve, including a chief, assistant chief, six clerks (presumably writers), and four support staff. The report provided full details on the duties, salary, civil service status, and previous experience of George Wharton, the Information Office chief, as well as the civil service appointment process for the office's assistant chief.

Last, Houston responded to the final question in the Humphrey resolution, which was Congressman Fowler's floor amendment. No, the Office of Information did not directly or indirectly help any private interests.

His report provided a statement on the "rules of engagement" for the Information Office, which clearly reflected lessons the department had learned from the Nelson fiasco. Here was a summary of principles that sought to decontroversialize department press offices: "It limits itself to the discussion of established facts and approved information. It has refrained from discussing personnel, entering into controversies, or commenting on legislation. It has not dealt with the policies of the department, discussed future measures, or praised individuals or organizations."[64] This description sought to move the image of an agency press office from one involved in policy disputes (potentially taking on a member of Congress) to a seemingly noncontroversial operation that even agency critics would accept. Both the description of the Office of Information mandate and the contents of the entire report were about as bland and boring as could be. The subtext of the secretary's report was "We have nothing to hide and, besides, this is not anything controversial." The bureaucracy was gradually learning a politically safe way to describe the activities and guiding principles of a public relations office that was inoffensive to prickly legislators. Houston's report concluded the episode. There were no follow-up requests for action from Humphrey or other members of Congress.

• • •

This chapter focuses on three formal investigations by Congress into the public relations activities of the Census Bureau and the USDA. These legislative reactions to agency public relations all ended after informational and investigative events, without ensuing authoritative congressional actions. Still, they conveyed an unambiguous message to federal agencies: external communications programs were highly sensitive and potentially controversial. They could easily be attacked by legislators and usually sympathetically publicized by the press. Therefore, while agency leaders were becoming increasingly aware of the integral nature of public relations to public administration, they were simultaneously absorbing the lesson that such activities needed to be handled gingerly and maintained in ways that would make them as bland and as defensible as possible politically.

CHAPTER 4

BANNING EMPLOYMENT OF
PUBLICITY EXPERTS, 1913–2004

*"No money appropriated by this or any other Act shall be used for
the compensation of any publicity expert unless specifically appropriated for that purpose."*

38 *Stat.* 212

Probably the most famous statutory reaction by Congress to muzzle
the bureaucracy was a 1913 law banning the employment of publicity experts in the federal government. This law is almost universally cited in the literature and viewed as the totemic event regarding
politicians' views of government public relations. It has been widely cited
in contemporary publications.[1] An indication of its significance, it was
also frequently referenced in earlier literature.[2] Though the details of the
enactment of the law were relatively brief and prosaic, its ongoing and
symbolic impact is of great importance. In fact, the largely ineffective
efforts to enforce this law reveal a pattern that presaged similar results
with other congressional efforts to silence the federal bureaucracy.

ENACTING THE BAN ON PUBLICITY EXPERTS

By 1913, the issue of agency publicity had been before Congress on and
off since the 1890s. For one congressman elected in 1892, the issue would

be quite familiar. He would have experienced the 1893–94 legislative debates on updating federal printing laws to reduce excessive government publications, the 1905 debate about a publicity agent at the Panama Canal Commission, the 1908 legislation banning some U.S. Forest Service publicity activities, the 1910 investigation of a publicity agent at the Census Bureau, and the inquiry in 1912 about USDA publicity activities. After two decades in the House, he would have been aware of the growing use of external communications techniques by federal agencies. That legislator was Frederick Gillett (R-Mass.).[3]

In mid-August 1913, the CSC issued a routine announcement of a competitive examination for a position in the classified service. The USDA's Bureau of Public Roads was seeking a "publicity expert."[4] The detailed position description was carried in the *New York Times* two weeks later. The duties of the job consisted of "preparation of news matter relating to the work of the office of Public Roads, and obtaining the publication of such items in various periodicals and newspapers, particularly in country newspapers." To qualify for the job, a man (women were excluded from applying) must have "had wide experience in newspaper work and whose affiliations with newspaper publishers and writers is extensive enough to insure the publication of items prepared by him."[5] Although the initial newspaper coverage was buried deep in the paper and in small print, an editorial writer saw it and thought it deserved comment. A few days after running the initial announcement, the *Times* published an editorial titled "Civil Service Needs No 'Publicity Experts.'" It stated that "what there is to know about good roads and bad the newspapers will find out and call to the attention of the public without the efforts of a public roads press agent. The need is not for an eight-dollar-a-day expert to inform the public what the department has been doing. . . . how the roads will profit thereby is far from clear."[6]

Given the readership of the *Times,* no doubt Gillett saw the editorial, even if he had missed the August 18 article or the later August 29 position description. Gillett acted as though he were unaware of such information activities occurring in federal agencies and, agreeing with the editorial, vowed to act as quickly as possible to scuttle the new job category in the federal government.[7] Three weeks later he had his opportunity. On September 6, the House was debating the proposed Urgent Deficiencies

Appropriation Bill. Gillett introduced a floor amendment to the bill that would add a proviso stating that "no money appropriated by this or any other act shall be used for the compensation of any publicity expert unless specifically appropriated for that purpose."[8]

Even before he had a chance to explain his amendment, a member asked him if it related to the 1908 limits on Forest Service publicity and if perhaps that 1908 legislation affected all units of the USDA, not just the Forest Service. If so, then the Bureau of Public Roads would already be under some publicity limitations. Gillett answered, "I am not aware of such legislation." Congressman Mondell interjected that he was the author of the 1908 Forest Service amendment and that it did not affect other bureaus in the USDA. Congressman Fitzgerald, who had first objected to the publicity agent at the Panama Canal Commission in 1905, chimed in his consistent opposition: "I do not believe that any department or bureau or service should employ men to extol its virtues or its activities."[9] Gillett confessed that he was equally unfamiliar with Fitzgerald's role vis-à-vis the Panama Canal. The "new" topic that Gillett thought he was bringing to light for the first time really was not so. When Gillett finally had a chance to explain his amendment, he articulated a classic rationale for Congress's anti-publicity stance:

> The different departments of the administration certainly are not very modest in finding men and means to put before the country in the press the duties and purposes of their administration, and I think they can do without the employment of a man like this who is avowedly simply a publicity agent. It does not seem to me that it is proper for any department of the Government to employ a person simply as a press agent to advertise the work and doings of the department. . . . In the ordinary work of the department, anything which requires the knowledge of the public certainly finds its way into the press.[10]

Now that Mondell, Fitzgerald, and Gillett had all pointed out how opposed they were to agency publicity activities, a few other contrary voices began being heard. Congressman Richard Austin (R-Tenn.) wondered if the House ought to postpone a vote on the amendment until it heard the rationale for the position from the department and bureau. After all, he said, "there is no subject now engaging the attention of the

American people that is of more interest."[11] Perhaps this new publicity expert in the Bureau of Public Roads would help provide information the public was seeking? Fitzgerald and Gillett hooted him down. Then Agriculture Committee chairman Lever joined the debate. Presaging his position the next year during the House hearing on the USDA Office of Information, he engaged in a key colloquy with Gillett:

> Lever: The gentleman [Gillett] has defined the publicity expert in his statement just now, to the effect that he is a man whose business it is to extol and exploit the virtues of this department. The gentleman does not undertake in this amendment to prevent some one employed in the Department of Agriculture, for instance, giving to the country information as to the work of the department?
> Gillett: Of course not . . .
> Lever: I do not mean in the capacity of one of the regularly employed editors, but I mean a man employed to make more democratic the reports of the Department . . . to put it in more popular language.
> Gillett: Of course, I do not object to that at all.[12]

By this exchange, Lever had cleverly created a legislative history of the author's intent. With his seemingly innocent and nonthreatening clarifications, he had gotten onto the record that, regardless of the wording of the amendment, it was not intended to affect the work of the department to popularize information. Gillett admitted that the amendment would not affect federal editors preparing publications or other information specialists who made sure all material was understandable to the lay public. Such information could be contained in reports, but also in virtually anything else pertaining to the work of the department. The only banned activity was extolling and exploiting the virtues of the department directly to the press. In legislative lingo, Lever had just created a loophole so large you could drive a truck through it. Probably trying to hide a smile or even a laugh at how effectively he had outmaneuvered Gillett, Lever sat down, satisfied. He would not oppose the adoption of the amendment. He did not need to; he had totally neutralized its impact.

After a few more short comments, the debate wound down. The whole debate had been very brief, less than three pages in the *Congressional Record*.

Gillett's amendment passed on a voice vote and had now been added to the House version of the bill. Democrats, as the majority party in the House, had no trouble accepting an amendment from a Republican, a member of the minority party, who was attacking an executive branch agency while a Democratic president was in the White House. It was another demonstration of the bipartisan appeal of anti-public relations legislation in Congress and of the weakness of presidents on this subject, even when their party was the majority party on Capitol Hill.

While the bill was being considered by the Senate (also with a Democratic majority), the progressive-leaning magazine *Outlook* editorialized against the Gillett amendment. It wrote that the rider would put Congress in a role to "exercise an executive function." Was Congress to decide if the USDA should use professional writers to convey information "in terms that the people can understand" or be limited to having its scientists write such reports? This kind of staffing choice, the magazine opined, was up to the executive branch to make, not Congress.[13] It was an argument calculated to appeal to President Wilson and his congressional supporters, given Wilson's expansive view of the role of the presidency versus the legislative branch. But the editorial was a voice in the wind, compared to the political appeal of bashing the bureaucracy and its self-serving publicists. Wilson's reaction came quickly, because the Senate left the Gillett amendment in the bill unmodified. It would go to the president as originally introduced.[14]

How did he feel about it, reporters asked President Wilson at a press conference in early October? (In those days, these sessions were more in the nature of briefings, with reporters prohibited from quoting the president verbatim or even attributing to him what they subsequently wrote.) First, they asked him if any cabinet secretaries had complained to him about the provision, perhaps even hoping for a veto. No, he said, and furthermore, "I am entirely against the way publicity agents have been used and I think that they [the departments] should have to provide publicity without special publicity agents." By his comment he clearly indicated that, like legislators, he was more than willing to criticize press bureaus in federal departments. But Wilson's motivation was different from the one at the other end of Pennsylvania Avenue. He was well informed about the scope of the Gillett amendment and told the reporters that "it won't affect [this] office. We'll have publicity, I can promise you that."[15] In other words, as president, he would be more than glad to limit agency publicity bureaus in order to magnify the role of a president in releasing information. Wilson was aware that agency public relations had expanded so significantly up to the beginning of his presidency that "some Washington reporters were living off executive department handouts, barely rewriting government press releases for their papers."[16] But the reporters at Wilson's press conference did not pick up the slight hint he embedded in his elliptical observation about publicity and did not ask him to elaborate. In fact, Wilson was privately toying with the idea of a centralized publicity bureau for the whole administration.[17]

At this point in the press session, the reporters reversed roles. Instead of the traditional function of such press conferences to pose questions to a president, the journalists began making the case that the emergence of publicity experts in departments and agencies was a positive development. They mentioned that those publicity staffers were one central point in a large agency for them to get information, that the current system worked well, that the handouts from the publicity experts were convenient for reporters and helped them do their jobs, and that in general these staffers were valuable to journalists.[18] Without saying it explicitly, they were urging a veto. This was a twist on most reporters' public posture of professional disdain for federal press agents; here, in private, they acknowledged the essential role these agency professionals played in helping them do their jobs.[19] Wilson did not take the bait. The press conference quickly moved on to another subject. Wilson signed the bill on October 22, 1913.[20]

Gillett's law continues to this day. Over the years, its wording has changed only a little, largely for stylistic reasons and to reflect changes in drafting guidelines. Its substantive meaning has not changed at all since being first adopted in 1913. Currently it states, "Appropriated funds may not be used to pay a publicity expert unless specifically appropriated for that purpose."[21]

ENFORCING THE BAN: AUTHORITATIVE INTERPRETATIONS BY THE GENERAL ACCOUNTING OFFICE

One did not have to be a lawyer to figure out how easy a bureaucracy could neutralize the effect of the Gillett law. The key was to be sure that no one engaging in any external relations activities in the agency had the formal title of "publicity expert." It did not much matter what they actually did, just as long as they were not called publicity experts. That title indeed vanished from usage in the federal executive branch almost instantaneously. Agencies began engaging in a "semantic double shuffle."[22] In 1917, there were publicity *bureaus* in the Post Office Department, the State Department, and the Treasury Department, but none employed publicity *experts*.[23] Two years later, the director general of the U.S. Employment Service was testifying at a public hearing of the House Appropriations Committee. He was required to submit a complete list of the agency's employees. In the area of public relations, his list included a director of information, assistant director of information, publicity director, assistant to the director of information, information secretary, and even a publicity *agent*, but no publicity experts.[24] In 1931, the *New York Times* reported that the U.S. Army had granted a reserve commission for a publicity expert, but apparently that was the newspaper's term, not an official title of a position.[25] An editorial in the *New York Times* in 1979 mocked the seemingly shorter and shorter shelf life of the euphemisms used in the Washington bureaucracy to mask this activity. "Public relations" became "public information," which begat "public affairs," the latter then replaced by several alternatives including "external affairs," "communications," "media liaison," and "public awareness."[26]

Still, it was a law on the books, and the General Accounting Office (GAO, in 2004 renamed the Government Accountability Office), a legislative branch agency, had the thankless task of enforcing it or, more specifically, disapproving any federal agency expenditure that violated it. From time to time, members of Congress asked it to investigate a specific public relations activity in a federal agency and decide if the Gillett provision had been violated. Generally, the GAO found it nearly impossible to enforce.

Its first formal reports on the 1913 ban did not occur until the mid-1930s, more than two decades after the passage of the law. In response to a 1935 inquiry from Congressman Sam Rayburn (D-Tex.), the comptroller general wrote that he believed the law was *intended* to identify "the border line" between permitted and prohibited public relations activities. The former would include situations when the statutory mission of an agency "would be aided by timely dissemination of accurate information." The latter would cover employment of experts "largely to publicize the activity or to encourage public approval or support" for the agency itself. Still, that was not what the law actually said. It was confined to the employment of federal employees who were appointed "*as* publicity experts" (emphasis in original). Given this "unfortunate" wording of the law, the comptroller general stated that the law was "ineffective."[27]

A year later, the GAO expressed a similar opinion to a different legislator. The agency pointed to the weakness of the statute by noting that "it cannot be said that every employee who gives out information or answers inquiries is a publicity expert. Neither can it be said that every employee who prepared a press release or a magazine article is a publicity expert." Similarly, it did not seem appropriate to penalize low-level employees by denying their salary, if they were just following instructions from senior agency officials. Therefore, the comptroller general suggested that Congress amend the wording of the Gillett law, so that it would penalize any senior agency official who "knowingly permits any subordinate to engage in any publicity activity not authorized by law."[28] No one took him up on that constructive suggestion.

Over the years, the GAO consistently maintained that interpretation of the law. In 1943, the comptroller general opined that a proposed law imposing controls on publications and publicity would "be much more effective" than the Gillett law.[29] In 1975, the GAO was still describing the 1913 law as "vague" and "difficult to apply."[30]

The only time that the GAO made a finding of a violation was in 1986, seventy-three years after the law had been enacted. It was asked to investigate the activities of the Chemical Warfare Review Commission, a presidential advisory council. Based on the few times over the years it had been asked to review the application of the law, the GAO's evaluation standard was that, if authorized by law, agencies *could* engage in activities that were "reasonably necessary to the proper administration of the laws for which the agency is responsible, to the general public or to particular inquirers." Anything violating that standard would be deemed a violation of the ban on publicity experts. Since this was an advisory commission, it did not have the customary basic authorization to disseminate information that most departments and agencies have in their statutory mission. Therefore, the GAO ruled that its public relations activities violated the ban on employment of publicity experts (as well as another anti-publicity law).[31] The issuance of this legal opinion with the finding of the violation was the end of the process. There were no further repercussions, partly because the commission dissolved after completing its assignment.

A much more contemporary GAO ruling related to this law occurred in 2004. It was asked to investigate the publicity activities of the Forest Service regarding a controversial management plan it had issued for a forest in the Sierra Nevada. The Forest Service had hired a private agency to help disseminate information explaining the decision and its rationale. This time, for its legal opinion, the GAO took a de novo look at the law. It concluded, breaking with all its decisions since the mid-1930s, that the legislative history of the adoption of the law was "particularly illuminating." Relying on the colloquy led by Congressman Lever, the GAO concluded that the scope of the law was to enforce a prohibition on hiring of employees "to extol or to advertise" the agency itself. Based on that new interpretation, the GAO concluded that the Forest Service had not violated the law. Rather, its public relations campaign had been aimed at disseminating factual information explaining its decision on the forest management plan.[32]

ENFORCING THE BAN: AUTHORITATIVE INTERPRETATIONS BY THE DEPARTMENT OF JUSTICE

The other major source within the federal government for authoritative legal interpretations is the Office of Legal Counsel (OLC) in the U.S. Department of Justice. That office is, in a sense, "the president's law firm" since it is frequently asked to provide interpretations of the law that would guide an administration's activities. The key point, of course, is that the Department of Justice is part of the executive branch and the attorney general is appointed by the president, serves at the president's pleasure, and is a cabinet member. Similarly, the OLC is headed by an assistant attorney general, also a presidential appointee. Therefore, the OLC views the president, not Congress, as its boss and client. As a result, legal opinions issued by Justice tend to be protective of executive branch behavior.

The first time the department issued an opinion about the law was in 1939. The previous year, Congressman J. Parnell Thomas (R-N.J.) twice attacked the growth in New Deal "propaganda" and wondered rhetorically if this was not a violation of the 1913 law.[33] Then, in 1939, he directly asked the attorney general to prosecute violations of the 1913 law because "numerous agencies in our Federal Government have not obeyed such mandate of Congress." His explanation of the need for such prosecutions captured well the way the conservative coalition in Congress zeroed in on agency public relations as an effective attack strategy on FDR's presidency. Such prosecutions, he wrote, would "demonstrate the extent to which Government agencies are annually expending millions of dollars of taxpayers' funds to perpetuate themselves in office on their present enormous scale. It would also show the degree to which certain agencies are resorting to the dissemination of propaganda to sell the public on the theory of Federal bureaucracy and collectivism."[34]

Given the relationship between the Department of Justice and the administration and given the naked political attack embodied in the letter, it was certain that the request would be deflected. But the rationale contained in the department's response was unusual. According Attorney General Frank Murphy, "the enforcement of this act is not vested in the Department of Justice, and that consequently I have no function to perform."[35] Strictly speaking, he was being accurate. The department prosecutes violations of the criminal code and the civil code, but this law—which had no penalties for violations—did not fit into either category. It was indeed a law establishing a crime, but it was unlinked to any of the routine enforcement structures or mechanisms of the federal justice system.

The matter lay dormant for a quarter of a century. Then, in 1963, the OLC prepared a review of the law, but not any official opinion. The memo noted that there was no authoritative interpretation of the meaning of the term "publicity expert" in any court decision or subsequent congressional enactment and that the law had never been enforced. It also noted the duality of congressional decisions: Congress has banned "publicity experts," on one hand, but conversely it "has long acquiesced to the existence of government information offices and has appropriated funds to maintain these offices." Therefore, "the line between information and 'publicity' is almost impossible to draw." The OLC concluded that it was "unable to offer any interpretation of this provision."[36]

The OLC issued the only formal legal opinion that covered the Gillett law about two decades later. As part of a larger discussion of laws controlling the work of the President's Council for International Youth Exchange, the opinion discussed the applicability of the ban on hiring publicity experts. After reviewing previous GAO opinions and the sparse involvement of the OLC, the opinion concluded, "We believe it is appropriate to accord considerable deference to decisions of the GAO."[37] So, for this particular law, the legal view of the executive branch was the same as the legislative branch's interpretation, an occurrence that was not automatic.

ENFORCING THE BAN: AUTHORITATIVE INTERPRETATIONS BY THE COURTS

There have been no federal court opinions that interpret the Gillett law. It has been mentioned only once in a Supreme Court opinion, and then only as an aside. That case dealt with the issuance of a press release by a federal agency that some of its former employees considered libelous. In a dissenting opinion, Justice Brennan observed, "To what extent is it in the public interest that the Executive Branch carry on publicity campaigns in relation to its activities? (Without reviewing all the history, one can say this is a matter on which Congress and the Executive have not always seen eye to eye. See 38 *Stat.* 212, 5 USC § 54)."[38] Brennan's digression succinctly summarized congressional efforts to mute the bureaucracy, with the counterpart resistance by the executive branch. As far as he was concerned, the Gillett law captured and symbolized the ongoing conflict over the entire issue.

DECLINING TO REVISE THE LAW

Regardless of GAO and OLC interpretations, the impotence of the law did not deter politicians and reporters from gleefully invoking it whenever the circumstances seemed propitious. Even though the GAO had only once identified a violation of it, accusations from legislators and reporters that agencies were violating the law were relatively common, especially during the New Deal. For example, syndicated political columnist (and conservative) Frank Kent referred to the law and the flagrant violations of it in three columns in the mid-1930s.[39] The *Wall Street Journal* "Washington Letter" feature did, too, in 1935.[40] That year, Senator Carter Glass (D-Va.) said in a floor statement that the USDA was flagrantly violating the Gillett law, and four Republican congressmen accused the Roosevelt administration of breaking it.[41] In 1939, after Attorney General Murphy had turned down his request for an investigation, Congressman Thomas introduced a resolution in the House calling for a special committee to investigate "to what extent, if any, the existing statute has been violated."[42] Although it did not pass, it garnered him some publicity.[43] The next year, during an appropriations committee hearing, Congressman Dudley White (R-Ore.) accused the head of the Bonneville Power Administration of having an employee who violated the Gillett law. The agency head firmly denied it, and the matter ended there. But White, like Thomas, got some sympathetic publicity from a conservative newspaper for making the charge.[44] When running for the Republican nomination for president in 1940, Senator Robert Taft (R-Ohio) attacked the estimated cost of the press relations activities of the Roosevelt administration but referred to the 1913 law as causing his estimates to be only near guesses: "This law perhaps accounts to some extent for the difficulty in determining how much is being spent for publicity purposes."[45]

Although the law was a useful tool for bureaucrat bashing by politicians, especially from the opposition party, it was a failure from an enforcement perspective. According to the consistent rulings of the GAO and the few opinions from the OLC, in its current form it was meaningless. From time to time the question was raised in Congress whether the law needed to be changed. The GAO had first suggested some specific amendments in 1936 (see above), when it proposed changing the focus to senior agency officials and to any publicity not authorized by Congress.[46] In 1942 and again the next year, in response to legislative requests, the GAO drafted a more extensive substitute to the Gillett law, focusing on a ban on any publicity unless specifically authorized and appropriated by Congress. It also required agencies to submit a copy of all publicly distributed material to Congress. The GAO believed the draft bill would "be much more effective in controlling expenditures for publicity purposes than the existing act."[47] It was, however, careful to note that it was providing the draft upon request, not necessarily endorsing it.

During the 81st Congress (1949–1950), the House created the Select Committee on Lobbying Activities to investigate the existing lobbying laws and identify possible reforms. At a hearing on "The Role of Lobbying in

Representative Self-Government," Frank Weitzel, assistant to the comp-troller general, was asked about the Gillett law. He said, "One of the great difficulties in enforcing that language is it is very, very rare, if ever, the case that a man is on the pay roll as publicity experts [sic]. He can be called almost anything else, and usually and frequently will have other duties, so that that in itself, is a very difficult statute to enforce."[48] But the committee issued no recommendations regarding the Gillett law.

Two decades later, another committee tiptoed through the topic. The Subcommittee on Foreign Operations and Government Information of the House Government Operations Committee held extensive hearings in the early 1970s on the executive branch's implementation of the 1966 Freedom of Information Act and other information-related laws. At several hearings, senior public information officials from federal agencies urged the committee to recommend repealing the Gillett law. One called it "archaic" and made the case to "supersede that ancient rider and to legitimize public affairs as a valid function of Government."[49] Another described the juxta-position of the Gillett law and the Freedom of Information Act as causing "a state of schizophrenia in the minds of many government public infor-mation employees."[50] Ultimately, the full committee tepidly recommended "that the appropriate committees of the Congress *consider* legislation that would repeal" the Gillett law.[51] None did. Notwithstanding the merits of the case, few politicians wanted to be subject to the criticisms of being soft on bureaucratic propaganda.

IMPACT OF THE LAW

The Gillett legislation has had negligible substantive effect on federal public relations activities. The GAO, which as a legislative branch agency would be expected to give the greatest deference to congressional enactments, viewed it as unenforceable. In the mid-1930s, two articles in academic journals stated flatly that "this law has been evaded" and had not had any significant substantive effect. That observation was confirmed almost thirty years later by Rourke and sixty years later by Fisher, who noted that the law was "circumvented" by use of other titles and also through Congress's own contradictory actions of retaining the 1913 ban but simultaneously funding agency programs that explicitly called for extensive public dissemination of information.[52]

On the other hand, research in the early 1990s documented that awareness of the Gillett law continued to be strong at the highest levels of agency public affairs offices and still perceived as delegitimizing their work.[53] That perception highlights the nonsubstantive impact of the law. Though impossible to enforce, it has served for nearly a century as a symbol of legislative hostility to the bureaucracy having a public voice and a useful congressional tool to invoke when the political occasion arises. The Gillett law is the perfect embodiment of the congressional effort to manage agency public relations—powerful symbolically but ultimately negligible in its real-world impact. According to DeSanto, "the intent of the legislators was to prevent incumbent government officials from using their power and positions to influence legislation. This single-minded idea, however, was in direct conflict with the principle that democracy relies on a relatively free communication structure providing information and methods of discussing issues to its citizens so they can make informed decisions. History, therefore, had its own plans for developing what legislation could not prevent."[54] The ban on publicity experts—focused on personnel as it was—failed because it was so easy for agencies to evade it by using other job titles and still be in ostensible compliance with the legal prohibition.

CHAPTER 5

CRIMINALIZING AGENCY LOBBYING, 1919–2002

No funds may be used if "intended or designed to influence in any manner a Member of Congress to favor or oppose, by vote or otherwise, any legislation or appropriation by Congress, whether before or after the introduction of any bill or resolution proposing such legislation or appropriation.

. . . Any officer or employee of the United States who . . . is found to have violated or attempted to violate this section, shall be removed by such superior officer from office or employment. Any officer or employee of the United States who violates or attempts to violate this section shall also be guilty of a misdemeanor and on conviction thereof shall be punished by a fine of not more than $500 or by imprisonment for not more than one year, or both."

41 *Stat.* 68

When Congress first began objecting to agency external communications, its focus was on publicity and press relations. In those situations the audience being targeted was the citizenry, whether directly through publications and speeches or indirectly through newspapers. Yet some legislators intuited that the public at large was not necessarily the end goal of these public relations activities.

Rather, they sensed that often the ultimate purpose of informing public opinion was to press Congress to be good to the agency. Comments along those lines had been made during the controversies over the Panama Canal Commission, Forest Service, Census Bureau, and USDA. For example, Congressman Humphrey had carefully described the chain of events that agency publicity would have, eventually culminating in a favorable public opinion that could force Congress to treat the agency generously. Similarly, Congressman Nelson had said, "The motive is self-aggrandizement of officials—intrenchment of officials in power. By magnifying, through publicity, the work of the officials and of the department they are able to command larger appropriations, enlarge the bureau, increase the number of employees and also the salaries of officials and employees."[1]

In that respect, press relations and publicity were sometimes more than public relations. They were also indirect lobbying of Congress. So, although the dominant legislative objection stated in the Canal, Forest Service, Census Bureau, and USDA cases was to press relations per se, an implicit objection was that publicity was connected to lobbying. Lobbying was just another form of external agency communications, whether intertwined or embedded in public relations or not.

BROADENING CONGRESSIONAL ATTENTION TO LOBBYING, 1912

In 1912, seven years after the first controversy involving the Panama Canal Commission, Congressman Solomon Prouty (R-Iowa) explicitly raised the issue of the propriety of direct lobbying of Congress by the bureaucracy. On April 5, he introduced a bill to regulate (and in some cases ban) lobbying by civil servants.[2] The specifics of the issue are a bit far afield of the subject of this inquiry. Prouty had heard that professional lobbyists were soliciting contributions from federal civil servants based in the capital (especially employees of the D.C. municipal government) in order to lobby Congress for pay raises and other benefits. He thought this was inappropriate and wanted legislation that would either ban the activity or force public disclosure by the lobbyists of the source of their funding.[3] Thus, the details of this incident related not to the institutional interests of a government agency but to the conditions of employment of its personnel. Still, Prouty's proposed legislation forced Congress to confront the general subject of legislative lobbying that was paid for (in this case indirectly) by federal funds. Without holding a public hearing, the House Committee on the District of Columbia quickly recommended Prouty's bill for passage. The committee report summarizing the rationale for this recommendation zeroed in on the crux of the issue: "We believe it is alike wrong for such employees to use money received from the Government to set in motion influences to secure more money from it."[4]

In other words, Congress objected to funding the lobbying of Congress. This statement of principle was enunciated specifically for the situation that Prouty's bill was addressing, namely, lobbying for the personal benefit of government employees, such as salaries and pensions. But a generalization of this doctrine was applicable to many other aspects of the broader subject. For example, this principle was later incorporated in federal law related to nonprofit organizations receiving federal funding. They were prohibited from using any federal money to lobby Congress.[5] Regarding this study of agency external communications and congressional reactions to it, the doctrine underlying the Prouty bill was also applicable. For such situations, the same principle would view lobbying of Congress by federal agencies to benefit their institutional interests to be equally as inappropriate as lobbying by federal employees to benefit their personal interests. If it was wrong to use federal funds received by federal civil servants to lobby Congress for more money for their salaries and benefits, then it was just as wrong for federal departments to use federal funds to lobby Congress for more appropriations.

These implications were unrecognized at that time. But Prouty's bill (which was not, ultimately, enacted into law) had several invisible effects that later became more apparent. First, his bill provided a principle that Congress could apply to legislative lobbying by federal agencies. That was to be deemed an objectionable activity. Second, highlighting such lobbying inevitably led to the recognition that agency legislative lobbying was part of the larger subject of agency external communications programs. If Congress wanted to silence the bureaucracy, it needed to expand its attention from just public and press relations (as it had up to this point) to legislative relations as well. All were external communications. Finally, if the ultimate goal of public and press relations was to influence Congress, then the Prouty principle could be applied to these indirect efforts to lobby Congress, not just to the direct ones (see chapter 9).[6]

It took less than a year before Prouty's prescient insights were applied. In early 1913, the House was debating the appropriation for the Government Printing Office for FY 1914 as part of the annual Sundry Civil Appropriation Bill. On February 21, 1913, Congressman Harvey Helm (D-Ky.) introduced a floor amendment because of his concerns about improper activities by the U.S. Army. The previous year Helm had chaired the Committee on Expenditures in the War Department and gained an extensive familiarity with the operations of the department. He believed that Congress was not adequately overseeing military spending.[7] Allied with that, he perceived increasingly explicit Army publicity and lobbying to affect congressional policymaking. Helm's amendment proposed to limit all War Department publications to those "authorized by law."[8] He said that he suspected the department was "employing a press bureau or a press agency" to promote its views on legislation pending in Congress. It was issuing publications that were intended "to create a sentiment in line with the views of the officers of the War Department." He characterized a specific publication he displayed during his speech as a "lobbying document."

Helm was operationalizing two aspects of Prouty's failed bill.[9] First, he connected agency publicity and press activities with lobbying. He showed that all external communications, whether ostensibly aimed at the public at large or at Congress, were intended to accomplish the same end goal of influencing federal policymaking to be supportive of an autonomy-seeking agency. Second, Helm verbalized the funding principle that Prouty had raised and applied it to this case. In his floor speech in favor of his amendment, he said, "I do protest most vehemently and in the strongest terms at my command against Congress putting at the command of the War Department, the Navy Department, or any other department, but more especially the Army and Navy, a sum of money which can be used for electioneering purposes."[10] In other words, Congress should not fund public relations programs aimed at influencing congressional decisions.

Helm's amendment was not adopted. Richard Hobson (D-Ala.) characterized the same pamphlet that Helm had objected to as "the compilation of expert opinions on technical matters [that] would be of great value,"[11] demonstrating that the same public relations product could be perceived as objectionable and as benign. Congressman Fitzgerald, who had vocif- erously denounced the publicity agent at the Panama Canal Commission in 1905 and now was chairman of the powerful House Committee on Appropriations, also opposed Helm's amendment, saying that it was poorly drafted, inappropriate for that particular bill given Helm's intent, and a violation of the parliamentary prohibition on new legislation within appropriation bills. Similarly, James Mann (R-Ill.) pointed to what was becoming increasingly obvious regarding the difficulty of drafting legisla- tive language related to agency external communications. In this case, since Helm's amendment limited the use of the printing appropriation for matters "authorized by law," would the War Department be prohibited from publishing a cookbook for use by all Army cooks unless Congress specifically authorized publication of Army cookbooks?[12] It was an effec- tive thrust. The amendment was rejected, 20–40.[13]

BANNING AGENCY LOBBYING OF CONGRESS

In 1919, six years after Helm's failed effort, Congress was dealing with the future of the U.S. Employment Service. First created within the Department of Labor by administrative action, the Employment Service was caught in the ideological and economic warfare between pro-labor Democrats and pro-business Republicans. Now it was facing extinction by the possibility of Congress not funding it any further. When the House Appropriations Committee was considering the third deficiency bill for the remainder of FY 1919, members said they were inundated with telegrams and mail urging them to continuing funding the Employment Service. As would be expected with an ideological issue such as this, some members were pleased since they supported the agency, and its opponents were dis- pleased. At a public hearing in February, John Densmore, the director general of the Employment Service, was asked about the lobbying. He said he had not asked any employees or friends of the agency to do that but indeed had disseminated information about its precarious status. He had done this in response to "vicious propaganda" carried out by opponents, and he singled out the National Metal Trades Association.[14] Densmore insisted that he had a right and obligation to disseminate factual infor- mation in response to negative publicity. He confirmed that he had asked the employees around the country to inform "the people themselves who had done business with the service, or the public at large, to give their opinions."[15] From their comments, it was clear that some committee members did not like being flooded by lobbying being orchestrated by a federal agency. But the issue did not yet have enough political critical mass for the committee to do anything about it. It reported the bill out without any sections related to improper agency lobbying.[16]

All the same, when the bill came up for floor debate, some members wanted to talk about it. On February 27, 1919, Congressman Albert Johnson (R-Wash.) raised the issue and objected to the "successful propaganda" from the Department of Labor "for the purpose of sustaining an appropriation." According to Johnson, "a very large part of the activities and energy of the departments of the Government are devoted to building up efforts to make it appear that their particular bureau is a very important one."[17] Joseph Moore (R-Pa.) agreed, decrying that "the tendency is for all departments to utilize the newspapers and their friends everywhere to impress upon Congress the importance of increased appropriations."[18] The next day, picking up where they left off, James Good (R-Iowa) introduced an amendment to prohibit the use of federal funds contained in the bill "for any personal services or to pay for any advertisement, telegram, letter, or circular designed to defeat or enact any proposed legislation by Congress, or to influence any Member of Congress to vote on any appropriation unless specifically authorized."[19]

The debate took an unexpected turn when James Gallivan (D-Mass.) suggested that the same standard should apply to legislators. They, too, should not be permitted to send telegrams urging support for their legislation. "Do not assume for ourselves something that we are not willing to give to the departments," he said.[20] This caught the attention of the House. It was one thing to choke the voice of the bureaucracy, but another to apply the same rules to themselves. A quick inspection of the wording of the amendment demonstrated that it applied only to the executive branch, and Gallivan did not go so far as to introduce a formal amendment to Good's amendment. Undoubtedly, it would have failed. After brief additional debate, Good's amendment was adopted by voice vote.[21]

The 65th Congress adjourned sine die before the bill passed both houses. Therefore, later in the spring of 1919 when the 66th Congress was sworn in, it still needed to act on such an appropriation bill, but it had to start the legislative process afresh. Now, though, there was a major change. As a result of the November 1918 election, the majorityship of the House had flipped from Democratic to Republican. Congressman Good became the chair of the House Appropriations Committee. As would be expected, when the committee reported out the third deficiency bill again, this time it included his anti-lobbying amendment, though with four significant changes from his earlier proposal:[22] it would apply not just to the funds contained in this bill but also to all other appropriation bills "hereafter"; it expanded the specific activities it was banning to include telephone and "any other device intended or designed to influence in any manner a Member of Congress"; it added clarifying language that the law would not affect formal communications from agencies to Congress "through the proper official channels";[23] and it added two penalty clauses. Violating the law would be a misdemeanor, punishable by a fine of up to $500 and imprisonment up to one year. The committee's recommendation to criminalize a violation of the ban was a major step. The other penalty was that any federal officer or employee who "violated or attempted to violate" the law would be fired.

During the floor debate on May 29, 1919, Good explained that the committee amendment was merely a continuation of the floor amendment adopted by the House during the preceding Congress. He asserted that the practice of agencies using appropriated funds to lobby Congress "has been indulged in so often, without regard to what administration is in power." He recommended adoption of the committee amendment because it would "absolutely put a stop to that sort of thing." After that comment, the *Congressional Record* noted "[Applause.]"[24] The amendment was adopted. Congressman Addison Smith (R-Idaho) tried to revise the language so that it would cover only "official" activities. He feared the committee's wording would prevent individual civil servants from communicating as constituents with their member of Congress, an issue that had led to the killing of the Prouty bill in 1912. But other members were concerned that Smith's wording created a glaring loophole in the committee's recommendation, and his amendment was rejected.[25]

The Senate Appropriations Committee accepted the premise of the House provision but sought further clarifying language regarding what agencies were permitted to communicate to Congress (added language italicized): " but this [law] shall not prevent officers and employees of the United States from communicating *to Members of Congress on the request of any Member or* to Congress, through the proper official channels, requests for legislation or appropriations which they deem necessary for the efficient conduct of the public business."[26] This was a significant watering down of the prohibition. It meant that agencies could communicate directly to Congress on a virtually unlimited basis, just as long as one senator or representative had "asked" them to do so. Considering the informal alliances that developed between agencies and some legislators, it would be quite easy to arrange for a friend on Capitol Hill to submit such a "request" to an agency.

Ultimately, the House members of the conference committee yielded and accepted the Senate's change to the original House version.[27] President Wilson signed the new anti-lobbying statute into law as part of the Third Deficiency Appropriation Act of FY 1919 on July 11, 1919.[28] The law continues to this day and is routinely referred to as Section 1913 (of Title 18 of the U.S. Code).[29]

USING THE LAW AGAINST ROOSEVELT ADMINISTRATION AGENCIES

The anti-lobbying law lay largely dormant for twenty years. There were no prosecutions, no GAO investigations or reports, no OLC opinions. It was "almost forgotten."[30] Then, the conservative coalition of southern Democrats and opposition Republicans rediscovered the law and used it to bash programs of Roosevelt's New Deal and Truman's Fair Deal that they *substantively* disagreed with. Here the congressional reaction to agency publicity was a tactic to accomplish a substantive goal by using a tangential issue to appeal for support. Yet the use of this tactic became so pervasive that it evolved into a larger strategy for picking issues that would help ultimately in negating the activities of these two liberal presidents. Silencing the bureaucracy was a line of attack that was more likely to garner agreement, broader support beyond ideological conservatives, and sympathetic press coverage than if the conservative coalition directly spoke of its ideological disagreement with these policies. It quickly became obvious that the

1919 anti-lobbying law was no more enforceable than the 1913 ban on publicity experts. Still, it was a great political battering ram for scoring hits against a specific program that particular politicians did not like.

Congressman Howard Smith (D-Va.) was a pillar of the conservative coalition on Capitol Hill. During the 76th Congress (1939–1941), he was appointed to chair a special committee of the House to investigate the National Labor Relations Board (NLRB). The NLRB embodied everything anti-union politicians hated about the legitimization of the right to organize. In February 1940, Smith submitted to Attorney General Robert Jackson some committee material about NLRB activities and asked him to determine if these were violations of the 1919 anti-lobbying law. As with the requests to the Department of Justice to enforce the ban on publicity agents (see chapter 4), this request was political mischief. NLRB activities that were "political" in the sense of advancing the administration's pro-labor stance would be unlikely to be deemed criminal by another member of the president's official family. Smith probably thought the request was a win-win situation, since if Jackson declined Smith could criticize him for not enforcing the law, and if Jackson prosecuted the NLRB then Smith would be vindicated.

Like the same situation regarding the publicity expert law, again the Department of Justice ducked the issue. Jackson wrote Smith that as a member of the executive branch he should not "render opinions" to the legislative branch. Based on the doctrine of separation of powers, he could not serve "two masters."[31] Responding, Smith argued that since the Department of Justice had the duty to prosecute violations of federal criminal laws, Congress would benefit from his judgment if the law needed to be amended to facilitate prosecutions. Again Jackson refused to be trapped. He answered that the law was "so uncertain in application" that he could not conceive of basing any prosecutions on it. Jackson tepidly asked the FBI to collect information, but it was hardly a prosecution-oriented investigation.[32] Smith, insisting on having the last word, concluded the correspondence by declaring that the anti-lobbying law was "clear and explicit" and posed no barrier to prosecution.[33] All these exchanges were conducted under the full glare of the media spotlight, with headlines such as "Lobby Curb Gives Problem to Jackson," "Jackson Is Asked to Prosecute NLRB," and "Prosecution of N.L.R.B.

Sought."[34] Meanwhile, the pro-labor members of the committee tried their best to neutralize Smith. When he attempted to put into the formal hearing record his assertion that the NLRB had indeed violated the anti-lobbying law, Congressman Abe Murdock (D-Utah) insisted in a closed committee session that Smith's statement be removed from the record. Smith relented.[35] Similarly, in their minority report the pro-labor members of the committee vociferously dissented from Smith's tactics, disagreed with his findings, and opposed any tightening of the 1919 law in its application to the NLRB.[36]

Stymied by the administration's refusal to consider criminal charges of violating the anti-lobbying law, Smith's allies on the House Appropriations Committee pushed for a legislative strategy to pursue their goal. But they too were blocked because general legislation (which is what the 1919 law was, even though it had been adopted as an amendment to an appropriation bill) could not be included in an appropriation bill, only funding and conditions attached to that specific pot of money. Some committee members sought an approach that could be viewed as a win for the conservatives but was so hollow that it would not be opposed by liberals. Their compromise was to insert in the bill providing the annual appropriation for the NLRB language "specifically inhibiting" any NLRB lobbying. But the committee report openly acknowledged that "this is already the law."[37] A friendly reporter characterized the provision as a "strengthening of anti-lobbying legislation," but it was not.[38] It was purely symbolic and for that reason no one opposed it throughout the rest of the legislative process. When President Roosevelt signed the bill into law in June 1940, the last line of the section of new law funding the NLRB for FY 1941 stated that "all expenditures under this title shall be made in strict compliance with the provisions of the Act of July 11, 1919 (18 U.S.C. 201)."[39] This bordered on being a legislative joke. A new law was directing the NLRB to be sure to follow another law. No wonder FDR was willing to sign the bill. Adding insult to injury, Smith's empty victory lasted only a year. The next year's bill dropped that meaningless section from the annual appropriation.[40]

During the 1940s, other members of the conservative coalition mounted an ongoing attack against New Deal agricultural policies by highlighting—among other issues—the anti-lobbying law. The same year as Smith's attack on the NLRB, the House Agriculture Committee accused the head of the Farm Credit Administration of violating the ban on lobbying and announced an investigation. This was major news.[41] The *New York Times* even listed it as one of the key news events on Capitol Hill that day.[42] Nothing came of any of these attacks legislatively, but the secretary of agriculture felt compelled the next year to issue an official memorandum reminding all departmental employees of the existing law banning the lobbying of Congress.[43]

Then, Republicans did well in the November 1942 elections (claiming bungling and inefficiencies in the administration's prosecution of the war). Democrats retained their majority in both houses, but their margins were significantly reduced. For Republicans, the 78th Congress (1943–1945) was their chance to leverage their 1942 victories toward winning the 1944 presidential election. They selected the anti-lobbying law as one of their key foci. Their continuing target was the USDA, in particular the Agricultural Adjustment Agency (AAA).[44] They charged that it had violated the ban on lobbying Congress (as well as the Hatch Act, which barred civil servants from partisan political involvement). They first brought it up in 1943, during the FY 1944 appropriations cycle.[45] The Farm Bureau Federation (a relatively conservative and right-leaning organization) testified at a House hearing that a provision should be inserted in the annual agricultural appropriation bill penalizing USDA employees who engaged in lobbying.[46] In an unusual political alliance, the National Farmers Union (a relatively liberal and left-leaning organization) agreed.[47]

Continuing attacks by Republicans (and some southern Democrats) on the USDA during the 78th Congress finally reached a critical political mass the next year, during the FY 1945 appropriations cycle. The House Appropriations Committee agreed to recommend the insertion of a new provision in the annual USDA funding bill that would require cutting off the salary of any full-time employee "who engages in any political activity or lobbying activity."[48] This was different from the 1919 law in that the salary cutoff would be invoked regardless of whether an employee was charged or convicted of the 1919 law. *Any* activity would require the salary shutoff.

The proposal sparked pointed floor debate. Congressman John Cochran (D-Mo.) called it "the most vicious limitation I have ever seen placed on an appropriation bill" and charged that the wording was a violation of the constitutional right of any citizen to petition Congress for redress of grievance.[49] He moved to delete that section of the bill. Significantly, rising to defend the provision was not a member of the majority party but Congressman Everett Dirksen (R-Ill.), who said, "Sometimes the most insidious, and certainly the most influential lobby activities in the Government are not pressure groups on the outside of Government, but pressure groups on the inside who consist of those who are on the pay roll."[50] Cochran's amendment lost, and so the committee recommendation stayed in the House-passed version of the bill.

Next, the Senate Appropriations Committee recommended deleting the House provision from the Senate version of the bill. According to the committee's report, the proposal "should be considered by the proper legislative committee [i.e., not in a funding bill], and . . . any changes proposed should be made equally applicable to all Departments and agencies of the Government." The committee had also solicited input from the comptroller general, who said that enforcing the proposed new law would be an administrative nightmare, especially since "nothing appears in the proposed appropriation restriction here involved to indicate the nature of the evidence to be required" for implementing it.[51]

A major floor debate took place in the Senate when John Danaher (R-Conn.), insisting on a separate vote for that committee recommendation, supported the House approach. This, according to the private diary of a wire service reporter covering it, "stirred up quite a tempest. . . . A lot of names were called in the process. Not since the soldier-vote fight [after Pearl Harbor] has politics come so close to the surface" in the Senate.[52] "The committee stand, stated reasonably by fleshy-faced, soft-voiced Dick Russell [D-Ga.], was that the Hatch Act covered all that anyway and therefore there was no reason for the amendment." He was supported by Kenneth McKellar (D-Tenn.), sarcastically described by the reporter as "violently sincere" in his comments during the floor debate, considering that he had taken the opposite position just a short time before.[53] Robert LaFollette, Jr. (R-Wis.), colorfully characterized the House provision as "a proposal to burn down the barn in order to get rid of a few rats." Answering him, Kenneth Wherry (R-Neb.) said that he had received "conservatively, thousands of communications" about legislation that were clearly stimulated by agency employees.[54] The committee's recommendation was ultimately endorsed and retained in the Senate-passed version of the bill.

Now the two houses were in disagreement, and the issue of USDA lobbying (and political activities) would be one of seventy-one differences between the two versions that a conference committee would have to resolve. The bill that emerged from conference contained compromises dealing with seventy items in the bill. The only one they could not agree on was the lobbying section.[55] Without debate, the Senate voted to insist on its position, but in the House Cochran tried to persuade members to recede from their position. This triggered an unusually extensive debate on the question of receding or insisting on the House provision; it covered five pages of dense text in the *Congressional Record*.[56] Even the chair of the House conferees suggested receding, but to no avail. The vote was 123 in favor of receding and 219 against. The conservative coalition was in control.

The conference committee now had to reconvene to deal with the only issue dividing the two houses on the bill and try to find a compromise on the lobbying issue that had evaded them previously. This time they agreed to recommend a new version that would deny a salary to any USDA employee *convicted* of violating the 1919 law.[57] The compromise was not controversial in either house and was accepted without serious floor debate in both.[58] As enacted into law, the provision stated that no funds in the bill could be expended by the USDA "for the payment of salary or travel expenses of any person . . . who has been found in accordance with the provisions of section 6 of the Act of July 11, 1919 (18 U.S.C. 201), to have violated or attempted to violate such section which prohibits the use of Federal appropriations for the payment of personal services or other expenses designed to influence in any manner a Member of Congress to favor or oppose any legislation or appropriation by Congress except upon request of any Member or through the proper official channels."[59]

The oddly quiet acceptance of the compromise by the House is striking since the substantive outcome clearly favored the Senate position more than the House's. Certainly, the tangible manifestation of inserting a new clause dealing with lobbying (and political activity) in the agriculture appropriation law could be viewed as a symbolic victory for the conservative coalition of the House. But the contents of the language favored the Senate's position much more. The compromise language was little more than a restating of the 1919 law, which itself had required the firing of federal employees convicted of violating or attempting to violate it. So the compromise language was little more than a rephrasing of existing law. It was a new law that said the old law would be upheld—and we really mean it this time! Also, the fact that no federal employee had ever been convicted of the 1919 law up through 1944 was another indication of the victory of the Senate's position over the House. It was highly unlikely that the new law would ever need to be invoked—something that could not be said of the original House-approved version. President Roosevelt signed the bill into law on June 28, 1944, with only three days left before the beginning of the new fiscal year.[60]

The next year, Congressman John Taber (R-N.Y.) maintained that the USDA continued to be "one of the worst offenders" in its lobbying activities, but that "the Attorney General will not do anything to enforce such law."[61] The FY 1945 anti-lobbying provision now became a permanent feature of the annual agricultural appropriation bill. It was routinely renewed every year through 1973, although slightly expanded in 1963 (see below).[62] In 1974, the language was slightly revised, but this time with no major substantive change.[63] Into the 1980s, it was still being included in the annual agricultural appropriation law.[64]

USING THE LAW AGAINST TRUMAN ADMINISTRATION AGENCIES

Republicans continued to use the anti-lobbying law as a weapon to bash the Truman administration. For example, in May 1946, Congressman Taber wrote the president and Attorney General Tom Clark with what he said was documentary proof that the head of the Office of Price Administration had violated the law prohibiting agencies from trying to influence congressional decisions.[65] As with Smith's 1940 correspondence with the attorney general, nothing came of it. Nonetheless, the publicity about his accusation gave momentum to the successful enactment of a FY 1947 appropriation rider banning this agency from "preparing or disseminating general propaganda in support of price controls," particularly regarding encouraging support for legislative proposals in Congress affecting the continuation of the agency.[66]

After gaining control of both houses in the November 1946 congressional elections, Republicans escalated their attacks on President Truman in an effort to help assure a victory in the 1948 presidential elections. (This was the Congress that Truman famously dubbed "The Do-Nothing 80th Congress" in his 1948 campaign.) Accusations of violations of the anti-lobbying law were part of that strategy. During the 80th Congress, Taber asked the GAO to decide whether recent actions of the Labor Department had violated the 1919 anti-lobbying law. The comptroller general responded discreetly that the departmental actions "would appear to contravene" the law, but he let the matter rest there; he did not refer it to the Justice Department for possible prosecution or suggest that Taber do so.[67] In 1950, the pro-business magazine *Forbes*, echoing Republican rhetoric, called the 1919 law the "most flagrantly-violated law in America."[68]

In particular, during the 80th Congress the House Republican majority established the Publicity and Propaganda Subcommittee of the House Committee on Expenditures in the Executive Departments. It was known as the Harness Committee, after its chairman, Congressman Forest Harness (R-Ind.).[69] Throughout 1947–1948, this committee issued a stream of reports claiming improper publicity and propaganda emanating from federal departments and agencies.[70] Specifically concerning the 1919 anti-lobbying law, some of these suggested that violations included lobbying activities by AAA committeemen in Nebraska, the Interior Department's Reclamation Bureau, and six agencies as part of the administration's push for national health insurance.[71] The committee asked the Department of Justice to prosecute, which it naturally declined to do.[72]

The last example deserves closer attention. Earlier discussions in this chapter focus on the difficulties with the 1919 law related to the Justice Department having responsibility to prosecute violations of the law but also being part of a president's administration. The assertion by the Harness Committee that agencies had violated the 1919 law highlights a different difficulty of that law. Here the president had made national health insurance one of the high priorities of his legislative program. A president is presumed to have an unfettered right to lobby Congress for his or her agenda, and that right is presumed extended to the official administrative "family" since a president cannot be expected to perform every action personally. When a federal agency produces informational products that provide a factual underpinning for the president's lobbying, is that proper or improper? Is it a violation of the 1919 law or not? Or is the law a constitutional infringement on the president's inherent powers and therefore unconstitutional?

The Harness Committee concluded that "the greatest and most effective lobby in the Nation today is that conducted by Federal administrative agencies." In general, the committee's perspective on the anti-lobbying law showed the close connection it made between the Republican Party's general ideology, its political attack strategy at that time, and the anti-lobbying law. "While most of the lobbying activity by Federal employees is aimed at specific legislation to increase the power and appropriations of specific departments and agencies, the over-all effect is a tremendous and constant pressure for more expensive government, and further encroachment upon the rights and liberties of individual citizens."[73] The minority reports of Democratic members of the subcommittee vociferously challenged the assertions that factual violations of the law had been identified.[74]

Also in 1948, the Housing and Rents Subcommittee of the Senate's Banking and Currency Committee held a hearing titled "Propaganda and Publicity in the Office of Rent Control." Notwithstanding the hearing's title, the committee meeting was actually about the rights of civil servants to express their views in-house on pending legislation. The issue arose after World War II when rent controls were still partially in place. Landlords and pro-business Republicans were generally for lifting all controls and letting the market set the rates. But those same Republicans were equally concerned about angry tenants penalizing them come the next election. For example, the subcommittee chair, Harry Cain (R-Wash.), had been picketed by his constituents and threatened with recall during a trip to his home state because of his stance on privatizing federal housing projects, and he was criticized at a conference in New York for a "tricky maneuver to weaken" some housing legislation.[75]

It was in this context that Cain convened a subcommittee hearing in 1948 to discuss with the head of the federal Office of Rent Control (his official title was Housing Expediter) an internal memo Cain had obtained written by the agency's Cleveland-based Midwest regional director. In it, the regional director commented on the status of pending rent control legislation. He suggested that the current proposal was "a victory for the opposition forces" who were trying to kill rent control. He noted the peculiarity of the legislative situation, namely, that a Republican majority that was philosophically opposed to rent control was writing a bill that supposedly extended rent control, but the bill was as weak and ineffective as possible. "One is astounded at a system of government which encourages legislative sabotage by giving the job of drafting legislation to people who are openly out of sympathy with the objective." He also pointed to the asymmetry of the subcommittee's public hearings, "gleefully pouncing on any statement derogatory to control and turning over under the microscope anything favorable." He characterized one of the elements of the new bill as "socialism in reverse."[76] Finally, he explicitly criticized Cain's role.

Chairman Cain and subcommittee member John Bricker (R-Ohio) were outraged by the memo. The regional director, they huffed, was "indicting the integrity of the Congress."[77] In their view, bureaucrats were to implement the law and confine all expressions to factual ones. It was acceptable to circulate an analysis of a law before it was passed, but no opinions about it were permitted. Bureaucrats were eunuchs, to be seen and not heard. They were not allowed to contribute to the development of an agency's position on the bill, regardless of their expertise. As a matter of fact, an agency should not, by definition, have positions on bills. Even if a bill would, say, weaken an agency to the point of having no tangible or effective powers, the agency's officials could not express a view about that. The senators behaved as though they were the direct bosses of the agency head, who was obligated to follow all directives of the subcommittee obsequiously—a position that was far from a bureaucrat's obligation to adhere to authoritative actions of Congress, such as a *law* approved by a majority of both houses of Congress and signed by a president (or a veto overridden by Congress). Cain and Bricker flailed at the agency's director until he promised to fire the official in Cleveland.[78] He did that, explaining in a public statement that the regional director had attempted to "influence" legislation and that this was grounds for firing. Firing back, the regional director denounced the "abuse of power by Congress."[79]

In retrospect, one can understand Cain's and Bricker's viewpoint in the context of an anti–big government conservative Republican majority in the 80th Congress facing an activist bureaucracy that had emerged under the liberal and Democratic presidencies of Roosevelt and Truman. For the 80th Congress, federal agencies were the enemy. Yet Cain and Bricker were trying to elevate their denunciations to the level of a disinterested review of the principle of separation of powers between the branches of government. In their worldview, bureaucracies were not independent actors. Rather, they were to be passive entities during congressional deliberations and decision making that would affect them significantly. A federal agency was not to have a view on legislation, let alone lobby in favor of that position. Hence, without even referring to the 1919 anti-lobbying law, Cain and Bricker were agreeing with its premise and trying to enforce it (administratively, not judicially) in this instance.

The rhetoric on Capitol Hill about agency lobbying and violations of the anti-lobbying law changed significantly after the 1948 elections. Not only had Truman won election to a full term, but the Democratic Party had resumed its majority in both houses of the 81st Congress.[80] One of the long-standing issues that Congress had dealt with unsuccessfully up to then was the regulation of lobbying. The House appointed a new Select Committee on Lobbying Activities to investigate and recommend statutory reforms. Though the main focus was on lobbying by private interests, the resolution establishing the committee also included in its jurisdiction administrative lobbying. For example, when the committee surveyed reporters for general information on lobbying, one of the questions invited them to inform the committee of their knowledge of violations of the 1919 anti-lobbying law.[81] The committee held extensive hearings, and some were dedicated to agency lobbying. When the GAO was asked to testify about the 1919 law, its representative emphasized that as a criminal law the 1919 act was not within the province of the agency. Rather, that role was the responsibility of the Justice Department. Also, clearly identifying an activity that was solely intended to lobby Congress was "quite elusive," the GAO said.[82]

The committee also requested the GAO to conduct some in-depth investigations of allegations of lobbying activities by agencies, in particular Republican claims that Secretary of Agriculture Brennan and other USDA staff had violated the ban at a 1950 meeting of the Production and Marketing Administration (the successor to the AAA) in Minnesota. The final conclusions of the GAO study vindicated the USDA.[83]

In its interim report in 1950, the committee tried as gently as possible to indicate that agency lobbying was necessary as a counterbalance to private interest lobbying. However, to retain some semblance of bipartisanship, it could not state that explicitly. Instead, it said so in a roundabout way: "We believe that there are interests in this Nation other than those which can be mobilized along group lines, and we believe that it is the responsibility of Government [i.e., the executive branch]—both morally and politically—to defend them. We believe, in sum, that Government must lead as well as follow; but at the same time we recognize that there are limits beyond which executive participation in legislative policy making may impinge on the authority of Congress and thus endanger our constitutional system."[84]

In its final report, the committee reviewed the 1919 law and concluded that it and other investigative and enforcement powers of Congress (such as appropriations committees, standing committees, and the GAO) could "provide adequate means for ascertaining and checking abuses" of agency lobbying. Therefore, "the long-established criminal statute . . . should be retained intact."[85] This was a safe and bipartisan political position, neither calling for repealing the law for its obvious ineffectiveness nor amending it to make it more enforceable.

USING THE LAW AGAINST KENNEDY ADMINISTRATION AGENCIES

The anti-lobbying bill was invoked only a few times during the Eisenhower presidency. The most prominent instance occurred when Congressman Daniel Reed (R-N.Y.), chairman of the House Ways and Means Committee, disagreed with the recommendation of the Eisenhower administration to extend a temporary excess-profits tax. This intraparty substantive policy disagreement led Reed to charge that the secretary and undersecretary of the treasury were violating the lobbying law when they tried to persuade several key national business organizations not to testify against the administration's position. Reed threatened to turn his evidence over to the Justice Department,[86] though he never followed through, in part because the accused officials had merely "discussed the tax program with them [business organizations] but never requested them not to testify."[87] Such fine distinctions contributed to the ineffectiveness of the law, although the Justice Department would certainly not have pursued prosecution even if it got that far. This row is emblematic of the impotence of the law, the willingness of the majority party to make such charges against a president from the same party, and the use of the law as a tactical and non-substantive device to pursue substantive goals. Another occasion involved a labor leader accusing an Eisenhower administration official of violating the anti-lobbying law over an issue the union and department disagreed about.[88] Again the charge was used to appeal for broader support while disguising the underlying substantive issue.

The anti-lobbying law was frequently invoked on Capitol Hill against the Kennedy administration's legislative program, affecting the Department of Health, Education, and Welfare, the State Department, the Department of Defense, and, especially, the USDA.[89] An incident with the USDA triggered the expansion of the 1944 USDA anti-lobbying provision. In April 1962, President Kennedy spoke about his farm policy to an assembly of the representatives of each state's Agricultural Stabilization and Conservation (ASC) committees, a part of the USDA. He reminded them that they were "prohibited by custom and law, quite rightly," from engaging in lobbying but continued, "We hope you will also see the Members of Congress and acquaint them and the Senators . . ." At that point he ended the incomplete sentence. After catching himself before saying what he should not, he jokingly added, "We don't want them to be, as the Secretary said, lonesome."[90] The audience roared in laughter. They could fill in the blank. They should promote the administration's farm policy on Capitol Hill but be aware of the constraints of the 1919 anti-lobbying law so that no one could complain that they were breaking the law. Press coverage of his speech said that the president had "delicately suggested" they meet with members of Congress.[91]

Kennedy's comments to the ASC committeemen caused a political uproar with Republicans. A few months later, when the annual agricultural appropriation bill was on the floor of the House, Congressman Robert Dole (R-Kans.) introduced an amendment banning use of funds contained in the bill for lobbying activities "in violation of present law."[92] He said, "The Kennedy administration has apparently adopted a double standard in dealing with lobbying activities of Federal employees designed to support or defeat pending legislation."[93] Dole quoted from a leaked USDA memo to all state ASC committeemen that summarized the administration's farm policy, was controversial (at least with Republicans) on Capitol Hill, and bemoaned a recent legislative setback in Congress. However, the statement emphasized, "we lost a battle but not the war."[94] In other words, the readers of the memo were encouraged to redouble their lobbying efforts. Dole spoke of the need to protect the "thousands and thousands" of federal employees being pressured to support President Kennedy's legislative proposals. "This type of activity should be stopped now and forever prohibited," he piously said.[95]

The Democratic floor manager of the bill answered that the subject of the amendment was already covered by the 1919 anti-lobbying law. Nothing was gained by adopting the amendment. Defensively, Dole responded that the 1919 law "needs some clarification" and "goes further than section 1913 of title 18."[96] Dole's amendment then triggered an unusually fierce and extensive debate, covering four pages of the *Congressional Record*. It was largely partisan, with Republicans supporting the amendment and Democrats opposing it. Substantively, the argument that the amendment was superfluous because it duplicated the 1919 law was valid. In a sense, it banned the USDA from spending money on an activity that was already criminal. The amendment was rejected, 118–172.[97]

A year later, Dole was at it again. This time the focus was on a referendum being conducted by the USDA among wheat farmers regarding a proposed administration policy. Dole, disagreeing with the substance of the proposal, vehemently objected to the "propaganda barrage" the USDA aimed at the wheat farmers before they voted—and he drew blood.[98] The majority party felt it could not totally ignore the topic, so during consideration of the annual agricultural appropriation bill the House Appropriations Committee's report mentioned the subject. It did not see any difference between "an effort to influence the vote of any participant in any referendum . . . or pending agricultural legislation." In other words, although the object of this lobbying was not Congress, it was similarly agency lobbying to influence policy. Therefore, "in the opinion of the Committee [it] would be completely unauthorized."[99] Still, the committee did not recommend any action, not wanting to give a partisan victory to the Republicans. Nevertheless, the fact that the majority felt compelled to address the issue in the report showed that it achieved a degree of critical mass.

The Senate Appropriations Committee went a step further. It recommended amending the 1944 USDA anti-lobbying provision by expanding it to refer not just to the 1919 law but also to efforts "to influence the vote in any referendum."[100] The Senate approved the recommendation, as did the conference committee.[101] By now it was December 1963 (a month after Kennedy's assassination and nearly six months into the fiscal year). President Johnson signed the bill into law on December 30, 1963.[102] The expanded ban on USDA lobbying continued being routinely renewed in the annual agricultural appropriation bill into the 1980s.[103]

Another attack on Kennedy administration lobbying was conducted by Congressman Glenard Lipscomb (R-Calif.) and Senator John Tower (R-Tex.) in the spring of 1962. They charged that Sargent Shriver, head of the Peace Corps (and the president's brother-in-law), had violated the 1919 anti-lobbying law when he sent a letter in April to all members of Congress summarizing the accomplishments of the agency and requesting support for authorizing and appropriating legislation.[104] They asked the GAO and then the Justice Department to rule on the propriety of the letter.[105] The comptroller general responded that indeed the costs of the communication from the Peace Corps had been paid from funds appropriated by Congress, thus bringing them under the scope of the anti-lobbying law. Beyond this documentation, though, the GAO said the allegations of violation were those of criminal law and not within its authority.[106] Tower and Lipscomb then asked the Department of Justice (headed by the president's brother) to bring criminal charges against Shriver for violating the law. In May, Assistant Attorney General Herbert Miller, Jr., responded. Despite the evidence and ruling of the comptroller general, he wrote, "no violation of the statute occurred." Citing the constitutional references to presidents communicating with Congress, Miller wrote, "Necessarily the President must entrust part of this function to subordinate officers with the executive branch." Therefore, "the Department is of the opinion that 18 U.S.C. 1913 cannot be construed to preclude the head of an executive agency from using its facilities to address an unsolicited letter to Members of Congress with respect to pending legislation."[107] Generally, the Department of Justice was to take the position that all presidentially appointed and Senate-confirmed officials were part of the presidency and therefore enjoyed all the freedoms of a president to lobby Congress or to urge the public to do so.

Lipscomb also charged more generally that Kennedy's appointees were frequently violating the 1919 act through "the barrage of letters, brochures, reports, folders, and other materials flooding congressional offices. So-called briefing sessions, for Members of Congress and aids [*sic*], are being held in great number." In terms of his political philosophy, these actions presented a "grave danger that individual rights and liberties in our Nation may be sacrificed on the alter of an all-powerful Federal Government."[108] Therefore, after being stymied by the position of the Justice Department, Lipscomb introduced a bill to revise the 1919 anti-lobbying law. His proposal was to amend the law "to make clear that the prohibition against lobbying with appropriated funds applies to the heads of executive departments and agencies."[109] In other words, members of the president's cabinet and other senior officials heading agencies could not lobby Congress on behalf of the president's legislative program. This would have been a major blow to the ability of presidents to pursue their goals in Congress. However, given that Lipscomb was a member of the minority party and the president was of the majority party, his bill died in committee and never had a chance. During the Johnson administration he introduced the bill in 1965 and again in 1967, but to no avail, with the Democrats continuing to be the majority party in the House.[110]

Aside from the two times Lipscomb reintroduced his bill during Johnson's presidency, the application of the anti-lobbying law came up only rarely. One example occurred in 1966, when Congressman John Ashbrook (R-Ohio) inserted in the *Congressional Record* the language of the anti-lobbying law with the cryptic comment that this reminder of the specifics of the law "might be useful for future reference."[111] Presumably he was hinting to agency officials as well as his colleagues of the need to remember the existence of the law and apply it more vigorously against alleged infractions. But the subject never became a big issue as it had been for Johnson's Democratic predecessors.

An early case of a congressional Democrat (then the majority party) using the law against a Republican president occurred during the Nixon administration. Congressman James Wright (D-Tex.) accused the Department of Transportation of violating the law with a staffer's behind-the-scenes involvement in criticizing Wright's role in the controversial Johnson-era legislation to remove billboards near highways.[112] It was the equivalent of a shot across the bow. A bland letter from the secretary, assuring him that department staff would be made even more mindful of the law, ended the matter.[113]

ENFORCING THE LAW: AUTHORITATIVE INTERPRETATIONS BY THE GAO

During all the presidencies from the enactment of the law in 1919 until Nixon, the utilization of the law, or at least references to it, were almost exclusively by legislators and only occasionally involved the GAO, Justice Department, or courts. Capitol Hill largely used the law as a political weapon to attack a president of the other party, with the roles of the GAO and Justice Department relatively tangential. This pattern changed during the shift from the Democratic presidency of Lyndon Johnson to Republican Richard Nixon. These outside players became much more involved in the application of the anti-lobbying criminal statute. For example, from 1919 to 1969, the GAO issued only five reports related to the law.[114] On the other hand, from then to about the beginning of the twenty-first century there were about fifty rulings, decisions, investigations, and testimony. Similarly, there was only one formal statement by the Department of Justice regarding the law before 1969 (cited in the Kennedy section, above), but ten afterwards. Finally, only one court decision mentioned the law before the Nixon presidency, but about half a dozen subsequently.

The GAO's involvement during the Truman and Kennedy administrations was minor. But, beginning in the mid-1970s, the pace of its role regarding the anti-lobbying law increased significantly. In one respect, the GAO position on the law did not change at all over time. The agency consistently noted that, because it was as a criminal statute, the Department of Justice was the only agency that had jurisdiction to determine whether or not to bring criminal charges. The GAO studiously refrained from ever stating that it believed a crime had been committed. Rather, it took the initiative to refer a case to Justice if it believed the facts it had developed warranted prosecutorial attention. (It also referred a case to Justice if a member of Congress specifically asked it to do so—without offering its own conclusions about whether the referral was justified.) The decision to refer or not refer a case to prosecutors required the GAO to develop standards and guidelines regarding what activities justified that. This was a de facto interpretation of the meaning of the law, even though such decisions would not automatically lead to criminal charges. Each situation involved a close reading, sometimes hairsplitting, of the anti-lobbying statute and its meaning. On most occasions, the GAO recited the Department of Justice's interpretations of the anti-lobbying law (see next section) and, without agreeing or disagreeing, deferred to those interpretations since they guided the prosecutorial decision-making process. Since no prosecutions ever occurred, this was all largely irrelevant. On at least one occasion, though, the GAO stated, "We share the department's view of the statute."[115]

As reflected in its own decisions, the GAO was gradually limiting the scope of the law by judging the following situations as *not* constituting grounds for a referral to the Department of Justice:

> Under the rubric of generally informing the public, a department could send mass mailings that included its policy positions, even regarding pending or potential legislation.[116]
>
> The law did not cover lobbying state legislatures, even if regarding ratifying a federal constitutional amendment or using federal funds for such lobbying.[117]
>
> The law did not cover lobbying a state's voters regarding an upcoming public referendum.[118]
>
> All routine and conventional forms of directly lobbying Congress, including initiating contacts and discussing issues not currently pending in the form of a bill, were generally acceptable.[119]
>
> Indirect lobbying was permissible if it did not involve expenditure of appropriated funds.[120]
>
> An agency could engage in communication activities informing the public of its views on particular pieces of legislation, as long as it did not explicitly ask the citizens to lobby Congress regarding that legislation.[121]

An appeal by local government employees (who worked in an agency that received federal funds) to lobby Congress was not a violation of the law because its scope was restricted to federal officials and employees. (That situation might, however, be in violation of a different federal law related to recipients of appropriated funds using that money to lobby Congress.)[122]

The military could provide free flights on military planes so that members of Congress could return to the capital to cast a vote on a matter affecting the military.[123]

The GAO was unable to opine about possible violations by the Central Intelligence Agency of the law because the agency declined to cooperate with its investigation.[124]

The law did not cover lobbying activities by the secretary of agriculture seeking to influence an *advisory* poll (in contradistinction to a binding referendum) of wheat farmers.[125]

A federal agency could encourage a citizen or corporation to lobby Congress for a legislative remedy to a specific problem the citizen or corporation faced, since the lobbying was not for a purpose that benefited the agency.[126]

Agency documents that demonstrated knowledge of a grassroots lobbying campaign did not necessarily prove the agency used federal funds to bring the lobbying campaign into existence.[127]

If an executive of a private corporation told a federal official about the lobbying efforts by the corporation, that did not prove the agency had originally encouraged the corporation to engage in such lobbying.[128]

The GAO accepted the explanation of the Justice Department's Public Integrity Section that a departmental newsletter urging the public to lobby Congress was not a violation because the contents of the newsletter were a "regurgitation" of a statement by the secretary of the department and all presidential appointees were permitted to urge the public to lobby Congress without violating the law.[129]

If a department encouraged a grassroots lobbying campaign but urged citizens to express their views to the department rather than to Congress (even though the subject was legislation pending in Congress), that did not violate the law.[130]

An e-mail that was a clear violation of the law did not warrant a referral to the Department of Justice, because the cost was "minimal."[131]

There were also specific activities that the GAO deemed prohibited by the law:

"A direct appeal addressed to members of the public" urging them to contact Congress to indicate their support or opposition to pending legislation was prohibited.[132]

"A primary purpose" of the law was to prohibit agencies from engaging in "indirect lobbying."[133]

The law prohibited federal agencies not only from asking citizens to lobby Congress but also asking private and nonprofit organizations to do so.[134]

All federal judges were included in the scope of the law.[135]

From the mid-1970s to early in the twenty-first century, the GAO referred at its own initiative (as opposed to on behalf of a member of Congress) only a handful of cases. For example, in 1982 it investigated the lobbying activities of the Department of Defense in cooperation with private corporations in support of acquisition of C-5B aircraft and found documentary evidence that Defense had privately encouraged and worked with private companies to conduct a grassroots campaign to lobby Congress on the subject.[136] Therefore, based on the Justice Department's own guidelines (large-scale, indirect grassroots lobbying of Congress; see next section), the GAO believed it had identified a clear violation of the law. Similarly, the next year the GAO examined a Department of Commerce article in a business magazine that specifically called on readers to lobby Congress in support of the department's position regarding pending legislation. The GAO found the elements of a violation as identified by the Department of Justice and decided to refer the case to it for possible prosecution.[137] However, no prosecutions materialized in either case.

Even though the GAO was a legislative branch agency, which presumably gave it great incentive to promote the positions of Congress, it failed to breathe any life to the 1919 anti-lobbying law. Given the reality that it could not bring criminal prosecutions, the weight of implementing the criminal law fell on the Department of Justice.

ENFORCING THE LAW: AUTHORITATIVE
INTERPRETATIONS BY THE DEPARTMENT OF JUSTICE

The Department of Justice (specifically its Criminal Division) has never prosecuted anyone under the 1919 anti-lobbying law.[138] During the Johnson administration it twice criticized agency actions but submitted no criminal charges in either case: In 1965 it criticized Commerce Department officials for, "at least inferentially," encouraging citizens to contact members of Congress in favor of a bill backed by the department. Three years later, it suggested that the unsolicited distribution of 100,000 copies of the president's farm message to Congress was a violation.[139] But no prosecutions followed. The Justice Department maintained the same approach with the next president. In 1973, Assistant Attorney General Henry Peterson, in charge of the Criminal Division, wrote of the Nixon administration's "Battle of the Budget" lobbying kit that it may have been "a technical violation of the law, which is questionable, [but] the situation, in its totality, must be regarded as de minimis."[140] In other words, only blatant and major violations would even rise to a *consideration* of potential criminal prosecution. Unstated was that Peterson served at the pleasure of the attorney general, who served at the pleasure of the president.[141]

Beginning in 1977, the OLC issued about ten formal interpretations of the law that gradually construed the statute more and more narrowly. This began when Assistant Attorney General John Harmon, head of the OLC, conducted a de novo review of the 1919 law in 1977. His premise was that the few previous observations about the law made by the department were "inconsistent with what we believe to be the correct interpretation" of the law.[142] He began his reinterpretation by first concluding that the 1919 law needed to be viewed as a legislative follow-up to the 1913 ban on publicity experts because Congress had sensed "the inadequacy of the earlier 'publicity expert' measure."[143] In that context, the 1919 law was about inappropriate public relations activities intended to influence Congress, not really about lobbying per se. This first premise permitted him to view the meaning of the law in a very different light. Second, he concluded that the 1919 law was "rather sweeping and unclear" and therefore needed more explicit interpretation.[144] For example, the law failed "to identify either the context in which its prohibition is to apply or the contents of such communications deemed to be offensive"—yet trying to do that would be "a practically hopeless exercise."[145] With those observations, Harmon practically negated the plain meaning of the law.

Now that he had emptied the law of much meaning, Harmon proceeded to enumerate what he deemed permissible and prohibited by the law.[146] Permissible activities included these guidelines:

A federal official "may say anything he wishes" as long as those statements are speeches, newspaper relations, and other activities clearly protected by the First Amendment. Such public statements can include urging citizens to lobby Congress on particular legislation.

The First Amendment also guarantees the "right to petition Congress for redress of grievance." Harmon said the right to petition would logically include executive support for legislative programs and executive interaction with citizen groups interested in particular legislation.

A federal official may mention "the need for support of a particular legislative proposal" in correspondence with individuals "with whom the official had had previous contact concerning related matters of policy."

Officials can talk freely on an informal basis with citizen groups, including discussing the merits of various lobbying strategies.

Federal officials may *initiate* contacts with members of Congress about desired legislation, even though the 1919 law permits that only in response to a request from a legislator. According to Harmon, notwithstanding the wording of the law, it could not be viewed as "an attempt to brush away, by implication, years of practice based on well-recognized practical and constitutional necessity."

Harmon identified only a few very specific prohibited activities:

Federal officials cannot use citizen groups as "a device" to promote legislation.

Officials cannot play so dominant a role in a citizen group as to make it an extension of a federal agency.

Executive branch officials cannot circulate a form letter to a large mailing list that mentions its position on legislation and urges recipients to lobby Congress.

Officials cannot ask a citizen group to disseminate a letter from a federal agency that requests lobbying of Congress on a particular matter.

Officials cannot give citizen groups information that the officials themselves would not properly collect or use themselves.

Harmon summarized his conclusions: "The Executive's untrammeled use of normal press channels, public forums, and routine personal contacts to gain legislative acceptance" is permissible within the scope of the 1919 law.

After Harmon's memo, additional interpretations of the 1919 anti-lobbying law were released frequently by the Department of Justice. In January 1978, the OLC opined that the intent of Congress "was to leave to the other branches of government the determination of what internal checks and methods of clearance would be appropriate."[147] This self-assignment meant that the executive branch had been delegated the power to decide the meaning of the law for the executive branch and how to implement it. Six months later, another opinion narrowed the law by declaring that an executive agency had unfettered power to inform the public about programs and policies, including "those that touch on legislative matters." The only prohibition of the 1919 law was that agencies could not explicitly "call for the reader to contact the Congress."[148]

In 1981, a summary of the law by the White House counsel further elaborated that it was not only permissible for officials to initiate contact with members of Congress to discuss legislation (as Harmon had ruled) but also to do so "whether or not specific legislation is pending."[149] Later that year, another OLC opinion summarized the meaning of the law as specifically prohibiting only "using federal funds to mount 'grassroots campaigns.'"[150] This was an even narrower construction of the statute than before. The meaning of the law was further limited when a 1987 opinion clarified that internal agency communications that mentioned legislation and even suggested lobbying by agency employees would not violate the law, assuming the agency was relatively small.[151]

The cheese paring continued. A 1988 opinion exempted grassroots lobbying for international treaties pending before Congress from the scope of the law since treaties were not laws. It also stated that grassroots lobbying of the public to raise money for foreign matters that did not involve Congress was also permissible.[152] The next year, the OLC engaged in a close reading of the section of the law that enumerated the methods of communication that were prohibited. First, the list prohibited virtually all forms of print communication but only certain forms of verbal communication such as by "telephone" and by "other device." Therefore, the Justice Department ruled, many other forms of verbal communication, such as speeches, were not covered at all by the law.[153] A federal official could call on the public to lobby Congress at, for example, a public forum. Second, the opinion noted the language of the law regarding activities that had the "express authorization of Congress." It suggested that when Congress funded certain senior positions in federal agencies, knowing that the responsibilities of those positions included lobbying, such appropriations were tantamount to "express authorization" for those officials to lobby without violating the law. Third, the opinion pointed out that the general principle of construction of criminal statutes was "lenity," that is, the narrowest possible meaning of the law. Fourth, the opinion noted the objection to a $7,500 expenditure in the original House floor debate. Using that as an expression of legislative intent, the memo suggested that the current value of $7,500 in 1919 would set a bright line between expenditures that were prohibited by the law and those that were not. According to the opinion's calculation, in 1989 the equivalent amount would be $50,000, implying that expenditures for lobbying less than $50,000 were acceptable under the law. Finally, the 1989 memo raised in detail several arguments that the law might well be totally unconstitutional because of its limitation on some of the constitutionally enumerated powers and duties of a president.

In 1995, the OLC released summary guidelines that provided a comprehensive compilation of its interpretations of the anti-lobbying law. By now, summing up all its previous opinions, not much was left. The law "might be unconstitutional," making it a nullity to be ignored. But, even if in force, its guidelines permitted "supporting an Administration's legislative program through direct communications with Congress; through communications with the public in speeches, writings, and appearances; or though most forms of private communications to members of the public."[154] The only things the act prohibited were "high-expenditure campaigns in which members of the public are expressly urged to write their Senators and Representatives." Between 1977 and 1995, the White House lawyers had gutted the law to near meaninglessness.[155]

ENFORCING THE LAW: AUTHORITATIVE INTERPRETATIONS BY THE COURTS

Federal courts have issued rulings related to the 1919 anti-lobbying law only a few times. In 1952, a district court referred to the law as an example of the difference between a criminal proceeding against a civil servant and a dismissal proceeding against the same person. Even if dismissal from federal employment would be prompted by a criminal activity (such as a violation of the 1919 law), the dismissal process itself (which is also part of the 1919 law) would not be a criminal action but rather the action of an employer against an employee.[156] In a 1973 case, a judge referred to the law as having been "dusted off" by the plaintiffs, using that characterization because of the law's "obscurity." He also noted that, unlike most laws, this one had neither the usual extensive legislative history nor a record of previously published court opinions that judges routinely rely on.[157]

Several cases have addressed whether the law can be used as a private course of action. Can a nongovernmental party have standing to initiate and bring suit against a federal officer or employee for allegedly violating the law? District courts have generally said no, as has the federal appeals court for the District of Columbia.[158] As an extension of that principle, a district court judge refused to issue an injunction barring a federal agency from continued distribution of a brochure expressing the administration's views on legislation.[159] In a clear reaction to these court rulings, when senators introduced a bill they titled the "Stop Government Propaganda Act" during the 109th Congress in 2005, they explicitly granted private citizens the right to bring civil suits against the government that alleged violations of their proposed law.[160] Had the courts ruled that the 1919 anti-lobbying law could be the basis for a private course of action, one can assume that its use would have exploded, with numerous special interest groups perceiving implied lobbying by an agency whenever it was on a subject or policy they disagreed with. Given that a definition of lobbying is in some respects in the eye of the beholder, presumably courts would have been inundated with such cases.

REVISING THE LAW: DECRIMINALIZATION, 2002

Up through the late 1970s there was no serious discussion of the need to revise the law so that violations would be prosecuted. This seems odd, given that the raison d'être of a legislative body is to pass laws. One would think that when it identified a flawed law it would immediately amend it to make it more operational. Yet this did not happen for nearly half a century after the law was adopted, during which time it was never prosecuted.

There was an initial tangential effort to give meaning to the law in 1977. The Senate Appropriations Committee inserted a new section into the bill providing appropriations for FY 1978 to the Department of Interior and several other agencies. It was reacting to some "colorful brochures printed and actively distributed" that extolled pending legislation. In the committee's view, those brochures were "in violation of the intent, if not the letter, of the Act" of 1919.[161] The new language added to the law stated that "no part of any appropriation contained in this Act shall be available for any activity or the publication or distribution of literature that in any way tends to promote public support or opposition to any legislative proposal on which congressional action is not complete, in accordance with the Act of June 25, 1948 (18 U.S.C. 1913)."[162]

With the explicit cross-reference to the 1919 criminal law banning agency lobbying, the committee was seeking to give new legal meaning to the moribund law by adding more specific statutory guidance. It was enacted into law. This was occurring, however, in an appropriation bill that controlled only the conditions attached to the spending of federal funds. It was not an add-on to the 1919 law itself and thus did not have any legal status as a revision of the criminal law. Still, the provision was routinely renewed in every annual Interior Department appropriation bill through 1981.[163] During that time, however, the GAO opined that the appropriation rider went beyond the scope of the 1919 law and therefore needed to be viewed as a separate law, unrelated to the criminal statute.[164] In 1982, Congress yielded to the reality that it could not strengthen the 1919 law through such funding provisos and dropped the cross-reference to the anti-lobbying law in that now-standard provision.[165]

Nevertheless, inserting items related to the 1919 law into appropriation bills was much easier than passing permanent law. A quarter-century later, a similar effort occurred in the annual funding for the Department of Energy. The FY 2003 appropriation bill prohibited the department from spending any appropriated funds for any "lobbying activity as provided in 18 U.S.C. 1913."[166] This was not much different from the 1977 proviso or even Congressman Smith's efforts against the NLRB in 1940. Here was a law directing a federal department to uphold another law. This still could not get around the key role of the Department of Justice in deciding what a violation of the law was and whether to prosecute. There was no way to bypass the Justice Department by inserting such provisions in appropriation bills. One way or the other, the implementation of the 1919 anti-lobbying law lay with the criminal justice system, not with Congress or any legislative agencies.

In the 1980s, several senators worked on bill drafts that would create a permanent law (as opposed to a provision in an annual appropriation bill) to state more explicitly permissible and impermissible roles of lobbying by executive agencies. The GAO commented on their drafts in order to strengthen the intent based on the experience with the 1919 criminal law.[167] But none of the senators pursued enacting their drafts. Also in 1985, the GAO was asked to evaluate agency legislative liaison activities. Based on interviews with liaison staff, the GAO reported that the criminal statute was "regarded as unclear, imprecise, and largely unenforceable."[168] Still, of forty-four people interviewed, only one recommended repealing it. Rather, forty of forty-four supported the (unsatisfactory) status quo compared to the alternative of "an expanded or stricter criminal law" that would be more precise and therefore easier to follow as well as prosecute.[169] Reacting to the results of its study, the GAO recommended counterbalancing the existing criminal law with a permanent civil law that gave more detail on permissible and impermissible lobbying.[170] It felt such a permanent law would have more impact than the unused criminal law and the riders routinely added to annual appropriation bills. The GAO renewed the suggestion in 1996,[171] but Congress took no such action.

In 2002, as part of an omnibus revision of Justice Department laws, Congress addressed a few of the weaknesses the GAO had identified in the anti-lobbying law over the years. It removed the criminal sanctions and converted the law into a civil law with nonincarceration penalties. It expanded the law's coverage from Congress to state legislatures as well and broadened the activities covered from legislation and appropriations to such other forms of legislative activity as treaty ratification.[172] This expansion of the law, however, was counterbalanced with a third major change that favored the executive branch: added was explicit language that the civil law would not apply to any situation that would "in the opinion of the Attorney General, violate the Constitution or interfere with the conduct of foreign policy, counter-intelligence, intelligence, or national security activities."[173] This language had the effect of giving formal status to all the opinions the OLC had issued interpreting the law, especially the suggestions that the law impinged on the president's constitutional prerogatives. The exception for any activity related to foreign policy and national security was a loophole that could be used to justify practically anything.

President Bush's signing statement made clear how significant a victory these changes were. He said that the executive branch would "construe" the new law "in a manner consistent with the President's constitutional authority . . . to supervise the unitary executive branch."[174] So, despite the substantial changes in the 1919 law, the revised 2002 version was no more enforceable or meaningful than before, probably less. After the decriminalization of the law, to date there have been no authoritative interpretations of its meaning and, of course, no prosecutions.[175]

IMPACT OF THE LAW

The pattern of public invocations of the anti-lobbying law after it was revised in 2002 showed little change from before. About a year after the law was decriminalized, some Democratic lawmakers accused the Environmental Protection Agency of the Bush administration of violating the law. The agency denied it.[176] In late 2003, an environmental advocacy group accused the Bush administration's Energy Department of violating the law.[177] In June 2004, lawyers at the National Park Service and Department of Interior confirmed that it would be legal for park superintendents to lobby the member of Congress in whose district that park was located.[178] When the ranking Democratic member of the House Judiciary Committee complained in 2004 of the attorney general's public advocacy of renewing the Patriot Act, the department's inspector general ruled that expenditures of appropriated funds for the cost of travel to venues where he made such comments did not violate the anti-lobbying law.[179]

These invocations of the revised law had about the same effect as when it was a criminal act. No one was ever charged with violating it, largely because the legal interpretations given to the content of the law were far from the plain meaning of its words. To a layperson, it appeared to ban agency lobbying of Congress except in some specifically described conditions. In reality, it was interpreted to mean that it applied only to behind-the-scenes and large-scale appeals from the agency to the public to lobby Congress specifically for or against something. Rather, the law had mostly extralegal uses—from the very beginning—as a political weapon that legislative (and other) opponents of a particular agency or president could use to bludgeon their adversaries with negative publicity. Little had changed over time.

Judgments about the effect of the law from academics and other observers have been relatively, but not totally, negative. Starting with the positive, in 1978, three faculty members of the Federal Executive Institute asserted that "in some cases departments have abused this [law], and Congress has responded sharply by cutting appropriations or otherwise restricting agencies," they but provided no specific examples or sources for their claim.[180] That same year, Louis Fisher, of the Library of Congress's Congressional Research Service, also concluded that the law had a positive, though modest, effect: The 1919 anti-lobbying law "is not the most potent weapon in the criminal code, neither it is as feckless as critics suggest. It stands as a warning against departmental efforts to mobilize grass-roots support for or against pending legislation."[181] Twenty years later, Fisher maintained that conclusion by observing that the law had been "somewhat effective" in preventing grassroots lobbying campaigns by federal agencies.[182]

Most other academic studies (although quite dated) have concluded with gloomier assessments. A study published in 1970 in a law review described the 1919 law (and others like it) as a "legal fiction," "ineffective," and "never enforced."[183] Harris, writing in 1972, viewed the law as "not enforced" though still giving opponents an opportunity to "raise a loud hullabaloo" about agency lobbying.[184] Key called that dynamic enforcement "by criticism."[185] Berman aptly pointed to Congress's "deeply ingrained institutional bias against 'administrative lobbying,'" although not enough to generate the energy and dedication to create enforceable laws.[186]

In all, efforts by Congress to gag the bureaucracy by criminalizing lobbying had been a failure. Still, of all the various silencing efforts, the 1919 law one was the most extensively invoked, especially prior to its decriminalization. This is probably due to the political sex appeal of a legislator being able breathlessly and publicly to accuse a bureaucrat and even a cabinet member of engaging in criminal conduct, of committing a crime. Such accusations were irresistible to the press since they subtly invoked the suspicion of government that is deeply embedded in American political culture. Yet awareness of the law continued to be an important requirement for senior bureaucrats.[187]

An insightful and concise summary of significance of the law was stated by the *New Republic* in 2001. It suggested that, given the previous uses of the law, there was about to be a partisan switch: instead of congressional Republicans accusing a Democratic president (Clinton) of violating the law in the 1990s, now it would be congressional Democrats accusing a Republican president (Bush II). According to the article, these partisan attacks would be relying on "what must be the most violated law in America: the Anti-Lobbying Act of 1919."[188] It was a fitting epitaph.

CHAPTER 6

LIMITING MACHINES —
NOT MEN, 1920

*"No journal, magazine, periodical, or similar Government publication,
shall be printed . . . unless the same shall have been authorized under
such regulations as shall be prescribed by the Joint Committee on
Printing . . . ; Provided further, That the foregoing provisions of this
section shall also apply to mimeographing, multigraphing and other
processes used for duplication of typewritten and printed matter."*

CR 59:5 (April 1, 1920): 5099

The ancien régime reflecting a nineteenth-century view of public administration sans any public relations was still manifesting itself into the second and third decades of the twentieth century. For example, in 1919 two legislators accused the War Department of violating federal postal and printing laws by sending to a list of 70,000 lawyers throughout the country the department's position in a controversy with the deposed judge advocate general. A senator called it "propaganda," as did a congressman.[1] All the same, the attorney general and the postmaster general (both cabinet members serving at the pleasure of the president, as was the secretary of war), ruled that no such legal violation had occurred. Attorney General A. Mitchell Palmer stated that if the secretary of war "believed it necessary to direct the printing and distribution of the letter here involved, to the end that what he regarded as *the truth might be available to the public,* his action cannot be called into question."[2] Although that may have settled the issue legally (as well as self-servedly by and for the executive branch), legislators and their allies in the press kept up the drumbeat of accusations during a Senate committee investigation (of the larger issue), claiming that the War Department had "established a propaganda bureau."[3] The charges were widely printed, indicating journalists' sympathy.[4] In their worldview, it was wholly inappropriate for public funds and federal employees to be dedicated to public information. Another example of the nineteenth-century perspective on agency external communications occurred when Palmer's successor, as part of the incoming Harding administration, was settling into office. Attorney General Harry Daugherty was quoted early in 1921 as saying that "he is against press agencing of his department. He has given orders that the department's record must speak for itself rather than speaking through publicity agents."[5]

But that worldview was increasingly anachronistic. Rosten observed that federal agencies became much more aware of the uses of publicity after World War I and then began significantly expanding their external communications activities and staffing.[6] For example, in 1922 a congressman who favored prohibition (and therefore favored publicity by the federal bureau enforcing it) acknowledged that "every department in our Government I know anything about, in order to save time, has a habit of giving publicity for the newspaper reporters in some kind of a systematic way."[7] Inevitably, with the growth and institutionalization of federal public relations came political criticism of it. From the criminalization of agency lobbying in 1919 until the beginning of Roosevelt's presidency in 1933, there were a few congressional initiatives to silence the bureaucracy, mostly through public condemnations. In 1922, Senator Heflin attacked propaganda from the Federal Reserve Banks and Congressman Hill tried to defund the public relations of Treasury's Prohibition Bureau. Legislators also attacked Hoover administration agencies for their publicity activities a few times. None of those initiatives produced any authoritative decisions by Congress.[8]

Congress's effort to ban publicity experts (chapter 4) in federal agencies was a tactic that focused on getting at a perceived problem by focusing on *personnel*. The criminalizing of lobbying was a subsequent effort that focused on an *activity* (chapter 5). A few years later Congress tried to muffle the bureaucracy's voice by going after *machinery*. This was an effort in 1920 to limit agency public relations by controlling mimeograph machines. Congress approved the bill and sent to the president. Although President Wilson vetoed the bill (and the veto was not overridden), for purposes of this study that legislative action was an official decision of Congress as an institution.

SENATOR SMOOT'S FOCUS ON MIMEOGRAPHING

In the late nineteenth century, Congress struggled with government printing and publications (see Prologue). Congressional efforts to control them continued into the twentieth century. Usually, Congress's attention to this subject was largely driven by costs, rather than as an explicit tactic in the larger strategy of silencing the bureaucracy,[9] but occasionally controlling publicity and propaganda was the motive. The issue was explicitly raised by Congressman Joseph Walsh (R-Mass.), who suggested during a floor debate in 1918 that enhancing congressional control of agency printing was a way to crack down on agency publicity and press agentry. He said bureaucracies had "an unappeasable appetite for pitiless publicity," and the only way to limit that was by controlling the paper they could consume for their publications.[10]

At that time, Senator Reed Smoot (R-Utah) was chair of the congressional Joint Committee on Printing. Because he was a fiscal conservative, the role was fitting; he persistently searched for ways to control federal agency publications and thereby reduce costs.[11] After an extensive review, in early 1919 the committee recommended revising some printing laws to increase congressional brakes on costs of agency publications. During the appropriations process for FY 1920, Smoot proposed a floor amendment to the omnibus legislative, executive, and judicial appropriations bill to reflect the committee's recommendations. The amendment would give the Joint Committee "additional authority to control public printing and binding and distribution of Government publications."[12] In the brief debate, he stated that his purpose was merely to "save some money."[13] It was approved and included in the law as signed by President Wilson.[14]

A year later (which was also a presidential election year) Smoot was singing a slightly different tune. In a floor speech he said that the goal of reducing federal printing costs was not only financially motivated but also intended to reduce agency "propaganda," such as the "wicked practice" of distributing copies of a speech given by the head of an agency.[15] This put the ongoing efforts of the Joint Committee on Printing in a new light. No longer were they focusing merely on the budget implications of federal agency printing. Now the issue was also agency publicity. Several other senators jumped into the discussion to agree with Smoot's new orientation. Senator Lawrence Sherman (R-Ill.) said that Congress needed to crack down on the publicity by executive branch agencies because "nearly every Government department is engaged in a crusade for the purpose of magnifying its own importance, and demanding additional powers and more appropriations."[16] He also said later that there were forty-three press agents working in federal agencies who were "issuing daily mimeographed accounts of the activities of the departments."[17] William King (D-Utah) joined the floor discussion by condemning a particular agency head who, he said, "spends hundreds and thousands of dollars of the people's money in carrying on an extensive propaganda throughout the United States in order to secure legislation to build up his department."[18] For these legislators, the goal was to save money on federal printing costs *and* to strangle the voice of the bureaucracy. Smoot had repackaged a relatively dull budgetary topic into one that now excited his colleagues.

Over the next few months, during the appropriations process for FY 1921, Smoot expanded the committee's agenda from controlling agency printing costs to congressional control of mimeograph machines owned by federal departments and agencies.[19] His felt that fewer mimeograph machines meant less agency publicity. A newspaper article captured his line of thinking and its relationship to the larger congressional reaction to agency publicity. Senator Smoot, it said, was seeking "still tighter restrictions on government press agent activities. It would forbid not only the publication of all governmental journals and magazines, but would *stop* also mimeograph 'hand outs,' which have been issued in such abundance by various departments in recent years, without specific authorization of the joint congressional committee on printing. . . . Armed with such authority, the joint printing committee is of the opinion that it can not only save much valuable print paper at a time when it is extremely scarce, but that it can also curtail the waste of thousands of dollars of expenditures on administration press agents' salaries."[20]

In April 1920, Smoot successfully attached a floor amendment to the annual legislative, executive, and judicial appropriations bill. It expanded the committee's jurisdiction over printing to include not just traditional printing but also "mimeographing, multigraphing, and other processes used for the duplication of typewritten and printed matter, other than official correspondence and office records."[21] The provision was included in the final version of the bill sent to President Wilson.[22]

PRESIDENT WILSON'S VETO

Wilson's secretary of the treasury (and former secretary of agriculture), David F. Houston, was exercised about Smoot's addition to the bill.[23] He had general concerns that the provision was yet another "congressional invasion of the executive field,"[24] and he specifically saw the implications of the Smoot language on executive agency publicity. Houston wrote President Wilson that the effect of the amendment would have Congress "enter into every department of the government and determine what information shall be made public." Congress would be able to "exercise a censorship" over all agencies. For example, it could second-guess his policy that "one of the first duties of the Treasury in particular [is] to make public information concerning its financial operations."[25]

Wilson was sympathetic to Houston's concerns, but the solicitor general saw no constitutional problems with the provision. Wilson could not justify a veto by arguing that the provision was unconstitutional. Nonetheless, he decided to veto the bill because of the mimeograph provision. He asked Houston to prepare a draft veto message.[26] In his message, Wilson explained that Congress should not have the "power to determine what information shall be given to the people of the country by the executive departments."[27] In response, Smoot argued that the veto should be overridden because congressional control of mimeograph machines was justifiable on the merits. He described the "the mass of such stuff with which the

departments have swamped the mails and the newspapers offices."
Exhibit A was a "Memo for the press" that the Navy Department had sent
to newspapers with an advance version of the Navy secretary's testimony
to Congress.[28] Further, the example subtly implied that the Navy was
disrespecting Congress by releasing information to the press even before
it was presented to Congress. The importance of Congress was being
diminished by an increasing agency orientation to press relations. Smoot
and Houston agreed what they were fighting about, namely, the degree
of freedom federal agencies and departments had to engage in public
communications. The differences in the congressional and executive perspectives were starkly apparent and self-interested.

Given how easy it is to sustain a veto (only one-third of one house),
Wilson won. Congress eventually repassed the identical bill sans the
mimeograph section. Smoot had, however, made an impression on agency
heads, agency publicity staffs, and reporters. He had established a direct
connection between his (somewhat ludicrous) effort to control mimeograph machines and the larger issue of congressional hostility to publicity
experts in the departments and agencies.

• • •

In 1927 and 1930, the *New York Times* referred back to this fight. When
commenting on the Treasury Department's innovative use of the radio
for publicity to sell U.S. Bonds in 1927, the newspaper observed, "Senator Smoot made a drive on mimeograph machines a few years ago from
which the departments have not yet recovered, and their publicity men
have to be disguised as 'editorial assistant' or 'chief of the division of
current information.'"[29]

Three years later, during the same week, four cabinet secretaries had
released their annual reports. This prompted the *New York Times* to suggest that these reports and the other publications of departmental public
relations offices "fail to give the public any adequate picture of the department and its activities." But taking steps to improve agency publicity might
not "escape the baleful eye of Senator Smoot, to whom a mimeograph
machine in a government office is a scandalous thing."[30] When it came to
external communications, the newspaper seemed to be saying, agencies
were in a no-win situation with Congress.

In the end, what the bureaucracy was using mimeograph machines for continued to be legal. Congressional efforts to limit agency public relations by statutorily overseeing the use of such equipment had been for naught.

CHAPTER 7

Limiting Public Relations One Agency at a Time: Attack of the Conservative Coalition, 1935–1950

Justice Department, 1936: *"For compensation and traveling expenses of special attorneys and assistants to the Attorney General . . . $600,000, no part of which, except for payment of foreign counsel, shall be used to pay the compensation of any persons except attorneys duly licensed and authorized to practice."*

49 *Stat.* 1326

Noncabinet Agencies, 1938: *"The committee views with disfavor the tendency to expend disproportionate sums for the printing of publications, often on high-priced paper and under expensive covers, the preparation of press releases, magazine articles, broadcasts, motion pictures, etc., the primary purpose of which is to build up a public demand for the services of the agency issuing the publicity. . . . the committee believes a substantial reduction of outlay in this quarter can be effected by many of the agencies without diminution of service."*

U.S. House, Committee on Appropriations, *Independent Offices Appropriation Bill, 1939*, report, 3

Interior Department, 1940: *"No part of this appropriation made available to the office of the Secretary by this section shall be used for the broadcast of radio programs designed for or calculated to influence the passage or defeat of any legislation pending before the Congress."*

54 *Stat.* 406

USDA Office of Information, 1943: *"No part of this appropriation shall be used for the establishment or maintenance of regional or State field offices or for the compensation of employees in such offices except that not to exceed $9,100 may be used to maintain the San Francisco radio office."*

57 *Stat.* 395

USDA Agricultural Adjustment Agency, 1943: *"None of the funds herein appropriated . . . shall be used to pay the salaries or expenses of any regional information employees or any State or county information employees, but this shall not preclude the answering of inquiries or supplying of information to individual farmers."*

57 *Stat.* 417

Interior Department Bureau of Reclamation, 1946: *"Not exceeding $150,000 of funds available for expenditure under this appropriation shall be used for salaries and expenses in connection with informational work."*

60 *Stat.* 364

The presidencies of Franklin Roosevelt and Harry Truman spanned the crest of authoritative congressional reactions to agency public relations. In part, this is understandable, given that the scope and size of the federal government expanded so significantly during those years. The New Deal and Fair Deal also crystallized the congressional conservative coalition, comprising southern conservative Democrats and Republicans as the minority party (during most of the time).[1] Sometimes they possessed an ideological majority on Capitol Hill and could get their way even though the Democratic Party was formally the majority party in both houses. For national legislators with a conservative political philosophy, big government was bad enough, but autonomous bureaucracies as distinct players in policy and decision making? Agencies with large and growing publicity and lobbying staffs? Bad, bad, bad. Limiting the federal bureaucracy's public relations was part of a larger strategy to restore government to the way they wished it to be, with executive branch agencies in a subordinate principle-agent relationship to Congress.

TOTAL WAR: TRYING TO SILENCE NEW DEAL AGENCIES

For congressional conservatives, new efforts to muzzle the bureaucracy made political sense. In general, they believed in smaller government, passive executive branch agencies, Congress as the alpha branch of the federal government, and members of Congress as the chief informational links to the citizenry. In particular, reactions by conservative legislators to the publicity activities of New Deal agencies can be seen as reflecting Carpenter's theory of autonomy (see Introduction). Carpenter identified publicity as one of the tools used by enterprising bureaucrats to achieve autonomy for their agencies. For all intents and purposes, if they succeeded, they reversed the traditional principle-agent relationship between Congress and executive branch agencies. In this context, the attack by the conservative coalition on agency publicity during the New Deal and the Fair Deal was precisely in order to thwart agencies from autonomizing. Opposing agency publicity was a de facto manifestation of opposition to the raison d'être of the agency itself.

For example, one of the innovative practitioners of New Deal agency publicity (and a former journalist) was Alfred Stedman, assistant administrator and director of information of the Agricultural Adjustment Administration (AAA). The agency's purpose was to stabilize farm income by enacting various planting quotas and subsidies per crop. These major policies were often enacted by referendum of the farmers who grew that crop.[2] This created an awkward public information role for the agency. Providing neutral information by a federal agency was relatively noncontroversial, but what about the agency proposing a policy for referendum that it, by definition, wanted to pass? To what degree could the AAA use its public relations tools to advocate passage of the referendum? Stedman took a relatively aggressive stance. He directed information campaigns to persuade farmers to vote in favor of a referendum but insisted that such external communications were *not* propaganda. This was new ground for agency public relations.

In a paper for a panel during the 1938 annual conference of the American Political Science Association, Stedman wrote that "a good many of those who have criticized the informational activities of the Agricultural Adjustment Administration have in reality been doing so on the broader ground that the entire farm program is unnecessary and inadvisable."[3] In other words, conservative coalition opposition to agency publicity was in reality a reflection of its opposition to the agency in toto. This underlying rationale helps explains a proclivity by some legislators to oppose external communications activities by federal agencies, as a way to stifle autonomizing efforts from becoming successful.

The effort by Capitol Hill conservatives to gag the bureaucracy was also part of a subtle strategy to defeat the New Deal by crippling it with nonsubstantive and indirect limitations to the point of losing viability. According to Burns, these politicians knew they could not defeat New Deal programs head on. These programs were too popular with too many voters. Instead, "what the coalition could and did do was to cut funds for those functions behind which no congressional bloc would rally, but which in the long run might critically influence the durability and impact of the programs—namely planning, research, statistical and economic analysis, scientific investigation, administrative management, information, staffing."[4]

At the other end of Pennsylvania Avenue, the Roosevelt administration took agency public relations and press relations activities to a new level.[5] A reporter (who was a conservative) wrote at the time, "The fact is the employment of newspaper men in this Administration is so far beyond that in any previous Administration that there is simply no comparison. There has never been anything like it at any time."[6] Sure, there had been press agents in the federal government since 1905 and observers had especially pointed to their pervasiveness in the Hoover administration.[7] But FDR's actions went beyond Hoover's. Roosevelt created dozens of new agencies, each of which eagerly sought to use publicity programs to inform the public, whether for pragmatic, democratic, or autonomistic purposes. According to Rosten, a "contagion of publicity-consciousness swept through the organs of the government."[8] The explosion in the scope and size of government necessitated such an escalation of agency public relations. This was an operationalization of the cliché "If a tree falls in a forest and no person hears it, does it make a sound?" In this case, the question was "If the government offered a new relief program for the unemployed, would they sign up for it if they didn't know about it?" Also, from the perspective of reporters covering government, a syndicated columnist admitted in late 1934 that "such a thing as really 'covering' Washington in the old newspaper sense is now out of the question."[9] Press agents were now vital to reporters being able to do their jobs, whether the journalists were willing to admit that or not. Yet, at the same time, the expansion of agency public relations in the New Deal prompted a reaction from Congress patterned after its earlier reactions in the twentieth century.

Some reporters called the attention of conservative politicians to publicity activities in federal agencies: "In 1935 dispatches began to reveal a more aggressive and critical journalistic temper."[10] Early headlines highlighting agency external communications included "The Press Agent," "Treasury Placed under Censorship," "40 Bureaus Tell Government News," "Fourth Estate Furnishes 150 New Deal Aids [sic]," and "Federal News Mill Runs at High Speed," and a pseudonymous book by two reporters was titled *Handout*.[11] The latter was a flat-out attack on New Deal external communications. The publisher claimed the book exposed "for the first time" the activities of "high-pressure propagandists" and "how important facts are being suppressed, misrepresented and distorted."[12]

Conservative politicians started sensing the political sex appeal of attacking New Deal public relations, but with an intensity and comprehensiveness greater than their criticisms during Hoover's presidency. Often they did not actually propose doing anything specific about it, just called for studies and investigations to expose the phenomenon, as had happened three decades earlier (chapter 3). In January 1935, Congressman Martin Dies (D-Tex.) called for a special House committee to investigate "the possibility of the shackling of the press by the administration."[13] The resolution's preamble, in outlining the problem to be investigated, charged the administration with having "a well-organized and highly developed plan of employing hundreds of newspapermen as press agents for various Federal activities; and that the administration requires such press agents to exercise favoritism and partiality in giving news releases."[14] The Dies resolution sparked extensive and largely sympathetic publicity in the *Washington Post, Chicago Tribune, Wall Street Journal,* and *New York Times*.[15] The House leadership, loyal to FDR, would not permit such an anti-administration effort to occur. But other politicians noticed Dies's media breakthrough. A few months later, Senator Lester Dickinson (R-Iowa) similarly submitted a proposal to investigate publicity activities of government agencies since March 4, 1933. Senator Hugo Black (D-Ala.) baited him on the floor by urging expanding the investigation "to include propaganda issued by any agency of any kind in the United States, including the chamber of commerce and the power companies."[16] Dickinson got the requisite publicity; the proposal was referred to committee and never heard from again.[17]

In 1936–38, Senator Harry Byrd (D-Va.), a "dedicated conservative, [and] grim opponent of waste in government," was chair of the Senate Select Committee on Investigation of Executive Agencies of the Government.[18] As part of the congressional reaction to the work of President Roosevelt's Brownlow Committee to reorganize the executive branch, Byrd (and counterparts in the House) had asked the Brookings Institution for its own report on reforming the federal government. At that time, the Brookings Institution was "earning a reputation as a locus of opposition to Franklin D. Roosevelt's recovery and reform programs."[19] A leader in the conservative coalition, Byrd sought to use both his committee chairmanship and the Brookings report to criticize the New Deal in general and its public relations activities in particular. For example, according to a front page article in the *New York Times,* "experts of the Brookings Institution . . . are now studying the publicity activities of the government, principally to ascertain how many press relations bureaus there are, what they do and how much they spend."[20] When it was released, only twenty-six pages (including an appendix) of the 500,000-word report were devoted to agency information activities.[21] Additionally, unlike most of the other sections of the report, this section contained no formal recommendations for changes, only "conclusions." Still, it was headline material. According to the *Times* headline, "More Than $500,000 Paid to Press Agents by Administration in a Year, Survey Shows."[22] The Brookings report provided grist for the (congressional) mill for years to come as the database for criticisms of agency external communications.[23]

Denunciations of propaganda by New Deal agencies became a staple of the conservative coalition's assault on the president.[24] As an outgrowth of these generalized attacks, there were also several ad hoc reactions on Capitol Hill to the public relations activities of specific agencies, such as an appropriations committee report criticizing publications of noncabinet agencies that would "build up a public demand for the services of the agency issuing the publicity."[25] I present some of the major efforts here by department and roughly in chronological order, in the sequence of when agency was first targeted. These events are an indication of the multiplicity of targets of the congressional effort to stifle the bureaucracy's voice during this period and the improvisational nature of the overall effort and sometimes serendipitous, even accidental, foci.

Justice Department, 1936

In August 1934, Attorney General Homer Cummings announced that he was hiring journalist Henry Suydam to be one of his special assistants. Suydam's main responsibility, said Cummings, would be "to inform the public of the problems and work of the department."[26] Suydam was one of the first people who built an entire career shuttling back and forth many times between journalism and government public relations, as opposed to the more routine practice of doing so just once, as a one-way career move of reporter to government information staffer. As the foreign correspondent for the *Brooklyn* (N.Y.) *Daily Eagle*, he had covered World War I from Europe. After the war, he was briefly the representative in Holland of the U.S. Committee on Public Information, the wartime presidential information agency headed by George Creel. In 1921, he was named by the secretary of state to head the publicity and press relations office of the State Department.[27] After serving a year, he resigned to become the Washington correspondent of the *Brooklyn Eagle*.[28] Now, after twelve years as a reporter, Suydam returned to government, this time the Department of Justice.

As the top public information officer for the attorney general, Suydam worked to improve the public image of the department in general. His activities were wide ranging: helping organize the administration's Crime Conference in late 1934, dealing with reporters, answering congressional mail, preparing press summaries for distribution within the department, advising on release of federal prison statistics, serving on a committee to explore the idea of a federal anti-crime "West Point," speaking to the public, and representing the department on a committee that sponsored the annual Community Chest fund-raising drive throughout the federal executive branch.[29]

But Suydam's major assignment was to improve the administration's crime-fighting image and to do that by working closely with the Federal Bureau of Investigation.[30] One newspaper described him as the "special press representative for the Attorney General *and* Director J. Edgar Hoover of the Federal Bureau of Investigation."[31] He worked closely with Hoover on "embellishing the bureau's image" and, conversely, worked "to eliminate the glamor that had been associated with gangland racketeers of that time."[32] President Roosevelt would benefit politically if these efforts received increased publicity. Indeed, Suydam helped tutor J. Edgar Hoover in maximizing press coverage and developing an image as a crime buster. Hoover was a quick study and eventually became the most successful bureaucrat to benefit from his agency's public relations activities. His image as the G-man who always got his man was extremely successful.

Though Roosevelt initially benefited from the association with Hoover's law-and-order popularity, the ideological differences between them gradually increased. In contradistinction to the normal legislative treatment of agency external communications, Hoover's public relations activities were popular with the conservative coalition on Capitol Hill. O'Reilly noted the double standard: "If conservative congressmen tended to support the FBI's media activities, they criticized the similar maneuverings of other New Deal agencies to publicize their programs and accomplishments."[33] Meanwhile, Hoover had gotten so good at public relations that he, straight-faced, testified before Congress that the FBI did not employ any writers, did not cooperate with Hollywood, and did not assist reporters covering his bureau.[34] Suydam's key role in improving the administration's crime-fighting image was demonstrated when, after resigning from the Department of Justice, he received a personal thank-you note from the president for his services—highly unusual treatment for a mere staff assistant to a cabinet secretary.[35]

Someone inside the Justice Department was out to get Suydam and tipped off some legislators about his salary and title.[36] At a routine appropriations subcommittee hearing on the department's FY 1936 appropriation in early 1935, chairman William Oliver (D-Ala.) pointedly asked for detailed information on all the special attorneys and special assistants employed at the department. The subsequent submittal listed Suydam as the highest-paid special assistant to the attorney general ($10,000 annual salary), with duties listed as "Special cases and matters to be assigned," a blanket phrase applied to about one-third of Justice's special assistants.[37]

The next year, the subcommittee was primed. First, a member asked the Justice Department to supply "a full statement showing the character of work" that each special assistant was engaged in. The blanket phrase the department had used the previous year would not work. The eventual list admitted Suydam's press work.[38] Shortly afterward, Attorney General Cummings testified before the subcommittee. Congressman Robert Bacon (R-N.Y.), the ranking minority member, read him the 1913 law banning publicity experts in federal agencies and then, in a carefully worded question, asked him point blank: "Are any of the men enumerated in the above list of special assistants or anyone else employed by the Department used for publicity purposes within the meaning of the statute I have just quoted?" "No, Mr. Bacon," Cummings responded, "There are no special assistants or other persons employed in the Department of Justice in contravention of the statute to which you refer."[39]Clearly Bacon was hinting at Suydam. But Cummings had parsed his response. He answered the first part of Bacon's question truthfully, but legalistically by relying on the poor drafting of the 1913 law.

The other shoe dropped in May 1936 when the conference committee released its report on the Justice Department's FY 1937 appropriation. Up to that point, the issue of Suydam had not been explicitly raised in any committee reports or floor amendments. Someone in the know on the conference committee was lying in wait for the right opportunity to strike. Out of the blue, "at the last minute," and "without knowledge of department officials," the conference committee inserted new language into the bill (which conference committees are permitted to do).[40] In the end of a section proposing a compromise between the different levels of funding for special assistants that had been approved by the two houses, a new clause was added—"a limitation that none of the funds may be used to pay anyone except a duly qualified and licensed attorney."[41] Suydam, who was not a lawyer, had just been pushed out of his job without his name ever coming up. Although Bacon was one of the House conferees, no one stepped forward to claim authorship. The conference committee report was accepted by both houses, and the new funding limitation became law.[42]

The "hit" on Suydam was news, with the Associated Press putting it on its national wire.[43] But Cummings was not going to be pushed around. He would, of course, abide by the letter of the law, but he found a loophole. A few weeks after the beginning of the new fiscal year, by using a different salary account he rehired Suydam as a special *executive* assistant rather than a special assistant.[44] But Suydam stayed less than a year after that contretemps. In March 1937 (before the annual appropriations process on Capitol Hill would heat up), he resigned to become an editorial writer with the *Newark Evening News*.[45]

Suydam left behind two legacies. The appropriation rider aimed at him was routinely renewed long after he had departed from the Justice Department; for example, exactly four decades later the anti-Suydam provision was still part of the annual Justice Department appropriation act.[46] And his four immediate successors, as heads of the department's public relations, continued to be called "special executive assistants" to continue evading the law that had been aimed at him.[47]

Interior Department, Division of Information, 1938–1941

Harold Ickes was the long-serving head of the Interior Department throughout the Roosevelt administration and the first two years of the Truman administration. Besides his secretaryship, he also held several other positions including heading the Public Works Administration and serving as the presidentially designated petroleum coordinator for the entire executive branch. He was equally active as a member of the president's political family, often giving speeches and radio appearances in support of administration policies (unrelated to his portfolios), was frequently quoted in the newspapers, offered the president advice on non-Interior matters, and made partisan speeches. He was about as involved and high profile as a cabinet secretary could be.

The highly public roles he played made him especially aware of the importance of public relations in public administration and the benefits that would accrue to improving the public information infrastructure of his department. Ickes especially envied the extensive apparatus of the central Office of Information at the USDA and wanted to copy that model to build a similar one. In September 1937, Ickes received permission from the Bureau of the Budget to establish a departmental Division of Information and for it to have its own line in the president's annual budget proposal to Congress.[48] The benefit of the latter seemingly minor detail was that it would formalize the office (if accepted by Congress) by being the recipient of its own appropriation, thus giving it relatively permanent stand-alone congressional sanction.

As part of the FY 1939 appropriations process in early 1938, Ickes made a point of bringing up the subject on his own initiative and asked for the approval of the House Appropriations Committee. He said, "We need one very badly. When we compare our situation with that of the Agricultural Department, for instance, we find that we have, perhaps, been rather derelict in not presenting the matter frankly."[49] Based on transfers from other units, the new Division of Information would be appropriated about $50,000 and twenty-one staff for FY 1939.[50] Besides relatively traditional activities such as publications, photography, and motion pictures, it would also have a teletype machine that would keep Ickes informed of important news developments throughout the day.[51] Congressman Robert Rich (R-Pa.) tried to bait him, asking if the new office would "have the same propaganda" as the USDA? Ickes dryly answered, "No. I do not think we could ever be so expert."[52]

Triggered in part by the request for a departmental Division of Information, the members of the committee asked about public information activities in some of the department's far-flung bureaus. They asked about publicity by the U.S. Geological Survey, the Office of Education (then in Interior), and the National Bituminous Coal Commission.[53] Ultimately, the committee turned down Ickes's request. It saw "no reason why this activity should be set up as a separate entity. Similar activity is now carried on under the existing appropriation for the Secretary's office."[54]

When the bill reached the House floor, Congressman John Taber (R-N.Y.) focused his criticism on publications of the Office of Education "as propaganda for promoting increased expenditures." He said those publications violated both the 1913 ban on publicity experts and the 1919 ban on lobbying Congress. A supporter of the department, Congressman Jed Johnson, Sr. (D-Okla.), challenged Taber to pinpoint any violations of the law in those publications. Taber could not and instead said, "I object to the whole thing."[55] Later in the debate, Congressman Rich moved to eliminate all funding for information activities in the secretary's office, arguing that its public information activities were "propaganda," "ridiculous," and not necessary since Ickes's "work ought to speak for itself." Again, Congressman Johnson rose to defend these activities, but as blandly as possible. He did not want to be put in the position of defending "propaganda" and wasteful spending. This was "nothing new" in the department, he said; all the other departments had information activities, and someone had to be there to answer public inquiries. "They are doing valuable work and are furnishing information that the public is entitled to have." On a voice vote, it appeared that the amendment had been defeated. But Rich then insisted on a head count, saying, "I want to find out whether we want propaganda here or not." But the implied political threat of being recorded as "favoring propaganda" did not work this time. The amendment was defeated 21–47.[56] For FY 1939, then, Ickes had the funding he wanted for a departmental Division of Information, but administratively it was part of his office, unlike the USDA's.

A year later, during the appropriations process in early 1939 for FY 1940, the topic naturally came up again. Ickes was asked about the work of the new Information Division within his office (but without its own budget line). He said that the new organizational structure was working "very satisfactorily. I think there is a better comprehension on the part of the people of the country of what the Department does." Ickes asked for an increase in the Information Division's budget, about $36,000 more. Subcommittee chair Edward Taylor (D-Colo.) asked how the new setup, including the requested increase, compared to that at the USDA. Assistant Secretary Ebert Burlew answered, "I believe the figure for the Department of Agriculture is higher." Again the subcommittee members also asked about public relations expenditures in the U.S. Housing Authority and by the Coal Commission.[57]

The committee eventually approved an expansion of the Information Division for FY 1940 but cut Ickes's request by $10,000. But then, when the bill reached the floor of the House, Congressman Dudley White (R-Ohio), a member of the subcommittee, submitted an amendment to deny any increases in the division's budget. He condemned the bureaucratic tendency to enlarge publicity activities and said the department was "trying to take a page out of Goebbels' book of propaganda."[58] Another subcommittee member, Charles Leavy (D-Wash.), tried to answer White, but without appearing to endorse propaganda. Avoiding even naming the topic under discussion (let alone defending it), he blandly said that, given the additional duties Congress had assigned the department in the past few years, "to say now that we should arbitrarily eliminate from this bill, without regard to the effect it might have on governmental activities, this particular item, or any item unless good cause exists, it seems to me, is unsound."[59] The amendment passed, 92–89. The conservative coalition had momentarily seized control of the legislative body, overturning the support for the administration's position by the Democratic leadership. This was the only amendment adopted to the bill in the House during that day's debate.[60] All other amendments were rejected. This exception is an indication of the strong political appeal that "cracking down" on propaganda had to legislators.

Radio Dramatizations

One of President Roosevelt's most powerful forms of communication was his "fireside chats." They were the most visible example of the use of radio by the federal government, but executive branch agencies followed suit and took full advantage of the relatively new medium.[61] Radio offered a way of communicating about their activities relatively inexpensively and efficiently, compared to print publications. In 1936, Ickes had used some Public Works Administration funds to install in the department's headquarters building a radio studio.[62] Besides the now-conventional communication activities the studio could be put to, he was especially mindful of the potential of "educational radio" by the Office of Education. It launched several series of educational programs and said it received significant positive response from listeners.[63] After a cabinet meeting in early 1938, the president suggested to Ickes creating a series of radio programs aimed at audiences in Latin America. He thought that would be an effective way to counter German and Italian propaganda broadcasts aimed there. He even suggested that the series be titled "University of the Air," even though it would not be formal pedagogy.[64] In all, the department studio was in heavy use.

In 1939, Ickes was testifying before the Interior Department subcommittee of the House Appropriations Committee on his FY 1940 budget request. When he was asked about the first year of the Division of Information, he casually mentioned as an aside a new project, a radio version of his annual report on the department's activities. It was called "My Dear Mr. President" and was a dramatization of the material in Ickes's routine annual (print) report. It had been broadcast on a national hookup.[65] Ickes was particularly proud of it and was glad to have the opportunity to boast about it. But the members of the subcommittee were not aware of it, and some did not have the same favorable opinion of such an innovation. Ickes had just provided grist for the mill. During the floor debate on his motion to deny the department any increase in its information budget, Congressman White said, "Mr. Ickes called attention to the fact that they had a very lovely entertainment not very long ago in the form of a radio broadcast dramatizing the annual report of the Secretary of the Interior to the President of the United States. I do not know whether they paid for the broadcasting time or not, but they certainly had to pay the cost of preparing the broadcast scrip [sic]. This, I think, is an example of exceeding the necessary boundaries of proper press relations work."[66] His amendment to cut the department's public information budget passed, partly because of this new phenomenon of radio dramatizations of annual reports.

The next year, the subcommittee members were ready to look into the matter more thoroughly. In his opening statement, Ickes tried to meet the apparent problem head-on. Trying to link the radio studio to Congress, he said, "I know of no more effective and economical method of securing the public cooperation essential to congressional policy and legislation than through this medium." He also emphasized that the studio operated with "a minimum skeleton staff." When questioned about the radio version of his annual report, he noted that "it was heard by millions of people, while not one-tenth of 1 percent of them would ever have read my report."[67] He was right, of course. The radio version of an annual report was an effective way for public administrators to fulfill their duty to engage in public reporting, as a way of contributing to an informed citizenry in a democracy.[68] Congressman Johnson, who had heard one of the department's other radio programs, said that "it was one of the most educational programs I ever listened to."[69] But his reaction was the exception to the rule. The average legislator disliked that an executive branch agency could describe its annual accomplishments to millions of listeners. After all, they thought, the department is accountable to us, to Congress. We are the ones who are accountable to the citizenry. It is our job to be the source of information about federal activities. What to Ickes was an exemplary activity was, to these legislators, more like waving a red cape in front of a bull.

When the bill reached the House floor, Congressman Taber's relatively predictable floor amendment to slash agency public relations budgets was quickly dispensed with on a party line vote of 73–107. But then freshman congressman Ed Gossett (D-Tex.) suggested a different approach. He proposed an amendment banning use of appropriated funds in the bill for "the broadcast of radio programs designed for or calculated to influence the passage or defeat of any legislation pending before the Congress." Congressman Johnson, who had been in Congress since 1927, took a quick look at the wording. He was familiar with the difficulty of drafting effective statutory language against public relations. Johnson concluded, to his delight, that "the amendment really does not amount to anything." He knew (unlike freshman Gossett) that it was not enforceable, given the GAO's track record up to that point with the 1913 law against publicity experts and the 1919 law against lobbying. With that acknowledgement, the amendment passed unanimously.[70]

The passage of the amendment was considered newsworthy, especially by anti-FDR newspapers like the *Chicago Tribune*, which trumpeted "House Puts End to Ickes' Use of Air Propaganda," and the *Los Angeles Times*, which headlined its story "House Votes Curb on Ickes Broadcasts."[71] Other press coverage was more restrained.[72] The provision was kept in by the

Senate, and President Roosevelt signed it into law on June 18, 1940.[73] The ban was routinely renewed in the annual Interior Department appropriation bill for several years after that.[74]

1942

The conservative coalition's assault on agency publicity reached a first crescendo in 1942, the first year of active U.S. involvement in World War II.[75] The attacks focused on executive branch activities that did not "directly" contribute to the war effort. Public relations was ideal low-hanging fruit. Conservative Democrats and minority Republicans went after it with unprecedented intensity and hostility. From the perspective of the early twenty-first century, Fleming noted that "lost to memory was the ferocious antagonism between Roosevelt and Congress" once the war began.[76] One of the sources and targets of that enmity was agency publicity.

Why did the legislative effort to silence the bureaucracy kick into high gear in 1942? One explanation would be that it was part of a larger trend on Capitol Hill that year. According to Caro, the antagonism was largely ideological and a reaction to Roosevelt's domination of Washington decision making. "Then bitterness began to mount on Capitol Hill—against the President, whom not a few conservative congressmen viewed as a would-be dictator; against his 'ass-kissing New Dealers'; against the administrative agencies which conservatives felt were misusing the powers granted by Congress to extend the New Deal under the cloak of wartime necessity. . . . Congress began attempting to reassert its status as a coequal branch of government."[77]

Catton saw these same developments more in terms of a tactical positioning by the conservative coalition. With the onset of the U.S. role in the war, conservatives were now able to exploit the new situation by creating a thematic yet nonideological opposition to the president that would resonate with the public:

> The we-hate-Roosevelt people were successful beyond their dreams during the war, and 1942 was the year of their first big triumph. . . .
> It began with the excellent assumption that any action which the administration might take (other than those actions directly concerned with military matters) was sure to be unsound and ill-advised

and was more than likely to be revolutionary; thus they always had something to criticize, and the criticism never had to be documented since it was based on an axiom rather than on facts and reasoning. Better yet, this created a game in which both ends could be played against the middle; for the very fact that this criticism was being made could then be used as a basis for further criticism, the idea being that there must be something terribly wrong or the administration would not be under so much attack.[78]

These different explanations are complementary, with Caro focusing on the larger institutional view and Catton on tactical political warfare. Since the long-standing legislative reaction to agency public relations had both institutional and ideological elements, 1942 had suddenly presented the conservative coalition with a perfect storm. Public relations could be criticized as wasteful (at all times), but especially so in wartime. It did not contribute to the war effort. As propaganda, it smacked of something unsavory and inappropriate in a democracy at war with evil. ("It's the other guys who use propaganda.") The image of former reporters, better paid now as civil servants, writing self-serving press releases for their agencies was a picture of malingerers evading their war duty who should be reassigned to something really important. It was time to strip the bureaucracy of luxuries and overhead costs—and public relations was at the top of the list. Also, if paper and ink were to be in short supply, should they be wasted on slick government publications instead of adequate supplies for the free press?

The cohesion of the attack was apparent as early as February 1942, just two months after Pearl Harbor. The *Congressional Record* printed four speeches criticizing federal agency publicity. Two were titled "The Government's Propaganda Bill" and "Propaganda Expenditure."[79] Another reprinted an editorial from the *Washington Times Herald* stating that the increase in federal information services "is building up in many people's minds a suspicion that this administration is putting together a propaganda ministry of the German, or Dr. Paul Goebbels' type, for use both during and after the war."[80] The fourth criticized "the growth of the publicity propaganda uses of the Federal Government."[81] More attacks continued in March and April: "New Deal Propaganda," "Government Press Agents," "Choked with Publicity," and a bill prohibiting any spending on services to the press, radio broadcasts, group contacts, exhibits, movies, lecture material, photography, and posters.[82] The assault continued for the rest of the year.

During 1942, significant cracks were appearing in the ranks of nominally pro-FDR Democrats. A Democratic member of the House Appropriations Committee, normally friendly to leadership and the administration, introduced a bill in July to impose strict controls on agency publicity and publications.[83] That signaled that the issue was becoming more mainstream politically. Another senior Democrat, head of the Committee on Public Buildings and Grounds, "joined yesterday in a congressional demand, heretofore spearheaded by Republicans, for curtailment of unnecessary governmental expenses." His key example and reason? The federal government's $50 million spending on printing, with "much of this printing being devoted to bureaucratic propaganda to enlarge and extend agencies which could either be diminished or eliminated."[84]

These events signaled that the conservative push was taking a toll and that politicians were positioning themselves on the safe side of a potentially big political issue. And the conservative coalition was winning some of the battles. Two months after Pearl Harbor, the Senate approved creation of a special subcommittee of the Appropriations Committee to investigate the transfer of federal employees from their regular positions to wartime agencies. The subcommittee was chaired by Senator Millard Tydings (D-Md.), another conservative.[85] The Tydings Committee generated significant amounts of anti-Roosevelt publicity, including attacks on agency public relations. For example, on May 28, Tydings made a floor statement criticizing the public relations activities of the Division of Information of the Office for Emergency Management. It reflected the long-standing conservative coalition's critique of agency external communications activities, now repackaged as a new attack on the administration's war effort: "Here is an agency, an emergency agency, set up with millions of dollars to aid in the war effort that actually has high-priced newspapermen, publicists, press agents, or whatever one may want to call them, turning out this drivel, using up good paper and ink and machines which often cost two or three thousand dollars apiece, and employing a large number of people."[86]

A few days later, Tydings articulated his view that agency public relations activities were "nothing more or less than pure propaganda, put out at government expense to promote a particular theory or point of view which is often highly controversial."[87] In other words, to the conservative coalition the fight over agency external communications was not merely one of a dozen targets of fiscal conservatives related to supposedly wasteful management overhead activities. Rather, it was also an attack on a tangible manifestation of the New Deal philosophy of government and on New Deal agencies' use of publicity to seek, and sometimes attain, autonomy. In the view of the conservative coalition, if it could choke off the external communications activities of federal agencies, then it would be preventing the persuasion of public opinion that Roosevelt's approach to government was superior to that of earlier administrations. Camouflaged by the wartime emergency, this was a battle for the hearts and minds of the American public over the direction government would take.

In its eventual report, the subcommittee conceded that some agency publicity was justified and limited those categories of activity to "regulatory, directive rules and regulations, production reports (crop and industrial), and certain information necessary for adequate and competent social protection." However, anything beyond that was "parasitic" and unnecessary. The report specifically objected to any external communications activities that had the effect of "the creation of additional sponsorship for the enlargement and/or continuation of the parent organization."[88]

The Tydings Committee report was then widely circulated to the national networks of conservative Democrats and Republicans. It was a "bible" that could be used by candidates, parties, and conservative publications to criticize Roosevelt's management of the war effort. The report was well timed (and not a coincidence) for the 1942 congressional elections, the first since Pearl Harbor. The results were a setback for Roosevelt and liberal Democrats.[89] The Tydings report was likely an important contributing factor to the electoral gains for the conservative coalition in the 78th Congress. As a result, the opposition to agency public relations was especially active during the Congress that was elected in November 1942.

Department of Agriculture, Office of Information, 1943

Ever since USDA's Office of Information was created in 1913 (chapter 3), it had largely succeeded in avoiding controversy or attracting attention from legislators interested in choking the bureaucracy's voice. In part, this was due to the special status that agriculture had on Capitol Hill, with many legislators coming from farm constituencies.[90] Also, one of the primary missions of the USDA was the dissemination of information to improve farm techniques. The office was usually successful when it argued that indirect dissemination of information to farmers through the press was efficient, cheaper, and faster than dealing on a retail basis with individual farmers. Finally, the department's *Agriculture Yearbook* was popular with members of Congress receiving large allotments that they sent to their constituents.[91]

The FY 1944 appropriation process in the spring of 1943 was, however, a break with past trends. The new Congress was seeking to flex its political muscle on all fronts in its war with President Roosevelt. Besides focusing on accusations of violations of the 1919 anti-lobbying law (see chapter 5) by the USDA and AAA, it targeted the department's Office of Information. At the initial House appropriations subcommittee hearing, the members drew a distinction between the Office's press relations (bad) and distribution of farmers' bulletins (good). They expressed disapproval of the high volume of press releases while criticizing the unit for delays of four to six weeks in responding to requests from farmers for information. In an echo of the 1908 controversy over Forest Service publicity (chapter 2), Congressman Everett Dirksen (R-Ill.) condemned the publication *Forest Outing,* saying, "I do not believe . . . that this sort of thing is justified at any time," whether in war or peace.[92]

As part of an effort to shift most field information programs to the Extension Service (see below), the American Farm Bureau—a conservative farmer organization—suggested moving all Washington-based information activities of the department's bureaus to the Information Office and eliminating as many USDA regional offices as possible. The latter suggestion would include the Office of Information's small field staff.[93] The Farm Bureau suggested that this reorganization could lead to a flatter organization and economies of scale, eventually reducing spending and staffing. The committee was listening. It recommended abolishing regional information offices.[94] But the related subject that its own members had raised during the hearings was equally important. The committee recommended shifting $20,000 in the Information Office's budget from press releases to farmers' bulletins.[95] When presenting the committee's report on the House floor, Congressman Malcolm Tarver (D-Ga.) explained that "we have decided that too much of the funds provided for this office has been expended in unnecessary and expensive publicity" and instead some of those funds should be shifted to permit responding "promptly" to farmers' requests for bulletins.[96] Both changes were adopted by the House.

The secretary of agriculture included these two items in his appeals to the Senate Appropriations Committee. In his testimony, the head of the Information Office told the senators that he had just "discontinued" the Field Information Service so that the ban was largely moot. He explained that the only field office left open was the San Francisco radio office, which consisted of two employees and was an "issuing office" for information rather than a "coordinating office" like all the other regional offices had been. The radio office originated important reports that were useful to West Coast farmers. Given the time zone difference between the capital and the particular agricultural foci in the West, he felt this service was irreplaceable. These arguments fell on sympathetic ears, since some of the members of the subcommittee were from Nevada, Arizona, New Mexico, and Oregon. He also asked the senators to undo the $20,000 transfer from press relations to farmers' requests. Because the overall budget request for the Office's operations had been going down (especially with the elimination of its field service), perhaps the $20,000 could be taken from the reduction, that is, the overall reduction be modified by $20,000. Then, the additional $20,000 could be dedicated to responding to farmers' requests for bulletins without penalizing the press office.[97]

The Senate Appropriations Committee agreed to both departmental requests. It recommended deleting the House ban on regional information offices, since they had already been abolished, and thereby implicitly permitted the San Francisco radio office to remain. It also proposed adding $20,000 to handling requests for information from the savings gained by the elimination of the Field Information Service while restoring the House's $20,000 cut in press services.[98] The committee's recommendations were accepted during the Senate floor consideration without debate.[99] In conference committee, the House accepted the Senate's position substantively but sought to prevail in a statutory sense. Therefore, instead of deleting the House language banning regional information offices, the compromise was to restore the ban but with the stated exception of the San Francisco radio office.[100] President Roosevelt signed the bill on July 12, 1943, twelve days into FY 1944. The statute read, "No part of this appropriation shall be used for the establishment or maintenance of regional or State field offices or for the compensation of employees in such offices except that not to exceed $9,100 may be used to maintain the San Francisco radio office."[101] That provision was routinely renewed in the annual appropriation bill over the next five years, with slight changes in the amount to reflect pay raises and inflation.[102] The issue and the statutory language disappeared after that.

Agricultural Adjustment Agency

Besides the attention to the USDA Office of Information during the FY 1944 appropriation process, the most serious attack on information activities in 1943 came from the conservative American Farm Bureau. In testimony before the House Agriculture Appropriations Subcommittee, it urged a major reorganization in this area, especially the field information activities of the AAA. The Farm Bureau proposed shifting all AAA information activities at the regional, state, and county levels to the Extension Service, commonly called county agents.[103] On the surface, these suggestions would appeal to the knee-jerk congressional dislike of agency public relations. But they reflected a more subtle power grab. The Extension Service in most states and counties was closely affiliated with the Farm Bureau. In some cases, the same employee worked part-time for both. Shifting all non-Washington-based information activities to the Extension Service would expand the ability of the Farm Bureau to dominate agricultural policy. Also, the AAA was viewed as a liberal and New Deal agency that was promoting concepts conservatives disliked. Its regional information offices were viewed as a mechanism for bypassing the conservative local power structure and disseminating information to farmers without the participation of the county agents.[104] Folding the AAA's information activities into the Extension Service would be a way of taming ideological messages the Farm Bureau disagreed with.[105]

Again, the Farm Bureau's suggestions fell on a receptive audience. The ideological issue revolved around distinguishing between *advocacy* aimed at farmers to persuade them to participate in new federal programs and *education and information* about the programs.[106] In and out of Congress, New Deal liberals supported advocacy whereas conservatives wanted only passive information. In its report, the House Appropriations Committee recommended a ban on informational activities by the AAA and a shift of the responsibility so that "such educational and informational activities will be carried on through the Extension Service."[107] However, during floor debate, the expansion of the Extension Service's duties to take over the AAA's informational activities was ruled impermissible parliamentarily because it was tantamount to new legislation, as opposed to an appropriation matter.[108] That left in the bill the ban on AAA field information activities, but without any reference to the Extension Service.

When the bill was before the Senate Appropriations Committee, the secretary of agriculture asked that the AAA section be deleted. In his formal submission to the committee he wrote, "The success of the food program, as any other program involving public participation depends largely upon public acceptance and understanding. The food program will be retarded if the Agricultural Adjustment Agency is restricted to the degree indicated by the House language, in explaining program provisions and pointing out the need and reason for public support."[109]

As a compromise, the department suggested maintaining the House ban on regional information offices but deleting the wording that applied to the state and county informational staff.[110] The Farm Bureau opposed that as an empty compromise. It blandly argued that the House language would "aid in reduction of expenditures and eliminate overlapping services."[111] The National Farmers Union, roughly the liberal counterpart of the Farm Bureau, stated bluntly that the seemingly money-saving idea was really an effort by the Farm Bureau "to break down the whole farm program into State units, where the organization has been successful at capturing control for its own purposes." It asked the Senate to delete from the bill the entire section banning AAA field information activities.[112]

The Senate Appropriations Committee chose to disregard the Farm Bureau's testimony and instead endorsed the department's proposed (and so-called) compromise of banning regional AAA information offices but not those at the state and county levels. Avoiding favoring agency publicity too specifically, the committee report merely stated that the USDA "would be seriously handicapped" if it had to close the AAA's state and county information offices.[113] In conference committee, the compromise between the two houses was to restore the House ban, but with the exception that the ban did not apply to providing information to individual farmers.[114] It was a loophole so large one could drive a tractor through it. The final version, as signed into law, stated that "none of the funds herein appropriated . . . shall be used to pay the salaries or expenses of any regional information employees or any State or county information employees, but this shall not preclude the answering of inquiries or supplying of information to individual farmers."[115]

A week after the bill was signed into law, the AAA issued directives to all its committeemen (i.e., farmers voluntarily serving on local committees, not agency employees) that the new law banned them from distributing AAA information to the press and radio. Predictably, members of Congress from farm areas complained that this might reduce the availability of important information to farmers. The agency innocently claimed that it was merely trying to be sure that it was fully complying with the new law. In reaction to congressional complaints, the AAA promptly withdrew the directive, saying instead that the committees could not "employ press agents."[116] Whether intended or not, it was a slick bureaucratic maneuver to dilute the new law further. As a result, it had now been clarified that committeemen could talk to reporters and on the radio, just that agency *employees* could not. It was another major loophole. After all, it would not be a big leap for AAA staff to provide background information that committeemen could then rely on for media relations. After 1943, the legal ban (with the loophole) was routinely renewed for thirty years with every annual agricultural appropriation bill, even after the AAA went out of existence and its programs merged fully into the USDA. After that, it was often referred to as the soil conservation program. The last time it was included in the law was 1973.[117]

TARGETING TRUMAN ADMINISTRATION AGENCIES, 1945–1950

Truman had been president for only a few months in 1945 when attacks on agency external communications resumed. As in 1942 and 1943, the intensity of some of the congressional criticisms was driven by political calculations. In the short term, Republicans were hoping to score points with public opinion and do well in the 1946 congressional elections. Then, regardless of those results, they wanted to keep softening Truman up to defeat him in 1948.[118]

The conservative-leaning *Nation's Business* ran an extensive article on federal publicity expenses in July 1945, three months after Truman assumed the presidency. It quoted several Democratic and Republican legislators on why the public should care. For example, Senator Robert Taft (R-Ohio) said, "Propaganda backed by the unlimited force of government funds, is likely to destroy democracy from within."[119] In early 1946, Congressman Richard Wigglesworth (R-Mass.) launched a major attack on the House floor on agency external communications. He estimated annual spending at about $75 million and nearly 46,000 employees. He emphasized that the end of the war was a particularly good time to cut these activities (although during the war he had argued that *that* was the time to cut nonessential wartime activities): "The war is over. It is time to call a halt to bureaucratic waste, extravagance, and deficit spending. . . . If we, as a Nation, are to escape financial disaster, the Congress must resume control over expenditures; the propaganda army of 45,778, recognized by the Bureau of the Budget as a tool of executive management, must be disbanded."[120]

Interior Department's Bureau of Reclamation, 1946

In the spring of 1946, the House Appropriations Committee focused on the public information activities at the Bureau of Reclamation. The bureau had extensive construction projects throughout the West, usually involving damming of rivers and construction of irrigation canals to distribute the captured water. After completion of construction, it maintained these facilities. The commissioner of reclamation, when asked during House appropriations hearings, listed several reasons for the size of the bureau's information staff, who were mostly attached to specific facilities in the field. His answers:

> "Inform all the people of their community of every action that the Bureau takes, the reason for it, the laws which require it, [and] of every contract let."

Photographing the facilities as part of the architectural and engineering records that must be kept of construction projects.

Using lower-salaried technicians to disseminate information "who take that burden off the higher salaried engineering groups, who do not like to perform that work."

"It is much easier to secure acceptance of the policies and the programs that are laid down here and also by law, than it is by so-called police action."

Preparing informational publications.

Offering guide services for public tours of dams.[121]

But the committee members, even ones supporting the bureau's projects, were startled by the size of the public relations staff—forty-eight in regional offices and twenty-six in Washington.[122] Some were against it on philosophical grounds, viewing this as propaganda. Others were opposed because it just seemed like a lot of money for an ancillary, even discretionary, activity. The committee's recommendations were blunt, calling for cutting the public communications budget in half. The bureau's budget request "contains a fantastic request for 72 employees for the Division of Information at an annual cost of more than $250,000. The committee has inserted a provision in the bill limiting all expenditures for the Bureau for this purpose to not more than $125,000."[123]

The cut was accepted by the House. Interior Secretary Julius Krug (Ickes's successor) put the topic on the short list of items he was appealing to the Senate to restore.[124] The chairman of the subcommittee for the Interior Department was Senator Carl Hayden (D-Ariz.). Given the large role of the bureau in his state, Hayden had a detailed knowledge of its work and a friendly inclination toward it. The bureau had been good to him, and he was glad to have an opportunity to reciprocate. He also understood the importance of having substantial informational staffs in regional offices. After all, those staffs were serving his constituents. When the subject came up at the hearing, Hayden gently inquired, "You are sure you are not carrying on a propaganda campaign?"[125] The commissioner of reclamation assured him nothing of the sort was occurring. That was good enough for Hayden.

The Senate committee recommended retaining the House's provision limiting public relations expenditures but changed the ceiling from $125,000 to $200,000. That was not a full restoration of the bureau's request ($250,000), but it was a major victory. Still, given the sensitivity of the subject, the committee report avoided the trap of defending agency external communications and stuck to vague generalities: "The expanding construction program and the increasing responsibilities of the Bureau of Reclamation as the custodian of a Federal investment of a billion dollars requires an adequate administrative and supervisory force. . . . Any reduction in the estimate for the fiscal year 1947 would seriously cripple the Bureau in carrying out specific mandates of the Congress."[126]

No senator challenged the committee's recommendation when the bill was debated on the floor.[127] In the conference committee, the two houses split the difference, but slightly in favor of the House position. The conferees compromised on $150,000, $25,000 more than the House had approved and $50,000 less than the Senate.[128] But it was still a major cut for the bureau, 40 percent less than its budget request. On July 1, 1946, the first day of the fiscal year, President Truman signed the bill into law. The congressional limitation on public relations stated "that not exceeding $150,000 of funds available for expenditure under this appropriation shall be used for salaries and expenses in connection with informational work."[129]

Interior Department's Division of Information, 1946

Echoes of the earlier controversies over the Interior Department's Division of Information resounded after World War II. Two demobilized veterans who had worked in the division before the war sought to exercise their reemployment rights. Therefore, in 1946 the department requested that Congress increase the division's budget by $8,840 in FY 1947 to cover their salaries rather than have to lay off other Information Division employees.[130] The House Appropriations Committee refused the request, as did the House.[131] Notwithstanding the relatively small amount, Secretary Krug included that item in the restoration requests he submitted to the Senate Appropriations Committee.[132] Acting like a court of appeals, the committee endorsed his request, and its recommendation was accepted by the Senate.[133] In conference, the House conferees were generally willing to accept the larger amount that the Senate had allocated to the budget of the secretary's office overall but insisted on maintaining cuts in just four activities in the Office of the Secretary, including the Division of Information. The Senate yielded.[134] The battle over this minor amount of money, and the unrelenting House opposition to it, was yet another signal of legislative hostility to agency external communications. To Senate conferees this was a piddling amount of money not worth fighting for or, worse, defending publicly.

The 80th Congress, 1947–1948

The November 1946 elections were even more of a Republican triumph than the preceding off-year elections in 1942. A war-weary public wanted to end economic controls as soon as possible and, in general, was ready for a change. Republicans were suddenly the majority party in both houses for the first time since 1928. For Republicans, the 80th Congress was the legislative opportunity of a generation. All of their criticisms against the New Deal could now be pursued to conclusion. Public relations was near the top of the list. According to Fitzpatrick, "attacks against 'propagandists' in the Democratic administration after the 1946 elections and early in 1947 were frequent."[135] Ten days after the election, Congressman Taber was already zeroing in on his goals as the incoming chair of the Appropriations Committee. He planned on "eliminating 'propaganda' bureaus in the government," limiting future agency bulletins to "legitimate information."[136] Later in the month, he elaborated on the $100 million cut he planned in agency publicity budgets. He said that agency publicity staffs "never tell the truth if they can help it, and these so-called public relations staffs were set up in the first place to cover up the iniquities of the departments." The problem was that "the people do not get the news—they are deceived by propaganda."[137] The *New York Times* editorialized in support of Taber goals, stating that "the danger in such propaganda campaigns . . . is that by appeal to mass emotion and ignorance, by the circulation of half-truths and by the technique of 'selling' a policy to one group on one basis and to another group on another basis, the whole democratic process is degraded."[138] Still, some in the Washington press corps were lukewarm about Taber's campaign, confronted with the reality of the indispensability of public information officers.[139]

As soon as the 80th Congress was sworn in, in January 1947, Congressman William Miller (R-Conn.) introduced a resolution to create a select committee to investigate "public relations activities of the executive branch."[140] When he made a floor statement a few weeks later in support of his proposal, a Democratic member asked him to define propaganda. At first Miller said it was an effort to make a program popular. Then, upon further challenge, he said it was "expensive lithograph illustrations." Finally, giving up, he said that a person "knows propaganda when he sees it."[141] Weeks later he was still trying. Propaganda was *not* employing "information specialists to help the radio and press get the facts." Rather, it was propaganda when the "real purpose is to convince Congress and the public that the . . . [agency] has been making a valuable contribution to the Nation."[142]

In lieu of Miller's proposal, the Republican majority created a Publicity and Propaganda Subcommittee of the House Committee on Expenditures in the Executive Departments. Informally it was called the Harness Committee, after its chair, Congressman Forest Harness (R-Ind.).[143] At its inception, Harness said he would expose $75 million in expenditures for publicity that "Congress never has authorized."[144] Yet when Secretary of State George Marshall pressed the issue, Harness quickly retreated, writing, "The Committee does not hold it to be unlawful or improper for officials or employes [*sic*] of the Federal government to express opinions or to impart factual information, if distinguished from propaganda."[145]

Nearly two years later, in its final report, the committee did not make any specific legislative recommendations to prevent or punish these alleged propaganda activities. The report conceded that "there is a fine line between legitimate information service" and propaganda. It even admitted that the propaganda activities it was objecting to "generally were conceived and carried on by officials who were in no manner connected with legitimate public-relations or information activity."[146] This awkward wording meant that it was objecting to a president and his appointees trying to persuade the public and Congress to support the president's legislative program. That this Congress and president were of different parties was the key. The 80th Congress was substantively in disagreement with Truman's proposals, which made his advocacy of them propaganda. The subcommittee had labored mightily and produced no tangible results. Yet its supporters viewed the committee's work as a success, since it generated huge amounts of highly partisan publicity that criticized Truman and promoted Republican views.[147]

Meanwhile, Congressman Taber was also busy trying to keep his promise. He had some success. He pressed for major cuts in Interior Department information programs and generally kept the subject on the legislative agenda. His push to cut agency external communications programs was so prominent it prompted a cover story in a trade journal for people working in the private sector in advertising and public relations. The issue's cover read "Memo to Congress: Should the Government Have a Public Relations Program?" Predictably, its answer was "yes."[148]

The USDA appropriation bill for FY 1948 in the spring of 1947 was an early opportunity for the Republican majority to enforce its views on agency public relations. The House Appropriations Committee report sought to cut the department's spending but openly admitted the difficulty of doing that through the appropriations process, supposedly Congress's more powerful tool: "It had been the purpose of the committee to reduce to 250 man-years the amount of work permitted to be done under this head [Public Relations and Publicity Activities] during the fiscal year 1948. However, it was found all but impossible to draft a provision in such terms as would not endanger the fundamental work of the Department in diffusing essential information pertaining to agriculture. The committee believes it is a matter which can be controlled by the more flexible device of administrative regulation, without injury to agriculture, and has decided to give the Department the opportunity to 'reform itself.'"[149] The Senate committee agreed, asserting that USDA public relations expenses "can well be reduced in the interest of economy and more wholesome public relations" but did not define how to differentiate between wholesome and unwholesome public relations.[150]

Here were candid admissions by hostile legislators of the gap between disapproving of publicity and operationalizing it. The House committee threw up its hands and asked the department to do what the committee could not, and the Senate committee called for only "wholesome" public relations but did not define it. Columnist Drew Pearson, a critic of Taber, claimed that at a closed meeting Taber railed against "propagandists" on the federal payroll. But when asked by committee members for specifics, he had little to offer except asserting that there were too many in the War Department.[151] During the floor debate on the Treasury and Post Office appropriation bill for FY 1949, Taber denounced "a well-oiled administration propaganda machine" that had succeeded in blunting his cuts to the IRS in the previous year. "The Government publicity boys, under orders from the administration's high command, oiled up their typewriters, inked up their mimeograph machines and went to work," but he had no specifics to offer.[152]

Meanwhile, media reports about Taber's USDA publicity cuts suggested that the funding reductions would severely harm farm programs. Taber lashed back, saying, "Perhaps the most disgusting criticism was that the Republican economy program had destroyed soil conservation. The cut was made because the committee knew than the Soil Conservation Service was spending too much money upon propaganda."[153]

At the same time, in early 1947, the Bureau of the Budget issued instructions to all federal agencies "prohibiting them from publicizing material prepared for congressional consumption." The instructions indicated that the ban was because of Taber's strict policies about government information activities. Yet Taber, the enemy of agency propaganda, was unhappy. He felt he had been sandbagged by the administration and made to look bad. He had not asked for the policy and was not responsible for it. He insisted that he opposed "limiting dissemination of information."[154] Whether intended or not, the Budget Bureau had called his bluff. It promptly withdrew the instructions. By now, just about every cabinet department (as well as their constituent bureaus) and independent agency had a public relations office that engaged in external communications. A survey published in 1949 identified 106 public information offices in the federal government.[155]

The Republican efforts during the 80th Congress to cut agency public relations spending were supported vigorously by the other partner in the conservative coalition, southern and conservative Democrats. For example, Senator Byrd, denouncing the maneuvers by federal agencies to blunt the Republican threat of cuts, said that they "do not hesitate to use the radio, the mails and other means to spread 'propaganda' at public expense to oppose any economies which affect them."[156] Byrd was considered by his allies an expert on Capitol Hill on this topic, having battled agency external communications with the special committees he chaired in 1937 and 1942. He was the "go-to" guy for Congress's sustained reaction to federal agency publicity programs.

In 1950, the Senate voted to limit all activities of the USDA Information Office to programs authorized by Congress, thus preventing any publicity for farm activities authorized by presidential executive orders—a favorite tactic of FDR, including the original establishment of the AAA.[157]

• • •

The congressional desire to silence the bureaucracy manifested itself in many distinct ways during the peak years of the war between the Democratic presidents Roosevelt and Truman and the conservative coalition on Capitol Hill. The loosely organized effort to reduce the bureaucracy's external voice showed flexibility and ability to take advantage of targets of opportunity.

The common thread of these diverse and successful efforts (at least in being enacted) was that they used annual appropriation bills to impose statutory limitations on agency public relations. Provisos tucked into funding bills were easier to pass than a free-standing law. After all, the annual departmental appropriation bills were on the short list of "must-pass" bills; otherwise, government would have to shut down. So, those bills could be counted on to be debated and eventually sent to the president. Compared to that, a proposal to change the law could be bottled up in a committee and die. In fact, given the plethora of bills introduced in every session of Congress, only a minute number ever come out of committee and become law.

Table 2 is a summary of the results of the efforts described in this chapter with a rough indication of winners and losers. It indicates that Congress won some of these battles, but in the end the bureaucracy prevailed most of the time. As a rough generalization, Congress was more often likely to impose its will successfully on individual agencies when it came to highly specific targets, such as the Department of Interior's radio dramatizations. However, the more amorphous the issue, the harder it was to beat the bureaucracy. According to this tally, agencies beat Congress two to one.

TABLE 2

Results of Efforts by the Conservative Coalition
to Control Individual Agency Publicity, 1935–1950

Subject	De jure Result	De facto Winner	De facto Loser
Noncabinet agencies: publications	Call for reduction in publications that "build up a public demand for the services of the agency"	Agencies (no mandatory action required)	Congress
Justice Dept.: press aide	Prohibit nonlawyers from serving as special assistants to attorney general	Agency (shifted public information officer to special executive assistant)	Congress
Interior Dept.: Office of Information with own budget line	Banned	Agency (budget included in secretary's office)	Congress
Interior Dept.: request for $36,000 increase in information office budget	Not adopted	Congress	Agency
Interior Dept.: radio programs	Banned radio programs intended to influence legislation	Agency (could continue radio broadcasts in general)	Congress
Agriculture Dept.: Information Office field offices	Banned except radio office in San Francisco	Agency (field service was disbanded only formally by shifting its activities elsewhere)	Congress
Agriculture Dept.: AAA field information activities	Banned (except answering inquiries, supplying information to individual farmers and nonemployees contacting the press)	Agency	Congress
Interior Dept.: Reclamation Bureau	Cut information budget by 40%	Congress	Agency
Interior Dept.: Information Office: rehire two vets without discharging replacements	Denied	Congress	Agency

Still, the relatively large number of enacted limitations on agency public relations spending (however diluted and weak) was an unmistakable signal to the bureaucracy. Departmental external communications programs were likely to be targets of congressional attacks. This was a perennially touchy subject. The best bureaucratic counterstrategy was to bury the programs deep in agency budgets with innocuous titles and categories. Further, following the political maxim that "You can't get in trouble for what you don't say," another agency counterstrategy was to avoid talking about these activities as much as possible. Never, ever, raise them in committee hearings and, when asked, give answers that are as brief and uninformative as possible.

CHAPTER 8

BANNING SPENDING ON
PUBLICITY AND PROPAGANDA,
APRIL 1951–2005

1951: *"No part of any appropriation contained in this Act shall be used for publicity or propaganda purposes not heretofore authorized by the Congress."*

65 Stat. 223

2005: No funds *"may be used by an executive branch agency to produce any prepackaged news story intended for broadcast or distribution in the United States unless the story includes a clear notification within the text or audio of the prepackaged news story that the prepackaged news story was prepared or funded by that executive branch agency."*

119 Stat. 301

Four major and authoritative congressional actions to silence the bureaucracy began in 1951, three in the consecutive months of April, May, and June. Some of those new laws were short-lived; others continue to this day. In chapters 8–10, I examine three of them in the chronological order in which they began. Unlike the examples in chapter 7, these three were across-the-board efforts to muffle all executive branch departments and agencies. The fourth dealt with the new 800-pound gorilla of the executive branch, the Department of Defense. It, too, began in 1951 with a focus on cutting the department's public relations funding. I have presented that story elsewhere and do not need to recount it here. Similarly, a related effort that began later in the 1950s focused on controlling the Pentagon's direct lobbying expenses. I have also detailed that initiative separately and therefore it, too, is omitted from this narrative.[1]

It is hard to pinpoint a single reason why this series of events all occurred in such a short timeframe. However, in a more general way, one can view the events of 1951 as the culmination of several interwoven trends. From the narrowest perspective, the legislative hostility to agency public relations since 1905 had greatly picked up momentum and support in the 1930s and '40s (see chapter 7); a cresting of this activity was relatively understandable. Expanding to a larger context, the broader war by the conservative coalition on the big government philosophies of President Roosevelt and his successor, Truman, included efforts to reverse the growth of the federal executive branch during their administrations. An unpopular president (as Truman was in the early 1950s) was a vulnerable target, and some wins could be accomplished. The broadest perspective entails the perennial constitutional power struggle between the legislative and executive branches. The events of 1951 reflected a resurgent Congress trumping an increasingly unpopular president who had been weakened by the Korean War, inflation, labor unrest, the Cold War, and accusations of Communists in the federal government. Finally, these initiatives can be seen as part of the partisan run-up to the 1952 presidential election.

THE SMITH AMENDMENT

On April 18, 1951, Congressman Lawrence Smith (R-Wis.) submitted a floor amendment during the House debate on the annual appropriation bill for the Department of Labor and other related agencies. Twice in 1943, Smith had complained about improper lobbying and political propaganda by the AAA (see chapter 5, note 46). Now, he proposed a simple amendment to ban the use of funds in the bill for "publicity or propaganda purposes not heretofore authorized by the Congress."[2] As the justification for the amendment, Smith argued that the Harness Committee hearings had documented efforts by executive branch officials to promote President Truman's legislative proposal for national health insurance. Since some of those officials worked at agencies funded by this bill, the need for the amendment was clear. During the debate, Congressman George Meader (R-Mich.) provided a classic description of the legislative rationale for silencing the bureaucracy: "It is necessary to strengthen the Congress in the interest of formulating national policy by the people themselves. It is a corollary to that principle that public opinion ought not be subjected to influence and direction by the executive agencies, the administrative branch of the Government, in the manner that it is today. . . . The people should not finance use of these agencies to foster and perpetuate the bureaucrats—not the people's objectives in national policy."[3]

But liberal Democrats did not want to hamstring agencies that had missions they supported. Labor and health agencies were at the heart of the New Deal and Fair Deal. Congressman Sidney Yates (D-Ill.) challenged Smith's amendment, saying, "Would not the effect of the gentleman's amendment in using the word 'propaganda' jeopardize publication by the Children's Bureau of pamphlets pertaining to the training and growth of children?" Smith denied that, saying it was easy to "distinguish" between propaganda and educational matter. Supporting Yates's argument, Congressman John Fogarty (D-R.I.) said to Smith, "You do not define in the amendment what propaganda is or what publicity is."[4] Even though the Democrats were the majority party, the conservative coalition was in control. Smith's amendment passed, 156–88.[5] Few elected officials wanted to be viewed as in favor of propaganda, especially given the Cold War fears of successful propaganda by Communists.

The Smith provision was retained in the version of the bill recommended by the Senate Appropriations Committee, which also cut the publications and reports staff of the Social Security Administration from forty-three to fifteen, a 55 percent cut.[6] When President Truman signed the bill into law on August 31, 1952 (two months into FY 1952), Smith's amendment (called here "Smith I" in contradistinction to "Smith II" in chapter 9) was included in the law's general provisions: "No part of any appropriation contained in this Act shall be used for publicity or propaganda purposes not heretofore authorized by the Congress."[7]

The amendment was routinely renewed in the annual appropriation bill for the Labor Department and over the next few years was gradually added as a permanent feature to most of the other annual appropriation bills Congress passed to fund the executive branch.[8] By the mid-1990s, the Smith I amendment (or slight variations) had been included in the annual appropriation bills covering the departments of Commerce, Justice, State, Defense, Treasury, Post Office, foreign operations, and other related smaller agencies.[9] By the beginning of the twenty-first century, the amendment and its minor variants had been extended to apply government-wide, affecting all executive branch departments and agencies.[10]

ENFORCING THE BAN: AUTHORITATIVE INTERPRETATIONS BY THE GAO, 1952–1987

The thankless task of trying to interpret what "publicity or propaganda purposes" meant was left to the GAO. The first year it was in effect, the NLRB (which was funded by the annual Labor Department appropriation bill) asked the comptroller general to clarify the implications of the law. He tried his best. Propaganda did *not* cover the "dissemination to the general public, or to particular inquirers, information reasonably necessary to the proper administration of the laws" the agency had the duty to implement.[11] What did it cover? Generally, "publicity of a nature tending to emphasize the importance of the agency or activity in question."[12] That was not much of an answer, but at least it gave agencies *some* guidance. The decision was considered important and precedent-setting enough to be included in the annual compilation of GAO decisions.

The GAO expressed its dissatisfaction at the position Congress had put it in. It bluntly stated that the provision was "too vague to clearly delineate unauthorized expenditures" given "the absence of adequate statutory standards."[13] For an agency of Congress, this was an unusually candid statement. So, for the first few decades of the Smith I amendment, the GAO limited its review to whether an incident was "so palpably erroneous as to be unreasonable" given the language of the law.[14] As long as an agency was able to provide the GAO with a "reasonable justification for its activities"[15] from the perspective of public administration, the GAO would deem it as not violating the Smith language. After investigating some of the publicity released by the Department of Health and Human Services in 2004 concerning changes in Medicare, the GAO concluded that even if the materials contained omissions of significant facts or included "some" political content, it would not consider the publicity to be a violation.[16]

Despite these problems, over the years the GAO "struggled to give meaning" to the Smith I amendment based on the accumulation of conclusions from specific incidents it investigated.[17] Thus, it was creating law through the case method. In this incremental way, it accrued a more nuanced and detailed explanation of the meaning of the law. The key was to differentiate legitimate from illegitimate activities. The GAO stated that a government agency had the legitimate right to (1) report on its activities to the citizenry, (2) justify its policies to the public and to Congress, and even (3) rebut attacks on it.[18] Activities that went beyond these purposes were violations. But "it is very difficult to distinguish" between the two.[19] By necessity, the GAO had to try to do so on a case-by-case basis.

From its 1952 NLRB decision, later GAO reports took the phrase "publicity of a nature tending to emphasize the importance of the agency" and christened it the "self-aggrandizement" principle. Did the dissemination of information tend to have any reasonable purpose other than aggrandizing the agency itself? This was sometimes also referred to as the "puffery" standard.[20] Another principle the GAO gradually developed hinged on whether the source of the news release seemed to be concealed. Preparation of "canned editorials" and letters to the editor coming ostensibly from private groups and individuals would violate this principle.[21]

On the other hand, even though it had some "reservations," the GAO did not deem the Peace Corps' dissemination of an article through a commercial news service a violation.[22] Similarly, some information that did not identify a government agency as its source was not a violation because that material was part of a packet and the other materials in the packet clearly listed the agency as the source.[23] When the Federal Trade Commission (FTC) distributed to reporters drafts of possible (critical) questions to ask the postmaster general (which it was fighting with at the time), the GAO was asked if that violated the Smith I amendment. It concluded that, although the proposed questions were "unquestionably propaganda," the FTC had not concealed its role but rather identified itself as the source of the packet that included the proposed questions.[24] What happened after that was not under the agency's control, so the resulting questions (or lack of) and subsequent articles (or lack of) were the responsibility of the reporters, who clearly were the independent actors for any subsequent follow-ups.

In the first half-century since its adoption in 1951, the GAO declared only three violations of the Smith I amendment. The first was in 1958. A speech by a deputy assistant Defense secretary had appealed to some military contractors to help persuade public opinion to support the U.S. military assistance program to foreign countries. This, the GAO decided, went beyond the ken of a legitimate effort to inform the public and constituted propaganda. However, because of the limited sums involved, it did not seek to recover any costs.[25] In 1986, almost three decades after the 1958 violation and thirty-five years since its adoption, the GAO found two violations of the Smith I amendment. It investigated the public affairs activities of the Chemical Warfare Review Commission and found numerous violations of federal laws, including the ban on spending for publicity and propaganda (see chapter 4). The GAO concluded that the violation had occurred because of the nature of the materials distributed by a consultant hired by the commission.[26] Therefore, it directed that the misspent appropriated funds be recovered.[27] And that same year it declared that the Small Business Administration (SBA) had violated the law. At that time, President Reagan had proposed merging the SBA into the Department of Commerce and eliminating some of its financing programs. The SBA prepared various materials explaining the president's proposal and its impact on SBA's clients and constituency. The GAO ruled that all of these materials conformed to the Smith I amendment except for "suggested editorials" that the agency prepared: the editorials, "for publication as the ostensible editorial position of the recipient newspapers, are misleading as to their origin and reasonably constitute 'propaganda.'"[28] Nonetheless, because "of the relatively small amount involved," the GAO did not seek to recover the misappropriated funds.

In 1987, the GAO made a finding of a major violation of the Smith I amendment by the State Department, so important that the decision was included in the annual volume of published comptroller general rulings. This was the first decision related to the Smith language to be published since the 1952 NLRB decision. At the time, the Reagan administration was deeply involved in Central America, especially trying to undermine the government of Nicaragua by supporting the Contras.[29] One of the elements of the general policy was the establishment in the State Department of the Office of Public Diplomacy for Latin America and the Caribbean, with the goal of promoting support for the administration's policies. The GAO declared that some of the activities of that office had violated the Smith I amendment because the office "arranged for the publication of articles which purportedly had been prepared by, and reflected the views of, persons not associated with the government but which, in fact, had been prepared at the request of government officials and partially or wholly paid for with government funds."[30] For example, the office prepared several op-ed pieces that were submitted to newspapers by a professor and by several of the Nicaraguan opposition leaders. Thus, the true source of the published columns was not identified. The GAO ruled that this "white propaganda" violated the principle of covert propaganda the GAO had developed to implement the Smith I amendment. The GAO was, however, unable to estimate the amount spent on such covert propaganda in contradistinction to the legal activities of the office. Therefore, it did not seek to recover the funds and instead recommended "that the Department of State take action to insure that violations . . . do not occur in the future."[31] This GAO finding of a violation was treated as significant news and covered by major newspapers.[32]

ENFORCING THE BAN: AUTHORITATIVE INTERPRETATIONS BY THE DEPARTMENT OF JUSTICE, 1982–2001

In the first fifty years after the Smith I amendment was enacted in 1951, the Office of Legal Counsel (OLC) of the Department of Justice issued only three opinions related to it. In those opinions, the OLC followed the lead the GAO had set in its decisions.[33] The first time the OLC commented on the Smith language was in 1982, three decades after the law was enacted. In a decision giving guidance to the U.S. Information Agency on the creation of the President's Council on International Youth Exchange, the OLC fully concurred with the GAO's decisions. It advised the agency that it could engage in an advertising campaign as long as it did not violate the

GAO principle of self-aggrandizement. Therefore, every ad "should be carefully tailored and scrutinized so that it does not unduly emphasize the accomplishments"[34] of the agency; rather it should be focused on the substantive goal of promoting international youth exchanges.

In 1988, the OLC sought to provide guidance to the administration in preparation for renewed lobbying in support of aid to the Contras in Nicaragua. It carefully reviewed the implications of the GAO's published decision the previous year on the "white propaganda" activities of the State Department's Office of Public Diplomacy for Latin America and the Caribbean. Accepting the validity of the GAO decision, the OLC advised that there would be no violations of the Smith I amendment (or several other relevant provisions) if the administration responded to media requests for interviews or op-ed pieces "by referring the media to supporters in the private sector, because such responses would not involve additional use of appropriated funds." Of course, among other things, the administration should be careful not to prepare materials that would subsequently be published in the name of private organizations or individuals.[35]

Three years later, the OLC issued a third opinion, this time advising the General Services Administration (GSA) regarding an advertising campaign it was considering to increase the awareness within other federal agencies of the services the GSA could provide them. The GSA had sought the opinion in advance to be sure that what it wanted to do would conform to applicable laws. Again, the OLC fully accepted GAO interpretations of the Smith I amendment. It advised the GSA that it could conduct the advertising effort without violating the Smith I amendment as long as it adhered to GAO guidelines. The keys would be for the GSA to be sure it could justify the rationale for the advertising campaign as "one means by which an agency achieves its mission," that the advertising would be "reasonable and carefully-controlled," and that it "not unduly emphasize the accomplishments of GSA or aggrandize the agency."[36]

VIDEO NEWS RELEASES, 2004–2005

Smith I roared back to life in 2004. That year the GAO declared that video news releases that were structured as free-standing news stories violated the Smith I language. By that time, the distribution of video materials (such as sound bites from senior officials, sometimes called B-roll) had become a common practice in federal agencies (as well as, of course, the private sector). These kinds of clips were viewed as consonant with Smith I, comparable to a print news release with an official's statement. However, in 2004, the Department of Health and Human Services (HHS) also released a new video product as part of its campaign about changes by Congress in Medicare, specifically the new drug benefit. It disseminated a video news release that could be used by TV news departments as a complete "package." In this package, a person who played the traditional role of a news correspondent did a standup at the beginning of the story leading in to an interview with an HHS official. Then another standup after the clip concluded with a wrap-up including the tag line, "In Washington, I'm Karen Ryan, reporting." The GAO ruled that this type of video release violated the Smith I amendment because it hid the true origin of the story. Viewers did not know that Karen Ryan was paid by HHS to play the role of a correspondent in the story, making it covert propaganda.[37] HHS said that such packages were the same as B-roll, since there was no way to control how the material was eventually used. The GAO disagreed, stating that, "in a modest but meaningful way, the publicity or propaganda restriction helps to mark the boundary between an agency making information available to the public and agencies creating news reports unbeknownst to the receiving audience."[38]

HHS estimated that it spent $42,750 on those video news releases. Based on its finding, the GAO directed HHS to implement the legal processes required for such incidents. The GAO report was considered major news and became part of the political battle in Washington leading up to the fall presidential election.[39]

A year later, the OLC broke for the first time with the GAO over the meaning of the Smith I amendment. It disagreed with GAO rulings that video news releases by HHS and the Office of Drug Control Prevention (colloquially called the "drug czar") had violated the law because they were covert propaganda, with the government sources of news stories concealed. The OLC instead focused on the meaning of the word "propaganda" as used in Smith I. Based on definitions in various dictionaries, the OLC concluded that propaganda consisted of communications that were intended to persuade the audience of the rightness of a certain opinion or position, often using misleading, emotional, or deceptive arguments. Since the HHS video news releases were ostensibly factual and intended merely to inform the audience of the scope of the new law, they were not propaganda and thus did not violate the Smith prohibition.[40] The opinion also tweaked Congress, the GAO's boss, by noting that the Smith language also applied to the appropriation law funding Congress itself—yet legislators were issuing video news releases routinely. This opinion put the OLC on a collision course with the GAO.

The fight over whether unsourced video releases were propaganda was joined when in February 2005 the comptroller general issued a government-wide circular, a relatively unusual action for the GAO. The purpose of his memo was to "remind" all executive branch departments and agencies of the Smith I law and of the GAO's interpretation that video news releases violated the law. He wanted to "advise vigilance to assure that agencies' activities comply with the prohibition."[41] That letter triggered a response from the executive branch. The next month, the director of the Office of Management and Budget disseminated to heads of all departments and agencies the opposite guidance. He forwarded a summary that the OLC prepared regarding its 2004 decision that permitted such video news releases.[42] In his cover letter, the director wrote that he wanted to be sure agency heads were "reminded that it is OLC (subject to the authority of the Attorney General and the President), and not the GAO, that provides the controlling interpretations of law for the Executive Branch."[43]

Agencies were now caught in the middle in a power struggle that went to the heart of the constitutional separation of powers. Congress controlled the purse strings, but agencies were in the executive branch. This was slightly different from the GAO-Justice disagreements regarding the anti-lobbying criminal statute (see chapter 5). In that case, the GAO had declined to declare if an activity was criminal and deferred to Justice, which did not prosecute. In the wake of that OLC ruling, a senior HHS official testified at a congressional hearing that he would not rule out using more videos on the new Medicare prescription drug benefit.[44] But the GAO would not flinch either. After the release of the OLC opinion and the Office of Management and Budget memo, a GAO official testified at another congressional hearing that it stood by its decision that video news releases, by definition, were a violation of the Smith I amendment.[45]

Congress quickly chose sides. When the Senate was debating an emergency appropriation bill in April 2005, Senator Robert Byrd (D-W.Va.) proposed an amendment to ban video news releases, or in the term used in his proposed legislation a "prepackaged news story," unless it contained clear notification "to the audience" that the story derived from a federal agency.[46] He began his floor remarks in support of the amendment by quoting the Smith I provision and then explained that the current law needed strengthening by explicitly banning video news releases. At first, two members of the majority (Republican) party opposed the amendment, trying to defend the administration. They reminded the Senate of the existing Smith I law and the criminal code provision. They also argued that the Byrd amendment imposed an impossible expectation on federal agencies, namely, to control what eventually reached the audience through the editing processes of TV stations. Surely no additional legislation was needed, they suggested. But Byrd quickly revised his draft to overcome that last concern by shifting from notification to the audience to "notification within the text or audio"—taking agencies off the hook if a TV news station edited out the notification. This change co-opted the "faultily drafted" argument of the majority to justify their opposition. Recognizing the political trap of defending government propaganda, the Republicans quickly folded. The revised Byrd amendment was adopted unanimously by a roll call vote.[47] This was a clear expression of legislative sentiment. It demonstrated that Congress was united in continuing its twentieth-century reaction to agency publicity into the twenty-first.

The issue then came up in conference committee, since the Senate had added it to the House-passed version of the bill. The House conferees (where the Republican Party was also the majority party) accepted the amendment without any substantive changes. But the language of the conference committee report went even further than Byrd's original legislative intent. In explaining the rationale for that section of the compromise bill, the committee report stated, "This provision confirms the opinion of the Government Accountability Office dated February 17, 2005 (B-304272)."[48] In other words, not only was Congress enacting legislation to ban an activity, but it was explicitly siding with the GAO's interpretation of Smith I in the showdown with the OLC and the executive branch. The Republicans, as majority party in the House and Senate, were unwilling to defend the public relations activities of a president of their own party. Congress's institutional antipathy to agency public relations trumped partisan solidarity.

The administration quickly backed down. When he signed the bill, President Bush noted that the executive branch disagreed with several provisions in the bill and therefore would "construe" those sections in ways that were consistent with its prior positions. The section relating to video news releases was not included in his list.[49] The Office of Management and Budget quickly issued an advisory memorandum to federal agencies essentially withdrawing its March 11 memo.[50] This one directed agencies to comply with the new law. The GAO and Congress had won in their showdown with the OLC and the president. In September 2005, the GAO released new opinions reinforcing its long-held interpretation of Smith I, labeling some departmental actions as covert propaganda and therefore clearly violating Smith I, even if they had occurred prior to the adoption of the Byrd amendment.[51]

IMPACT OF THE LAW

The 1951 Smith I amendment had been relatively dormant and largely ineffective for over half a century. During that time, the GAO had major difficulties implementing the law because it was so hard to define in any operational and meaningful way the distinction between "publicity or propaganda" and acceptable external communications activities by federal agencies. Nonetheless, the GAO gradually accumulated a series of decisions that provided some understandable way to interpret the Smith language. During these first fifty years of the law, the GAO described scores of situations in which agency activities did not violate the Smith proviso and only three that did. Similarly, the OLC issued only three decisions during those five decades, all agreeing with the GAO. Furthermore, there had been no significant court decisions defining the meaning and application of the law.

But suddenly, when the subject of video news releases became a big issue beginning in 2004, the Smith I amendment roared back to life. Based on prior GAO decisions, the 1951 law had some impact, clearly designating a certain activity as unlawful. With the adoption of the 2005 Byrd amendment providing a modern-day updating of Smith I, the original law can be judged to have made a modicum of difference.[52] Still, in the larger context of the entire history of the application of the Smith I amendment, one would have to judge it as having a minor to negligible effect in the overall operation of federal agency external communications activities, given the many ways that its scope was circumscribed.

CHAPTER 9

Banning Spending on Indirect Lobbying, May 1951–1996

1951: *"No part of any appropriation contained in this Act . . . shall be used for publicity or propaganda purposes to support or defeat legislation pending before the Congress."*

65 Stat. 247

1973: *"No part of any appropriation . . . shall be used, other than for normal and recognized executive-legislative relationships, for publicity or propaganda purposes for the preparation, distribution, or use of any kit, pamphlet, booklet, publication, radio, television, or film presentation designed to support or defeat legislation pending before the Congress, except in presentation to the Congress itself."*

87 Stat. 129

1984: *"None of the funds made available by this Act shall be used in any way, directly or indirectly, to influence congressional action on any legislation or appropriation matters pending before the Congress."*

98 Stat. 1904

In 1922, Congressman Albert Johnson (R-Wash.) was in the midst of a running vendetta against the USDA. He proposed several hostile amendments during the floor debate on the department's appropriation bill for FY 1924; one proposed to ban use of any money contained in the bill for funding any departmental "advocacy of or in opposition to legislation or bills before the Congress of the United States."[1] Even though Johnson was a member of the majority party, the Republican leadership opposed all his amendments. Without a debate on the merits of this proposal, it failed by a vote of 35–50. In retrospect, though, Johnson had identified a new approach to silencing the bureaucracy. In 1919, Congress had passed a permanent statute that criminalized agency lobbying of Congress (chapter 5). Johnson was going after the same activity, but using a different legislative tool. Rather than focusing on permanent law, he was suggesting a rider to a funding bill. The provision would last only one year, but it would cover all spending by the department for that year. Also, to be enacted, it needed only to be added as an amendment to an appropriation bill, a much easier task than the long and drawn-out process of passing a separate bill. Three decades later, his idea was revived and passed.

A DIFFERENT SMITH AMENDMENT

A month after Congressman Lawrence Smith (R-Wis.) had first introduced his amendment to the annual Department of Labor appropriation bill to ban agency publicity and propaganda (chapter 8), he proposed another amendment when the House was debating the annual Department of Interior funding bill. In his introductory remarks he said this amendment was "in effect" the same as the one in April.[2] But it was not. The April amendment to the Labor appropriation bill was a flat ban on "publicity or propaganda." His proposed change to the Interior funding bill had an additional clause tacked on at the end of the earlier wording: "No part of any appropriation contained in this act . . . shall be used for publicity or propaganda purposes designed to support or defeat legislation pending before the Congress."[3] In his floor remarks, Smith did not explain why the wording of this proposal was different. It was narrower than the April amendment in that it applied only to publicity and propaganda intended to influence legislative decision making. He was focusing on "indirect lobbying" by federal agencies—activities that sought to influence public opinion and would, in turn, influence Congress. In a sense, Smith was proposing an appropriation rider that would be a counterpart to the 1919 criminal law banning agency lobbying. This would be a civil law prohibition on similar activities, although applying only to indirect lobbying.

Several other Republicans stated their support for the amendment, one particularly referring to what he claimed were propaganda activities in the Interior Department, especially the Bureau of Reclamation (chapter 7). From the other side of the aisle, Congressman Henry "Scoop" Jackson (D-Wash.) opposed the amendment, but without defending agency publicity. Instead, he said the Smith amendment was "simply surplusage" because it largely duplicated other laws on the books. As he had done when Congress was debating the Smith I amendment, Congressman John Fogarty (D-R.I.) pointed out that this second amendment from Smith had the same weakness as the first version: it provided no definition of propaganda. Therefore, "it does not mean anything." Also, Jackson chimed in, it had no penalties.[4] In their brief instant critiques, Fogarty and Jackson had immediately identified crucial problems with the Smith II amendment that would plague the GAO perennially.[5] Nonetheless, the Smith II amendment passed by voice vote. Again, as with the Smith I amendment, the conservative coalition was in charge on the floor of the House, not the Democratic leadership. However, the Senate Appropriations Committee chose to substitute an amendment from Senator Harry Byrd (D-Va.) (see chapter 10) for the Smith II amendment, and in floor debate the change was unopposed.[6] In conference, the House conferees (dominated by Democrats, the majority party) were willing to give up on that Republican amendment from their house in favor of a Democratic amendment from the other house.[7]

Smith was nothing if not persistent. On May 4, 1951, two days after the House had accepted his amendment to the Interior Department funding bill, he proposed the same amendment to the Independent Offices appropriations bill. This time it passed without even any debate.[8] Democrats like Jackson and Fogarty knew the outcome was preordained. Again, the Senate substituted the Byrd amendment for the Smith approach. This time, however, the conference committees deadlocked on the subject, twice.[9] The House conferees felt they had to represent the clear position of their house vigorously. Eventually the two houses compromised, deciding to include both Byrd and Smith amendments in the bill.[10] It became law on August 31, 1951.[11]

Two weeks after the House adopted the Smith II amendment for the Independent Offices bill, the next annual appropriation bill, for the USDA, was being debated. Again Smith proposed the Smith II amendment as the last amendment submitted for the bill.[12] In the brief debate, two other Republican congressmen spoke in support of the amendment's particular relevance to the USDA, given the criticisms of it by the Harness Committee and other legislative critiques (chapter 7).[13] The only majority party member to speak was Jamie Whitten (D-Miss.), the floor manager of the bill, who said that all the language accomplished was an absurdity. The amendment prohibited an activity "which they [USDA] have no authority to do" and no funding to do it, either. Without defending USDA public relations, he reminded the members that there would always be disagreement about whether an agency's communication "is propaganda or good, sound argument. That difference of opinion will always exist."[14] Having made his point, Whitten said he would not oppose the amendment, and it was adopted. The Senate again accepted it, and it also became law on August 31, 1951.[15] The Smith II amendment was now part of two appropriations acts. From that point on, it was routinely renewed for those annual bills and gradually expanded to affect all executive branch departments and agencies. It then lay dormant for a decade.[16]

USING THE LAW AGAINST KENNEDY ADMINISTRATION AGENCIES

The 1950s were dominated by a Republican presidency, with Eisenhower elected in 1952 (a year after the Smith II amendment was adopted) and reelected in 1956. During that time, there were no efforts to invoke Smith II. But as soon as control of the White House shifted to a Democrat, congressional Republicans resuscitated it, seeing Smith II as an effective tool for bashing the Kennedy administration. In February 1962, Civil Service Commission chair John Macy issued a memorandum of guidance titled "Role of the Career Official in Support of Federal Programs." In it he reminded federal employees of the Smith II amendment but also said that, regarding pending legislation, civil servants "may explain the position of the administration in the proposed legislation before interested public groups" without violating the law.[17] Congressional Republicans cried foul, accusing the administration of trying to politicize the civil service and force federal employees to promote publicly legislation they might not agree with.[18] Trying to ride out the negative publicity, Assistant Attorney General Nicholas Katzenbach issued a ruling that there was "nothing in the language of these statutes which renders it illegal for a career official to make an explanation of an administration legislative proposal or position to a public gathering." What if the staffer publicly disagreed with the proposal? Katzenbach stated that that would be "a serious impropriety." In his view, the administration was "entitled to his [a staffer's] cooperation and support."[19]

In late March, Senator John Williams (R-Del.) proposed a floor amendment to a FY 1963 appropriation bill expanding the scope of Smith II. He wanted to add a second paragraph that would similarly ban paying "the salary of any civil service employee who appears before public groups for the purpose of supporting or opposing the administration's position on pending legislation."[20] By April, the ruckus raised by Williams and other congressional Republicans seemed to be gaining traction. Williams was persistent, keeping the issue alive through floor speeches, committee testimony, and press coverage.[21] His amendment had forced Democrats into vaguely defending the administration without saying they were in favor of politicizing the civil service. At one point, a Senate Appropriations Committee report defensively stated that "the committee is in sympathy with the objectives sought to be accomplished by the amendment. . . . The committee proposes that this matter be studied further by the staff in cooperation with the Civil Service Commission and it is proposed to consider the amendment further."[22] There was a chance that Republicans would succeed in embarrassing both the White House and the majority party in both houses into passing the amendment. That would certainly be interpreted as a political loss for the president and a win by opposition Republicans in Congress. Finally, the administration backed down. Minutes before the Williams amendment was about to come up for a vote, Macy called Williams and said he would issue another memo that withdrew from the original memo the offending sentence.[23] That mooted the amendment and Williams withdrew it.

Other congressional Republicans occasionally invoked the Smith II amendment to bash the Kennedy administration. For example, it was mentioned twice in mid-1962. When debating increasing the federal government's public debt limit, Congressman John Byrnes (R-Wis.) suggested that the Kennedy administration was lobbying Congress with "executive pressure" and even "blackmail" even though Congress's enactment of Smith II was "prohibiting that kind of conduct."[24] A month later, Congressman Glenard Lipscomb (R-Calif.) again denounced administration propaganda and lobbying in a floor speech (see chapter 5), and John Rhodes (R-Ariz.) publicly reminded the House that "there is a law against any Department of Government using appropriated funds for the purpose of influencing Members of Congress." Rhodes suggested that the State Department activities Lipscomb was criticizing "might well be prohibited."[25] But these were all examples of using Smith II for political and rhetorical attacks, since individual members of Congress could not enforce the law. Similar to the criminal code provision banning agency lobbying, enforcement and sanctions were beyond their reach. Only institutions such as the GAO or Department of Justice could enforce it.

ENFORCING THE BAN:
AUTHORITATIVE INTERPRETATIONS BY THE GAO

Even though Smith II was enacted in 1951, for the first decade of its existence the GAO was not actively involved in defining and enforcing it. However, beginning in 1961, it was increasingly called on to judge the precise meaning and scope of the law (which was routinely renewed by Congress in annual appropriation bills). The GAO's first official opinion on Smith II was issued in May 1961, ten years after Smith II was first introduced and only a few months into the Kennedy presidency. In rapid succession, several Republican legislators asked the GAO to rule on whether Smith II had been violated. These requests initiated a gradual process whereby the GAO developed guidelines on its interpretation of the law and what constituted violations of it.

According to the GAO, presidents and their appointees as well as the top management of all federal agencies had legitimate reasons to communicate openly about their positions on issues of public and legislative concern.[26] Therefore, merely stating a position on bills pending in Congress was not a violation of the law, whether communicated directly to legislators (since this by definition would not involve propagandizing the public) or expressed in a reasonable way in a public forum.[27] Still, the line separating such legitimate communications and propaganda was, the GAO admitted, "a finely drawn one."[28] For example, a "concerted effort" aimed at "the molding of public opinion" to influence Congress would be a violation.[29]

Gradually, the GAO evolved a criterion to judge violations: it declared that activities constituting "grass roots" lobbying were prohibited by Smith II. If an agency reached out to many individual citizens—that is, the grassroots of the public at large—and urged them to lobby members of Congress on specific legislation, then the law had been violated.[30] A determination of a violation necessitated "circumstances which leave no room for doubt as to the prohibited nature of the expenditure involved."[31] Yet, even when the GAO ruled that Smith II had been violated, if the expenditure "was small and commingled with proper expenditures," the GAO would not pursue the matter further.[32] Alternately, the GAO sometimes concluded that it would be "relatively futile to try to attach a specific dollar amount to the violation." For example, in 1982, the GAO ruled that the Air Force and Defense Department had committed an "egregious" violation of Smith II when they worked behind the scenes with the Lockheed Corporation to lobby Congress to buy the C-5B airplane.[33] Still, "we do not believe it would be practical to recover amounts illegally spent."[34]

The Kennedy era rulings largely set the precedents for scores of subsequent GAO reviews of possible violations of the law. Requests for such inquiries typically came from legislators who were not of the party of the sitting president. Democrats worried about violations by a Republican administration, and vice versa. So, for example, Senator Edmund Muskie (D-Maine) complained about activities of the Nixon administration,[35] and minority leader John Rhodes (R-Ariz.) complained about activities of the Carter administration.[36] This partisan pattern of seeking to enforce Smith II is another demonstration that the statute served partisan political purposes of legislative-executive conflict rather than more substantial statutory and legal purposes.

Generally, the GAO's post-Kennedy decisions reflected the precedents set by those early decisions, interpretations that largely made Smith II impotent in any practical effect.[37] Over the years, the GAO further clarified the scope of the law. It ruled that the original Smith II (and some of its subsequent versions; see below) did not cover:

> lobbying to influence state-level elections or referenda[38]
>
> lobbying financed by nonappropriated funds[39]
>
> lobbying to influence state legislation[40]
>
> situations that lacked "a specific exhortation for people to write to their Congressman to actually take some action"[41]
>
> participation by students of the federal National War College in meetings with Members of Congress as part of the curriculum of a class on the legislative process[42]
>
> lobbying by the federal judicial branch[43]
>
> the Defense Department providing free air transportation to legislators to Washington to be present for a key vote[44]
>
> speeches urging public expressions of support to Congress for general policy goals and principles rather than specific legislation[45]
>
> grassroots lobbying if the Smith II provision had temporarily lapsed or did not cover a particular agency[46]
>
> statements to the public about a legislative proposal that only implied contacting legislators[47]

Occasionally, though, the GAO did find Smith II and its successor versions to have been violated in a manner significant enough to require action. In 1981, it declared that local anti-poverty agencies affiliated with the federal Community Services Administration had violated the law. It directed that agency to "take action to recover such illegal expenditures."[48] Four years later, it found that the Defense Department's Chemical Warfare Review Commission had illegally hired a lobbyist to promote specific legislation. It declared that all payments by the Review Commission to the lobbyist "were illegal," as was its employment of a public relations firm to promote its legislative views with the public.[49] In 1995, the GAO declared that an employee of the Interior Department's Fish and Wildlife

Service had violated the version of the ban applying to the department, but it accepted as an adequate departmental response the promulgation of new guidelines clarifying the meaning of the law for all departmental employees.[50] Four years after that, it found that the USDA's Forest Service Communications Plan was a violation of the law but again accepted the department's commitment to develop legal guidelines for its employees specifying how to operationalize the ban.[51]

ENFORCING THE BAN: AUTHORITATIVE INTERPRETATIONS BY THE DEPARTMENT OF JUSTICE

In 1977, Assistant Attorney General John Harmon, head of the OLC, submitted to the White House a comprehensive review of legal restraints on executive branch lobbying. He wiped the slate clean by stating at the beginning of his opinion that previous observations about these laws made by the department were "inconsistent with what we believe to be the correct interpretation" of the law.[52] Though most of the memo dealt with the criminal law against agency lobbying (see chapter 5), Harmon also addressed the variations of Smith II then in effect. His central interpretation greatly narrowed its plain meaning: "The appropriation rider should be read as principally designed to meet the immediate evil perceived by Congress—the unchecked growth of a government public relations arm used to disseminate agency appeals to the public at large—not as an effort to interfere unduly with the normal and healthy functioning of the body politic."[53]

The operational guideline he stated was that what executive branch officials "must avoid is any effort to serve as their own press by cranking out their own propaganda for distribution via any of a variety of media or by shifting personnel into the field of public relations without congressional authorization."[54] In terms of specifics, he was slightly stricter than the GAO's precedents. Harmon suggested that the lack of "magic words" (e.g., "contact your Congressman to oppose . . .") would not necessarily provide automatic protection from violating the law.[55] Similarly, he cautioned against excessive distribution of even "neutral material."[56]

Harmon's view of Smith II set the trend for future interpretations of the law by successive administrations. In 1981, White House counsel Fred

Fielding advised members of the White House staff to be careful about the appropriation rider because "any disallowed expenditures [by the GAO] would have to be borne by the individual supervising the activity that resulted in the unauthorized use of government funds."[57] The examples and guidelines he provided generally followed the Harmon memo, but he was careful not to allege blanket exemption for the president and his personal staff. Generally, he equated the application of the law to White House staff the same as it would apply to senior managers in executive branch agencies.

During the Reagan administration, the OLC issued an opinion stating that generally the Department of Justice interpreted Smith II "in much the same way" as the GAO,[58] but it declared that Smith II covered legislation only, and therefore grassroots and indirect lobbying related to Senate consideration of international treaties was permissible. It also reminded executive branch officials that indirect and grassroots lobbying of specific legislation were legal until that legislation was formally introduced in Congress. This was a relatively explicit hint to the White House and agencies to choreograph the administration's legislative program carefully to delay the introduction of legislation until the later stages of the policy advocacy process. An OLC opinion released during the Clinton administration, addressed mostly to the anti-lobbying criminal statute, also touched on Smith II by restating the comptroller general's interpretations of the law, but it left open the option of differing future opinions by stating that it had never "set out a detailed, independent analysis" of that law.[59] Finally, during the Bush (II) administration, the Department of Justice's inspector general investigated the attorney general's public campaign to promote renewal by Congress of the Patriot Act and, based on GAO guidelines, ruled that those activities had not violated Smith II because the law did not prohibit departmental representatives "from making public speeches conveying the DOJ's view regarding the merits of the Patriot Act" and because there was no documentation that the attorney general had "urged his audiences to contact their elected representatives."[60]

In summary, the legal opinions of various executive branch officials, whether during Republican or Democratic presidencies, have tended to support the GAO's interpretations of the law, largely because they posed no vital obstacles to the interests of the administration in power. Still, all the opinions carefully preserved the option of future, more detailed, reviews of the law that might differ from the comptroller's guidelines.

ENFORCING THE BAN:
AUTHORITATIVE INTERPRETATIONS BY THE COURTS

Two court decisions in the early 1980s referred to the Smith II law. In the first case, the American Trucking Associations sued the U.S. Department of Transportation, alleging that it had at least twice violated Smith II in public communications that supported deregulating the trucking industry. The federal district judge dismissed the suit, ruling that "the harm alleged [is] so generalized that it does not support standing" for the Trucking Association to pursue the lawsuit.[61] With that ruling, the court did not definitively rule on whether private citizens (and corporations) had standing to pursue alleged violations of Smith II. In 1982, however, a different federal district court ruled more definitively in a similar case, this time related to alleged violations of Smith II by the Legal Services Corporation. In this lawsuit, several U.S. senators alleged the violation by a federal agency. The court concluded "that an implied cause of action was not intended by Congress when it adopted" any specific version of Smith II and dismissed the case.[62]

Taken together, the few court decisions related specifically to Smith II have paralleled judicial decisions related to other congressional efforts to silence the bureaucracy. In all these situations, the courts have ruled that private citizens were not granted the right to bring suits to force an agency to cease violating the law. In legal terms, they did not have standing. Like all the other provisos and riders that Congress enacted to stifle federal agencies, this was a law that could be invoked and enforced only by official bodies.

REVISING THE LAW: 1973 AND 1984

Since its original enactment in 1951, Smith II would usually be automatically renewed in successive annual appropriation bills, occasionally not renewed, and sometimes reworded to have slightly different scope of coverage. The GAO summarized these changes in the mid-1990s by stating that, "over the years, these restrictions have applied at different times, to different agencies and have used different wordings."[63] At a congressional hearing in 1996, it identified five different versions of Smith II and, about a decade later, at least four.[64]

For example, in 1973, based on a floor amendment offered by Senator Hubert Humphrey (D-Minn.) to a supplemental appropriation bill, the language of Smith II was substantially modified to make more explicit what it covered and what it did not.[65] The new wording specifically exempted from the ban any activities involving "normal and recognized executive-legislative relationships" and any "presentation to the Congress itself." On the other hand, it elaborated the scope of the ban as including "the preparation, distribution, or use of any kit, pamphlet, booklet, publication, radio, television, or film presentation designed to support or defeat legislation pending before the Congress."[66] So, although the new language was more detailed than the original Smith II about what was and was not acceptable, it still was worded in a way that was open to highly different and contradictory interpretations.

A similar provision was included that year in the annual funding bill for the departments of Labor and Health, Education, and Welfare. Senator Warren Magnuson (D-Wash.) complained that public information officers at the National Institutes of Health were ghostwriting editorials for small-town newspapers criticizing how Congress was handling the agency's budget request.[67] His ire led to unusually strong language in the committee's report: "Federal workers have been directed by their respective agencies to prepare documents solely for propaganda purposes. These documents serve as the basis for speeches, editorial pieces, and media broadcasts, aimed at lobbying for or against legislation pending before the Congress. In some cases, this material goes so far as to attack specific Members of Congress. The committee is adamantly opposed to such activities."[68]

This statement rather bluntly identifies an underlying rationale for Smith II and other congressional efforts to silence the bureaucracy. Certainly, the oft-stated reason is related to institutional interests of a legislative branch to maintain supremacy and control over executive branch agencies; this is a motivation that relates to political power. But another motivation for controlling the voice of the bureaucracy is also clear here. As elected officials, legislators fear the ability of the bureaucracy to defeat them for reelection. According to Holtzman, "congressmen do not like to be threatened," not just in relation to institutional etiquette and prerogatives but especially in terms of the most basic of all considerations: political survival.[69] Should an agency that has attained autonomy be successful at publicly depicting an elected official as harming the agency's efforts to continue providing a popular service, then the legislator's very political survival is at stake. The legislator does not want to be "exposed" back home by a government agency as supposedly working against the interests of the constituents. With the emergence of the administrative state, the ability of agencies to communicate publicly was becoming more and more of a threat not only to legislative preeminence but to a legislator's own political career. As would be expected, even the glimmer of the potential of such a threat would electrify legislators into decisive action to protect themselves—regardless of party, ideology, or policy subject. Given that, the House conferees had no problem accepting Magnuson's Senate amendment.[70]

In 1978, in response to a GAO ruling that the lobbying of state legislatures by the Legal Services Corporation was legal, Congress promptly expanded the scope of the appropriation provision to cover lobbying activities by the agency directed at state as well as federal legislation.[71] Another later version of Smith II enacted in 1984 prohibited agencies from "directly or indirectly" lobbying to influence Congress.[72] However, not all proposals to renew or revise Smith II were adopted. In 1983, when the House Appropriations Committee added Smith II to the FY 1984 funding bill for the Treasury Department and Post Office, a member raised a point of order during floor debate that the amendment violated the prohibition on inserting new legislation in appropriation bills. His point of order was upheld, and Smith II was removed from the bill, suggesting that earlier challenges might have been successful as well.[73]

The impotence of Smith II, including its later versions, was highlighted in 1976, when the Air Force carefully arranged for the cost of food served at its congressional briefings in support of the B-1 bomber to be paid for by the nonprofit Air Force Association. This meant—supposedly—that no appropriated funds had been expended on the briefings, thereby showing how easy it was to skirt the law, even if deferring to its literal meaning.[74] A *New York Times* article about the incident quoted a source as saying that "Congress generally winks at the frequent violations of the law" by the military.[75] Then, in 1982, a House Armed Services sub-committee investigated what the GAO had called "egregious" violations of the law regarding the Air Force campaign for the C-5B airplane. But the subcommittee refused to condemn the military. Instead, it merely concluded in its report that the law was "imprecise, vague and largely unenforce-able." It hazily recommended that the appropriate committees review the law and recommend legislation "to correct any such defects and clarify" the boundaries between acceptable and unacceptable agency lobbying of Congress.[76]

Reacting to the same case, Senator David Pryor (D-Ark.) introduced a bill to ban, even more explicitly, direct and indirect lobbying by federal agencies.[77] Pryor's proposal had the advantage of shifting from annual appropriation riders to regular federal law that governed the use of appro-priated funds. It also established a more detailed definition of appropriate and banned activities. The comptroller general told the Armed Services Committee that Pryor's bill or something along its lines should be approved. If Congress wanted the GAO to enforce a ban on indirect lobbying, then it needed to enact legislation that was "easier to apply" and that would clearly "delineate the extent of permissible executive branch lobbying activities."[78] Pryor was, however, a member of the minority party, so his bill did not pass or even receive a public hearing.[79] Two years later, the GAO recommended that the more detailed and updated version of Smith II be shifted from its status as an annual appropriation restriction to "permanent law."[80] In the end, Congress took no concrete actions in response to those 1980s recommendations.

A relatively major effort to improve the impact of Smith II occurred in the mid-1990s (Republican Congress, Democratic president). In 1996, Senator Ted Stevens (R-Alaska) and Congressman William Clinger, Jr. (R-Pa.), introduced the Federal Agency Anti-Lobbying Act.[81] The purpose of the bill was to revise the law by "providing for easier enforcement, and [to help] clear up any ambiguities." It sought to ban, effectively, "what has become in essence a grassroots lobbying operation at taxpayer expense," said Stevens.[82] The central concept of the bill involved shifting Smith II from an annual appropriation rider to permanent prohibition in civil law regarding the spending of federal funds. Hence, it was a continuation of the principle of trying to silence the bureaucracy through appropriation limitations, just changing from annual riders to a permanent one. The wording of the bill addressed some of the problems with Smith II (and other parallel efforts). Specifically, it banned expenditure of any funds for indirect lobbying "however small" the amount, expanded coverage to include international treaties and confirmation of nominations, and included actions "intended" to spur public lobbying even if the "magic words" were not used. Finally, the bill declared that the inherent right of presidents and their administrations to state publicly their views on legislation could not be delegated to the middle and lower echelons of federal agencies. These were all clear responses to the problems and issues the GAO had identified. The bill also put all departmental and agency inspectors general under the jurisdiction of the GAO for purposes of enforcing the law. On the other hand, the bill did not permit individual citizens to have standing to bring suits alleging violations, nor did it specify any explicit civil penalties for violating the proposed law.

The chief sponsor of the House version was the chair of the Committee on Government Reform and Oversight. He convened a public hearing on the bill in May 1996. The hearing reflected the highly charged partisan atmosphere of the era, with Republican members promoting the bill and attacking the administration while Democrats opposed the bill and defended the president of their party. The Department of Justice submitted a prepared statement suggesting that the bill was an infringement on the constitutional duties and prerogatives of a president. Representatives of two legislative branch agencies, the GAO and the Congressional Research Service, also testified.[83] In a nonpartisan tone, they reviewed the problems with the various current laws (not just Smith II but also, e.g., the 1919 criminal penalty) and, generally, supported in principle legislation such as this one that would address and resolve the defects in enforcing the laws. Inexplicably, however, even though the Republicans were the majority party in Congress and the bill was sponsored by the committee chairman, he never scheduled a committee vote on it and so the bill was never reported out of committee. The companion bill in the Senate was never given a hearing. Therefore, the proposal died at the end of the 104th Congress in early 1997. At the time of this writing, the different variations of Smith II are routinely being renewed as part of the annual appropriations process.[84]

IMPACT OF THE LAW

The conventional wisdom about the impact of restrictions such as Smith II is that they are "legal fiction."[85] Still, in terms of tangible impact, documents such as Fielding's legal advice to White House staff in the early 1980s demonstrated a clear desire for executive branch officials to steer clear of the law's prohibitions.[86] According to Holtzman, the law "imposes a degree of restraint upon their behavior," but that is more a reference to lobbying discretely rather than crudely, not to lobbying at all.[87] Even when the GAO determined that the law had been violated, it normally deemed the financial terms of the violation minor or commingled with valid expenditures. For a law that had been in effect for more than half a century, the GAO's findings of violations including requirements for financial recovery could be counted on one hand, with fingers left over. In that context, Fielding's advice seems more political than legal. Further, the OLC's careful protection of its prerogative in future cases to interpret the law differently from the GAO has preserved a potentially significant option for inventing new in-house legal guidelines to protect executive branch agencies from particular accusations of violations.

With its impotence as a legal restriction, the main impact of Smith II—like so many other congressional efforts to silence the bureaucracy—rests with a combination of publicity and political factors. Given the democratic underpinnings of government, even for such a vast infrastructure as the federal government, the power of negative publicity can be a potent tool for punishing alleged wrongdoers. The same is true of Smith II's effect on the *potential* of negative publicity as a restraint on *future* behavior. Yet, if Smith II is largely enforced by publicity or the threat of it, then it truly has shifted from a legal and institutional weapon in the legislative struggle for predominance over the bureaucracy to a political and partisan one. From the resurrection of Smith II by congressional Republicans during the Kennedy administration to the present, the kabuki-like predictability of such incidents has nearly become ossified. For example, during the 1973 confirmation hearing of Lewis Helm to be assistant secretary for public affairs of the Department of Health, Education, and Welfare, Senator Walter Mondale (D-Minn.) accused the nominee of acquiescing to breaking the law because, Mondale claimed, the law prohibited spending any appropriated funds to *criticize* Congress.[88] At the time, the presidency was held by Republican Richard Nixon. As long as one knows the party affiliation of the president, one can with a high degree of certainty correctly predict the partisan affiliation of congressional critics alleging violations of Smith II.

This particular role of Smith II also poisoned congressional consideration of the 1996 legislative proposal to clarify the law and make it permanent. The endorsement of some legislation along those lines by the GAO and Congressional Research Service indicated that, from an institutional and nonpartisan perspective, the proposal had merit. But the bill was being considered after half a century of legislative partisans using Smith II to bash a president of the other party or a bureaucracy they were at war with. Given that, it was impossible to consider the proposed legislation on its merits. Such an outcome is not only a shame from the perspective of government as constructive machinery but an indication of how far gone the situation had become. Beginning with an institutional concern by Congress about the potential power of the administrative state, the effort to silence the bureaucracy in this instance had deteriorated largely to just one more piece of rhetorical ammunition in Washington's seemingly perpetual, gridlocked partisan warfare. Instead of a tool in the legislative reaction to agency publicity, Smith II had devolved into political cannon fodder. It was now part of the verbal congressional arsenal used in the perpetual partisan combat over separation of powers, but little more.

CHAPTER 10

DEFINING PUBLIC RELATIONS
BEFORE CUTTING IT, JUNE 1951–1956

A 25 percent cut in appropriated funds spent "in the performance of—

functions performed by a person designated as an information specialist, information and editorial specialist, publications and information coordinator, press relations officer or counsel, photographer, radio expert, television expert, motion-picture expert, or publicity expert, or designated by any similar title, or

functions performed by persons who assist persons performing the functions described in (1) in drafting, preparing, editing, typing, duplicating, or disseminating public information publications or releases, radio or television scripts, magazine articles, photographs, motion pictures, and similar material."

65 Stat. 189

A month after Congressman Smith introduced his ban on agency spending for publicity intended to influence Congress (chapter 9) and two months after his more general ban on agency publicity and propaganda (chapter 8), Senator Harry Byrd (D-Va.) tried a different approach to silencing the bureaucracy. Even though he had been attacking agency public relations since the New Deal (chapter 7), he felt his efforts had been largely unsuccessful. One of the causes of his failures, he believed, was that so much of agency external communications occurred under innocuous and even misleading titles—whether titles of staffers, programs, or budget lines. The problem of effective wording of statutory language to curb agency publicity had plagued the effort since it first began in 1905. Byrd decided to try to finesse these definitional tactics by addressing the issue head-on.

THE BYRD AMENDMENT

On June 19, 1951, Byrd introduced a floor amendment to the FY 1952 Independent Offices appropriations bill. It would cut by 25 percent all agency spending in the area of public relations (in lieu of the Smith II amendment that the House had added to the bill). But the twist he added to his rider was that the limitation applied not only to people with obvious titles reflecting involvement in public information but also to staff who engaged in such activities, regardless of title. His amendment described the *functions* that would be covered by the spending limit as including "drafting, preparing, editing, typing, duplicating, or disseminating public information publications or releases, radio or television scripts, magazine articles, and similar material."[1] Byrd thought that he had finally figured out a way to neutralize agency efforts to camouflage their external communications programs. He said his new approach "is the only way I know of that the abuse—and it has been a great abuse—can be corrected."[2] Ever since the beginning of Congress's reaction to agency publicity, difficulties with legislative drafting and definitions had been a persistent and perennial obstacle. Byrd thought that imposing an activity-based definition of public relations on the agency would finally cut this Gordian knot.

Byrd's amendment prompted some automatic support from senators who denounced executive branch propaganda, but other senators raised concerns. Majority leader Ernest McFarland (D-Ariz.) wondered if the cut would be so severe that agencies would then rightly be criticized for not releasing adequate information to the public.[3] Clinton Anderson (D-N.Mex.) flatly opposed the amendment and addressed the standard congressional shibboleths regarding agency publicity head on. Yes, senators had had a good laugh a few years earlier when a member ridiculed a USDA booklet on fleas. But, he said, that booklet had been requested during World War II by the military to help its doctors deal with health problems faced by servicemen stationed in North Africa, where fleas were particularly prominent as disease transmitters. Similarly, if the Byrd amendment were to be adopted, it would hamper the efforts of the Atomic Energy Commission to educate school children about atomic power. He was joined by William Benton (D-Conn.), who pointed out that what some legislators denounced as publicity was really education and instruction, such as extension activities of the USDA.[4] With such counterarguments articulated so boldly, Byrd shrewdly asked that his amendment be voted on in a recorded vote. He knew that some senators who privately agreed with Anderson and Benton would not want to give a potential opponent an easy target for criticism, by supposedly voting to support bureaucratic propaganda. Byrd's amendment passed by a comfortable 63–10 vote.[5] But a reporter noted "a curious voting line-up" triggered by the unexpected opposition to cutting agency publicity.[6]

Twice, the conference committee was unable to resolve the differences between the Senate's Byrd amendment and the House's Smith II amendment (along with many other items, of course). Neither side was willing to defer to the other house's position.[7] Eventually, in a floor maneuver to overcome the conference committee deadlock, each house voted to include both the Byrd and Smith amendments in the bill.[8] It became law on August 31, 1951.[9] Byrd's legislative success in this matter was considered important enough for it to be mentioned in a biography published in the 1990s.[10]

Byrd thought he had made a breakthrough. And he was on a roll. As more of the annual appropriation bills were reaching the Senate floor, he was ready with his amendment. He successfully proposed adding it to bills funding the USDA and the Army Corps of Engineers.[11] Sensing the desires of the body, the Senate Appropriations Committee took the initiative and added the Byrd amendment to several bills before sending them to the floor, obviating the need for Byrd to introduce his proposal as a floor amendment. The committee included the Byrd amendment in the Interior Department bill, funding for the Import-Export Bank, and the Department of Labor and the Federal Security Agency appropriations.[12]

For the latter bill, however, the committee softened the now-standard wording by exempting any federal agency that had four or fewer public information staffers.[13] In conference, the two houses again were unable to agree on the Byrd amendment.[14] Finally, through floor maneuvers, in the House supporters of the two agencies funded by the bill succeeded in adding two more softenings of the Byrd amendment that the Senate then accepted. One was an exemption for all "technical, scientific, or research publications, the reporting or dissemination of the results of research or investigations, [and] the publishing of other work required by law to carry out the[ir] duties," other than media relations. With the other, for all other agencies affected by earlier enactments of the Byrd amendment, any public relations activities they engaged in that involved interacting with the public regarding defense mobilization or defense production were exempt.[15] These two additional loopholes were so broadly worded that they practically negated the impact of the Byrd amendment. Liberal Democrats in the House had succeeded in protecting the information activities of the domestic agencies they liked without facing any politically awkward recorded votes, and the Democratic majority leadership had protected a presidential administration of its own party by invoking the sacred cow of national defense.

Congressman Smith also jumped on the Byrd bandwagon. Since the Constitution requires that all appropriation bills start in the House of Representatives, he would get first crack at funding bills before Byrd. Seeing that Byrd's amendment was acceptable to the Senate, Smith started proposing variations of it when three other appropriation bills were debated on the House floor. That approach had a tactical advantage. If Smith could get the House to add the Byrd amendment when the bill was still in the House—and then the Senate, of course, would go along— the issue could not come up in conference committee since both houses had approved it. It would not be in play. This was a distinct benefit— avoiding, for example, kinds of deadlocks just faced with the Independent Offices and Interior Department appropriations. In those cases, the eventual compromises were not particularly bad outcomes from Smith's perspective, but other times he did not like the result. For example, later, when the conference committee faced bills that added the Byrd amendment in the Senate, the House conferees could insist on weakening it, since the House-passed version had no such provision. For the Army Corps of Engineers bill, the House conferees succeeded in exempting the Panama Canal Zone government from the Byrd amendment. Since Smith considered his general goal to be the same as Byrd's, he could strengthen the effectiveness of Byrd's approach by proposing it (or variations on it) in the House. It would prevent a conference committee dominated by the leadership from tampering with it.

On July 26, Smith introduced the Byrd amendment on the House floor during the debate on the annual funding bill for the State Department. The bill's floor manager, John Rooney (D-N.Y.), raised the point of order that, as drafted, Smith's amendment was new legislation and therefore out of order as an amendment to an appropriation bill. The presiding officer upheld the point of order.[16] Smith then redrafted the amendment so that it complied with House rules and reintroduced it. This time Rooney openly opposed it, blandly urging his colleagues to vote against it because "it does not belong in this bill."[17] As a member of the minority party, Smith thought he might lose a partisan-based vote. He hoped a counted vote (rather than voice vote) would more likely overcome that obstacle. At first he lost 131–137. Then he called for an even more formal counted vote (but not a roll call vote), and more members scrambled to the floor. Amazingly, he lost on a tie vote, 154–154.[18] The Democratic leadership had shown that it could protect a presidential administration of its own party as long as there was no record of how each member voted.

A month later, the House was debating a bill that provided additional funding for most of the executive branch's departments and agencies. This time Smith introduced a variation of the Byrd amendment, upping the ante by requiring a 50 percent cut in public relations spending for all domestic activities, compared to the 25 percent cut in Byrd's version. He was engaging in partisan one-upsmanship, proving that he, as a Republican, was more opposed to agency publicity than Byrd, a Democrat. Apparently not wanting to risk losing as they nearly did on the State Department vote, the Democratic leadership let the amendment pass without challenge and it became law.[19] The same scenario played out with another supplemental funding bill in October.[20]

REENACTING THE BYRD AMENDMENT, 1952–1956

The next year (1952, for FY 1953), as the annual funding bills were being considered by Congress, the Byrd amendment was routinely renewed for the Independent Offices bill and the bill funding the Department of Labor and Federal Security Agency.[21] It was also included in the Interior Department and USDA bills, but this time calling for only a 10 percent cut in external communications spending. Also, both departments were given major exemptions from the Byrd cuts. [22] For the Department of Interior, all technical publications and all publications of the National Park Service were exempt. For the USDA, the list of exemptions was even longer, including technical publications, the *Agricultural Yearbook* (popular with legislators to distribute free to constituents), the Farm and Home Hour radio program, and anything related to "information on the protection of natural resources against fire, insects, and disease." This last clause covered just about everything the USDA did, including the Forest Service's "Smokey the Bear" campaign. Clearly, Byrd's sway was fading as more and more legislators stepped in to protect the external communications activities of their pet agencies and programs.

A year later (1953, for FY 1954), congressional consideration of the next funding cycle would occur in a very different legislative and political context. As a result of the November 1952 elections, the presidency had shifted from Democrat to Republican (Truman to Eisenhower), and the majority party in both the House and Senate also shifted from Democratic to Republican. Republican legislators, who had felt so comfortable as part of the congressional conservative coalition in opposing bureaucracy and its public relations programs, now found themselves with the shoe on the other foot. Budget requests for agency funding would now be coming from their president. And, as the majority party, it was their responsibility to govern, to provide for the smooth functioning of the federal government. Suddenly, in this topsy-turvy political upheaval, everything looked different. The "us versus them" partisan mentality was now reversed. As always in politics, where you stand depends on where you sit. The Republican majority in Congress was sitting in a very different place than a year before. Given this political earthquake, the automatic renewal of the Byrd amendment looked very different to one of the partners in the conservative coalition. Maybe it was not such a good idea after all? It was included in only one funding bill, the Independent Offices bill. And even for that, it was watered down. Exempted from the cut were all agencies with two or fewer information staffers, the operations of the *Federal Register,* and all external communications of the Civil Service Commission related to recruitment of new employees.[23] For FY 1955, the Byrd amendment disappeared from the bill.

Aside from the Independent Offices bill, the Byrd language survived beyond the 1952 Republican election victories in only one other limited situation. The Interior Department had long been in the gun sights of the conservative coalition, with numerous attacks on its external communications in the late 1940s (chapter 7). For the last appropriations cycle before the November 1952 election, for FY 1953, the Byrd amendment had been included in the annual Interior Department appropriation bill, although with some exemptions, along with the ongoing annual limitation on Bureau of Reclamation publicity. Now the Republican-majority House Appropriations Committee needed to decide what to do in the FY 1954 Interior bill both regarding the Byrd amendment's application to the entire department and the spending limitation on the Bureau of Reclamation. It decided to impose an overall cap of $100,000 for all departmental information programs. This, of course, was a major cut, considering that just one bureau within the department, the Reclamation Bureau, had been allowed $150,000 in publicity spending the previous year. However, to reflect partisan solidarity, the committee's report blandly stated that "it is the committee's desire that the Secretary give this matter very careful study also."[24] The report also included other major budget and staffing cuts.

The department's leadership did not even wait for the bill to reach the Senate. In early May 1953, only a few weeks after the House report was released, the department announced that in time for the beginning of the next fiscal year on July 1 it would lay off about two thousand employees (involved in all aspects of operations, not just publicity) to meet the targets set by the House committee report.[25] The Bureau of Reclamation was hit hardest by the cuts, where firings would include many of the bureau's "press agents."[26] It was an effective maneuver, at least regarding the department's public relations. Congress beat something of a hasty retreat. The Senate Appropriations Committee stated that the House limitation of $100,000 was "not adequate for a sound information program" and recommended increasing it to $250,000.[27] In conference, the compromise was to accept the higher Senate figure but to apply it to all activities falling under the Byrd language used in the bill the previous year (including some exemptions), not just the department's publicly acknowledged information budget.[28] Byrd's amendment had shown itself useful for those legislators seeking the broadest possible net for information cuts. On July 31, 1953, a month into the fiscal year, President Eisenhower signed the bill.[29] The next year (1954, for FY 1955), the compromise for the Interior Department from the previous year, including the Byrd language, was routinely renewed, except with the ceiling reduced from $250,000 to $200,000.[30] Again the following year, the Byrd wording was included in the maintenance of the $200,000 limit for FY 1956.[31] This was, however, the last time the Byrd approach appeared in the law. It then totally disappeared from the statutes.

IMPACT OF THE LAW

In all, Byrd's supposed breakthrough in identifying all agency information programs for reductions had lasted only five years, from its unveiling in June 1951 through the end of FY 1956 on June 30, 1956. Why was it so short-lived compared to Smith I and Smith II? The changed political context was probably a secondary, though discernable, factor, considering when and how quickly Congress stopped renewing the Byrd language. But there was a much more dominant reason for the demise of the Byrd amendment: it had a fatal flaw.

Although Byrd thought he had slyly overcome the longtime problem of defining public relations, his solution had merely shifted the problem to a slightly different locus. This would be a new but equally difficult approach to Congress imposing its will on unwilling agencies. Cutting 75 percent (or any other percentage) from an unknown sum still leaves an unknown sum. How could Congress, or the GAO on its behalf, judge if the Byrd amendment was being properly implemented by federal agencies? There was no measuring stick, no quantified baseline. In all, there is virtually no documentation that Byrd's amendment (with the exception of the Interior Department announcement of impending firings), when imposed on various departments and agencies, had any significant effect on the levels of public information spending and staffing.

In his sustained effort, Byrd had accomplished a public relations victory by inserting his provision in the statutes, but little more. In part, Byrd had no one to blame but himself. After years of his persistent attacks on agency public information, it was no wonder that public information staffers in these agencies were so well hidden with misleading job titles and equally opaque budget lines from which they could not be identified. There was no line in each agency's budget titled "public relations" or "public information." These activities had become, in a sense, beyond the reach of Congress. Congress's vaunted power of the purse had bumped up against the desire of autonomizing agencies to protect their publicity activities and lost.

CHAPTER 11

DIFFERENTIATING
BAD PR FROM GOOD PR

"Publicity, instead of serving as an incident to Government func-
tions, has become an end in itself."

"Why not help . . . make information available to all the busi-
nessmen of the country?"

Congressman Everett Dirksen (R-Ill.), *CR* 88:4
(May 28, 1942): 4735; *CR* 89:3 (April 7, 1943): 3084

The preceding chapters identify the separate and distinct legislative efforts to limit or prohibit different aspects of agency external
communications throughout the executive branch: publicity experts,
propaganda, direct lobbying, and indirect lobbying. All these initiatives,
whether across-the-board or agency-specific, were uniformly negative in
orientation and largely ineffective. This chapter examines the obverse,
instances of positive views of agency public relations by the GAO, as
Congress's instrument.

Some of the previous discussions identify various drafting problems
related to the statutory limitation on congressional management of
agency publicity. These program activities within federal departments and
agencies were difficult to define in legal language and had boundary

lines that were equally hard to draw. Even Senator Byrd's effort to finesse definitional problems by imposing an all-inclusive definition of public relations on executive branch agencies based on activities rather than formal personnel and budget titles (chapter 10) was a failure. As a legislative branch agency, it fell to the GAO to breathe life into these disparate, sometimes overlapping, and often poorly drafted laws. This was an unenviable and thankless job. For each of the specific legal bans and restrictions, the GAO did its best to provide tangible interpretations of the scope of the law.

Along with implementation problems of the initiatives covered in the preceding chapters, two others were equally problematic. Beginning in 1951 and especially during the 1960s and '70s, Congress tried to limit public relations spending in the Defense Department. The GAO examined Defense Department claims that it implemented those budget cuts and noted the arbitrary way the department categorized what constituted public relations–type activities subject to the spending cuts and what did not.[1] The same happened with a separate congressional initiative to control the direct lobbying expenses of the Pentagon.[2]

In all its good-faith efforts to apply the legal limitations on agency public relations, the GAO consistently emphasized that some external communications activities by federal agencies, whether directed at the public at large or at Congress, had a valid and justifiable role in modern public administration. The legislative branch could not simply wave a magic wand and outlaw them all. The GAO recognized that a president and his administration had explicit obligations and implicit rights to communicate with Congress and the citizenry. Even setting aside constitutional separation-of-powers arguments, the GAO acknowledged that, with the emergence during the twentieth century of the administrative state, federal agencies *needed* to communicate externally. Sometimes these duties related to specific statutory responsibilities, such as the USDA disseminating information on the latest farming techniques to farmers.

The GAO also recognized a more generalized role of public administrators to promote an informed citizenry in a democracy, account for stewardship of public funds, and be as transparent as possible befitting the public sector. In its case-by-case decision making, the GAO was gradually

creating a comprehensive definition of the scope of acceptable and justifiable public relations in federal administration. This was an incremental
effort gradually to undo the Gordian knot that had frustrated both legislators and federal managers by providing some concrete guidelines as to
what was acceptable and what was not. Whether it wanted to or not, the
GAO was defining with some specificity the precedents of "good" public
and legislative relations that executive branch agencies could rely on as
defensible from congressional criticism, or at least from GAO sanctions.
Given the dominant role of lawyers in U.S. government, the GAO's approach
was understandably comparable to the "stare decisis" doctrine of the
legal system: each individual decision was to be an extrapolation of earlier
ones so that the body of law that gradually emerged was consistent as to
the principles being applied.

GAO DECISIONS ON
ACCEPTABLE PUBLIC RELATIONS, 1920s–1950s

The GAO began its long involvement in interpreting the propriety of
agency public relations programs with a strict interpretation of federal
law. What was allowed was only what was expressly permitted by the
statute or was very directly tied to implementing law. The GAO was first
asked to rule on the general public relations activities of a federal agency
in 1927. The Treasury Department, in its efforts to publicize U.S. Savings
Bonds, had bought time on a national radio network to carry brief talks
by senior departmental officials explaining the nature and purpose of the
bonds. The comptroller general ruled that the department had crossed a
line between acceptable and unacceptable public relations. Traditional
promotional activities that were legitimate included press coverage in
newspapers of statements issued by departmental spokespersons as well
as printing and displaying posters in federal buildings. But radio was still
a relatively new medium, and appropriations to the department did not
outright permit using such a "modernism." Though the GAO permitted
payment of the bills for the radio talks that had already occurred, it declared
that future recurrences would not be permitted under the current wording
of the law. A few months later, Treasury asked the comptroller general to
reconsider his decision. He refused.[3]

In 1935, the GAO ruled that the Federal Housing Administration could not engage in a public information campaign to encourage owners of residential property to repair and modernize their buildings. This, it felt, went beyond the statutory powers of the agency. Yes, the Housing Administration could "disseminate authentic information as to the benefits" that the agency paid out to eligible beneficiaries, but a public information campaign to promote property maintenance would go too far beyond a close relationship to the agency's statutory duties.[4] Two years later, the GAO ruled that the USDA could expend funds to create recordings of agency officials discussing soil conservation and provide those tapes to radio stations. However, consistent with its earlier rulings, the GAO relied on whether it could identify *specific* statutory language to permit such a public relations activity. In this case, the GAO deemed that the law authorizing the department's secretary "to make public such information as he deems necessary to carry out the provisions" of congressionally approved goals for the agency provided the kind of explicit legal permission it insisted was needed.[5]

Four years later, the comptroller general ruled that the Veterans Administration could not participate in the series of national radio programs called "United States Government Reports" sponsored by the White House's National Emergency Council because its statutory powers did not confer any precise authority to spend funds "for the dissemination of information by any means." It would have permitted the expenditure if the agency could have demonstrated that a particular information activity was "essential to the administrative duties and functions conferred upon you [the Veterans Administration] by statute."[6]

In all these rulings the GAO was doing more than engaging in a strict interpretation of federal law. It was following a principle that an information activity was justified only if it could be shown that it was directly helpful in the effective administration of an agency's specific duties and statutory programs. In other words, publicity that was integral to, and inextricably intertwined with, public administration was permissible. Though strict, for agency managers this was a relatively clear and helpful principle.

Without diverging from that principle, in the 1940s the GAO began accepting more liberal justifications of what an agency's duties required in terms of informational efforts. In 1942, it ruled that the costs of making and printing pictures of farmers serving on local advisory committees to federal agencies would be permitted. It accepted the argument of the AAA that the visual images of these committee members would contribute to area farmers recognizing them and, therefore, being more willing to sign up for production control programs enacted by Congress. As long as the publication of these photos logically and arguably helped "carry out the provisions" of the law, the GAO would approve the expenditure.[7] Similarly, in 1947, the comptroller general approved the U.S. Employment Service releasing during a parade balloons containing information for employers and for returning veterans seeking employment.[8] The GAO thought its basic principle had been met by the agency, because the release of the balloons with the information they contained was directly related to accomplishing the agency's statutory duties.

In the 1950s, the GAO permitted a federal agency to conduct public fora and record them for later review at agency headquarters, since those activities could be justified as part of the agency's duty, as stated in an executive order, to "inform the public."[9] Similarly, if a scientific journal charged authors some ancillary production costs for publishing scientific papers, the Public Health Service could make such payments on behalf of its employees because the end result entailed fulfilling the agency's statutory goal of disseminating information about public health.[10] More and more, the GAO was accepting the rationale that information collection and dissemination were inherent parts of an expansive view of public administration, wholly exclusive of rationales for public relations related to democracy and separation of power between the legislative and executive branches.

GAO DECISIONS ON
ACCEPTABLE PUBLIC RELATIONS, 1960s–2004

Beginning in the 1960s and continuing to the present, the GAO has further liberalized its interpretations of acceptable activities that could be financed with appropriated funds. For example, during the 1960 presidential election it was asked whether certain activities of executive branch agencies were intended by the outgoing Republican administration to help elect the Republican presidential nominee. The GAO declared that the public relations activities would have "to be so completely devoid of any connection with official functions" to deem them in violation.[11] Similarly, in 1962, the Democratic administration involved federal agencies in "White House Regional Conferences." The GAO declared that it would not second-guess the decisions of presidentially appointed heads of departments to involve their agencies in such activities as long as there was a "reasonable basis" to conclude that the events' role related in some way to "official duties."[12]

Still reflecting the literal emphasis of some of its decisions earlier in the century, in 1964 the GAO ruled that the Bureau of Engraving and Printing could not legally expend federal funds for a publicly available book commemorating the Bureau's one-hundredth anniversary because there was no statute authorizing the agency to do that.[13] But, beginning two decades later, the GAO inverted this legal interpretation, approving similar kinds of activities as long as they were not explicitly prohibited by law. This was signaled in 1971 when the GAO permitted some Department of Defense public relations programs because "we are not aware of any existing statute that would preclude DOD from incurring these costs."[14] Between 1983 and 2003, it permitted these activities:

> Army prints wall calendars for publicity purposes.[15]
>
> IRS buys crepe paper for events publicizing U.S. Savings Bonds.[16]
>
> Environmental Protection Agency buys buttons and magnets to promote clean air.[17]
>
> Veterans Administration distributes matchbooks and grip openers for jars at a state fair.[18]
>
> Forest Service buys ads in newspapers to inform the public of activities and events at a nearby U.S. forest.[19]
>
> Bureau of Land Management prints a brochure containing pictures of lighthouses.[20]
>
> Immigration and Naturalization Service purchases medals commemorating its seventy-fifth anniversary (the opposite of its 1964 decision regarding the Bureau of Engraving's one-hundredth anniversary book)[21]

The GAO evolved three other standards to judge external communications activities: information versus advocacy, fair and reasonable definitions, and truthfulness. It assessed whether a federal agency was disseminating information or was promoting an activity in order to generate public demand for it. An agency could inform the public about the metric system, for example, but could not advocate its adoption.[22] Yet even the issue of advocacy was a nuanced one, because the GAO deemed the courts had acknowledged that government agencies could publicly express their views, even when such opinions were controversial.[23] Yet, again, for the GAO an agency merely presenting its views (even when disputed by others) was inherently different from promoting those views. The GAO also sought to promote uniform definitions for public affairs and congressional relations activities. Based on its experiences trying to apply various statutes, it promoted the need to adopt consistent and standard definitions of external communications activities, including for use by the Defense Department when accepting or rejecting cost claims of defense contractors.[24] Finally, the GAO held all government agencies to a standard of truthfulness and accuracy. Even if a specific piece was not financed with appropriated funds, all publicly released products from a federal agency (e.g., statements, brochures, publications) must be accurate and avoid misleading information. Otherwise, the citizenry would assume that the connection of the material to the government indicated a "seal of approval."[25]

Overall, the GAO did about as well as could be expected with such a difficult subject. Besides interpreting the specific meaning and applications of various congressional riders and statutes, its decisions also had the effect of gradually constructing an outline of agency external communications that were appropriate and on the "right" side of the confusing and fuzzy boundary separating legitimate from illegitimate communication activities. Given the inherent difficulties of defining such concepts as propaganda with any degree of operational specificity, the GAO had thus performed a positive service. This was a constructive contribution in a difficult environment. In that respect, it was the GAO, not Congress, that was managing the practice of public relations in federal administration by providing relatively helpful guidelines to agencies on what, specifically, they could do.

GOOD PR VS. BAD PR:
535 DIFFERENT DEFINITIONS ON CAPITOL HILL

As a legislative branch agency serving Congress, the GAO was seeking to develop guidelines of acceptable and unacceptable public relations to apply uniformly to all agencies. Its efforts were based on interpreting the authoritative actions of Congress. But individual legislators did not feel compelled to accept such an approach. Rather, the 100 senators and 435 representatives at times enunciated standards that were not uniform, instead reflecting their individual views of a particular agency. This decentralized political environment promoted the cynical view that agency propaganda was akin to the floating definition of pornography: "I'll know it when I see it." This created a frustrating and unstable political environment for federal agencies seeking to engage in robust public relations without raising the ire of anyone on Capitol Hill.

Congressional efforts to silence the bureaucracy sometimes occurred without a specific violation of a particular existing law. Sometimes a specific activity would trigger ad hominem attacks on just about any agency's external communications. One congressman called overall agency public relations spending "almost shocking" and "pork barrel" at its worst.[26] A Democratic congressman complained during a Democratic administration about the "mammoth" spending in the executive branch on public relations.[27] Others complained about excessive advertising spending,[28] the volume of movies produced by federal agencies,[29] audiovisual services at the Department of Defense,[30] public relations at NASA,[31] and agency inserts with monthly Social Security checks.[32]

An archetypal such incident occurred in 1979, when a Senate committee chairman (a Democrat) and the ranking minority member (a Republican) asked the GAO to evaluate the effectiveness of federal public information programs.[33] Subsequently, the chairman attacked the federal executive branch (headed by a Democratic president) for propaganda, "runaway flacksertism," lack of accountability in public relations spending, and the fact that it was "virtually impossible" to even estimate federal publicity expenditures.[34] Rourke described the impact of such rhetorical and position-taking attacks (per Mayhew's typology) as "the use of exposure as a method of constraint."[35]

Legislators tended to categorize the external communications of an agency whose mission they disagreed with as "propaganda" and what agencies they liked were doing as "information." Amusingly, members of Congress had little difficulty denouncing agency propaganda in one breath and praising the information programs of another agency in the next. For example, Congressman Everett Dirksen (R-Ill.) had been particularly vociferous in his denunciations and floor maneuvers to limit the external communications activities of the USDA and cut the funding of Roosevelt's Office of Government Reports and other information agencies.[36] In his view, "publicity, instead of serving as an incident to Government functions, has become an end in itself."[37] But a year later he was unhappy when the Bureau of the Budget (under a Democratic president) recommended defunding the Commerce Department's field information offices and the House Appropriations Committee (in a Democratic majority Congress) concurred. Dirksen introduced a floor amendment to restore the funding fully. He explained that the cuts would be "short-sighted economy" and that it was vital "to make information available to all the businessmen of the country." These were the kinds of arguments that normally opponents of his attacks on agency public relations would make. His amendment lost.[38]

Similarly, Congressman Malcolm Tarver (D-Ga.), who had denounced USDA publicity and press releases in 1943, the next year bemoaned the cuts in the USDA's Office of Information since its work was "of inestimable value" to farmers.[39] Nearly comically, during the same Senate hearing Guy Cordon (R-Ore.) first denounced the Interior Department's Division of Information "because I do not like the Government to go into propaganda" and then, a few minutes later, praised the department's publications and information program: "I congratulate the Department of the Interior on just doing its job rather than proselytizing."[40]

The way things looked to lawmakers, unaffected by the GAO's imperative for clarity and consistency, was that agency public communications could certainly be acceptable, but that conclusion was in the eye of the beholder, just as bad publicity was. It was simply a matter of friends and enemies, not substance or laws.

CHAPTER 12

BALANCING CONGRESSIONAL AND BUREAUCRATIC INTERESTS: A SISYPHEAN STRUGGLE

A summary of the results of the case studies presented in this volume and elsewhere is relatively easy to depict. Table 3 is a concise review of this historical study, including the results of the agency-by-agency attacks of the conservative coalition depicted in table 2 (chapter 7).

The trend reflected in this narrative and in table 3 is quite plainly in sight: in a showdown between congressional power and bureaucratic autonomy over agency public relations, the bureaucracy has usually won. Sometimes agencies did have to keep a low profile for their external communications effort, but these defensive behaviors were quite different from ceasing such activities. Congress's exoskeleton for agency publicity was soft and stretchable, not firm and constraining. This is a somewhat arresting conclusion given the perception that Congress's law-making powers, and especially its power of the purse, are control mechanisms par excellence. It turns out that laws and funding were not necessarily the last word.[1]

A CONTINUING BATTLE IN THE TWENTY-FIRST CENTURY

Yarwood and Enis have identified at least five ways that agencies can circumvent legislative initiatives to manage their public relations activities:

TABLE 3

Results of Congressional Efforts to Control Executive
Branch Public Relations in the Twentieth Century

Subject/Source	De jure Result	De facto Winner	De facto Loser
Panama Canal public relations staffer (chap. 1)	Ban on a Literary Bureau; public relations staffer hired	Agency	Congress
Public relations by U.S. Forest Service (chap. 2)	No direct payments to newspapers	Agency	Congress
Ban on hiring publicity experts (chap. 4)	Law on books, public relations staffers hired with other titles	Agencies	Congress
Criminalizing agency lobbying (chap. 5)	Law on books, law never enforced	Agencies	Congress
Regulating mimeo-graph machines (chap. 6)	Presidential veto	Agencies	Congress
Attacks by conservative coalition on individual agencies (chap. 7; see table 2)	Banned spending on highly specific activities and programs	Agencies (6 of 9) Congress (3 of 9)	Congress (6 of 9) Agencies (3 of 9)
Ban on spending for propaganda (chap. 8)	Annually renewed appropriation ban, almost never enforced	Agencies	Congress
Ban on spending for indirect lobbying (chap. 9)	Annually renewed appropriation ban, almost never enforced	Agencies	Congress
Congressional definition of public relations (chap. 10)	Not successfully enforced	Agencies	Congress
Limiting Defense Dept. spending on public relations[a]	Annual cap on spending in appropriation bills	Agency	Congress
Limiting Defense Dept. spending on legislative liaison[b]	Annual cap on spending in appropriation bills	Agency	Congress

[a] Lee, "When Congress Tried," 144–148.
[b] Lee, "Too Much Bureaucracy," 343–344.

taking advantage of the unrealistic basis of a law, aggressive action by high-level officials, inconsistent personnel classifications, lack of uniform budgeting formats, and contradictory justifications and explanations.[2] These kinds of counterstrategies were apparent in this recounting. The law criminalizing agency lobbying was unrealistic in that the Department of Justice would be unlikely to charge officials of the administration with such conduct (chapter 5). Similarly, Smith I was not a realistic law because it did not define propaganda (chapter 8).

Roosevelt's attorney general acted aggressively to retain the services of a public relations official. When Congress banned him from employing a nonlawyer as a special assistant, he simply rehired Henry Suydam and, later, several of his successors as special executive assistants (chapter 7). Regarding personnel classifications, the ban on employing publicity experts was easily ignored by giving these staffers other titles (chapter 4). Similarly, the military defined many bona fide public relations activities as recruiting efforts and therefore exempt from the congressional spending limitation on public relations. The Navy used contradictory explanations to justify continuing the operations of the High School News Service.[3] The legislative reaction to agency publicity created a kind of tit-for-tat arms race that showed inventiveness by both combatants.

During the second term of President George W. Bush (2005–2009), various incidents related to public relations in the bureaucracy continued to trigger the attention of Congress. This was an indication that the legislative effort to silence the bureaucracy was still being fought as vigorously as before, just as it was entering its second century of the conflict. Some of the contretemps during this presidency related to extant legislative control efforts and are discussed in preceding chapters: the scope of the law criminalizing lobbying (chapter 5), the ban on using appropriated funds for propaganda (chapter 8), the ban on using appropriated funds for indirect lobbying (chapter 9). Other attacks on agency publicity had been more generalized, as though the mere accusation of their existence was enough to justify their condemnation and cessation—even if untied to any specific legal prohibitions or limitations.

For example, during President Bush's unsuccessful push in 2005 to restructure Social Security to include private accounts, civil servants in the Social Security Administration complained that they were being pressured to limit their public statements to support the president's position.[4] Predictably, outraged minority-party Democrats pounced on the issue as a violation to the neutral status of civil servants and an impairment of Congress's ability to receive expert opinion.[5] Similarly, information sheets that the agency inserted in mailings to Social Security beneficiaries were alleged to justify Bush's legislative solution to the fund's long-term financial solvency. The Social Security commissioner, a presidential appointee, quickly backed down, saying that no pressure would be placed on the agency's employees to support the president's proposal and that all agency publications would be limited to factual statements about the financial status of the program.[6] The controversy over whether video news releases violated the ban on propaganda (chapter 8) also led to broader criticisms by congressional Democrats about the amount of spending by agencies on public relations. They accused the Bush administration of spending unprecedented amounts on agency public relations, far more than the previous Democratic administration. Conceding that "not all public relations spending is illegal or inappropriate," the minority party nonetheless asserted that such large amounts of expenditures must be, in and of themselves, a bad thing.[7] The media ate it up.

Other aspects of agency public relations became headline issues around the same time. The U.S. Department of Education had paid a TV commentator to promote the No Child Left Behind law as part of a $9 million budget for public information.[8] The USDA paid a freelance writer to prepare "articles" for hunting and fishing magazines.[9] The Environmental Protection Agency hired the Weather Channel to produce and broadcast stories about climate change.[10] These incidents triggered attention for several reasons, including whether the line separating reporting by independent journalists had been blurred, if agencies were covertly inserting "news" into the public realm, if legitimate and factual public information activities of federal departments and agencies had morphed into propaganda, and if agencies were now spending too much on public relations. According to the *New York Times*, the cumulative effect of such incidents during Bush's second term demonstrated that agency publicity activities "have been considerably more pervasive than previously known" or practiced.[11] Congressional criticisms (usually from minority party Democrats) followed in short order.[12] The template of the legislative reaction to agency publicity, as already fully developed by the 1910s, continued with vitality a century later. It needed little change and adaptation in the twenty-first century to be invoked with the full force of its enduring congressional values.

A new front in this reaction was gradually emerging at the beginning of the twenty-first century. A rider attached to one of the FY 2001 appropriation bills was known as the Information Quality Act.[13] Its goal was generally to enforce standards of quality, objectivity, utility, and integrity on federal agencies. Though not specifically oriented to public relations, it inevitably could encompass those activities. In 2002, as required by the act, the Office of Management and Budget issued guidelines to help agencies implement the act. The guidelines specifically excluded press releases from the scope of the act. But not all external distribution of information is formally in the template of a press release. In 2005, Kosar opined that it was too early to tell what impact the act and these new guidelines would have on agency public relations.[14] Given the trend toward digital dissemination of information, there likely could be an effect, perhaps even a significant one. However, based on the agency behaviors identified throughout this study, countermeasures by federal departments and agencies to negate the potential restraining effects of the act are most likely to occur.

The pattern explored in this volume seems to be a perpetual effort by Congress to dominate the bureaucracy, especially to muffle it voice. For example, in 2008 congressional attention was reactivated when the *New York Times* reported that the Pentagon had given private briefings to the military analysts of the various news networks regarding the Iraq war, allegedly to help spin their views to be more pro-military.[15] Congress promptly added to the Defense Department authorization bill for FY 2009 a directive to the GAO and Defense inspector general to investigate the practice and report back to Congress. In the meantime, the law banned the use of any funds for "publicity or propaganda purposes within the United States not otherwise specifically authorized by law," a slightly broader prohibition than bans that had been routinely included in annual spending bills.[16] That this was included in the annual authorization bill, rather than the common practice of inclusion in the appropriation bill, was an indication of expanding congressional interest in the subject.[17]

PUBLIC RELATIONS STASIS: CONGRESS'S SHORT-TERM INTERESTS VS. LONGER-TERM BUREAUCRATIC GOALS

External communication is inherent to public administration. Agencies seek to identify citizens eligible for a new program, inform the public of new laws and regulations that may affect them, conduct public information campaigns to promote safe and healthy lifestyles, and recruit the public to serve as eyes and ears of a law enforcement agency. These pragmatic functions are efficient and low-cost ways to implement an agency's mission. In other situations, agency external communication is driven by democratic rationales, such as engaging in media relations or being accountable to the citizenry through public reporting. These various purposes of agency external communications demonstrate that public relations is integral to government management. It is probably impossible to have the latter without the former. Yet public relations is also one of the methods that bureaucracies can use to achieve autonomy from political oversight. This is the central prism by which to analyze congressional efforts to control agency public relations.

In this descriptive historical theory of the congressional reaction to agency public relations and subsequent effort to manage it, I view departmental publicity as one of several key tools that an agency can use to achieve autonomy. Congressional influence over an agency that achieves autonomy is greatly reduced. Hence, the congressional reaction to public relations in public administration reflects the legislative logic of retaining leverage to impact the agency's fate. The success or failure of particular congressional proposals to limit agency public relations has been based, in part, on politicians trying to assess their constituents' opposition to bureaucratic publicity versus the popularity (and therefore degree of autonomy) of an agency. The floating majority that decides the passage or rejection of any particular publicity control proposal reflects shifting coalitions which, in turn, reflect political interpretations of those conflicting values.

Should readers be bothered by the apparent failure of all of these legislative efforts to dominate the bureaucracy? In some respects, the tug-of-war presented in this inquiry is about two institutions, both of which are held in low esteem in our political culture; Congress and the bureaucracy are both unpopular with the American citizenry. The average American may not care which of the two "wins" these battles, figuring that in the simplistic world of mass public opinion neither should.

Still, in classical democratic theory, no institution should be able to flout the decisions of the elected institutions of democratic government. This somewhat unsophisticated approach is premised on a principal-agent dynamic in democracy, of public administrators as the passive agents and implementers of decisions of Congress and the president. In early public administration, this was called the politics-administration dichotomy. The legislative and executive branches (the latter referring to the president) were the comanagers the bureaucracy, giving it marching orders. They were assumed to be dominating the administrative apparatus. Yet, based on how relatively easily federal departments and agencies were able to negate the intended impact of congressional controls over public relations, the relationship between elected institutions and federal agencies emerges as quite different from these expectations.

What comes into view is a confirmation of Carpenter's larger framework of the autonomizing forces of bureaucracy and, especially, the central role of public relations. To paraphrase Schattschneider's term of only a "semi-sovereign people" underlying modern U.S. democracy, perhaps it would be accurate to describe the bureaucracy as semi-sovereign, even in relation to Congress.[18] Another similarly descriptive term that could be resurrected is Riggs's "semi-powered bureaucracy" that operates within the U.S. political system.[19] Just as presidents have learned that they cannot control the executive branch with the stroke of a pen, similarly, Congress still has some learning to do. What is somewhat surprising about the sum total of this historical narrative is how little institutional memory Congress has displayed. Almost no feedback loop seems apparent. Congress has continued acting as though all that is needed is just another law, just another appropriation rider, just another prohibition. This inquiry has demonstrated how naïve such an approach always is, and yet that it continues to be employed throughout the twentieth century and in the twenty-first.

Perhaps there is some method in this apparent illogic of an unelected public institution being able to checkmate an elected one. After the 2008 crash of the global financial system and the Great Recession that followed, one of the most widely held critiques was that Wall Street had in place only incentives to maximize short-term profits. The previous regulatory framework had been denuded during the deregulation mania in the 1990s. In retrospect, it was government regulation that was viewed as being the counterweight to such short-term financial perspectives, having the de facto impact of imposing a longer-term perspective on these financial institutions. A parallel dynamic emerges from this historical inquiry. Congress, as an elected institution, is bent on short-term rewards, given that all members of the House face the electorate every two years, along with a third of the Senate. Legislators have inherent incentives for short-term gains, quick fixes, actions that appeal to the political culture of public opinion, and decisions that—at least—*look* good. Balancing Congress, the bureaucracy can be seen as a countervailing institution. Government agencies are (almost always) permanent institutions with long-term goals of survival, stability, and growth. Congressional efforts to choke off the bureaucracy's public voice are a threat to such long-term survival and autonomy. So, without overtly violating congressional prescriptions, government agencies seek to have a modicum of viable public relations as part of their inherent genetic desire to live on. This brings a certain stasis and balance to the relationship between Congress and the bureaucracy. Congress's failure to control in toto executive branch public relations suggests a surprising positive outcome, of a balance between short-term political decision making with the longer-term perspectives of public administration. If so, then the conclusions of this historical investigation are not ones to be greatly exercised by. Rather, they are somewhat reassuring about the future. In the long run, bureaucracy brings some balance to the always-teetering federal political system, with no one branch truly dominating the other. This creates a dynamic that has some positive aspects, especially given alternate scenarios.

Furthermore, more and more of (domestic) public administration is being transformed into the dissemination of information. This includes government-to-citizen contacts (e.g., agency web pages with helpful information about such topics as weather, traffic, flight status, crime locations, and property assessments) and citizen-to-government transactions (such as paying taxes, paying parking tickets, and renewing drivers' licenses). Web-based communication permits agencies to e-mail relevant information to individuals based on previously expressed interests, to deliver electronic payment of government benefits, and even to conduct e-voting. In such circumstances, the role of public relations (broadly defined) increases. Given that public relations *is* the dissemination of information, and as more and more of public administration becomes digital information interactions, the public voice of the bureaucracy becomes nearly tantamount to public administration in toto. That makes it even more difficult for Congress to differentiate between good and bad public relations.

As discussed in the Introduction and demonstrated in the case studies presented here, the purposes and effects of government public relations overlap. In the digital era, more and more agency contacts with the citizenry will be fully justifiable to Congress on the pragmatic and democratic rationales of such activities. However, the self-serving benefits to the agency in terms of generating public support are inextricably embedded in them. Therefore, Congress will likely continue to react negatively to agency use of publicity to increase autonomy, but simultaneously Congress will have ever greater difficulty separating out what a legislative majority might define as bad public relations from good.

One can reasonably expect that, into the indefinite future, there will continue to be ad hoc and occasional majorities in Congress trying to control agency publicity and trying to prevent external communication activities from contributing to the autonomizing goal of the federal bureaucracy. And it will continue to be well nigh an impossible and Sisyphean quest.

NOTES

ABBREVIATIONS

Comp. Gen.	*Comptroller General Decisions* (regularly published compilation of major GAO decisions)
CR	*Congressional Record*
F. Supp.	*Federal Supplement* (regularly published compilation of major decisions of U.S. district courts)
Op. OLC	*Opinions of the Office of Legal Counsel* (regularly published compilation of major opinions)
P.L.	Public Law
Stat.	*Statutes at Large* (all laws and regulations passed by Congress, published by the Office of the Federal Register)
USC	United States Code

INTRODUCTION

1. See chap. 1. Roosevelt parsed his public commitment closely and figured out a way to circumvent his pledge without explicitly violating it.

2. 119 *Stat.* 301.

3. Emmerich, *Essays on Federal Reorganization,* 33–60; Simon, Smithburg, and Thompson, *Public Administration,* chaps. 18–19; Fenno, *President's Cabinet,* 228–229; Roberts, *Collapse of Fortress Bush,* 72.

4. Carpenter, *Forging of Bureaucratic Autonomy,* 355. In a 2009 management advice best seller, Daniel H. Pink argued more broadly that human behavior was largely

driven by a desire for autonomy and that all managers should base their organizational oversight on this principle (*Drive: The Surprising Truth about What Motivates Us*. New York: Riverhead, 2009).

5. Carpenter, *Forging of Bureaucratic Autonomy*, 1.

6. Arnold, *Logic of Congressional Action*, 7.

7. Carpenter, *Forging of Bureaucratic Autonomy*, 380n47, emphasis added.

8. Schick, "Congress and the Details."

9. Carpenter, *Forging of Bureaucratic Autonomy*, 364.

10. Lippmann, *Public Opinion*, 218.

11. Carpenter, *Forging of Bureaucratic Autonomy*, 354, quoting Herring, "Social Forces and the Reorganization," 191.

12. Herring, "Official Publicity," 170–171, 174.

13. Herring, *Public Administration*, 375.

14. McCamy, *Government Publicity*; and "Public Relations in Public Administration."

15. This typology of McCamy's research into agency publicity is mine, not McCamy's. For a more recent overview of the purposes of public relations in public administration, see Lee, *Government Public Relations.*

16. Lippmann, *Public Opinion*, 229.

17. Beyle, *Governmental Reporting in Chicago*; National Committee on Public Reporting, *Public Reporting*. For a more detailed discussion of the significance of McCamy and Beyle's writings, see Lee, "Herman Beyle."

18. McCamy, *Government Publicity*, 25, emphasis added.

19. McCamy, "Public Relations," 303.

20. Graham, "Trends in Teaching," 73; Simon, Smithburg, and Thompson, *Public Administration*, 415; Pimlott, *Public Relations and American Democracy*, 88, 72.

21. Rourke, *Bureaucracy, Politics, and Public Policy*, 3rd ed., 50. Rourke originally made this observation in 1969 in the first edition of the book (12–13) and retained it unchanged through to the third and last edition in 1984.

22. Caro, *Master of the Senate*, 315; Sheehan, *Fiery Peace*, 391.

23. Carpenter, *Forging of Bureaucratic Autonomy*, 373n8.

24. "Maps for Gold Searchers," *New York Times*, April 8, 1894, 24.

25. Bertelli and Lynn, *Madison's Managers*, 105ff.

26. Meier and O'Toole, *Bureaucracy in a Democratic State*, 66.

27. Shipan, "Congress and the Bureaucracy," 444–445. My appreciation to one of the anonymous reviewers for suggesting using congressional *reaction* to agency public relations as a unifying theme for this inquiry.

28. The focus here on authoritative congressional actions was partly influenced by Orren and Skowronek's emphasis on authority as a key component of their definition of political development (*Search*, chap. 4).

29. Liu and Horsley, "Government Communication Decision Wheel."

30. R. W. Pullman, "Foes of Conservation Want Check on Federal Publicity," *Atlanta Constitution*, August 14, 1910, C8.

31. U.S. House, Select Committee on Lobbying Activities, *Role of Lobbying in Representative Self-Government*, 146, 149.

32. Kosar, "Executive Branch and Propaganda," 794–795.

33. Lee, "Public Relations Program."

34. Lee, "Case Study"; "Congressional Controversy"; and "Public Affairs."

35. Mayhew, *Congress*.

36. Brookings: U.S. Senate, Select Committee to Investigate the Executive Agencies, *Investigation of Executive Agencies*, 528–553; Tydings: U.S. Senate, Committee on Appropriations, Subcommittee on Senate Resolution 223, *Transfer of Employees*; Harness: U.S. House, Committee on Expenditures in the Executive Departments, Publicity and Propaganda Subcommittee, *Investigation of the Participation of Federal Officials in the Formation and Operation of Health Workshops*; *Investigation of Agricultural Adjustment Agency*; *Investigation of Bureau of Reclamation*; *Investigation of Participation of Federal Officials of the Department of the Army*; and *Final Report*.

37. Horn, *Unused Power*, 186; Kirst, *Congress without Passing Laws*.

38. *CR* 40:1 (December 6, 1905): 177.

39. *CR* 40:1 (December 15, 1905): 442.

40. *CR* 40:1 (December 16, 1905): 500.

41. *CR* 40:2 (January 26, 1906): 1686.

42. *CR* 42:5 (March 30, 1908): 4137.

43. *CR* 42:5 (March 30, 1908): 4139.

44. *CR* 42:6 (May 7, 1908): 5870.

45. *CR* 42:6 (May 9, 1908): 6021.

46. U.S. House, Committee on the Census, *Press Bureau*, 24.

47. U.S. House, Committee on Rules, *Department Press Agents*, 6.

48. Ibid., 17.

49. *CR* 40:2 (January 29, 1906): 1688.

50. U.S. Senate, Committee on Agriculture and Forestry, *Agricultural Appropriation Bill*, 14–15.

51. *CR* 42:6 (May 7, 1908): 5870.

52. Warren B. Francis, "Reorganization Plan Scored as Taber Seeks to Block Move," *Los Angeles Times*, April 27, 1939, 6.

53. U.S. House, Committee on Armed Services, *Allegations of Improper Lobbying*, 199.

54. Safire, *Safire's Political Dictionary*, 581–582; Walton, *Media Argumentation*, chap. 3.

55. Berry, "Nonprofits and Civic Engagement," 571.

56. Sproule, *Propaganda and Democracy*, chap. 2.

57. *CR* 40:1 (December 6, 1905): 193. Clearly, an unnecessary expenditure is different from an improper one, the latter the normative critique summarized in the preceding categories.

58. *CR* 40:2 (January 23, 1906): 1441.

59. *CR* 40:1 (December 15, 1905): 442.

60. *CR* 40:1 (December 16, 1905): 500.

61. *CR* 40:1 (December 6, 1905): 184.

62. *CR* 42:5 (March 30, 1908): 4137.

63. Ibid., 4140.

64. *CR* 42:6 (May 7, 1908): 5870.

65. AP, "Carter Blames Pinchot for Disastrous Forest Fires," *Los Angeles Times,* August 30, 1910, I13.

66. U.S. House, Committee on Rules, *Department Press Agents,* 6.

67. *CR* 40:1 (December 6, 1905): 193.

68. *CR* 42:7 (May 11, 1908): 6073.

69. *CR* 42:5 (March 30, 1908): 4140.

70. *CR* 40:2 (January 23, 1906): 1441.

71. *CR* 40:1 (December 6, 1905): 181.

72. *CR* 42:5 (March 30, 1908): 4137.

73. Ibid., 4139.

74. U.S. House, Committee on Rules, *Department Press Agents,* 5.

75. Houston, *Eight Years,* 201.

76. U.S. House, Committee on Rules, *Department Press Agents,* 12 (Hunt quote), 7 (Nelson quote).

77. "Frenzied Publicity" (editorial), *Atlanta Constitution,* February 11, 1918, 4.

78. Delorme and Fedler, "Journalists' Hostility."

79. Two of the few exceptions to the rule were editorials endorsing the value of the public information staff at the USDA: "The Government and Publicity" (editorial), *Outlook* 105 (September 27, 1913), 148* (asterisk in original); and "The Press Agents" (editorial), *Washington Times,* July 23, 1914, 6.

PROLOGUE

1. John, *Spreading the News,* 68.

2. Cutlip, "Unseen Power," 23.

3. Stiles, *First Tycoon,* 256, 580.

4. Ritchie, *Press Gallery,* chap. 7. I suggest a distinction between USGS public relations by Powell and earlier external communications by the USDA. At about the same time as Powell's and Croffut's publicity efforts, Agriculture secretary Jeremiah Rusk (1889–93) was overseeing an extensive and innovative expansion of departmental public information programs too. Those activities included broad dissemination of brochures and pamphlets, an extensive press relations program,

and development of the department's yearbook as a popular publication for mass distribution (White, *Republican Era*, 241–242). However, these activities were aimed at reaching farmers, the department's central constituency. They were not aimed at the public at large, opinion leaders, and the like. These early external communication activities by the USDA would be comparable to USGS publications oriented solely to scientists. Unlike the USDA, Powell also wanted his publications to reach larger portions of the citizenry.

5. Terrell, *Man Who Rediscovered America*, 4.

6. U.S. Senate, Committee on Printing, *Public Printing*, 234, emphasis added.

7. Darrah, *Powell of the Colorado*, 278.

8. Ritchie, *Press Gallery*, 196.

9. "Uncle Sam Is an Editor," *Boston Globe*, November 25, 1894, 14.

10. White, *Tale of a Comet*, 108.

11. 28 *Stat.* 601. Congress passed the bill in 1894, but it was not signed into law until early 1895.

CHAPTER 1

1. Gould, *Modern American Presidency*, 21–22; Ponder, *Managing the Press*, chap. 2. Gould argues that the first modern president was McKinley, but the consensus of historians and political scientists seems to give the nod to Roosevelt.

2. "Cannon Pokes Fun at Others' Hobbies," *New York Times*, February 16, 1910, 3.

3. Ponder, *Managing the Press*,18.

4. When Roosevelt inquired with his attorney general about developing a post hoc legal justification for his actions, Philander Knox responded, "Oh, Mr. President, do not let so great an achievement suffer from any taint of legality" (Boot, *Savage Wars of Peace*, 134).

5. Roosevelt set another precedent when he visited the canal in 1906. Up till then, no sitting president had ever been outside the country. His trip prompted concerns about its very constitutionality: Could a president leave the country and still hold that office? Could a president exercise his powers while outside the United States? Characteristically, Roosevelt brushed those concerns aside and went ahead with his trip. The precedent was so unusual that it was not repeated until 1919, when President Wilson went to Paris for the post–World War I peace conference.

6. Bishop had written the "official" Roosevelt biography used in the 1904 campaign, leading the *New York Times* to editorialize that Bishop's appointment as Panama Canal Commission secretary was simply a reward for his campaign work ("Money for the Canal" [editorial], *New York Times*, December 12, 1905, 8).

7. McCullough, *Path between the Seas*, 536.

8. "Anti-Odell Men Plan Fight to Name Root," *New York Times*, May 9, 1904, 3. Also, "Bishop Makes a Denial," *New York Times*, May 10, 1904, 1.

9. Roosevelt had been President McKinley's vice president and then became president when McKinley was assassinated in 1901, only six months into his second term.

10. "Railroads Fear Federal Action," *Chicago Tribune*, February 23, 1905, 8.

11. Sproule, *Propaganda and Democracy*, 22.

12. Cutlip, *Unseen Power*, 20–21; "Educational Campaign Begun," *New York Times*, May 27, 1905, 8.

13. "Roads Accused by Press: Western Editors Charge 'Bribery' in Rate Campaign," *Chicago Tribune*, October 1, 1905, G21.

14. "Big Railroad Bureau Dies: Sudden Demise of Organization to Create Public Sentiment," *Chicago Tribune*, November 12, 1905, 1.

15. The secretary of war was the head of the Department of the Army (sometimes called the War Department), the civilian agency overseeing the U.S. Army. Similarly, there was a secretary of the navy who, as head of the Navy Department, oversaw the U.S. Navy. Both were cabinet secretaries. In the post–World War II reorganization of the military, the secretary of war was renamed the secretary of the army. Then, all such posts (including the new Air Force secretary) were significantly downgraded with the merger of all the military services and their respective civilian departments into the Department of Defense, headed by the secretary of defense. Now only the Defense secretary has cabinet rank. Taft was designated by Theodore Roosevelt to be his successor, when Roosevelt chose not to run for a full second term in 1908. However, the two had a falling out during Taft's term as president, and Roosevelt ran against him when he sought reelection in 1912. The split in the Republican vote led to the election of Woodrow Wilson, only the second Democratic president since the Civil War.

16. Speech by Secretary of War William Howard Taft to the St. Louis (Mo.) Commercial Club, November 18, 1905 (*CR* 40:1 [December 7, 1905]: 241). A partial transcript of the speech, including most of this quotation, was also printed in the *New York Times*, where it differed from the "official" version only in minor stylistic and grammatical details ("Real Work on Canal Is Being Done—Taft," November 19, 1905, 5).

17. U.S. Senate, Committee on Appropriations, *Panama Canal*, 88, 92–93.

18. Ibid., 58–59. Known as "Pitchfork Ben," Senator Tillman was a virulent racist, demagogue, and political terrorist who built and maintained his political career on white supremacy. He helped repeal state Reconstruction laws and replace them with the Jim Crow regime. At the beginning of his political career he was a leader of vigilantes who used terrorism and mob violence to disenfranchise African American voters (Kantrowitz, *Ben Tillman*).

19. "Names Canal Press Agent," *Washington Post*, September 6, 1905, 2. See also "Office for J. B. Bishop," *New York Times*, September 6, 1905, 4; and "Press Agent for a Canal: Joseph B. Bishop Well Fitted for the Work by His Experience," *Washington Post*, September 16, 1905, 4. Bishop's duties were not mentioned in

the official commission resolution hiring him, but external communications responsibilities were formally part of his job. For example, in an official communication
to a member of Congress, Shonts wrote, "In addition to the duties set forth in
the resolution cited, Mr. Bishop has charge of the publicity and literary branches
of the Commission's work. He prepares the various statements which the chairman
or the Commission as a body may desire to make public" (*CR* 40:1[December 13,
1905]: 346).

20. "Names Canal Press Agent," *Washington Post,* September 6, 1905, 2.

21. Although the construction "speaker's bureau" is still in wide usage in
the twenty-first century, use of its relative, the "literary bureau," has lapsed.
These were related terms, mostly referring to the activities of political parties
and campaigns in late nineteenth-century. The former supplied speakers and
the latter provided written materials. Contrary to the contemporary meaning of
"literary," the term as used then did *not* apply to Bishop's responsibility for
writing the official history of the canal. Rather "literary bureau" was often used
as a synonym for "publicity bureau" or "press bureau," with the title literally
focusing more on the act of writing than on the subsequent dissemination of
that written information.

The phrase "literary bureau" was mostly used in reference to the publicity
activities of political parties and election campaigns. Credit for the concept and
term is given to Samuel J. Tilden, in his successful race for governor of New
York in 1874. In 1876, he partially used a literary bureau approach in his (unsuccessful) campaign as the Democratic nominee for president. His innovation was
gradually incorporated during the 1880s and '90s by both national parties as a
standard component of their campaign efforts (McGerr, *Decline of Popular Politics,*
chap. 4). Still, "literary bureau" was also sometimes used by businesses and non-
profit organizations for their public information offices.

References to literary bureaus in government agencies, rather than politics,
were less frequent, especially as a formal and official title. An example of the
term's usage as a formal title was for an office established by New York City to
disseminate information about public health threats and guidelines for prevention ("Streets Must Be Clean," *New York Times,* January 12, 1895, 9). In the federal
government, usage appears to have been limited solely to informal titles, usually
with a derogatory meaning. For example, in 1899 the lobbying effort by the
Department of Treasury was described by a newspaper as a "literary bureau,"
though that was not the formal name of the office ("National Capital Topics,"
New York Times, June 18, 1899, 13). That same year, critics of the U.S. Pension
commissioner, annoyed at the good press he was getting, criticized him for
apparently maintaining a literary bureau within his office ("Evan's 'Literary Bureau,'"
New York Times, September 6, 1899, 4). In 1902, during a House floor debate, a
speaker mocked a well-written committee minority report as probably having
been secretly drafted by the "literary bureau" of the federal agency seeking to

promote its view of the legislation (*CR* 35:3 [March 3, 1902]: 2315). In 1907, during the controversy over the U.S. Forest Service's press releases (see chapter 2), the *Washington Post* referred negatively to the Forest Service press office as a "literary bureau" ("Pinchot Likes Puffs," August 11, 1907, E1).

22. Bishop, *Notes and Anecdotes*, 125.

23. U.S. Senate, Committee on Appropriations, *Panama Canal*, 87.

24. "Panama Board Annuls $50,000,000 Contract," *New York Times*, October 12, 1905, 2.

25. "No Plan to Dig Canal Made by Commission," *New York Times*, October 24, 1905, 7.

26. "$129,262 to Dig Canal, $784,085 for Salaries: Secretary of Commission Tells How $4,009,959 Was Spent," *New York Times*, October 29, 1905, 6.

27. U.S. Senate, Committee on Appropriations, *Panama Canal*, 79.

28. Ibid., 87.

29. "$129,262 to Dig Canal," *New York Times*, October 29, 1905, 6.

30. U.S. Senate, Committee on Appropriations, *Panama Canal*, 93.

31. "Hot Time in Prospect for Canal Commission: First Report to Congress May Cause Trouble," *New York Times*, November 23, 1905, 5.

32. "The Muzzle Order Revoked" (editorial), *New York Times*, November 7, 1905, 8, quoting from an earlier story in the *New York Evening Post*; U.S. Senate, Committee on Appropriations, *Panama Canal*, 79, 82.

33. U.S. Senate, Committee on Appropriations, *Panama Canal*, 83.

34. Ibid., 63–64.

35. "No Plan to Dig Canal Made by Commission," *New York Times*, October 24, 1905, 7.

36. "The Muzzle Order Revoked" (editorial), *New York Times*, November 7, 1905, 8.

37. Quoted by the *New York Times* in editorial (ibid.).

38. Bishop, *Notes and Anecdotes*, 126–128.

39. A. Maurice Low, "Criticism of the Panama Salaries," *Boston Globe*, December 8, 1905, 16.

40. The cycles of congressional sessions during the nineteenth century and extending into the beginning of the twentieth were different from contemporary practice. A new Congress, even though it was elected in November of an even-numbered year, would not take office until about a year later. This first session of a Congress was sometimes called the "long session." Congress's second session (aka "short session") would usually begin late in the even-numbered (election) year and conclude the next spring. Presidents were inaugurated toward the end of the second session. Then, Congress would promptly adjourn sine die. The newly elected Congress would convene for its first session about nine months after the president took office. In contemporary terms, the second session was always a "lame duck" session, occurring after an election. However, given the

mores and slower pace of life of the nineteenth and early twentieth centuries, political perceptions of the second session of a Congress did not discount as steeply its actions as would be the case a century later. Nowadays, it is rare for a Congress to take any significant new action after the November election. A major exception to this generalization was the House vote to impeach President Clinton in December 1998.

41. *CR* 40:1 (December 4, 1905): 55.

42. *CR* 40:1 (December 6, 1905): 177.

43. Ibid., 44. Given that the bill proposed spending $16.5 million and Bishop's salary was $10,000 a year, the debate could be seen as a manifestation of Parkinson's Law of Triviality: "The time spent on any item of the agenda will be in inverse proportion to the sum involved" (Parkinson, *Parkinson's Law*, 40). Yet the unprecedented step of hiring a press agent in a federal agency was new and significant, thereby negating somewhat Parkinson's cynical perspective.

45. *CR* 40:1 (December 6, 1905): 181–182.

46. Ibid., 198, 193. The latter statement was made by Congressman Henry Clayton (D-Ala.), who was also quoted by the *Washington Post* as saying, "What does the Canal Commission want of a $10,000 press agent? Why, you can go out and hire two cheap Congressmen anywhere for that sum of money" ("Press Agent Secrecy," December 7, 1905, 4). That indiscreet comment and insult were omitted, for understandable reasons, from the printed record of the floor debate in the *Congressional Record.*

47. *CR* 40:1 (December 6, 1905): 193.

48. "Attack Begun in House on the Canal Account," *New York Times,* December 7, 1905, 1; "$16,500,000 Ready for Panama Canal," *Chicago Tribune,* December 7, 1905, 4; and Dickinson, "Three $10,000 Men," *Washington Post,* December 8, 1905, 1. (During the shift from the journalistic custom of non-bylined newspaper articles to bylined ones, sometimes only the last name of the reporter was provided.)

49. "Press Agent Secrecy," *Washington Post,* December 7, 1905, 4; "Canal Bill Threatened with Opposition in Senate," *New York Times,* December 8, 1905, 4. The article mistakenly listed Bishop's salary as $9,000 a year instead of $10,000.

50. U.S. Senate, Committee on Appropriations, *Panama Canal,* 59, 70 (Tillman), 64 (Hale).

51. "Probe for Panama," *Washington Post,* December 14, 1905, 1.

52. U.S. Senate, Committee on Appropriations, *Panama Canal,* 92; *CR* 40:1 (December 15, 1905): 441.

53. U.S. Senate, Committee on Appropriations, *Panama Canal,* 92. Taft's and Shont's testimony covered seventy-eight pages of the hearing transcript, Bishop's only sixteen.

54. *CR* 40:1 (December 13, 1905): 336–337; "Taft Agrees to Accept $11,000,000 for Canal," *New York Times,* December 13, 1905, 4.

55. *CR* 40:1 (December 14, 1905): 388ff.

56. *CR* 40:1 (December 15, 1905): 441–442.

57. Ibid., 442.

58. Ibid., 449.

59. "Tillman Won't Be Stumbling Block," *Chicago Tribune*, December 16, 1905, 6; "Tillman Angered," *Washington Post*, December 16, 1905, 1.

60. *CR* 40:1 (December 16, 1905): 500.

61. Ibid.

62. Ibid., 502.

63. "Bishop Called Off: Senator Hale Announces End of Canal Press Agency," *Washington Post*, December 17, 1905, 1; "Emergency Canal Bill Passed by the Senate," *New York Times*, December 17, 1905, 1.

64. *CR* 40:2 (January 23, 1905): 1441.

65. "How to Place Bishop, Roosevelt's Problem," *New York Times*, December 18, 1905, 4; "Hasn't Seen Bishop's Resignation," *Washington Post*, December 19, 1905, C1.

66. John Callan O'Laughlin, "President Makes J. B. Bishop Member of Canal Commission," *Chicago Tribune*, December 20, 1905, 8; "To Lift the Lid," *Los Angeles Times*, December 21, 1905, I1.

67. Many other political reasons were at play as well, such as the eternal struggle for predominance between the two branches, factional rivalries, partisanship, and backlash against Roosevelt's popularity.

68. "Bishop Is Opposed," *Washington Post*, March 21, 1906, 4; "Bishop Not on List: President Names New Panama Canal Commission," *Washington Post*, July 3, 1906, 3.

69. Bishop, *Notes and Anecdotes*, 124.

70. Bishop, *Panama Gateway*; Bishop and Bishop, *Goethals*.

71. McCullough, *Path between the Seas*, 536.

72. *CR* 42:7 (May 11, 1908): 6071.

73. *CR* 42:6 (May 9, 1908): 6022.

74. *CR* 50:5 (September 6, 1913): 4411.

CHAPTER 2

1. Although this chapter is based mostly on primary sources, some excellent published and unpublished research helped me identify some of those primary sources (Ponder, *Managing the Press*; "Executive Publicity"; "Gifford Pinchot"; "Progressive Drive"; and "Publicity in the Interest"; Goodman, "Origins of a Continuing Conflict").

2. There was also a West versus Washington element in this conflict (Harrison, *Congress, Progressive Reform*,169).

3. For a discussion of the conservation movement within the broader context of the Progressive Era, see McGerr, *Fierce Discontent*, 164–169.

4. As is usual in political conflict, the specifics of the issue that prompted Heyburn's call for a congressional investigation were eye-glazingly technical. In this case, the federal government was seeking to reobtain the title to some lands it had deeded to the railroads as part of the land grant policy. The government sought the lands in order to designate them as forest reserves. In return, the railroad would be permitted to obtain titles to an equal amount of acreage of other federally owned lands, even in another state. Heyburn was complaining that the state (in this case Idaho) where federal lands were being transferred *to* the railroad was being victimized by events originating in another state. This inter-state trading of lands by the federal government and the railroads, he argued, was deleterious to his state because it reduced the amount of federal land in Idaho that could be developed by industry and business or settled by newcomers.

Committee members gently argued with him that these precise kinds of transfers were explicitly permitted by legislation passed in 1901. Heyburn had developed a hair-splitting interpretation of the language of that act, claiming that the transfer power delegated to the president was much more circumscribed and, for some kinds of transfers, was not permitted explicitly by the law. Therefore, he argued, the conveyance of titles to federal lands in Idaho to the railroads in return for designating former federal lands held by railroads in other states as forest reserves was illegal.

5. U.S. Senate, Committee on Public Lands, *Forest-Reserve Lands,* 7.

6. For a more detailed review of Heyburn's position on forestry, see Cook, "Study of the Political Career," chap. 4.

7. Carpenter, *Forging of Bureaucratic Autonomy,* especially chap. 8.

8. Miller, *Gifford Pinchot;* McGeary, *Gifford Pinchot;* Pinkett, *Gifford Pinchot.*

9. Quoted in Ponder, *Managing the Press,* 45. By now Roosevelt had been reelected to a full term, and this occurred a few months after his inauguration. In those days, presidential inaugurations were in March. During his presidency, Franklin Roosevelt permanently moved the date up to January 20 to shorten the interregnum.

10. "Heyburn Attacked Policy: President Refused to Permit Politics to Affect Forest Reserves," *Washington Post,* September 28, 1905, 2.

11. Sheingate, "'Publicity and the Progressive Era," 469–470.

12. U.S. House, Committee on Agriculture, *Agricultural Appropriation Bill,* 276.

13. Ibid., 276–277.

14. Pinchot, *Breaking New Ground,* 156.

15. Quoted in Steen, *U.S. Forest Service,* 86.

16. Carpenter, *Forging of Bureaucratic Autonomy,* 1, 275–288.

17. Ponder, *Managing the Press,* 39.

18. *CR* 42:5 (March 30, 1908): 4138.

19. U.S. Senate, Committee on Agriculture and Forestry, *Agricultural Appropriation Bill,* 16.

20. Miller, *Gifford Pinchot*, 158–159; Ponder, *Managing the Press*, chap. 3; McGeary, *Gifford Pinchot*, 50–51, 60; Pinkett, *Gifford Pinchot*, 81–86.

21. "Pinchot Likes Puffs," *Washington Post*, August 11, 1907, E1.

22. That was how the House Appropriations Committee had treated the bill providing additional funding for the Panama Canal's construction in late 1905 (chapter 1).

23. That sole hearing was on preservation of historic and prehistoric ruins located on federal lands.

24. Notation in the bound minutes of the Committee on Public Lands during the 59th Congress for its meeting on January 17, 1906 (e-mail to the author from Rod Ross, Archivist, Center for Legislative Archives, April 25, 2005). The custom of the U.S. Congress is to publish transcripts of committee *hearings*, but not of committee *meetings*. As a result, there is no verbatim record of Heyburn's comments that day. Searches of the archival holdings related to Heyburn at the Idaho State Historical Society and the special collections of the University of Idaho Library did not locate any material related to his comments at this meeting (e-mail from Carol Bowler, Archivist, Idaho State Historical Society, April 27, 2005; and e-mail from Terry Abraham, Head, Special Collections and Archives, Library, University of Idaho, April 22, 2005).

25. "Senator Heyburn Attacks the Bureau of Forestry," *Washington Post*, January 18, 1906, 4. The *Post* coverage contained a relatively important error, referring to the committee holding a public hearing rather than convening for a business meeting.

26. *CR* 40:2 (January 29, 1906): 1686. Tillman was being consistent; he had also criticized Bishop's press activities at the Panama Canal Commission (chapter 1). The agency's name had been changed to Forest Service in 1905, but Tillman was still using its previous name.

27. Ibid., 1688. The term "combination" was used with a meaning that is archaic in the twenty-first century. It meant a group working together for negative purposes. It was common for Roosevelt to denounce industrial and economic combinations, such as illegal cooperation by supposed competitors for economic advantage. Heyburn was mocking Roosevelt's rhetoric by describing the Forest Service's press bureau and its cooperation with the White House as a combination.

28. Ibid.

29. "Another Press Agency Attacked by Senator," *New York Times*, January 30, 1906, 4; "Aired the Boycott," *Washington Post*, January 30, 1906, 4. A summary of Heyburn's speech was in the second half of the *Post* article. The first half (and headline) dealt with a Chinese boycott of U.S. products, in reaction to discriminatory treatment in the United States of Chinese immigrants and temporary workers.

30. U.S. House, Committee on Expenditures in the Agricultural Department, *Expenditures in the Department of Agriculture*, 17.

31. Ponder, *Managing the Press*, 45.

32. "Pinchot Likes Puffs," *Washington Post,* August 11, 1907, E1.

33. The U.S. Constitution requires that all taxing and spending bills originate in the House. That creates an inevitable legislative dynamic of the Senate acting akin to a court of appeals for those who are unhappy with provisions in the House-approved version of a bill.

34. U.S. House, Committee on Agriculture, *Agricultural Appropriation Bill,* 276–277.

35. Pinchot's diaries are in the collection of the Manuscript Division at the Library of Congress. Unfortunately, the collection does not cover all the years of his career. Container No. 4 ends with 1907 and Container No. 5 begins with 1910. Therefore, Pinchot's private ruminations about the congressional initiative in 1908 to circumscribe Forest Service public relations remain unknown.

36. *CR* 42:5 (March 30, 1908): 4137. Mondell, despite his earlier alliance with western interests, had shifted sides and in 1903 agreed to sponsor legislation transferring forest management to Pinchot's bureau (Carpenter, *Forging of Bureaucratic Autonomy,* 280–282). See also Herold, "Historical Perspectives on Government Communication," 15.

37. *CR* 42:5 (March 30, 1908): 4137.

38. *CR* 42:5 (April 1, 1908): 4241. A few days later, Pinchot formally responded to the charge, unequivocally denying Mondell's charges.

39. Ibid., 4140; "Assail Forestry Head," *Washington Post,* March 31, 1908, 4; "Pinchot Defends His Policy," *Washington Post,* April 4, 1905, 4. The identical issue arose nearly a century later regarding video news releases (chapter 8).

40. U.S. Senate, Committee on Agriculture and Forestry, *Agricultural Appropriation Bill,* 11, 14.

41. *CR* 42:6 (May 9, 1908): 6020.

42. *CR* 42:6 (April 24, 1908): 5151.

43. U.S. Senate, *Attendance of Members of Forest Service at Meetings; A Statement of the Attendance of Members of the Forest Service.*

44. Ponder, *Managing the Press,* 45.

45. *CR* 42:6 (May 5, 1908): 5731.

46. *CR* 42:6 (May 7, 1908): 5870–5872; (May 9, 1908): 5984–6022; 42:7 (May 11, 1908): 6055–6075.

47. *CR* 42:6 (May 9, 1905): 6020.

48. *CR* 42:7 (May 11, 1908): 6073.

49. Ibid.

50. Ibid., 6074.

51. "Pinchot Likes Puffs," *Washington Post,* August 11, 1907, E1.

52. *CR* 42:7 (May 11, 1908): 6075.

53. "Forest Sum Doubled," *Washington Post,* May 12, 1908, 4. The second subheadline, "Press Bureau Is Shut Out," was an inaccurate characterization of the meaning of the Warren amendment that was adopted.

54. Ibid.; "Declares Franks Misused," *Washington Post*, May 10, 1908, 7.

55. U.S. Congress, Committee of Conference, *Agricultural Appropriation Bill*, 1, 5. The compromise language recommended by the conference committee contained a few minor and nonsubstantive changes in the wording of the Mondell and Warren amendments, so the final statutory language that was enacted was not exactly what had been adopted by the House and Senate.

56. "Bill Is Cut $480,380," *Washington Post*, May 20, 1908, 4; *CR* 42:7 (May 21, 1908): 6679–6680; 35 *Stat.* 259.

57. There were several negative references to Forest Service public relations in the Senate floor debate, including by Heyburn, but there were no motions or amendments (*CR* 43:4 [February 25, 1909]: 3088–3104); 35 *Stat.* 1048.

58. *CR* 45:2 (February 1, 1910): 1338–1360.

59. *CR* 45:2 (February 3, 1910): 1444–1446; "Agricultural Bill Passed," *Washington Post*, February 4, 1910, 2.

60. The bill allocated funding to the legislative and judicial branches and to miscellaneous federal departments and agencies that did not have their "own" annual appropriation bill.

61. *CR* 45:3 (March 11, 1910): 3073–3078.

62. "Taft Gag Is Loosened: Dickinson's Bureau Chiefs May Talk Discreetly— Press Agents May Go," *New York Times*, December 8, 1909, 1.

63. Unusually, this bill required three conference committees before passing.

64. 42 *Stat.* 521; 16 *USC* 556. In 1955, the comptroller general offered in a formal opinion that the provision also affected scientific publications, not just lay-oriented ones (35 *Comp. Gen.* 52–55). In reaction, Congress enacted in 1958 language exempting "scientific and technical articles prepared for or published in scientific publications" from the restrictions of the 1908 law (72 *Stat.* 218). In 1993, the General Accounting Office issued another interpretation of the law, clarifying that paid advertising by the Forest Service to promote public awareness of, and attendance at, events related to National Fishing Week were permissible (U.S. GAO, Decision B-251887, July 22, 1993).

65. Steen, *U.S. Forest Service*, 86.

66. McGeary, *Gifford Pinchot*, 90.

67. Ponder, "Executive Publicity," 183.

68. Pinchot continued to use publicity as a device for pursuing the Forest Service's political autonomy even after leaving office. In December 1921, he mailed out six thousand copies of a press release to daily newspapers around the country opposing the proposed transfer of the Forest Service from the USDA to the Interior Department (McCartney, *Teapot Dome Scandal*, 105). At the time, Interior secretary Albert Fall was lobbying President Harding for the transfer of the Forest Service to his department. Pinchot's (and others') efforts were successful. The Forest Service has remained in the USDA to the present. Secretary Fall, it later turned out, was the corrupt federal official at the center of the Teapot

Dome scandal. Presumably, had Fall gotten control of the Forest Service, he could have shifted its policies to promoting development and exploitation over conservation—while pocketing graft from those he gave such privileges to.

69. Hutchinson, "Public Relations;" Smith, *Forest Service*, 96–97, 104–105.

70. U.S. Department of Agriculture, Forest Service, *Public Relations Course.*

71. Kaufman, *Forest Ranger*, 195–197.

CHAPTER 3

1. Taft had been secretary of war during the controversy over Bishop's work as a press agent at the Panama Canal Commission and defended the practice at a Senate committee hearing (chapter 1).

2. U.S. House, Committee on Rules, *Department Press Agents*, 10. According to Carpenter, the USDA was a hotbed of autonomizing bureaus during this period (*Forging of Bureaucratic Autonomy*).

3. Executive Order 1101, June 29, 1909. Besides its issuance as a free-standing legal document, the text of the executive order was reproduced in the CSC's annual report for FY 1909 (U.S. Congress, *Twenty-Sixth Annual Report of the United States Civil Service Commission*, 132).

4. Ibid. This was quite a slam at the CSC and the premise that merit-based appointments would yield the best candidate.

5. This was a relatively common practice at the time in Washington, D.C. A cursory review of all executive orders signed by presidents in the late nineteenth and early twentieth centuries reveals scores of such actions.

6. Smith, "Old-Time Publicity Bureaus."

7. Proctor, "First Marine Corps Publicity Bureau."

8. "Army and Navy Gossip," *Washington Post*, June 29, 1913, ES2.

9. Lindsay, *This High Name*, chap. 2. The "Publicity Bureau" terminology sank deep into the lingo of the military services, even after the ban on employing publicity experts was enacted in 1913 (see chapter 4). After World War I, the Marine Corps still had a Publicity Bureau ("Marine in Bronze Bought by Marines," *Boston Globe*, July 13, 1919, 42). The nomenclature continued in use decades after the ban. For example, in 1943 the U.S. Army still had a unit called the Recruiting Publicity Bureau ("Bricker Attacks Government's $100,000,000 Publicity Staff," *American Press*, 61:9 [July 1943], 4). A 1951 House Appropriations Committee report explicitly referred to *maintaining* funding for the Marine Corps' "Publicity Bureau" (U.S. House, Committee on Appropriations, *Department of Defense Appropriation Bill, 1952*, 60)—this in a year when congressional efforts to control agency public relations were at their peak (see chapters 8–10). It is somewhat amazing that the military would still have any unit called, formally, a "publicity bureau" after the 1913 ban on publicity experts in federal employment. They were opening themselves up to the charge that some of the employees in the publicity bureau

must be, by definition, publicity experts. But in the inscrutable and serendipitous way that politicians pick and skip targets, the military's publicity bureaus seemed exempt from the generic legislative hostility to overt public relations activities by federal agencies.

10. Ponder, *Managing the Press*, 85–86, 89.

11. The related phenomenon of public information specialists appointed by cabinet secretaries and serving as their "special assistant" sometimes prompted congressional criticism beyond that leveled at press officers in the line bureaus of the departments. They were accused not only of promoting the work of the department but also of promoting the vanity and political career of the secretary.

12. "Taft Gag Is Loosened: Dickinson's Bureau Chiefs May Talk Discreetly—Press Agents May Go," *New York Times*, December 8, 1909, 1; "Washington Gossip: Departmental Press Agents," *Editor and Publisher* 11:48 (May 18, 1912): 2. The passage of the 1913 ban on all federal "publicity experts" can be seen as a delayed implementation of that goal (see chapter 4).

13. Goodman's unpublished thesis, "Origins of a Continuing Conflict," was very helpful in providing me leads to original sources relevant to this section and the next one.

14. Robinson was a rising star in the Democratic Party. After his service in the House, he was elected governor, then elected to the U.S. Senate. He was selected by New York governor Al Smith in 1928 to be Smith's vice presidential running mate (the ticket lost to Herbert Hoover) and was the Senate's majority leader during Franklin Roosevelt's first term.

15. U.S. House, Committee on the Census, *Press Bureau*, 4, 15.

16. Ibid., 2.

17. Writing nearly four decades afterwards, Catton contended that Osgood "did not deal with the Washington press corps direct: he mailed his releases out and shunned personal contacts" with reporters (Catton, "Handouts," 161). However, Durand testified unequivocally that, besides mailing press releases, Osgood also dealt directly with Washington-based reporters who visited the Census Bureau in search of information and stories (U.S. House, Committee on the Census, *Press Bureau*, 19). Given his direct participation and Catton's predilection for drama over accuracy, Durand deserves the benefit of the doubt. (Catton, for example, got the date of the opening scene in his *War Lords of Washington* memoir wrong.)

18. *CR* 45:1 (January 15, 1910): 665.

19. "Charges Political Activity: Representative Roberts [*sic*] Says Census Bureau Spreads Republican Doctrines," *Washington Post*, January 19, 1910, 5.

20. Catton, "Handouts," 160. Catton was familiar with government public relations because of his career as a Washington reporter and nationally syndicated columnist for Scripps-Howard and then as a public information officer from 1941 to 1948 (Lee, "Origins of the Epithet").

21. As the twentieth century wore on, hearings became more and more events where members who disagreed with a person's testimony would argue with, even harangue, a witness.

22. U.S. House, Committee on the Census, *Press Bureau* (in order of presentation), 6 (Hamlin), 10 (Robinson), 12 (Hamlin), 18–19 (Robinson), 2–3 (Crumpacker), 5 (Hughes), 8 (Foelker), 15 (Slemp), 4 (Godwin).

23. Ibid., 12–14.

24. Ibid., 9–11. It must be remembered that this occurred before the coalescing of the conservative coalition in Congress (conservative southern Democrats and Republicans) during the New Deal. In the early twentieth century, the Republican Party was still somewhat the more liberal and pro–civil rights party that had supported of the goals of Reconstruction. Conversely, the Democratic Party was largely the conservative and racist party. Robinson was also trying to raise, indirectly, the specter that a Republican-tilted census would seek to maximize the count of blacks, thereby disadvantaging racist Democratic candidates.

Three years later, Jones was again involved in a matter related to African Americans. In 1913, as a "special agent" of the District of Columbia's Bureau of Education, he was active in an effort to promote the work of rural industrial schools serving black students ("Negro Educators Plan to Co-operate," *New York Times,* April 18, 1913, 6).

25. U.S. House, Committee on the Census, *Press Bureau*, 1; *Christian Science Monitor*, January 21, 1910, 7.

26. Ibid., 24. Godwin was the only Democratic member of the committee who refused to sign the minority report.

27. *CR* 45:1 (January 24, 1910): 921.

28. *CR* 45:2 (January 28, 1910): 1216.

29. *CR* 45:9 (Index): 249. Two years later, another congressman claimed that as a result of Robinson's charges the Census Bureau sent press releases to newspapers in Robinson's district attacking him for his criticisms of the Bureau (U.S. House, Committee on Rules, *Department Press Agents*, 13). This allegation needs to be viewed with skepticism since it was second-hand, provided no specific examples, and had partisan overtones. Probably most significant, it reflected the double standard of congressional culture that it was acceptable for a legislator to attack an executive branch agency but not for the agency to respond in any way. Like children in the Victorian world, agencies should be seen but not heard. In 1932, Robinson, then the Senate's Democratic leader, attacked the Hoover administration for the USDA's publicity activities (Lee, "Government Public Relations," 57).

30. For a discussion of the battle to impose government standards on the meat packing industry within the broader context of the Progressive Era, see McGerr, *Fierce Discontent*, 160–163.

31. Nelson was part of the LaFollette progressive movement, which had won control of the Wisconsin Republican Party from the Stalwart (i.e., big business) wing.

32. "Bad Meat Inquiry Today: Congressman Nelson Aroused by Agricultural Department Statement," *New York Times*, May 8, 1912, 22.

33. "Near Blows at Query: Meat Probe Causes Nelson and McCabe to Grow Hostile," *Washington Post*, May 15, 1912, 5.

34. Given the prevalence of both morning and afternoon newspapers in most major cities (sometimes referred to as AMs and PMs), reporters were always looking to top their hometown competitors. These USDA releases gave journalists new angles for the next news cycle.

35. U.S. House, Committee on Rules, *Department Press Agents*, 14–15.

36. "Wiley May Back Mrs. Crane," *Chicago Tribune*, May 17, 1912, 7.

37. "Accused of Giving Out False News," *New York Times*, May 19, 1912, 6. Even though this article was not bylined, it almost certainly was written by Charles Willis Thompson (U.S. House, Committee on Rules, *Department Press Agents*, 14–18).

38. "Beef Indictment Called 'Frame-up,'" *Chicago Tribune*, May 19, 1912, 2.

39. *CR* 48:7 (May 20, 1912): 6851.

40. U.S. House, Committee on Rules, *Department Press Agents*, 4.

41. Ibid., 8–9.

42. Ironically, Gregg later became the chief of the Information Service of the Post Office Department ("National Leaders Express Sorrow," *New York Times*, December 31, 1931, 7). In its obituary, the *Times* described Thompson as "one of the foremost newspaper reporters in this country during the first two decades of this century" ("C. W. Thompson Dies; Editor, Reporter," September 9, 1946, 9). Even if that may have been an exaggeration, he was a major player in the Washington press corps (Ritchie, *Press Gallery*, 186, 191, 204, 215).

43. U.S. House, Committee on Rules, *Department Press Agents*, 18. In his testimony, Hunt also referred to other departmental press agentry, saying that "the State Department had one which I think Congress has abolished—the Bureau of Information" (ibid., 10). However, working with the State Department's Office of the Historian, I was unable to identify such a departmental activity or documentation of a congressional action terminating it (e-mail message, November 17, 2005). The State Department at that time had a *Division* of Information, but it provided information to U.S. embassies and did not distribute material to D.C.-based reporters. The Division of Information was still in existence at the time of the congressional hearing, so Hunt could not have been referring to it, given that he used the past tense in his testimony.

44. Ibid., 28.

45. Press coverage of the hearing included "Press Agent Quiz On," *Washington Post*, May 22, 1912, 4; and "Tell How Federal Press Agents Work," *New York Times*, May 22, 1912, 6.

46. U.S. House, Committee on Rules, *Department Press Agents*, 17. It had been the Committee on Expenditures in the Agriculture Department that held the hearings on Nelson's original resolution regarding USDA meat inspections. All these committees were merged into the single Committee on Government Operations at midcentury.

47. "Still Room for Inquiry," *Washington Star*, May 22, 1912, 2.

48. Houston, *Eight Years*, 202. In his autobiography, Houston claimed that it was his idea to invite Page to look over the department's publicity program. A contemporaneous newspaper article indicated that it was the other way around ("Page's Idea That U.S. Reports Be Made 'Popular' Adopted," *Washington Post*, June 3, 1913, 4). For Page's biography, see "Walter Hines Page Dies at Pinehurst," *New York Times*, December 23, 1918, 11.

49. Houston, *Eight Years*, 203. See also Harding, "Genesis," 231.

50. Based on my review of USDA annual reports from 1913 to 1918.

51. "Page's Idea That U.S. Reports Be Made 'Popular' Adopted," *Washington Post*, June 3, 1913, 4.

52. "G. W. Wharton, 59, Magazine Director, Dies," *Washington Post*, July 10, 1934, 4.

53. *CR* 51:14 (August 27, 1914): 14339; "Several Tests for Government Services Coming," *Christian Science Monitor*, April 21, 1914, 7.

54. *CR* 51:14 (August 27, 1914): 14338.

55. U.S. Congress, *Annual Reports of the Department of Agriculture for the Year Ended June 30, 1913*, 34. In those days, such annual reports were taken much more seriously and the secretary was more involved in their preparation. For example, in his memoirs Houston wrote that his campaigning for Democratic candidates in the 1914 congressional elections was delayed because "I had . . . my Annual Report to write" (Houston, *Eight Years*, 211). The publication's plural title (*Annual Reports*) hints at how successfully some of the USDA's bureaus had achieved autonomy. They functioned like independent entities, with the departmental superstructure presenting publicly only a thin veneer of a supposed unitary department. To the bureau heads, the department was little more than a loose federation of largely autonomous subunits.

56. "Houston Proposes More Aid to Farmer," *New York Times*, December 8, 1913, 7.

57. *CR* 51:12 (June 20, 1914): 12409. Humphrey was sometimes confused with colleague Benjamin Humphreys (D-Miss.).

58. U.S. House, Committee on Agriculture, *Press Agency*.

59. *CR* 51:14 (August 17, 1914): 13862.

60. Ibid. To provide some context, what was to be called World War I had begun on August 1 (although the United States did not enter the war until 1917).

61. Ibid., 13861.

62. *CR* 51:14 (August 27, 1914): 14338–14341.

63. The 1915 annual report from the head of the USDA Division of Publications (wholly separate at that time from the Office of Information) noted an inversion of the phenomenon the secretary described. The Office of Information quietly, but quickly, expanded the topics covered by its press releases, not limiting them to subjects of existing USDA brochures. Newspaper coverage of those kinds of press releases also prompted requests to the Division of Publications from farmers for more information, but in these situations no bulletins existed. The division would have to answer those requests individually or consider publishing new brochures for particularly popular topics (U.S. Congress, *Annual Reports of the Department of Agriculture for the Year Ended June 30, 1915*, 269). In other words, the tail was now wagging the dog, in contrast to what the secretary had stated in his response to the Humphrey resolution in 1914.

64. *CR* 51:14 (August 27, 1914): 14339. The statement became safe boilerplate wording that could be reused whenever needed. For example, it appeared, almost verbatim, in the department's 1914 annual report (U.S. Congress, *Annual Reports of the Department of Agriculture for the Year Ended June 30, 1914*, 35).

CHAPTER 4

1. In reverse chronological order: Webb and Salmon, "United States Government and Public Relations," 877; DeSanto, "Public Affairs," 38–39; Ponder, *Managing the Press*, 86–87; Fisher, *Politics of Shared Power*, 58–59; Short, "Effect of the Gillett Amendment."

2. In reverse chronological order: Herold, "Historical Perspectives," 15; Runyan, "Development of Public Information Laws," 55–56; Marbut, *News from the Capital*, 196; Rosapepe, "Neither Pinkertons"; Holtzman, *Legislative Liaison*, 44; Spitzer, "Information and Policy," 51–52; Rourke, *Secrecy and Publicity*, 184; Pimlott, *Public Relations*, 69–72; Fitzpatrick, "Public Information Activities," 530–531; McCamy, *Government Publicity*, 6; Larson, "How Much Federal Publicity," 636–637.

3. It is sometimes misspelled "Gillette" (Rosapepe, "Neither Pinkertons," 14; McCamy, *Government Publicity*, 6). Pimlott got it right in the text but misspelled it in the index.

4. "Seek Publicity Expert for Roads," *New York Times*, August 18, 1913, 6. Oddly, the position description reprinted in the *Congressional Record* is dated *September* 15, 1913, a week *after* it had been inserted there (*CR* 50:5 [September 6, 1913]: 4409). This is no doubt a typo. It probably should have been August 15.

5. "The Civil Service," *New York Times*, August 29, 1913, 15.

6. "Topics of the Times," *New York Times*, August 20, 1913, 8.

7. Fitzpatrick suggested that the whole controversy was due to a blunder that could have been avoided. The request from the Bureau of Public Roads had reached the CSC "in the summer, when most of the higher officials were on vacation. It was considered a routine matter" and an announcement issued ("Public Information Activities," 530). This implies that the higher-ranking CSC executives

would have realized the sensitivity of the topic and done something, such as changing the title of the position. However, Fitzpatrick included no citations to document this assertion. There is no assurance that senior CSC officials would have stopped the announcement or even felt the title needed to be changed. The earlier controversies related to publicity/press agents and bureaus had not entailed civil service positions. Therefore CSC officials would not necessarily have made a connection between them and the request from the Bureau of Public Roads, especially since it used slightly different terminology.

Coincidentally, a few days later the CSC issued an announcement of the examination for the chief of the new Office of Information at the USDA. The latter announcement (also issued while senior CSC officials were on vacation) attracted no negative publicity. Therefore, it seems more likely that the attention given the publicity expert circular by the *New York Times* editorial was the key factor in turning one CSC announcement into a public controversy and not the other. It is the serendipity of politics and journalism that one led to a political furor and the other passed unnoticed.

8. *CR* 50:5 (September 6, 1913): 4409.

9. Ibid., 4409, 4410.

10. Ibid., 4409.

11. Ibid., 4410.

12. Ibid., 4411.

13. "The Government and Publicity" (editorial), *Outlook* 105 (September 27, 1913), 148*, asterisk in original.

14. Gillett went on to become Speaker of the House and then a senator. In a profile marking his ascendancy to the speakership, a reporter subtly and perhaps mischievously referred back to the 1913 amendment by describing Gillett as "eschewing publicity agents" ("Gillett, the New Speaker, Forecasts War Criticism," *New York Times*, March 2, 1919, 37). Gillett's interest in government public relations was episodic and inconsistent. On one occasion during World War I, he criticized the public relations activities of Wilson's Committee on Public Information ("Creel under Fire, Defends His Work, "*New York Times*, December 15, 1917, 2), but on another he defended it ("Funds for Creel Reduced by House," *New York Times*, June 18, 1918, 7).

15. Hilderbrand, *Complete Press Conferences*, 260–261.

16. Ritchie, *Press Gallery*, 206.

17. Ponder, *Managing the Press*, 84; Hilderbrand, *Power and the People*, 109. Wilson did not pursue the idea during his first term. But once the country entered World War I, he established by executive order the Committee on Public Information in the White House, which functioned as a centralized publicity bureau in the way he had earlier envisioned. Throughout its existence, the Committee was under constant criticism from Congress as a presidential propaganda agency. Congress defunded it shortly after the war was over. For contemporary

discussions of the Committee on Public Information, see Axelrod, *Selling the Great War;* Adams, *Progressive Politics,* 118–131.

18. Hilderbrand, *Complete Press Conferences,* 261–262.

19. Their comments largely echoed an article in *Editor and Publisher* two years earlier that pointed out the positives for reporters of having agency publicity staffs, even though the article largely focused on the negatives ("After Press Agents," 11:49 [May 25, 1912] 1, 8).

20. 38 *Stat.* 212.

21. 5 *USC* 3107.

22. Kell, "Research and Evaluation," 1.

23. "MacAdam Gets Hawaii Job," *Washington Post,* February 1, 1917, 5; "Lansing Defends Gag," *Washington Post,* May 9, 1917, 2; "Liberty Dollars Presage Victory," *Christian Science Monitor,* October 31, 1917, 6.

24. U.S. House, Committee on Appropriations, *Third Deficiency Appropriation Bill, 1919,* 66th Cong., 1st sess., hearing, 252–253.

25. "Gets Reserve Commission: W. H. Rankin Is Named Lieutenant Colonel as Publicity Expert," *New York Times,* March 26, 1931, 8.

26. "In Media's Rays" (editorial), *New York Times,* March 13, 1979, A18.

27. U.S. GAO, Report A-61553 (May 10, 1935). Later, Rayburn was Speaker of the House during all the Congresses with a Democratic majority from 1940 to 1961. He nurtured the career of congressman, senator, and majority leader Lyndon Johnson (D-Tex.), having served with Johnson's father in the Texas State Legislature.

28. U.S. GAO, A-82332 (December 15, 1936).

29. U.S. GAO, B-26689 (May 4, 1943). See also discussion of the Tydings Committee in chapter 8.

30. U.S. GAO, B-181254 (February 28, 1975), 6. The GAO issued two documents to Congressman John Moss (D-Calif.) that day with the same file number. This quote comes from the letter signed by the deputy comptroller general and not the one signed by the assistant comptroller general.

31. U.S. GAO, B-222758 (June 25, 1986), 9–10.

32. U.S. GAO, B-302992 (September 10, 2004), 12.

33. *CR* 83:9 [Appendix] (March 2, 1938): 887–888; *CR* 83:10 [Appendix] (June 1, 1938): 2294–2296.

34. *CR* 84:2 (February 28, 1939): 2016.

35. *CR* 84:11 [Appendix] (March 20, 1939): 1069.

36. Memo from Norbert A. Schlei, Assistant Attorney General, Office of Legal Counsel to Joseph F. Dolan, Assistant Deputy Attorney General, "Request of House subcommittee for interpretation of 5 U.S.C. §§ 54," March 1, 1963.

37. 6 *Op. OLC* 547.

38. Barr v. Matteo, *United States Supreme Court Reports,* 3 L ed 2d 1452 (1959).

39. Frank R. Kent ,"The Great Game of Politics" (syndicated column), *Los Angeles Times,* May 7, 1935, 6; April 12, 1937, 4; and April 15, 1937, 8. Kent was

based at the *Baltimore Sun* and was the first of the semianonymous authors of the long-running "TRB" column in the *New Republic* magazine, a progressive weekly (Ritchie, *Reporting from Washington*, 134; Ritchie, *Electing FDR*, 78).

40. Thomas W. Phelps, "Washington Letter," *Wall Street Journal*, March 5, 1935, 1.

41. *CR* 79:5 (March 29, 1935): 4699; "Glass Attacks Use of Press Agents by Secretary Wallace," *Chicago Tribune*, March 30, 1935, 9. A comparison of these two sources demonstrates either the way floor statements are "improved" before publication in the *Congressional Record* or poor note taking by a reporter. According to the *Record*, this was the exchange between Glass and Senator Bennett Clark (D-Mo.): Clark: "The Senator knows as well as I do that it [violation of the law] has been done." Glass: "That is what I am complaining of now." And this was the version in the newspaper: Clark: "The senator knows that the law is being violated." Glass: "Of course it is. That's what I'm objecting to." On the accusations from the GOP congressmen, see Arthur Sears Henning, "Press for Full White House Lobby Inquiry," *Chicago Tribune*, July 7, 1935, 1.

42. *CR* 84:3 (March 20, 1939): 3013.

43. *CR* 84:15 [Index]: 883; "For Inquiry on Publicity," *New York Times*, March 21, 1939, 19.

44. Willard Edwards, "Bare New Deal Use of U.S. Cash in Utility Drive," *Chicago Tribune*, March 5, 1940, 8.

45. "Taft Hits Expense of New Deal News," *New York Times*, May 4, 1940, 18.

46. U.S. GAO, Report A-82332 (December 15, 1936).

47. U.S. GAO, B-26689 (May 4, 1943), 3. This was released in relation to a request from the Tydings Committee (see chapter 8).

48. U.S. House, Select Committee on Lobbying Activities, *Role of Lobbying*, 156.

49. U.S. House, Committee on Government Operations, *U.S. Government Information Policies*, 1661.

50. Ibid., 2155–2156.

51. U.S. House, Committee on Government Operations, *Administration of the Freedom of Information Act*, 84, emphasis added.

52. Hanson, "Official Propaganda," 176; Larson, "How Much Federal Publicity," 637; Rourke, *Secrecy and Publicity*, 190; Fisher, *Politics of Shared Power*, 59.

53. Short, "Effect of the Gillett Amendment." A related effect of the congressional hostility to the open practice of public relations in federal agencies was the short life of American University's Institute for Government Public Information Research, founded in 1978 but lasting only three years (Lee, "Rise and Fall").

54. DeSanto, "Public Affairs," 39.

CHAPTER 5

1. U.S. House, Committee on Rules, *Department Press Agents*, 8.

2. *CR* 48:5 (April 5, 1912): 4364.

3. "Denies Police Lobby," *Washington Post,* April 7, 1912, 8; *CR* 48:5 (April 23, 1912): 5202–5203.

4. U.S. House, Committee on the District of Columbia, *Prohibit Raising Funds for Lobbying,* 1.

5. 31 *USC* 1352.

6. Prouty's bill did not pass when Congress realized that it would unintentionally limit the right to petition Congress for redress of grievance, a principle embodied in the First Amendment. There were political calculations as well. President Taft had issued a so-called gag order banning employees of the executive branch from initiating contacts with Congress without his approval. By defeating the Prouty bill, Congress could show that it was open to free communications while the president was not. Finally, it did not want to discourage whistle-blowers from contacting it. Congress eventually enacted legislation formalizing this approach, providing legal guarantees that civil servants, as individuals, could contact Congress on an unlimited basis without any penalty regarding personal employment issues or for other purposes such as whistle-blowing. This form of communication, of course, was the opposite of civil servants contacting Congress for purposes of advancing the interests of their agency. The former was acceptable, the latter eventually banned.

The issue of an administration allegedly violating that law by trying to prevent civil servants from providing information directly to Congress because that might contradict the administration's policy would arise from time to time. For example, in 1963 President Kennedy was asked at two press conferences about supposedly blocking the State Department's director of security from providing information to the Senate's Internal Security Committee (the Senate's counterpart to the House Un-American Activities Committee) (Chase and Lerman, *Kennedy and the Press,* 503–504, 513). In 2004, the administration of President Bush (II) was accused of preventing Congress from obtaining from a staffer at the Department of Health and Human Services estimates of the cost of a proposed Medicare drug benefit that contradicted the "official" estimates (Amy Goldstein, "Official Says He Was Told to Withhold Medicare Data," *Washington Post,* March 13, 2004, A01). These incidents are, however, about a president allegedly trying to muzzle the bureaucracy, not about Congress doing so.

7. "$1,896,893,428 Spent on Army in 13 Years," *New York Times,* February 12, 1912, 6.

8. *CR* 49:4 (February 21, 1913): 3597.

9. Helm was a Democrat and Prouty a Republican, demonstrating the bipartisanship of the congressional reaction to agency external communications.

10. *CR* 49:4 (February 21, 1913): 3597. In the context he used it, Helm clearly meant "electioneering" in the generic sense of seeking to persuade public opinion, not involvement in a particular partisan election campaign.

11. Ibid., 3598.

12. Ibid., 3597.

13. Ibid., 3599.

14. U.S. House, Committee on Appropriations, *Third Deficiency Appropriation Bill, 1919*, 65th Cong., 3rd sess., hearing, 412–413. Deficiency bills covered unanticipated expenditures above and beyond the routine annual appropriation bill for each department and agency. They were relatively common during World War I and immediately afterwards, and then again during the Great Depression and World War II.

15. Ibid., 414.

16. U.S. House, Committee on Appropriations, *Third Deficiency Appropriation Bill, Fiscal Year 1919*, 65th Cong., 3rd sess., H. Rep. 1148.

17. *CR* 57:5 (February 27, 1919): 4515.

18. Ibid.

19. *CR* 57:5 (February 28, 1919): 4624.

20. Ibid., 4625.

21. Ibid., 4627.

22. At a conference in 1953, a speaker asserted that the 1919 law was passed "largely as a result of friction between the Army and Navy" (Wagner, "Government Public Relations," 20). I have not found such a direct link in the legislative history of the law or press coverage about the legislation, although these kinds of incidents may well have contributed as contextual factors. For example, Congressman Helm's failed 1913 floor amendment was triggered specifically by what he considered military lobbying.

23. U.S. House, Committee on Appropriations, *Third Deficiency Appropriation Bill, Fiscal Year 1919*, 66th Cong., 1st sess., H. Rep. 11, 5.

24. *CR* 58:1 (May 29, 1919): 403.

25. Ibid., 425–426.

26. The original handwritten amendment by the clerk of the Senate Appropriations Committee, Wm. Tyler Page, is on page 85 of the bill's Confidential Subcommittee Print (File H.R. 3184–H.R. 3478; Box Sen. 66A-C1, Bills and Resolutions Originating in the House of Representatives, 66th Congress; Record Group 46 [Records of the United States Senate], Center for Legislative Archives, National Archives). The proposed inserted text was eventually presented as part of the floor debate on the committee's recommended version of the bill (*CR* 58:1 [June 10, 1919]: 911).

27. U.S. Congress, Committee of Conference, *Deficiency Appropriation Bill*, 6.

28. 41 *Stat.* 68.

29. A 1948 recodification of Title 18 of the U.S. Code led to an updating of the wording of the 1919 law, but with no substantive changes (U.S. House, Committee on the Judiciary, *Revision of Title 18, United States Code*, A130). It also shifted its statutory citation, making it 18 USC 1913 (62 *Stat.* 792–793), a reference that has continued to this day. It is important not to confuse the 1913 *law* against

publicity experts with *Section* 1913 of the U.S. Code, which deals with lobbying Congress. To reduce confusion, I refer primarily to the law criminalizing lobbying as the 1919 law rather than as Section 1913.

30. AP, "Lobby Curb Gives Problem to Jackson," *Washington Post,* March 3, 1940, 5.

31. U.S. House, Special Committee to Investigate the National Labor Relations Board, *National Labor Relations Act,* 156. Jackson's response was considered such major news that it was one of the twenty questions in the weekly quiz in the Sunday *New York Times* called "Who's Who, What's What: Twenty News Questions" (March 3, 1940, 2E, 5E).

32. AP, "Rep. Norton Calls for Vote on Labor Issue," *Washington Post,* March 9, 1940, 2.

33. The entire correspondence is in Appendix B of the committee report (U.S. House, Special Committee to Investigate the National Labor Relations Board, *National Labor Relations Act*).

34. AP, *Washington Post,* March 3, 1940, 5; *New York Times,* March 19, 1940, 18; AP, *Los Angeles Times,* March 19, 1940, 11. Besides several other articles in the *Times* covering the controversy, Smith also received a sympathetic portrayal in Arthur Krock's regular column ("In the Nation: Mr. Smith Puts a Problem before Mr. Jackson," February 29, 1940, 18). As the *New York Times* Washington bureau chief, Krock was probably the most influential Washington-based reporter at the time, notwithstanding his recurring criticisms of FDR and relatively consistent support for conservative political positions (Ritchie, *Reporting from Washington,* 12–13).

35. John B. Oakes, "Ruling Sought on NLRB's Alleged Lobby," *Washington Post,* February 14, 1940, 2.

36. U.S. House, Special Committee to Investigate the National Labor Relations Board, *Intermediate Report, Minority Views,* 51–52.

37. U.S. House, Committee on Appropriations, *Department of Labor, Federal Security Agency,* 36.

38. Joseph B. Oakes, "Labor Board Funds Slashed by Committee," *Washington Post,* March 22, 1940, 2.

39. 54 *Stat.* 595.

40. 55 *Stat.* 495.

41. "Lobbying Charged to FCA Governor," *New York Times,* April 25, 1940, 13; Felix Cotten, "FCA Head Accused of Lobbying," *Washington Post,* April 17, 1940, 1; "The 'Liberal Credit' Campaign" (editorial), *Hartford* (Conn.) *Courant,* April 22, 1940, 8; CR 86:15 [Appendix] (April 26, 1940): 2459–2460.

42. "The Day in Washington," *New York Times,* April 25, 1940, 13. A few days later, Congressman Frank Horton (R-Wyo.) accused the Office of Government Reports of violating the anti-lobbying law and introduced a resolution calling for an investigation that would include recommendations for "remedies, both

in the form of new legislation and for the proper enforcement of existing statutes" (*CR* 86:5 [April 29, 1940]: 5191).

43. U.S. Senate, Committee on Appropriations, *Agricultural Appropriation Bill for 1944,* hearings, 869.

44. Before February 1942, it was an independent agency called the Agricultural Adjustment Administration.

45. U.S. House, Committee on Appropriations, *Agriculture Department Appropriation Bill for 1944,* hearings, 743.

46. Ibid., 1486–1487. See also comments by Congressman Lawrence Smith (R-Wis.) echoing the complaints of the Farm Bureau (*CR* 89:9 [March 12, 1943]: A1165-A1166; *CR* 89:11 [June 10, 1943]: A2917). Smith was later active in the 1951 offensive against agency external communications (see chapters 8–9).

47. U.S. Senate, Committee on Appropriations, *Agricultural Appropriation Bill for 1944,* hearings, 836–837. This odd alliance reflected the opposing political perceptions by each organization. The Farm Bureau wanted to blunt the institutionalization of the liberal agricultural policies of the Roosevelt administration, whereas the Farmers Union wanted to sever the strong unofficial links between local USDA employees and the Farm Bureau.

48. U.S. House, Committee on Appropriations, *Department of Agriculture Appropriation Bill, Fiscal Year 1945,* 19.

49. *CR* 90:3 (March 24, 1944): 3094.

50. Ibid.

51. U.S. Senate, Committee on Appropriations, *Agricultural Appropriation Bill, 1945,* 10.

52. The 1944 election would be the first presidential election after Pearl Harbor. Congressional politics in 1943–44 was dominated by partisan maneuvering over a bill to facilitate voting by members of the armed forces. Republicans feared that this vote would go predominantly for Roosevelt, should he run for a fourth term.

53. Drury, *Senate Journal,* 174.

54. *CR* 90:4 (May 17, 1944): 4589, 4591.

55. U.S. Congress, Committee of Conference, *Department of Agriculture Appropriation Bill, 1945,* H. Rep. 1605, 9.

56. *CR* 90:5 (June 20, 1944): 6278, 6290–6296.

57. U.S. Congress, Committee of Conference, *Department of Agriculture Appropriation Bill, 1945,* H. Rep. 1714.

58. *CR* 90:5 (June 22, 1944): 6481–6482 (Senate), 6557–6558 (House). See also Jerry Kluttz, "The Federal Diary" (daily column for federal employees), *Washington Post,* June 23, 1944, 3.

59. U.S. Congress, Committee of Conference, *Department of Agriculture Appropriation Bill, 1945,* H. Rep. 1714, 1–2.

60. 58 *Stat.* 450.

61. *CR* 91:2 (February 28, 1945): 1576.

62. 87 *Stat.* 487.

63. 88 *Stat.* 1829.

64. 95 *Stat.* 1476.

65. *CR* 92:4 (May 22, 1946): 5440–5441; *CR* 92:11 (May 24, 1946): A2945.

66. Mansfield, *Short History of OPA,* 306.

67. U.S. GAO, Report B-76695 (June 8, 1948).

68. "Most Flagrantly-Violated Law in America," *Forbes* 66:7 (October 1, 1950): 15.

69. Although formally a subcommittee, it was often referred to as a committee, especially in the press. The two terms are used interchangeably here. The work of this (sub)committee is also discussed briefly in chapter 7.

70. For a lay summary of the work of the committee from its chairman's perspective, see Harness, "Federal Thought Control." It was published by the National Industrial Conference Board (now the Conference Board), an organization of business executives. Two years later, *Forbes* published an unauthored article with an identical headline. It appeared to be an edited and rewritten version of Harness's earlier piece ("Federal Thought Control," *Forbes* 66:7 [October 1, 1950]: 14–17).

71. On the AAA, see U.S. House, Committee on Expenditures in the Executive Departments, Publicity and Propaganda Subcommittee, *Investigation of Agricultural Adjustment Agency.* This was a continuation of charges of lobbying violations made against the AAA during the Roosevelt administration. On the Reclamation Bureau, see "Downey Says Straus Violated Lobbying Law," *Fresno* (Calif.) *Bee,* December 19, 1947, 1; AP, "Downey Hurls Lobbying Charge," *Los Angeles Times,* May 13, 1948, 24; AP, "Straus Denies Talks Violated Lobbying Act," *Washington Post,* June 16, 1948, 9; AP, "Abuses Charged in Reclamation: Willful Violation of Law Is Laid to Bureau by Harness in Report to House," *New York Times,* August 5, 1948, 22. On health insurance, see U.S. House, Committee on Expenditures in the Executive Departments, Publicity and Propaganda Subcommittee, *Investigation of the Participation of Federal Officials in the Formation and Operation of Health Workshops.*

72. U.S. House, Committee on Expenditures in the Executive Departments, Publicity and Propaganda Subcommittee, *Investigation of the Participation of Federal Officials in the Formation and Operation of Health Workshops,* 7; and *Final Report,* 8. The political shoe was on the other foot in 2005, when congressional Democrats complained that the Social Security Administration was violating the anti-lobbying law in its actions vis-à-vis President Bush's proposal for major changes in Social Security; see chapter 12.

73. U.S. House, Committee on Expenditures in the Executive Departments, Publicity and Propaganda Subcommittee, *Final Report,* 7–8.

74. Ibid., 11–12; U.S. House, Committee on Expenditures in the Executive Departments, Publicity and Propaganda Subcommittee, *Investigation of Agricultural Adjustment Agency,* 10–19.

75. "Senator Cain Is Picketed," *New York Times*, July 4, 1947, 15; "Strong Bill Urged at Housing Parley," *New York Times*, May 4, 1948, 3.

76. U.S. Senate, Committee on Banking and Currency, Subcommittee on Housing and Rents, *Propaganda and Publicity*, 18–19, 23.

77. Ibid., 27.

78. Ibid., 34–35.

79. "Ohio Rent Official Ousted," *New York Times*, March 14, 1948, 44.

80. Up till then, Truman had been filling out the term that the Roosevelt-Truman ticket had been elected to in 1944.

81. "Lobbying Data Is Requested," *Washington Post*, December 17, 1949, B7.

82. U.S. House, Select Committee on Lobbying Activities, *Role of Lobbying*, 157–159; C. P. Trussell, "Government Held to Lobby Elusively," *New York Times*, March 31, 1950, 24.

83. U.S. House, Select Committee on Lobbying Activities, *Legislative Activities*, 59–306; "Brennan Cleared on Lobby Charge," *New York Times*, July 1, 1950, 7.

84. U.S. House, Select Committee on Lobbying Activities, *General Interim Report*, 62.

85. U.S. House, Select Committee on Lobbying Activities, *Report and Recommendations*, 36.

86. Charles F. Barrett, AP, "Humphrey Draws Warning on 'Lobbying' for Tax Extension," (Burlington, N.C.) *Daily Times News*, June 3, 1953, 1; John D. Morris, "Lobbying Warning Given to Humphrey," *New York Times*, June 4, 1953, 1; John Fisher, "Treasury Aids' [*sic*] Moves for Tax Extension Hit," *Chicago Tribune*, June 4, 1953, F9.

87. John Fisher, "Truce in Korea Won't Cut Tax, Treasury Says," *Chicago Tribune*, June 6, 1953, 8.

88. "Union Charges Summerfield Violates Law," *Chicago Tribune*, April 9, 1954, A2; Jerry Kluttz, "The Federal Diary" (daily column for federal employees), *Washington Post*, April 9, 1954, 31.

89. For challenges against the Department of Health, Education, and Welfare related to health policy and legislation, see "Ribicoff Accused of Lobby Activity," *New York Times*, May 10, 1962, 27; John D. Morris, "Kennedy Reopens Drive for Health Care for Aged," *New York Times*, November 19, 1963, 22; Eve Edstrom, "Celebrezze Insists Medicare Foes Quit Personal Attacks," *Washington Post*, November 19, 1963, A11; Eve Edstrom, "Mundt Says HEW Sabotages State-Run Medicare Program," *Washington Post*, November 20, 1963, A2. On challenges related to education policy and legislation, see John D. Morris, "College Aid Bill Beaten in House," *New York Times*, September 21, 1962, 12; AP, "Celebrezze Is Accused of Breaking Law," *Chicago Tribune*, October 3, 1962, 3. On the State Department, see *CR* 108:5 (April 4, 1962): 5926–5927. The accusations against the State Department were made by Congressman Frank Bow (R-Ind.), who before his election to Congress had been the general counsel of the Harness Committee

(see also chapter 7). On the Department of Defense, see *CR* 108:8 (June 14, 1962): 10490.

90. Kennedy, *Public Papers of the Presidents,* 290. The same quote in the *New York Times* did not contain the "as the Secretary said" aside ("Kennedy Accused of Farm Lobbying," April 5, 1962, 68). The *Times* columnist, Arthur Krock, published a third version: "you won't let your Congressman feel lonely" ("In the Nation" column, May 18, 1962, 30).

91. *CR* 108:11 (July 25, 1962): 14738.

92. Ibid., 14736.

93. *CR* 108:11 (July 31, 1962): 15090.

94. Ibid.

95. Ibid., 15091.

96. *CR* 108:11 (July 25, 1962): 14736.

97. Ibid., 14739.

98. *CR* 109:7 (May 14, 1963): 8525. The wheat referendum became such a major news story that President Kennedy was asked about it at two press conferences (Chase and Lerman, *Kennedy and the Press,* 440, 446, 448–449).

99. U.S. House, Committee on Appropriations, *Department of Agriculture and Related Agencies Appropriation Bill,* 28–29.

100. U.S. Senate, Committee on Appropriations, *Department of Agriculture and Related Agencies Appropriation Bill,* 23.

101. U.S. Congress, Committee of Conference, *Department of Agriculture and Related Agencies,* 10.

102. *77 Stat.* 827.

103. *95 Stat.* 1476.

104. Shriver's letter was reprinted in *CR* 108:6 (May 15, 1962): 8449. See also UPI, "Shriver's Letters on Funds Upheld," *New York Times,* May 15, 1962, 27.

105. This double-barreled approach was an innovation that was subsequently adopted by some other legislators pursuing similar issues.

106. U.S. GAO, Report B-145883 (April 20 and 27, 1962). Reprinted in *CR* 108:6 (May 15, 1962): 8449–8450. The GAO responded similarly a few months later to an inquiry about "White House Regional Conferences." U.S. GAO, Report B-147578 (November 8, 1962), 3.

107. Letter of Assistant Attorney General Herbert J. Miller, Jr., to Congressman Glenard P. Lipscomb, May 10, 1962. Reprinted in *CR* 108:6 (May 15, 1962): 8451. See also UPI, "Shriver's Letters on Funds Upheld," *New York Times,* May 15, 1962, 27.

108. *CR* 108:6 (May 15, 1962): 8449.

109. Ibid., 8460.

110. *CR* 111:1 (January 11, 1965): 501; *CR* 113:1 (January 10, 1967): 112.

111. *CR* 112:19 (October 5, 1966): 25370. Ashbrook ran unsuccessfully against President Nixon in the 1972 Republican primaries, arguing that Nixon had not been conservative enough.

112. Letters from Congressman James Wright to Transportation Secretary Claude S. Brinegar, April 12 and 18, 1973 (Anti-Lobbying [Highway Bill] Folder, Box 18, Alpha—Subject Files, Michael Raoul-Duval Papers, Staff Member and Office Files, White House Central Files, Nixon Presidential Library, National Archives).

113. Letter from Transportation Secretary Claude S. Brinegar to Congressman James C. Wright, Jr., April 20, 1973 (Anti-Lobbying [Highway Bill] Folder, Box 18, Alpha—Subject Files, Michael Raoul-Duval Papers, Staff Member and Office Files, White House Central Files, Nixon Presidential Library, National Archives).

114. One was described in the preceding Truman section and two in the section on Kennedy. The other two are U.S. GAO, B-76695 (June 8, 1948) and B-139134-O.M. (June 17, 1959).

115. U.S. GAO, Report B-256340 (September 6, 1994), 22.

116. U.S. GAO, B-159835 (July 18, 1975), 5.

117. U.S. GAO, B-182398 (October 14, 1975), 4–5; B-214455 (October 24, 1984).

118. U.S. GAO, B-130961 (September 30, 1976), 32.

119. U.S. GAO, B-129874 (July 27, 1977), 4.

120. 56 *Comp. Gen.* 889 (August 10, 1977); U.S. GAO, Report B-192658 (September 1, 1978), 4.

121. 59 *Comp. Gen.* 115 (December 3, 1979).

122. U.S. GAO, Report B-202975 (November 3, 1981), 5.

123. U.S. GAO, B-215746 (January 18, 1985), 4.

124. U.S. GAO, B-221041 (December 5, 1985), 3.

125. U.S. GAO, B-226449 (April 3, 1987); B-226449 (October 23, 1987), 37.

126. U.S. GAO, B-229275-O.M. (November 17, 1987), 4.

127. U.S. GAO, B-229069.2 (August 1, 1988), 4.

128. U.S. GAO, B-261929 (October 19, 1995), 5.

129. U.S. GAO, B-270137 (November 30, 1995), 3.

130. U.S. GAO, B-270875 (July 5, 1996), 4.

131. U.S. GAO, B-285298 (May 22, 2000), 4.

132. U.S. GAO, B-114839 (May 24, 1976).

133. U.S. GAO, B-164497(5) (March 10, 1977).

134. U.S. GAO, B-209049 (September 29, 1982), 17.

135. 63 *Comp. Gen.* 624 (September 26, 1984).

136. U.S. GAO, Report B-209049 (September 29, 1982). See also Morton Mintz, "Defense Officials Held to Violate Lobby Law in Transport Campaign," *Washington Post*, October 1, 1982, A2; Morton Mintz, "Pentagon Denies GAO Charges," *Washington Post*, October 2, 1982, A2; Brad Knickerbocker, "Pentagon's Lobbying for Favorite Weapons May Be Illegal—GAO," *Christian Science Monitor*, October 6, 1982, 3.

137. U.S. GAO, B-212235(2) (November 17, 1983), 4. See also Cass Peterson, "Inside: Commerce Department," *Washington Post*, August 1, 1983, A13.

138. U.S. GAO, Office of the General Counsel, *Principles of Federal Appropriations Law*, chap. 4, 194–195.

139. Memos from John W. Barnum, General Counsel, U.S. Department of Transportation, Re: Statutory Prohibitions Against Lobbying, February 18, 1972 and April 20, 1973 (Anti-Lobbying [Highway Bill] Folder, Box 18, Alpha—Subject Files, Michael Raoul-Duval Papers, Staff Member and Office Files, White House Central Files, Nixon Presidential Library, National Archives, 2.)

140. Quoted in Louis Fischer, "White House-Congress Relationships: Information Exchange and Lobbying," CRS Report for Congress, Congressional Research Service, Library of Congress, July 7, 1978, 68.

141. This inherent conflict of interest played out that same year over a much larger issue—Nixon's effort to have Peterson keep him apprised of the Criminal Division's investigation into the Watergate break-in.

142. Memorandum to Robert J. Lipshutz, Counsel to the President, from John M. Harmon, Assistant Attorney General, "Statutory Restraints on Lobbying Activity by Federal Officials," November 29, 1977, 1.

143. Ibid., 2.

144. Ibid., 8.

145. Ibid., 9–10,

146. Ibid.

147. 2 *Op. OLC* 32 (January 30, 1978).

148. 2 *Op. OLC* 160–161 (July 18, 1978).

149. Memorandum for Members of the White House Office Staff, from Fred F. Fielding, Counsel to the President, "Support of Administration Legislative Programs," February 23, 1981, 1. The memo is reproduced as Appendix IV in U.S. GAO, Report B-129874 (March 20, 1984).

150. 5 *Op. OLC* 184 (June 17, 1981).

151. Memorandum for John R. Bolton, Assistant Attorney General, from Charles J. Cooper, Assistant Attorney General, "Applicability of 18 U.S.C. 1913 to Contacts between United States Attorneys and Members of Congress in Support of Pending Legislation," October 27, 1987.

152. 12 *Op. OLC* 30 (February 1, 1988). See also 14 *Op. OLC* 7 (January 25, 1990).

153. 13 *Op. OLC* 302 (September 28, 1989).

154. Memorandum for the Attorney General and the Deputy Attorney General, from Walter Dellinger, Assistant Attorney General, "Anti-Lobbying Act Guidelines," April 14, 1995.

155. Along with the OLC, the Criminal Division of the Department of Justice would be involved in any decisions about prosecuting the law. In the 1970s, it generated two documents related to the anti-lobbying law: a 1973 letter from the assistant attorney general heading the Criminal Division and a 1979 memo from the chief of the Criminal Division's Public Integrity Unit to his boss, the assistant attorney general in charge of the division. In response to a Freedom of Information request I submitted in 2005 for those two documents, the division responded that it could not find the 1973 letter and denied release of the 1979

memo. Letter to Mordecai Lee from Thomas J. McIntyre, Chief, Freedom of Information/Privacy Unit, Office of Enforcement Operations, Criminal Division, U.S. Department of Justice, July 13, 2005. My appeal of the decision was denied (Letter from Richard L. Huff, Co-Director, Office of Information and Privacy, U.S. Department of Justice, September 6, 2005). The ruling stated that because of the exemption from the Freedom of Information Act for "intra-agency memorandums or letters which reflect the predecisional, deliberative processes of the Department, and/or which consist of attorney work product prepared in anticipation of litigation," the entirety of the sixteen-page memo was exempt.

The rationale for the denial was significant, because it implied that the memo covered the internal decision making and standards used to justify prosecuting or not prosecuting an alleged violation of the anti-lobbying law and that those considerations were still relevant in 2005. Given that the Criminal Division had never prosecuted a violation of the law, the reason given for the denial also raised the possibility that the document baldly discussed the prosecutability of violations of the law and that (for whatever reason) the department did not want this to be public information, even more than twenty-five years later.

156. Angilly v. U.S., 105 *F. Supp.* 259 (1952).

157. National Association for Community Development v. Hodgson, 356 *F. Supp.* 1403 (1973). Even though the judge ruled that the case could proceed, I was unable to locate any subsequent decisions related to that lawsuit.

158. Examples from district courts include American Public Gas Association v. Federal Energy Administration, 408 *F. Supp.* 640 (1976); American Trucking Associations v. Department of Transportation, 492 *F. Supp.* 566 (1980); and Grassley v. Legal Services Corporation, 535 *F. Supp.* 818 (1982). The only time when the judge had ruled preliminarily that the law could be used as a private course of action was National Association for Community Development v. Hodgson, 356 *F. Supp.* 1403 (1973). However, the consistency of all decisions issued after that decision appears to be decisive. The Court of Appeals case is National Treasury Employees' Union v. Campbell, 1981 *U.S. App.* LEXIS 12598.

159. American Public Gas Association v. Federal Energy Administration, 408 *F. Supp.* 640 (1976). The judge in that case was John Sirica, famous for his role as the judge in the trial of the original Watergate burglars.

160. Several Democratic senators had introduced the proposal in reaction to the controversy over video news releases (see chapter 8). Given their minority party status, the bill (S. 266, 109th Congress; *CR* [February 2, 2005]: S895–898) had no chance of passage.

161. U.S. Senate, Committee on Appropriations, *Department of the Interior,* 5.

162. 91 *Stat.* 307.

163. 95 *Stat.* 1416.

164. 59 *Comp. Gen.* 118–119 (December 3, 1979).

165. 96 *Stat.* 1996.

166. 117 *Stat.* 149.

167. U.S. GAO, Report B-206391 L/M (July 2, 1982); GAO Document 128354 (October 30, 1985).

168. U.S. GAO, Report B-129874 (March 20, 1985), 6.

169. Ibid., 26–27.

170. Ibid., 32.

171. U.S. GAO, Congressional Testimony GAO/T-OGC-96–18 (May 15, 1996).

172. U.S. Congress, Committee of Conference, *21st Century Department of Justice*, 177.

173. 116 *Stat.* 1778.

174. George W. Bush, "Statement on Signing the 21st Century Department of Justice Appropriations Authorization Act," November 2, 2002, *Public Papers of the Presidents of the United States: George W. Bush, 2002,* Book 2:2011.

175. U.S. GAO, Office of the General Counsel, *Principles of Federal Appropriations Law,* chap. 4, 190.

176. Eric Plainin, "Democrats Decry EPA Ads on Bill; Lawmakers Cite Anti-Lobbying Laws," *Washington Post,* October 15, 2003, A10.

177. National Resources Defense Council, "NRDC Questions Legality of Secret Dealings; Files FOIA Request with Energy Department" (press release), December 18, 2003.

178. Al Kamen, "They Wouldn't Wait in the Lobby," *Washington Post,* June 11, 2004, A23.

179. Letter from Glenn A. Fine, Inspector General, Department of Justice, to Congressman John L. Conyers, Jr., Ranking Minority Member, Judiciary Committee, October 22, 2004.

180. Murphy, Nuechterlein, and Stupak, *Inside the Bureaucracy,* 31.

181. Louis Fisher, "White House-Congress Relationships: Information Exchange and Lobbying," Congressional Research Report for Congress (July 7, 1978), 50 (unpublished).

182. Fisher, *Politics of Shared Power,* 60.

183. Engstrom and Walker, "Statutory Restraints."

184. Harris, *Congress and the Legislative Process,* 165.

185. Key, *Politics, Parties, and Pressure Groups,* 702.

186. Berman, *In Congress Assembled,* 81.

187. Cummings, "Working with Congress," 226.

188. Ryan Lizza, "Root Cause" ("White House Watch" column), *New Republic* 224:13 (March 26, 2001): 14.

CHAPTER 6

1. "Senator Assails Military Court Propaganda Plan," *Christian Science Monitor,* April 9, 1919, 1; "Postal Laws Broken: Johnson So Asserts, Attacking Col. Wigmore's Propaganda," *Washington Post,* April 19, 1919, 2.

2. "Finds Wigmore Violated No Law," *New York Times*, May 2, 1919, 11.

3. U.S. Senate, Committee on Military Affairs, *Establishment of Military Justice*, 167–169, 231–232.

4. For example, "Army Law Critics Were Disciplined," *Washington Post*, August 27, 1919, 9; "Charges Army Heads Ran a Press Bureau," *Boston Globe*, August 27, 1919, 4; AP, "Ansell Tells of Propaganda," *Los Angeles Times*, August 27, 1919, 16.

5. M. E. Hennessey, "Things Are Stirring down Washington Way," *Boston Globe*, March 13, 1921, 44.

6. Rosten, *Washington Correspondents*, 69.

7. *CR* 64:1 (December 8, 1922): 219.

8. Lee, "Congressional Controversy;" and "Case Study of Congressional Hostility."

9. White, *Trends in Public Administration*, 146, 156.

10. "Government Waste of Paper Attacked," *New York Times*, September 15, 1918, 21.

11. Merrill, *Reed Smoot*, 358–359.

12. U.S. Congress, Committee of Conference, *Legislative, Executive, and Judicial Appropriation Bill*, 65th Cong., 3rd sess., 7.

13. *CR* 57:4 (February 20, 1919): 3865.

14. 40 *Stat.* 1270.

15. *CR* 59:3 (February 5, 1920): 2492; "Smoot Condemns Print Paper Waste," *New York Times*, February 6, 1920, 23.

16. *CR* 59:3 (February 5, 1920): 2493.

17. Arthur Sears Henning, "Skids Greased for U.S. Paid Press Agents," *Chicago Tribune*, March 29, 1920, 1,

18. *CR* 59:3 (February 5, 1920): 2493.

19. U.S. Congress, Joint Committee on Printing, *Government Periodicals*, 8, 40.

20. "Senate Finds 2 More Sources of Extravagance: Press Agents and Bureau of Efficiency," *Chicago Tribune*, April 3, 1920, 3, emphasis added.

21. *CR* 59:5 (April 1, 1920): 5099.

22. U.S. Congress, Committee of Conference, *Legislative, Executive, and Judicial Appropriation Bill, 1921*, 9.

23. Houston played a major role in the establishment of the USDA Office of Information (chapter 3).

24. Houston, *Eight Years*, 71.

25. Ibid., 73,

26. Link, *Papers of Woodrow Wilson*, 65:264.

27. U.S. Congress, *Veto Message on Legislative, Executive, and Judicial Appropriation Bill*, 2. This sentence was in Houston's draft and was unaltered by Wilson (Link, *Papers of Woodrow Wilson*, 65:266). Apparently, however, Houston did not consider it a very important sentence. In his memoirs, he did not include it within the text of the abridged version of his draft (Houston, *Eight Years*, 78).

28. *CR* 59:7 (May 14, 1920): 7034.

29. "Moderation in the Treasury" ("Topics of the Times" feature), *New York Times,* September 24, 1927, 16.

30. "Congested Annual Reports" (editorial), *New York Times,* December 7, 1930, 55. Smoot lost reelection in the Roosevelt landside of 1932.

CHAPTER 7

1. Patterson, *Congressional Conservatism.*

2. Howard, "Agricultural Referendum." After changes in its title, the third "A" in its abbreviation later stood for "Agency" rather than "Administration."

3. Stedman, "Development of an Informational Policy," 228. The original paper is in the collection of the USDA Library: Alfred D. Stedman, "Public Policies in Information Developed by the AAA," December 29, 1938. The panel was part of the track on public opinion at the conference. The title of the session was "Government: Source and Target of Propaganda," organized and chaired by Harwood Childs (*American Political Science Review* 33:1 [February 1939]: 94). The cited 1939 publication is a section of an annual report by the head of the AAA, and Stedman's authorship of that section is not listed in the annual report. However, Stedman acknowledged his authorship of that section of the annual report both in the American Political Science Association paper and in a later publication ("Public Information and the Preservation of Democracy," 1075n1).

4. Burns, *Roosevelt,* 370.

5. Lee, *First Presidential Communications Agency;* Ritchie, *Reporting from Washington,* 17; Rosten, *Washington Correspondents,* 70–71; Herring, *Public Administration,* chap. 22; McCamy, *Government Publicity.*

6. Kent, *Without Grease,* 49.

7. Lee, "Government Public Relations."

8. Rosten, *Washington Correspondents,* 70.

9. Kent, *Without Grease,* 51.

10. Rosten, *Washington Correspondents,* 53.

11. Kent, *Without Grease,* 48; *New York Times,* November 21, 1933, 4; *New York Times,* September 30, 1934, 36; *Washington Post,* October 10, 1934, 24; Frank George, *New York Times,* November 4, 1934, XX1; Michael, *Handout.*

12. Advertisement for *Handout, New York Times,* May 7, 1935, 21.

13. *CR* 79:1 (January 14, 1935): 429. Dies later went on to fame and notoriety as chair of the House Un-American Activities Committee.

14. Text of H. Res. 52, 74th Congress, 1st session, 1. The significance of this first congressional attack on agency public relations during the Roosevelt administration was signaled when the book *Handout* reprinted the entire Dies resolution in its foreword as a comprehensive and accurate outline of the problems the book would be exposing (Michael, *Handout,* vii–ix).

15. AP, "Democrats Warned against Smothering Censorship Quiz," *Washington Post*, January 15, 1935, 2; "Democrats Put 'in Middle' over Censor Charge," *Chicago Tribune*, January 15, 1933, 20; "Freedom of Press Probe," *Wall Street Journal*, January 15, 1933, 4; Paul Mallon, "Has the New Deal Colored the News?" *New York Times Sunday Magazine*, February 17, 1935, 6.

16. *CR* 79:7 (May 7, 1935): 7044.

17. "Dickinson of Iowa Asks Senate Quiz of New Deal 'Press,'" *Chicago Tribune*, May 8, 1935, 7; Raymond Clapper, "Between You and Me" (syndicated column), *Washington Post*, May 16, 1935, 2; *CR* 79:7 (May 13, 1935): 7352–7353; *CR* 79:14 (Index): 706.

18. Drury, *Senate Journal*, 483. For the larger political context of this committee, see Heinemann, *Harry Byrd of Virginia*, 179.

19. Smith, *Brookings at Seventy-Five*, 25.

20. Turner Catledge, "Federal Bureau for Press Urged," *New York Times*, December 29, 1936, 1.

21. U.S. Senate, Select Committee to Investigate the Executive Agencies of the Government, *Investigation of Executive Agencies*, 528–553.

22. AP, *New York Times*, June 14, 1937, 4.

23. For examples, see *CR* 83:11 [Appendix] (June 16, 1938): 3202–3205; 97:5 (June 19, 1951): 6734.

24. Some 1936–40 examples, in chronological order: *CR* 80:3 (February 20, 1936): 2455–2456; Robert C. Albright, "3-Way Split in New Deal Imperils Aid," *Washington Post*, April 19, 1936, M1; Walter Trohan, "Ballyhoo Corps Finds New Way to Boost WPA," *Chicago Tribune*, December 16, 1937, 8; AP, " Propaganda Cost Set at $50,000,000 a Year," *Los Angeles Times*, January 12, 1938, 9; AP, "Business Offers President Help," *Los Angeles Times*, April 27, 1938, 5; *CR* 83:11 [Appendix] (June 16, 1938): 3202–3205; *CR* 85:1 (October 10, 1939): 257–258; "Taft Hits Expense of New Deal News," *New York Times*, May 4, 1940, 18.

25. U.S. House, Committee on Appropriations, *Independent Offices Appropriation Bill*, 3.

26. "Suydam Named Aid to Cummings," *Washington Post*, August 29, 1934, 7. See also "Suydam Is Cummings's Aide," *New York Times*, August 29, 1935, 15. O'Reilly mistakenly set Suydam's hiring in 1933 instead of 1934 ("New Deal," 644).

27. "Post for Henry Suydam," *New York Times*, April 29, 1921, 11.

28. "Henry Suydam Resigns," *New York Times*, February 15, 1922, 22. Suydam had spoken at a 1931 conference on reporters' perspective when covering federal agencies (*Conference on the Press*, 66–72).

29. U.S. House, Committee on Appropriations, *Department of Justice Appropriation Bill for 1937*, 350; Swisher, *Selected Papers of Homer Cummings*, 271; "Anti-Crime 'West Point' Is Ordered," *New York Times*, January 25, 1935, 44; AP, "Crime Plan Aides Picked," *Los Angeles Times*, January 25, 1935, 7; "Henry Suydam Will Address Woman's Club," *Washington Post*, February 17, 1935, SS4; "Draper to

Head Federal Group in Chest Drive," *Washington Post,* October 25, 1936, M16. "Community Chest" was the term for the United Way at this time.

30. Burrough, *Public Enemies,* 517. The book was the basis of the 2009 film *Public Enemies.* Sudyam appeared in the movie as well. See the script, pages 14–17, at www.mediafire.com/?mwnmicywmmi (accessed November 2010).

31. "Cummings Names Dean as Assistant," *Lost Angeles Times,* March 19, 1937, 3, emphasis added.

32. O'Reilly, "New Deal," 644; "Henry Suydam, 64, Dies; News Chief for Dulles," *Washington Star,* December 12, 1955.

33. O'Reilly, "New Deal," 639n.

34. U.S. Senate, Committee on Appropriations, *Departments of State, Justice, Commerce, and Labor,* 162–164. According to O'Reilly, Hoover and his sycophants tried to revise history by erasing Suydam's original contributions to the design and establishment of the FBI's tremendously effective public relations ("New Deal," 644n).

35. O'Reilly, "New Deal," 644.

36. O'Reilly suggested that it was Hoover (ibid., 644n).

37. U.S. House, Committee on Appropriations, *Department of Justice Appropriation Bill for 1936,* 212, 216.

38. U.S. House, Committee on Appropriations, *Department of Justice Appropriation Bill for 1937,* 347, 350.

39. Ibid., 357.

40. Warren B. Francis, "New Deal Rapped in Postal Mix-up," *Los Angeles Times,* August 2, 1936, C7; "Cummings' Aide Unseated by Bill," *Washington Star,* July 1, 1936.

41. U.S. Congress, Committee of Conference, *State, Justice, Commerce, and Labor Departments Appropriation Bill,* 1937, 5.

42. 49 *Stat.* 1326.

43. AP, "Suydam Is Ousted by Clause in Bill," *Washington Post,* July 2, 1936, X2; AP, "Cummings Aide Loses His Job," *New York Times,* July 2, 1936, 2.

44. "Suydam Returns as Cummings Aid [*sic*]," *Washington Post,* July 25, 1936, X9; "Suydam Given New Post by Cummings," *Washington Star,* July 25, 1936; AP, "Cummings Aide Returns to Job with New Title," *Los Angeles Times,* July 26, 1936, 6.

45. "Suydam Resigns D. J. Post Mar. 31," *Washington Star,* March 4, 1937. Suydam's "in and out" career continued after that. He resigned his journalism job in 1953 to become the spokesman for Secretary of State John Foster Dulles in the Eisenhower administration (Edward T. Folliard, "Suydam Succeeds M'Dermott as State Dept. Press Officer," *Washington Post,* September 30, 1953, 2). He died, on the job, in 1955 ("Henry Suydam, 64, Press Aide, Dead," *New York Times,* December 12, 1955, 31).

46. 90 *Stat.* 947.

47. "Named Cummings Aide," *New York Times*, March 19, 1937, 12; "Murphy Picks Press Aide," *New York Times*, June 16, 1939, 22; "Fahy Is Nominated to Succeed Biddle," *New York Times*, October 30, 1941, 24.

48. U.S. House, Committee on Appropriations, *Interior Department Appropriation Bill for 1939*, hearings, 21–23.

49. Ibid., 21.

50. Ibid., 90.

51. Ickes, *Inside Struggle*, 298.

52. U.S. House, Committee on Appropriations, *Interior Department Appropriation Bill for 1939*, hearings, 23.

53. Ibid., 396–397 (Geological Survey); 687–689 (Office of Education); 133, 161, 163–164 (Coal Commission).

54. U.S. House, Committee on Appropriations, *Interior Department Appropriation Bill, Fiscal Year 1939*, report, 3–4. See also United Press, "Ickes Assailed on Bill to Hire Publicity Staff," *Washington Post*, February 26, 1938, X3; "Ickes Funds Bill Attacked in House," *New York Times*, February 26, 1938, 5.

55. *CR* 83:3 (February 25, 1938): 2469–2470. Johnson was the second-ranking majority party member (outranked only by the chairman) of the Interior Department subcommittee of the House Appropriations Committee.

56. *CR* 83:3 (February 28, 1938): 2545–2546. See also "Ickes Fund Upheld under House Fire," *New York Times*, March 1, 1938, 14.

57. U.S. House, Committee on Appropriations, *Interior Department Appropriation Bill for 1940*, hearings, 21–22; 192–193 (Housing Authority); 634–635, 674–676, 679 (Coal Commission).

58. *CR* 84:3 (March 14, 1939): 2729. White's comparison of federal public relations to the work of Nazi Propaganda Minister Joseph Goebbels is another example of the over-the-top rhetoric that the conservative coalition continued using to attack Roosevelt and the New Deal long after the realities of the pre-war Nazi regime were widely known.

59. Ibid., 2730.

60. "Ickes Publicity Item Cut," *New York Times*, March 15, 1939, 4. See also "What's News," *Wall Street Journal*, March 15, 1939, 1.

61. Lee, *First Presidential Communications Agency*, 43, 85; McCamy, *Government Publicity*, 94–99.

62. "Interior Department Plans Studios for Bureau Talks," *Christian Science Monitor*, April 22, 1936, 8.

63. U.S. House, Committee on Appropriations, *Interior Department Appropriation Bill for 1939*, hearings, 663–666; *Interior Department Appropriation Bill for 1940*, hearings, 881–883. See also James McConaughy, "U.S. Education Radio Programs Prove Popular," *Washington Post*, November 22, 1936, F1–F2; "Radio Experts Help U.S. Office of Education Make Programs Interesting and Worth-while," *Washington Post*, March 21, 1937, TR5; "10 Air Programs Added to Educational Series," *Washington Post*, July 30, 1938, X24.

64. Ickes, *Inside Struggle*, 317. An indication of Roosevelt's in-depth knowledge of the details of federal government operations: when he wanted improved coordination of all federal radio activities, he specifically referred to Interior's radio studio as a key unit that needed to be integrated into an overall plan (Harold Smith, dictated summary of daily activities, September 29, 1939; and dictated summary of conference with the President, October 3, 1939, Smith Papers, Roosevelt Library). For more information on federal radio coordination during that time, see Lee, *First Presidential Communications Agency*, 94–95.

65. U.S. House, Committee on Appropriations, *Interior Department Appropriation Bill for 1940*, hearings, 21–22.

66. *CR* 84:3 (March 14, 1939): 2730.

67. U.S. House, Committee on Appropriations, *Interior Department Appropriation Bill for 1941*, hearings, 4, 20. For a partial text of one of the radio dramatizations, in this case dealing with oil supply (another of Ickes's responsibilities), see *CR* 86:13 [Appendix] (March 1, 1940): 1124.

68. Lee, "Intersectoral Differences."

69. U.S. House, Committee on Appropriations, *Interior Department Appropriation Bill for 1941*, hearings, 23.

70. *CR* 86:3 (March 7, 1940): 2506–2508.

71. Willard Edwards, "House Puts End," *Chicago Tribune*, March 8, 1940, 11; Lorania K. Francis, "House Votes Curb," *Los Angeles Times*, March 8, 1940, 8.

72. AP, "House Votes $118,000,000 for Interior," *Washington Post*, March 8, 1940, 2; "House Votes Ickes $118,578,187 Funds," *New York Times*, March 8, 1940, 13.

73. 54 *Stat.* 406.

74. 55 *Stat.* 304; 56 *Stat.* 506.

75. The war began on September 1, 1939, with the German invasion of Poland. Germany and the Soviet Union were allies and, a few weeks later, Stalin followed up with a preplanned and coordinated invasion of Poland from the east. The United States did not become a combatant in the war until more than two years later, after the Japanese attack on Pearl Harbor (December 7, 1941). The second crescendo was in 1951; see chapters 8–10.

76. Fleming, *New Dealers' War*, 558.

77. Caro, *Master of the Senate*, 74.

78. Catton, *War Lords*, 180.

79. *CR* 88:8 (February 6, 1942): A414–A415; (February 9, 1942): A488.

80. *CR* 88:2 (February 23, 1942): 1513. This appalling hyperbole helps convey the hysterical hatred by Republican newspapers and legislators of Roosevelt. By the time this statement was made, the United States was in a state of war with Germany, so the odious comparison was to a declared enemy of the nation. In a mild excuse for their rhetoric, the ultimate meaning of Nazi propaganda and the regime's beyond-belief deeds (such as the Holocaust) were not known at that time. Still, many of Hitler's horrific views and policies were known by then.

81. *CR* 88:1 (February 9, 1942): 1150.

82. *CR* 88:8 (March 2, 1942): A788; (March 9, 1942): A924; *CR* 88:9 (April 21, 1942): A1480–481; *CR* 88:3 (April 14, 1942): 3485–3486, 3488.

83. *CR* 88:5 (July 24, 1942): 6574.

84. AP, "Lanham Joins Drive to Curb U.S. Spending," *Washington Post*, December 17, 1942, 10.

85. *CR* 88:1 (February 17, 1942): 1311. Strictly speaking, Tydings chaired a subcommittee of the Appropriations Committee, but it was commonly referred to as the Tydings Committee. Tydings was such an implacable conservative opponent of the New Deal that he was one of the Democratic senators Roosevelt unsuccessfully tried to deny renomination as a Democratic Party's candidate.

86. *CR* 88:4 (May 28, 1942): 4684. The Office for Emergency Management (OEM) was the civilian wartime agency in the Executive Office of the President that Roosevelt created as a kind of administrative "holding company" for the scores of temporary agencies he established to handle distinct nonmilitary aspects of the war effort. The Division of Information was an agency within the OEM and the largest public relations office in the federal government at that time. Going against the desire by each federal agency for its own public relations office (as part of an autonomy-seeking goal), the Division of Information provided public relations services to all the other OEM agencies. The division was headed by Robert W. Horton, a former reporter. Horton's philosophy of government public relations was canonized by Bruce Catton in his memoir *War Lords of Washington*. Horton had hired Catton, a reporter, to be one of the public information officers the division supplied to other agencies. In an effort to fend off increasingly effective conservative attacks on agency public relations in 1942, Roosevelt signed an executive order abolishing the Division of Information and several other public relations units (including the Office of Government Reports) when he merged them into the new Office of War Information in June.

87. "Official 'Deluge' of News Assailed," *New York Times*, May 31, 1942, 33.

88. U.S. Senate, Committee on Appropriations, Subcommittee on Senate Resolution 223, *Transfer of Employees*, 16.

89. Fleming, *New Dealers' War*, 151–161. To Roosevelt's great disappointment, the U.S. invasion of North Africa did not occur until just after the November elections.

90. This was especially so in the House until the principle of one-person-one-vote fully controlled reapportionment of congressional districts.

91. For a circa 1940 summary of the operations of the USDA Office of Information, see Gaus and Wolcott, *Public Administration*, 359–364.

92. U.S. House, Committee on Appropriations, *Agriculture Department Appropriation Bill for 1944*, hearings, 134–141, 596 (Dirksen).

93. Ibid., 1513–1517.

94. U.S. House, Committee on Appropriations, *Department of Agriculture Appropriation Bill, Fiscal Year 1944*, report, 15.

95. Ibid., 5.

96. *CR* 89:3 (April 14, 1943): 3354.

97. U.S. Senate, Committee on Appropriations, *Agricultural Appropriation Bill for 1944,* hearings, 2, 4–5, 76–80.

98. U.S. Senate, Committee on Appropriations, *Agricultural Appropriation Bill, 1944,* report, 14–15.

99. *CR* 89:4 (June 7, 1943): 5419.

100. U.S. Congress, Committee of Conference, *Department of Agriculture Appropriation Bill, 1944,* 2, 9.

101. 57 *Stat.* 395.

102. 58 *Stat.* 428 ($13,900); 59 *Stat.* 138 ($11,856); 60 *Stat.* 272 ($9,000); 61 *Stat.* 525–526 ($10,000); 62 *Stat.* 510 ($10,000).

103. U.S. House, Committee on Appropriations, *Agriculture Department Appropriation Bill for 1944,* hearings, 1483, 1486, 1488–1489, 1504–1505.

104. Frischknecht, "State Extension Services," 423.

105. Knapp, "Congressional Control," 267–268.

106. Frischknecht, "State Extension Services," 424.

107. U.S. House, Committee on Appropriations, *Department of Agriculture Appropriation Bill, Fiscal Year 1944,* report, 15.

108. *CR* 89:3 (April 16, 1943): 3493.

109. U.S. Senate, Committee on Appropriations, *Agricultural Appropriation Bill for 1944,* hearings, 29.

110. Ibid., 413.

111. Ibid., 727.

112. Ibid., 836, 880.

113. U.S. Senate, Committee on Appropriations, *Agricultural Appropriation Bill, 1944,* report, 7.

114. U.S. Congress, Committee of Conference, *Department of Agriculture Appropriation Bill, 1944,* 6–7, 13.

115. 57 *Stat.* 417.

116. AP, "AAA 'Gag' Is Withdrawn," *New York Times,* July 30, 1943, 9.

117. 87 *Stat.* 486.

118. With Truman winning in 1948, Republicans kept the issue alive. For example, half a year before the midterm 1950 elections, a Republican congressman from California reported to his constituents that the agency implementing the Marshall Plan to reconstruct postwar Europe had "just hired five new ones [press agents] at $39,450, nearly $8000 a year each; and also engaged a magazine 'consultant' who will get $50 a day every time he is consulted. It is proposing . . . to hire more press agents. . . . [Its] appropriation for publicity is $285,000 for the year" ("The Budget Down to Earth" [editorial], *Los Angeles Times,* April 15, 1950, A4).

119. Junius B. Wood, "Ballyhoo Runs Wild," *Nation's Business* 33:7 (July 1945): 65. See also "U.S. Propaganda Cost Set at 300 Million a Year," *Chicago Tribune,* July 5, 1945, 15.

120. *CR* 92:1 (January 23, 1946): 274.

121. U.S. House, Committee on Appropriations, *Interior Department Appropriation Bill for 1947,* hearings, 144, 146.

122. Ibid., 126–127.

123. U.S. House, Committee on Appropriations, *Interior Department Appropriation Bill, 1947,* report, 16.

124. U.S. Senate, Committee on Appropriations, *Interior Department Appropriation Bill for 1947,* hearings, 41–43.

125. Ibid., 557.

126. U.S. Senate, Committee on Appropriations, *Interior Department Appropriation Bill, 1947,* report, 21.

127. *CR* 92:6 (June 18, 1946): 7075.

128. U.S. Congress, Committee of Conference, *Interior Department Appropriation Bill, 1947,* 9, 27.

129. 60 *Stat.* 364.

130. U.S. House, Committee on Appropriations, *Interior Department Appropriation Bill for 1947,* hearings, 68. Even before reaching that specific request during the House appropriations hearings, several congressmen had already taken the initiative to ask about the size and budget of the department's Information Division (ibid., 13–14, 35). This was an indication of Congress being ever alert to bureaucratic public relations, no matter how well buried in budget documents.

131. U.S. House, Committee on Appropriations, *Interior Department Appropriation Bill, 1947,* report, 5.

132. U.S. Senate, Committee on Appropriations, *Interior Department Appropriation Bill for 1947,* 2, 4, hearings, 417.

133. U.S. Senate, Committee on Appropriations, *Interior Department Appropriation Bill, 1947,* report, 2.

134. U.S. Congress, Committee of Conference, *Interior Department Appropriation Bill, 1947,* 23.

135. Fitzpatrick, "Public Information Activities," 538.

136. Laurence Burd, "G.O.P. to Fire Million, Save 9 Billion," *Chicago Tribune,* November 16, 1946, 1.

137. AP, "Republicans to 'Scrutinize' Culture Funds," *Washington Post,* November 27, 1946, 2.

138. "The Cost of Propaganda" (editorial), *New York Times,* November 30, 1946, 12.

139. James J. Butler, "Taber Blast on Press Agents Fails to Excite Washington: Correspondents Regard Some as Helpful in Official Maze," *Editor and Publisher* 79:49 (November 30, 1946): 10, 60.

140. *CR* 93:1 (January 16, 1947): 385; "Propaganda Study Asked," *New York Times,* January 17, 1947, 6.

141. *CR* 93:1 (January 23, 1947): 542–543. Seventeen years later, that was the definition U.S. Supreme Court Justice Potter Stewart famously used for pornography.

142. *CR* 93:1 (February 10, 1947): 948–949.

143. Like the Tydings Subcommittee being referred to as a committee, the same occurred in this case.

144. AP, "House Inquiry Set on Publicity Expense," *New York Times,* May 28, 1947, 19.

145. "Harness Gives Aim in Marshall Plan," *New York Times,* August 20, 1947, 9.

146. U.S. House, Committee on Expenditures in the Executive Departments, Publicity and Propaganda Subcommittee, *Final Report,* 9.

147. Harness, "Federal Thought Control." Besides daily newspaper coverage, see also "Federal Thought Control," *Forbes* 66:7 (October 1, 1950): 14–17. The Harness Committee's work was recycled as a 1950 report to the Hoover Commission on reforming the federal government, but Hoover and the other commissioners displayed no interest in pursuing the topic (Lee, *First Presidential Communications Agency,* 190–191; "The Government and PR," *Tide* 24:40 [October 6, 1950]: 49; *CR* 96:17 [September 22, 1950]: A6861–A6866; *CR* 96:18 [September 23, 1950]: A7175–A7176).

148. Millard C. Faught, "Government Public Relations," *Tide* 21:20 (May 16, 1947): 17–19.

149. U.S. House, Committee on Appropriations, *Department of Agriculture Appropriation Bill, Fiscal Year 1948,* 8.

150. U.S. Senate, Committee on Appropriations, *Agricultural Appropriation Bill, 1948,* 4.

151. Drew Pearson, "Washington Merry-Go-Round" (syndicated column), *Washington Post,* February 5, 1947, 5.

152. *CR* 94:2 (March 11, 1948): 2598. A slightly different quote is in "Postal and Treasury Budgets Whittled in Passage by House," *Chicago Tribune,* March 12, 1948, 2.

153. "Farm Bill Gets House Clearance," *New York Times,* May 27, 1947, 29.

154. "News Source Is Stopped," *New York Times,* January 31, 1947, 28.

155. Prince, *Washington Book Mart,* 2–45.

156. "Senate Democrats Try to Force GOP to Fulfill Economy Pledges," *Wall Street Journal,* May 23, 1947, 2.

157. AP, "Truman Said to Fight Cut in Appropriation," *New York Times,* July 19, 1950, 13; John W. Ball, "Gifts to U.S. Agents Cited in Grain Quiz," *Washington Post,* March 21, 1952, 16.

CHAPTER 8

1. Lee, "When Congress Tried" and "Too Much Bureaucracy?"

2. *CR* 97:3 (April 18, 1951): 4098.

3. Ibid., 4099.

4. Ibid., 4098, 4100.

5. Ibid.

6. U.S. Senate, Committee on Appropriations, *Labor-Federal Security Appropriation Bill, 1952*, 9.

7. 65 *Stat.* 223.

8. 66 *Stat.* 372; 67 *Stat.* 259.

9. U.S. GAO, Congressional Testimony T-OGC-96–18 (May 15, 1996), Attachment 1, 1.

10. U.S. GAO, Report B-301022 (March 10, 2004), 2. For an example from 2008, see P.L. 110–329, 46.

11. 31 *Comp. Gen.* 314.

12. Ibid., 313.

13. U.S. GAO, Report B-145883 (April 5, 1971), 3.

14. Ibid.

15. U.S. GAO, B-114823 (December 23, 1974), 4.

16. U.S. GAO, B-302504 (March 10, 2004), 10–12. See also Robert Pear, "A Watchdog Sees Flaws in Bush's Ads on Medicare," *New York Times*, March 11, 2004, A23.

17. U.S. GAO, Report B-303495 (January 4, 2005), 6.

18. U.S. GAO, B-284226.2 (August 17, 2000), 5.

19. U.S. GAO, B-178528 (July 27, 1973), 3.

20. U.S. GAO, B-212069 (October 6, 1983), 3.

21. U.S. GAO, B-129874 (September 11, 1978).

22. U.S. GAO, B-145883 (April 5, 1971), 4.

23. U.S. GAO, B-301022 (March 10, 2004), 4.

24. U.S. GAO, Office of the General Counsel, *Principles of Federal Appropriations Law*, chap. 4, 202; U.S. GAO, B-229257 (June 10, 1988).

25. U.S. GAO, B-136762 (August 18, 1958).

26. U.S. GAO, B-222758 (June 25, 1986), 9.

27. Ibid., 14.

28. U.S. GAO, B-223098, B223098.2 (October 10, 1986), 9.

29. This led to the Iran-Contra scandal.

30. 66 *Comp. Gen.* 708.

31. Ibid., 710.

32. Richard L. Burke, "State Dept. Linked to Contra Publicity," *New York Times*, October 5, 1987, A3; David Rogers, "Administration Broke Rules of Congress in Funding of Propaganda, GAO Says," *Wall Street Journal*, October 5,

1987, 54; Doyle McManus, "GAO Says State Dept. Ran Illegal Propaganda Effort," *Los Angeles Times*, October 5, 1987, 1-1.

33. In 1957, the Bureau of the Budget indirectly opined that expenditures by the State Department for public opinion polls were not violations of Smith I, although the Bureau—understandably—mostly focused on budgeting and accounting proprieties rather than issues of publicity and propaganda (Brown, "Demise," 6).

34. 6 *Op. OLC* 549.

35. 12 *Op. OLC* 40.

36. Memorandum Opinion from Daniel Koffsky, Acting Deputy Assistant Attorney General, OLC, to the Acting General Counsel, General Services Administration regarding "General Services Administration Use of Government Funds for Advertising," January 19, 2001, www.usdoj.gov/olc/gsafinal.htm (accessed November 2010).

37. In its defense, HHS provided the GAO with identically styled products produced in 1999 during the Clinton administration. The GAO ruled that the fiscal statute of limitations had already expired on those uses, but substantively they too were covert propaganda (Decision B-302710 [May 19, 2004], 13).

38. U.S. GAO, Decision B-302710 (May 19, 2004), 13.

39. May 20, 2004: Robert Pear, "Ruling Says White House's Medicare Videos Were Illegal," *New York Times*, A24; Amy Goldstein, "GAO Says HHS Broke Laws with Medicare Videos," *Washington Post*, A1.

40. Memorandum Opinion from Steven G. Bradbury, Principal Deputy Assistant Attorney General, OLC, to the General Counsel, Department of Health and Human Services regarding "Expenditure of Appropriated Funds for Information Video News Releases," July 30, 2004, www.usdoj.gov/olc/opfinal.htm (accessed November 2010).

41. U.S. GAO, Memo B-304272 (February 17, 2005), 1. See also Anne E. Kornblut, "Administration Is Warned about Its Publicity Videos," *New York Times*, February 19, 2005, A11; Christopher Lee, "Prepackaged News Gets GAO Rebuke," *Washington Post*, February 21, 2005, A25.

42. Memorandum from Steven G. Bradbury, Principal Deputy Assistant Attorney General, OLC to General Counsels of the Executive Branch regarding "Whether Appropriations May be Used for Informational Video News Releases," March 1, 2005.

43. Memorandum from Joshua B. Bolten, Director, Office of Management and Budget to Heads of Departments and Agencies regarding "Use of Government Funds for Video News Releases" (M-05–10), March 11, 2005. See also Christopher Lee, "Administration Rejects Ruling on PR Videos," *Washington Post*, March 15, 2005, A21.

44. Tony Pugh, "Medicare Administrator Won't Rule Out Government-Produced Video News Releases," Knight Ridder Tribune News Service, April 5, 2005.

45. U.S. GAO, Congressional Testimony 05–643T (May 12, 2005).

46. He was not related to Senator Harry Byrd (D-Va.).

47. *CR* (April 14, 2005): S3630–S3641.

48. U.S. Congress, Committee of Conference, *Making Emergency Supplemental Appropriations*, 159.

49. George W. Bush, "Statement on Signing the Emergency Supplemental Appropriations Act for Defense, the Global War on Terror, and Tsunami Relief Act, 2005," May 11, 2005. *Public Papers of the Presidents of the United States: George W. Bush, 2005*, Book 1:784–785. The Byrd amendment became Section 6076 of P.L. 109–13, 119 *Stat.* 301.

50. Memorandum from Joshua B. Bolten, Director, Office of Management and Budget, to Heads of Departments and Agencies regarding "Statutory Provision on Video News Releases" (M-05–20), July 21, 2005.

51. U.S. GAO, B-304228, B-305368, B-306349 (September 30, 2005). See also Robert Pear, "Buying of News by Bush's Aides Is Ruled Illegal," *New York Times*, October 1, 2005, A1. In 2006, the advocacy group Center for Media and Democracy reported on the continuing use of video news releases by local TV stations without source disclosures. Of the ones they identified, "only a few came from government agencies or non-profit organizations," with most coming from for-profit corporations; www.prwatch.org/fakenews/execsummary (accessed November 2010).

52. The FY 2009 Defense Department authorization bill included a slightly reworded version of Smith I: "No part of any funds authorized to be appropriated in this or any other Act shall be used the Department of Defense for publicity or propaganda purposes within the United States not otherwise specifically authorized by law" (Section 1056, P.L. 110–417).

CHAPTER 9

1. *CR* 64:1 (December 21, 1922): 829.

2. *CR* 97:4 (May 2, 1951): 4741.

3. Ibid.

4. Ibid., 4742.

5. I designated this amendment from Congressman Smith the "Smith II amendment" to avoid confusion with the "Smith I amendment" related to banning agency publicity and propaganda in general, regardless of the intent or purpose (chapter 8).

6. U.S. Senate, Committee on Appropriations, *Interior Department Appropriation Bill, 1952*, 34; *CR* 97:6 (July 5, 1951): 7651.

7. U.S. Congress, Committee of Conference, *Interior Department Appropriation Bill, 1952*, 15.

8. *CR* 97:4 (May 4, 1951): 4913–4914.

9. U.S. Congress, Committee of Conference, *Independent Offices Appropriation Bill, 1952*, 82nd Cong., 1st sess., 1951. H. Rep. 753, 14; H. Rep. 869, 15.

10. *CR* 97:8 (August 15, 1951): 10065.

11. 65 *Stat.* 291.

12. *CR* 97:4 (May 17, 1951): 5474.

13. U.S. House, Committee on Expenditures in the Executive Departments, Publicity and Propaganda Subcommittee, *Investigation of Agricultural Adjustment Agency.*

14. *CR* 97:4 (May 17, 1951): 5475.

15. 65 *Stat.* 247. Even though President Truman signed the USDA and Independent Offices bills on the same day, he signed the USDA bill first. Therefore, USDA's appropriation was technically the first enactment of Smith II into law.

16. In 1953, the Smith II amendment was in the USDA bill (67 *Stat.* 225) and the two separate bills passed to cover all of the independent agencies (67 *Stat.* 195, 316).

17. *CR* 108:2 (February 7, 1962): 1989.

18. Ibid., 1988–1990; *CR* 108:3 (March 1, 1962): 3155–3157.

19. *CR* 108:4 (March 28, 1962): 5287.

20. Ibid., 5281.

21. Ibid., 5281–5287; *CR* 108:3 (March 29, 1962): 5459–5468; U.S. Senate, Committee on Appropriations, *Second Supplemental Appropriation Bill for 1962,* hearings, 428–443; AP, "5 Billion Fund Bill Is Voted by Senate," *New York Times,* March 30, 1962, 3.

22. U.S. Senate, Committee on Appropriations, *Second Supplemental Appropriation Bill, 1962,* report, 21.

23. *CR* 108:5 (April 16, 1962): 6615–6616.

24. *CR* 108:8 (June 14, 1962): 10490.

25. *CR* 108:11 (July 20, 1962): 14334.

26. U.S. GAO, B-116331 (May 29, 1961), 7; B-148206 (March 20, 1962), 2; B-147578 (November 8, 1962), 4.

27. U.S. GAO, B-93353 (September 28, 1962); B-148206 (March 20, 1962), 2–3.

28. U.S. GAO, B-148206 (March 20, 1962), 3.

29. U.S. GAO, B-116331 (May 29, 1961), 7; B-93353 (September 28, 1962), 4.

30. The GAO's substantive guidelines for interpreting Smith II (including its successive versions) did not change significantly over the years, but the adoption of the shorthand term "grass roots" as signifying a prohibited activity was not used until 1981 (U.S. GAO, Decision B-202787 [May 1, 1981]). After that, it became common nomenclature in GAO decisions and guidelines.

31. U.S. GAO, Report B-147578 (November 8, 1962), 4.

32. U.S. GAO, B-116331 (May 29, 1961), 7.

33. U.S. House, Committee on Armed Services, *Allegations of Improper Lobbying,* Hearing HASC 97-65, 194, 188.

34. U.S. GAO, Report B-209049 (September 29, 1982), 20. See also Charles Mohr, "Pentagon Accused by G.A.O. of Illegal Lobbying," *New York Times,*

October 1, 1982, A23. Usually, agencies meekly accept GAO findings and recommendations. In this case, the Department of Defense and the Air Force mounted a major effort to rebut and discredit the GAO report, prompting the GAO to issue a point-by-point surrebuttal of the critique of its original report (U.S. House, Committee on Armed Services, *Allegations of Improper Lobbying,* Hearing HASC 97-65, 307–326). The counterattack on the GAO was so successful that the House subcommittee conducting the investigation ended up disagreeing with the GAO and siding with Defense (U.S. House, Committee on Armed Services, *Allegations of Improper Lobbying,* Committee Print 24). The comments and questions by subcommittee members at the hearing tended to be supportive of the military-industrial complex and the economic benefits of such spending in their districts. Hence, here was a situation where parochial political and constituency interests trumped the generalized institutional hostility of legislators to agency public relations and lobbying.

35. U.S. GAO, Report B-178448 (April 30, 1973).

36. U.S. GAO, B-192658 (September 1, 1978).

37. For example, U.S. GAO, Report B-118638 (August 2, 1974); Report B-114823 (December 23, 1974); Report B-159835 (July 18, 1975); Report B-128938 (July 12, 1976).

38. U.S. GAO, Report B-130961 (September 30, 1976), 32.

39. 56 *Comp. Gen.* 891 (August 10, 1977).

40. U.S. GAO, Report B-199777 (August 28, 1980), Appendix I, 15.

41. U.S. House, Committee on Armed Services, *Allegations of Improper Lobbying,* Hearing HASC 97-65, 207, emphasis added.

42. U.S. GAO, Report B-209584 (January 11, 1983).

43. 63 *Comp. Gen.* 624–631 (September 26, 1984).

44. U.S. GAO, Report B-215746 (January 18, 1985).

45. U.S. GAO, B-216239 (January 22, 1985).

46. 64 *Comp. Gen.* 281–282 (February 19, 1985).

47. U.S. GAO, Report B-304715 (April 27, 2005). The legislators (Democrats, during a Republican presidency) seeking a declaration of a violation of Smith II argued that the law covered *implied* requests for grassroots lobbying when the *intent* of the agency's communication is obvious. Otherwise, they argued, agencies were wholly exempt from the ban as long as they did not use the "magic words" of explicitly asking the public to contact Congress on a specific bill. The GAO rejected that argument based on a position it had articulated in 1982 (U.S. House, Committee on Armed Services, *Allegations of Improper Lobbying,* Hearing HASC 97-65, 207).

48. U.S. GAO, Decision B-202787 (May 1, 1981), 3. This was at the beginning of stricter federal oversight of expenditures by recipients of federal funds. The prohibition on lobbying or engaging in political activities by recipients of federal funds gradually evolved into a major regulatory and enforcement effort directed

at, for example, state and local governments, nonprofit agencies delivering federal services, and defense contractors. Besides Congress, the executive branch also became substantially involved this oversight effort, including, for example, OMB Circular A-110 (Uniform Administrative Requirements for Grants and Other Agreements with Institutions of Higher Education, Hospitals and Other Non-Profit Organizations), Appendix A, Section 7; OMB Circular A-122 (Cost Principles for Non-Profit Organizations); 5 *Op. OLC* 180 (June 17, 1981); and 31 USC 1351. However, restricting third parties from using federal funds for lobbying and public relations is beyond the scope of this inquiry into direct congressional efforts affecting federal agencies.

49. U.S. GAO, Report B-222758 (June 25, 1986), 8. See also John H. Cushman, Jr., "Illegal Military Lobbying on Chemical Arms Seen," *New York Times,* August 4, 1986, A15.

50. U.S. GAO, Report B-262234 (December 21, 1995), 10.

51. U.S. GAO, B-281637 (May 14, 1999), 21.

52. Memorandum from John M. Harmon, Assistant Attorney General, OLC, to Robert J. Lipshutz, Counsel to the President, regarding "Statutory Restraints on Lobbying Activity by Federal Officials," November 29, 1977, 1.

53. Ibid., 6.

54. Ibid., 8.

55. Ibid., 7n17.

56. Ibid., 8.

57. Memorandum from Fred F. Fielding, Counsel to the President to Members of the White House Office Staff, regarding "Support of Administration Legislative Programs," February 23, 1981, 4. The memo is reproduced as Appendix IV in U.S. GAO, Report B-129874 (March 20, 1984).

58. 12 *Op. OLC* 36 (February 1, 1988).

59. Memorandum from Walter Dellinger, Assistant Attorney General, OLC, to the Attorney General and the Deputy Attorney General, regarding "Anti-Lobbying Act Guidelines," April 14, 1995, 3.

60. Letter from Glenn A. Fine, Inspector General, Department of Justice, to Congressman John Conyers, Jr., Ranking (minority) Member, Committee on the Judiciary, October 22, 2004, 6.

61. American Trucking Associations v. Department of Transportation, 492 *F. Supp.* 570.

62. Grassley v. Legal Services Corporation, 535 *F. Supp.* 826.

63. U.S. GAO, Report B-270875 (July 5, 1996), 3.

64. U.S. House, Committee on Government Reform and Oversight, *H.R. 3078,* 159–160; U.S. GAO, Office of the General Counsel, *Principles of Federal Appropriations Law,* chap. 4, 204–205.

65. *CR* 119:14 (May 31, 1973): 17692–17695.

66. 87 *Stat.* 129.

67. U.S. Senate, Committee on Appropriations, *Departments of Labor and Health, Education, and Welfare and Related Agencies Appropriations for Fiscal Year 1974,* hearings, 196–200. During the same time as this brouhaha, Magnuson was profiled in a book about the legislative process, written by his former legislative assistant (Redman, *Dance of Legislation*). The former aide depicted Magnuson as one of the Senate's workhorses, in contradistinction to its showhorses (i.e., publicity hounds). If this is accurate, then Magnuson's strong reaction to the potential political threat of agency public relations carries more weight than if it had come from a showhorse senator excessively preoccupied with his or her media image and quick on the trigger to complain publicly about the bureaucracy.

68. U.S. Senate, Committee on Appropriations, *Departments of Labor, and Health, Education, and Welfare, and Related Agencies Appropriation Bill, 1974,* report, 101.

69. Holtzman, *Legislative Liaison,* 64–70; U.S. Congress, Committee of Conference, *Making Appropriations for Departments of Labor, HEW,* 30.

71. U.S. Senate, Committee on Appropriations, *Departments of State, Justice, and Commerce,* 78; *CR* 124:13 (June 14, 1978): 17641–17644.

72. 98 *Stat.* 1904; U.S. GAO, Report B-222758 (June 25, 1986), 7.

73. *CR* 129:21 (October 27, 1983): 29629–29630. Apparently the action was intended to undergird a later point of order on another provision in the bill, one banning any federal funding for abortions, rather than as substantive opposition to Smith II.

74. This claim would have ignored the use of appropriated funds for the salaries of the staff involved, transportation costs, copying costs, and so forth.

75. John W. Finney, "Air Chief's Briefing for Senate Aides on B-1 Was Funded by Private Group," *New York Times,* July 30, 1976, 6. The article mistakenly dated the law to 1948 instead of 1951.

76. U.S. House, Committee on Armed Services, *Allegations of Improper Lobbying,* Committee Print 24, 3.

77. S. 1969, 97th Congress; *CR* 127:24 (December 15, 1981): 31373. Pryor was mostly interested in getting at the lobbying costs of federal defense contractors and being sure they could not be financed with federal funds. Pryor resubmitted his bill as an amendment to the FY 1982 Defense appropriation bill. It was adopted on the floor (*CR* 127:22 [November 30, 1981]: 29180), but it did not survive the conference committee (*CR* 128:11 [June 30, 1982]: 15397).

78. U.S. House, Committee on Armed Services, *Allegations of Improper Lobbying,* Hearing HASC 97-65, 188.

79. *CR* 127:25 [Index]: 2436; 128:25 [Index]: 2396.

80. U.S. GAO, Report B-129874 (March 20, 1984), 32.

81. S. 1617 and H.R. 3078, 104th Congress, 2nd session. For text, see U.S. House, Committee on Government Reform and Oversight, *H.R. 3078,* 3–4.

82. *CR* 142:4 (March 14, 1996): 4968.

83. U.S. House, Committee on Government Reform and Oversight, *H.R. 3078,* 76–77, 155–174.

84. For the version adopted in 2008 for funding the federal government during the first half of FY 2009, see P.L. 110–329, 142.

85. Engstrom and Walker, "Statutory Restraints"; Freeman, *Political Process*, 39.

86. Memorandum from Fred F. Fielding, Counsel to the President to Members of the White House Office Staff, regarding "Support of Administration Legislative Programs," February 23, 1981, 4. The memo is reproduced as Appendix IV in U.S. GAO, Report B-129874 (March 20, 1984).

87. Holtzman, *Legislative Liaison*, 45.

88. U.S. Senate, Committee on Finance, *Nominations of James S. Dwight, Jr., William A. Morrill, and Lewis M. Helm*, 31–32.

CHAPTER 10

1. *CR* 97:5 (June 19, 1951): 6733.

2. *CR* 97:5 (June 20, 1951): 6795.

3. C. P. Trussell, "President's Funds Slashed in Senate," *New York Times*, June 20, 1951, 28.

4. *CR* 97:5 (June 20, 1951): 6797–6799. Rosapepe misattributes this comment to Anderson ("Neither Pinkertons," 17). Benton was a former assistant secretary of state for public affairs (1945–47), so he knew whereof he spoke (Lee, "Public Affairs Enters," 188–189).

5. *CR* 97:5 (June 20, 1951): 6799.

6. Robert C. Albright, "Funds for 27 Agencies Voted after More Cuts by Senate," *Washington Post*, June 21, 1951, 13.

7. U.S. Congress, Committee of Conference, *Independent Offices Appropriation Bill, 1952*, H. Rep. 753, 14; H. Rep. 869, 15. Rosapepe mistakenly concluded from this that the Byrd amendment had been killed and never incorporated into the final version of the bill that was signed into law ("Neither Pinkertons," 17).

8. *CR* 97:8 (August 15, 1951): 10065.

9. 65 *Stat.* 291–292.

10. Heinemann, *Harry Byrd of Virginia*, 302.

11. *CR* 97:7 (July 27, 1951): 8990–8991; 65 *Stat.* 248; *CR* 97:8 (August 15, 1951): 10036–10037; 65 *Stat.* 622. The House insisted on excluding the Panama Canal Zone government from the Byrd amendment to this bill (U.S. Congress, Committee of Conference, *Civil Functions Appropriation Bill*, 2–3, 5).

12. U.S. Senate, Committee on Appropriations, *Interior Department Appropriation Bill, 1952*, 34; 65 *Stat.* 266; U.S. Senate, Committee on Appropriations, *Treasury and Post Office Departments*, 8; 65 *Stat.* 189; U.S. Senate, Committee on Appropriations, *Supplemental Appropriation Bill*, 28–29. Two years later, the Federal Security Agency was renamed the Department of Health, Education, and Welfare.

13. U.S. Senate, Committee on Appropriations, *Supplemental Appropriation Bill*, 29.

14. U.S. Congress, Committee of Conference, *Supplemental Appropriation Bill*, 12.

15. *CR* 97:10 (October 20, 1951): 13707, 13761–13762; 65 *Stat.* 759.

16. *CR* 97:7 (July 26, 1951): 8981–8982.

17. Ibid., 8984.

18. Ibid.

19. *CR* 97:8 (August 20, 1951): 10409; 65 *Stat.* 759. This meant, incomprehensibly, that the same law contained Smith's 50 percent cut in all domestic public relations, the Byrd amendment cutting the Labor Department and the Federal Security Agency by 25 percent, and the three exemptions for press offices with four or fewer people, scientific publications, and defense-related work.

20. *CR* 97:10 (October 10, 1951): 12904; 65 *Stat.* 767.

21. 66 *Stat.* 419; 66 *Stat.* 372–373. This renewal included the exemption added by the House the previous year for technical publications.

22. 66 *Stat.* 462; 66 *Stat.* 357.

23. 67 *Stat.* 317.

24. U.S. House, Committee on Appropriations, *Interior Department Appropriation Bill, 1954,* 28.

25. "Cut of 1,000 Employees Ordered in Reclamation," *New York Times,* May 8, 1953, 50.

26. AP, "Interior to Drop 2,098," *New York Times,* May 20, 1953, 30; "Cut 1,322 from Reclamation Bureau Rolls," *Chicago Tribune,* May 8, 1953, 2.

27. U.S. Senate, Committee on Appropriations, *Interior Department Appropriation Bill, 1954,* 27.

28. U.S. Congress, Committee of Conference, *Interior Department Appropriation Bill, 1954,* 12.

29. 67 *Stat.* 276.

30. 68 *Stat.* 374–375.

31. 69 *Stat.* 151–152.

CHAPTER 11

1. Lee, "When Congress Tried," 145–148.

2. Lee, "Too Much Bureaucracy," 340–344.

3. AP, "Treasury Warned over Radio Ad Cost," *Washington Post,* September 23, 1927, 11; "Treasury Officials Charged for Talks," *New York Times,* October 2, 1927, XX16; "McCarl Ruling Bars Radio in Bond Deal," *Washington Post,* January 7, 1928, 20.

4. 14 *Comp. Gen.* 641.

5. U.S. GAO, Report A-82749 (January 7, 1937), 3.

6. Lee, *First Presidential Communications Agency,* 26–27, 43–44; 18 *Comp. Gen.* 979.

7. U.S. GAO, Report B-15278 (May 15, 1942), 3.

8. U.S. GAO, B-62501 (January 7, 1947).

9. 32 *Comp. Gen.* 361.

10. 32 *Comp. Gen.* 487–488.

11. U.S. GAO, Report B-144323 (November 4, 1960), 4.

12. U.S., GAO, B-147578 (November 8, 1962), 5.

13. 43 *Comp. Gen.* 564–567.

14. U.S. GAO, Report B-169242 (June 29, 1971), 6.

15. U.S. GAO, Decision B-211477 (July 14, 1983).

16. 1987 *U.S. Comp. Gen.* LEXIS 1022, B-225006 (June 1, 1987).

17. 72 *Comp. Gen.* 73–75.

18. U.S. GAO, Decision B-247563.2 (May 12, 1993).

19. U.S. GAO, B-251887 (July 22, 1993).

20. U.S. GAO, B-290900 (March 18, 2003).

21. U.S. GAO, B-280440 (February 26, 1999).

22. U.S. GAO, Office of the General Counsel, *Principles of Federal Appropriations Law,* chap. 4, 231.

23. The 1995 court decision *Donaggio v. Arlington County, Virginia,* contained a footnote emphasizing that Congress had expressly exempted government agencies from lobbying registration, a requirement that applied to all private and nonprofit sector lobbyists (880 *F. Supp.* 455). The GAO interpreted that footnote as meaning that Congress categorized statements by federal agencies on controversial legislative topics as implicitly permissible, since this was a form of lobbying that was exempt from federal lobbying controls—as long as such a role was consistent with other federal laws related to agency direct and indirect lobbying.

24. U.S. GAO, Report B-161939/B-144618 (January 18, 1979), 4–8; Report B-216239 (October 29, 1984).

25. U.S. GAO, B-130961 (January 6, 1978), 2.

26. *CR* 113:7 (April 10, 1967): 8826.

27. Robert Coffey, "Taxpayers Footing Bill for Army of Admen," *Chicago Tribune,* April 23, 1978, 1.

28. U.S. GAO, Reports B-144618 (March 18, 1977 and July 12, 1977).

29. "Government Film Activity Called Peril to Movie Unions," *New York Times,* August 10, 1972, 26.

30. "Hidden Spending Laid to Pentagon," *New York Times,* August 22, 1971, 17.

31. U.S. GAO, Report B-161939 (April 4, 1974); Report B-271957 (September 27, 1996).

32. "Aged Get Pamphlets on Nixon's Order," *New York Times,* October 16, 1972, 32.

33. U.S. Senate, Committee on Governmental Affairs, *Lack of Accountability,* 7–49.

34. Ibid., 2, iii. See also James M. Perry, "Washington PR Staffs Dream Up Ways to Get Agencies' Stories Out," *Wall Street Journal,* May 23, 1979, 1, 28. These attacks and their stridency were especially ironic because the senator making them, committee chair Abraham Ribicoff (D-Conn.), had himself been accused of employing "highly paid publicity experts" when he was governor of

Connecticut ("Connecticut G.O.P. Attacks Ribicoff," *New York Times*, January 26, 1958, 54) and of violating federal lobbying laws when he later was secretary of the Department of Health, Education, and Welfare in the Kennedy administration ("Ribicoff Accused of Lobby Activity," *New York Times*, May 10, 1962, 27).

35. Mayhew, *Congress*; Rourke, *Secrecy and Publicity*, 183.

36. Lee, *First Presidential Communications Agency*, 67–70, 148.

37. *CR* 88:4 (May 28, 1942): 4735.

38. *CR* 89:3 (April 7, 1943): 3083–3084, 3087.

39. *CR* 90:3, 2941 (March 22, 1944).

40. U.S. Senate, Committee on Appropriations, *Interior Department Appropriation Bill for 1947*, hearings, 417, 426.

CHAPTER 12

1. Kosar, "Executive Branch and Propaganda."

2. Yarwood and Enis, "Problems in Regulating," 33–36.

3. Lee, "When Congress Tried," 145.

4. Robert Pear, "Agency Running Social Security to Push for Change," *New York Times*, January 16, 2005, 1, 21. This issue was a repeat, except with partisan positions switched, of Republican congressional complaints about Kennedy administration pressures on USDA employees (chapters 5, 9).

5. Minority Staff, House Committee on Government Reform, "The Politicization of the Social Security Administration," February 2005, www.yuricareport.com/Corruption/PoliticizationOfSSA.pdf (accessed November 2010).

6. Robert Pear, "No Call for Agency to Sell Fix for Social Security, Aide Says," *New York Times*, January 17, 2005, A15.

7. Minority Staff, House Committee on Government Reform, "Federal Public Relations Spending," January 2005, 1. www.house.gov/dingell/documents/pdfs/federal_public_relations.pdf (accessed November 2010).

8. Office of the Inspector General, U.S. Department of Education, "Review of Formation Issues Regarding the Department of Education's Fiscal Year 2003 Contract with Ketchum, Inc. for Media Relations Services," Report ED-OIC/A19-F0007, April 2005, www.ed.gov/about/offices/list/oig/auditreports/a19f0007.doc (accessed November 2010). See also Ben Feller, AP, "U.S. Education Dept.'s PR Budget More than $9 Million," *Charleston* (W.Va) *Gazette*, May 6, 2005, 10A.

9. Christopher Lee, "USDA Paid Freelance Writer $7,500 for Articles," *Washington Post*, May 11, 2005, A15.

10. Christopher Lee, "EPA Paid Weather Channel for Videos," *Washington Post*, July 18, 2005, A13.

11. David Barstow and Robin Stein, "Under Bush, a New Age of Prepackaged Television News," *New York Times*, March 13, 2005, 1.

12. The controversy that began in December 2005 regarding Defense Department payments for articles and ads in Iraqi newspapers is beyond the scope of

this inquiry since it relates to propaganda by the federal executive branch to audiences abroad, which Congress has generally authorized. In part, these overseas activities seemed to resonate with some on Capitol Hill because they ostensibly paralleled the contemporaneous public relations activities of federal executive branch agencies of the Bush II administration domestically. For general coverage, see Josh White and Bradley Graham, "Military Says It Paid Iraq Papers for News," *Washington Post*, December 3, 2005, A01; Jeff Gerth, Carlotta Gall, and Ruhullah Khapalwak, "Military's Information War Is Vast and Often Secretive," *New York Times*, December 11, 2005, 1; Mark Mazzetti and Kevin Sack, "The Challenges in Iraq: Planted PR Stories Not New to Military," *Los Angeles Times*, December 18, 2005, A1.

13. P.L. 106–554.

14. Kosar, "Executive Branch and Propaganda," 787–788, 790.

15. David Barstow, "Behind TV Analysts, Pentagon's Hidden Hand," *New York Times*, April 20, 2008, A1.

16. Section 1056, P.L. 110–417.

17. Defense appropriation bills are handled by the appropriations committees, whereas the legislation that must precede them, called defense *authorization* bills, go through the armed services committees. The latter often have members who are more pro-military than Congress as a whole.

18. Schattschneider, *Semi-Sovereign People*.

19. Riggs, "Bureaucracy and the Constitution," 67. Riggs repeated the term many times in his in later writings, sometimes hyphenating the phrase, sometimes not.

BIBLIOGRAPHY

PUBLISHED PRIMARY SOURCES

Bush, George W. *Public Papers of the Presidents of the United States: George W. Bush, 2002,* Book 2. Washington, D.C.: GPO, 2005.

———. *Public Papers of the Presidents of the United States: George W. Bush, 2005,* Book 1. Washington, D.C.: GPO, 2007.

Chase, Harold W., and Allen H. Lerman, eds. *Kennedy and the Press: The News Conferences.* New York: Thomas Y. Crowell, 1965.

Hilderbrand, Robert C., ed. *The Complete Press Conferences, 1913–1919.* Vol. 50, *The Papers of Woodrow Wilson.* Princeton, N.J.: Princeton University Press, 1985.

Ickes, Harold L. *The Inside Struggle, 1936–1939.* Vol. 2, *The Secret Diary of Harold L. Ickes.* New York: Simon and Schuster, 1954.

Kennedy, John F. *Public Papers of the Presidents of the United States: John F. Kennedy, 1962.* Washington, D.C.: GPO, 1963.

Link, Arthur S., ed. *February 28–July 31, 1920.* Vol. 65, *The Papers of Woodrow Wilson.* Princeton, N.J.: Princeton University Press, 1991.

Swisher, Carl Brent, ed. *Selected Papers of Homer Cummings: Attorney General of the United States, 1933–1939.* 1939; reprint, Holmes Beach, Fla.: Gaunt, 1996.

GOVERNMENT DOCUMENTS

U.S. Congress. *Annual Reports of the Department of Agriculture for the Year Ended June 30, 1913.* 63rd Cong., 2nd sess., 1914. H. Doc. 653.

———. *Annual Reports of the Department of Agriculture for the Year Ended June 30, 1914.* 63rd Cong., 3rd sess., 1914. H. Doc. 1437.

———. *Annual Reports of the Department of Agriculture for the Year Ended June 30, 1915.* 64th Cong., 1st sess., 1916. H. Doc. 903.

———. *Twenty-Sixth Annual Report of the United States Civil Service Commission for the Year Ended June 30, 1909.* 61st Cong., 2nd sess., 1910. H. Doc. 135.

———. *Veto Message on Legislative, Executive, and Judicial Appropriation Bill.* 66th Cong., 2nd sess., 1920. H. Doc. 764.

U.S. Congress. Committee of Conference. *21st Century Department of Justice Appropriations Authorization Act.* 107th Cong., 2nd sess., 2002. H. Rep. 107–685.

———. *Agricultural Appropriation Bill.* 60th Cong., 1st sess., 1908. H. Rep. 1698.

———. *Civil Functions Appropriation Bill, 1952.* 82nd Cong., 1st sess., 1951. H. Rep. 1197.

———. *Deficiency Appropriation Bill.* 66th Cong., 1st sess., 1919. H. Rep. 44.

———. *Department of Agriculture Appropriation Bill, 1944.* 78th Cong., 1st sess., 1943. H. Rep. 571.

———. *Department of Agriculture Appropriation Bill, 1945.* 78th Cong., 2nd sess., 1944. H. Rep. 1605.

———. *Department of Agriculture Appropriation Bill, 1945.* 78th Cong., 2nd sess., 1944. H. Rep. 1714.

———. *Department of Agriculture and Related Agencies.* 88th Cong., 1st sess., 1963. H. Rep. 1088.

———. *Independent Offices Appropriation Bill, 1942.* 77th Cong., 1st sess., 1941. H. Rep. 335.

———. *Independent Offices Appropriation Bill, 1952.* 82nd Cong., 1st sess., 1951. H. Rep. 753.

———. *Independent Offices Appropriation Bill, 1952.* 82nd Cong., 1st sess., 1951. H. Rep. 869.

———. *Interior Department Appropriation Bill, 1947.* 79th Cong., 2nd sess., 1946. H. Rep. 2329.

———. *Interior Department Appropriation Bill, 1952.* 82nd Cong., 1st sess., 1951. H. Rep. 888.

———. *Interior Department Appropriation Bill, 1954.* 83rd Cong., 1st sess., 1953. H. Rep. 947.

———. *Legislative, Executive, and Judicial Appropriation Bill.* 65th Cong., 3rd sess., 1919. H. Rep. 1146.

———. *Legislative, Executive, and Judicial Appropriation Bill, 1921.* 66th Cong., 2nd sess., 1920. H. Rep. 835.

———. *Making Appropriations for Departments of Labor, HEW for Fiscal Year Ending June 30, 1974.* 93rd Cong., 1st sess., 1973. H. Rep. 93–682.

———. *Making Emergency Supplemental Appropriations for the Fiscal Year Ending September 30, 2005, and for Other Purposes.* 109th Cong., 1st sess., 2005. H. Rep. 109–72.

————. *State, Justice, Commerce, and Labor Departments Appropriation Bill, 1937.* 74th Cong., 2nd sess., 1936. H. Rep. 2574.

————. *Supplemental Appropriation Bill, 1952.* 82nd Cong., 1st sess., 1951. H. Rep. 1222.

U.S. Congress. Joint Committee on Printing. *Government Periodicals and Field Printing.* 66th Cong., 2nd sess., 1920. S. Rep. 265.

U.S. Congress. Joint Committee on Reduction of Nonessential Federal Expenditures. *Reduction of Nonessential Federal Expenditures (Preliminary Report).* 77th Cong., 1st sess., 1941. S. Doc. 152.

————. *Reduction of Nonessential Federal Expenditures (Additional Report).* 78th Cong., 1st sess., 1943. S. Doc. 140.

U.S. Department of Agriculture, Forest Service. *Public Relations Course.* Washington, D.C.: GPO, 1941.

U.S. General Accounting Office, Office of the General Counsel. *Principles of Federal Appropriations Law* (aka the *Red Book*). 3rd ed., Vol. I, GAO-04–261SP. 2004. www.gao.gov/special.pubs/3rdeditionvol1.pdf, accessed November 2010.

U.S. House. Committee on Agriculture. *Agricultural Appropriation Bill.* 60th Cong., 1st sess., 1908. Public hearings.

————. *Press Agency in the Department of Agriculture.* 63rd Cong., 2nd sess., 1914. H. Rep. 1092.

U.S. House. Committee on Appropriations. *Agriculture Department Appropriation Bill for 1944.* 78th Cong., 1st sess., 1943. Public hearings.

————. *Department of Agriculture Appropriation Bill, Fiscal Year 1944.* 78th Cong., 1st sess., 1943. H. Rep. 354.

————. *Department of Agriculture Appropriation Bill, Fiscal Year 1945.* 78th Cong., 2nd sess., 1944. H. Rep. 1271.

————. *Department of Agriculture Appropriation Bill, Fiscal Year 1948.* 80th Cong., 1st sess., 1947. H. Rep. 450.

————. *Department of Agriculture and Related Agencies Appropriation Bill, 1964.* 88th Cong., 1st sess., 1963. H. Rep. 355.

————. *Department of Defense Appropriation Bill, 1952.* 82nd Cong., 1st sess., 1951. H. Rep. 790.

————. *Department of Defense Appropriations for 1972: Operation and Maintenance, Part 4.* 92nd Cong., 1st sess., 1971. Public hearings.

————. *Department of Justice Appropriation Bill for 1936.* 74th Cong., 1st sess., 1934. Public hearings.

————. *Department of Justice Appropriation Bill for 1937.* 74th Cong., 2nd sess., 1936. Public hearings.

————. *Department of Labor, Federal Security Agency, and Related Independent Offices Appropriation Bill, Fiscal Year 1941.* 76th Cong., 3rd sess., 1940. H. Rep. 1822.

————. *Independent Offices Appropriation Bill, 1939.* 75th Cong., 3rd sess., 1938. H. Rep. 1662.

————. *Interior Department Appropriation Bill for 1939, Part I.* 75th Cong., 3rd sess., 1938. Public hearings.

———. *Interior Department Appropriation Bill, Fiscal Year 1939.* 75th Cong., 3rd sess., 1938. H. Rep. 1855.

———. *Interior Department Appropriation Bill for 1940,* Part I. 76th Cong., 1st sess., 1939. Public hearings.

———. *Interior Department Appropriation Bill for 1941,* Part I. 76th Cong., 3rd sess., 1940. Public hearings.

———. *Interior Department Appropriation Bill, 1941.* 76th Cong., 3rd sess., 1940. H. Rep. 1709.

———. *Interior Department Appropriation Bill for 1947,* Part 1. 79th Cong., 2nd sess., 1946. Public hearings.

———. *Interior Department Appropriation Bill, 1947.* 79th Cong., 2nd sess., 1946. H. Rep. 1984.

———. *Interior Department Appropriation Bill for 1947,* Part 2. 79th Cong., 2nd sess., 1946. Public hearings.

———. *Interior Department Appropriation Bill, 1954.* 83rd Cong., 1st sess., 1953. H. Rep. 314.

———. *National War Agencies Appropriation Bill for 1944.* 78th Cong., 1st sess., 1943. Public hearings.

———. *Third Deficiency Appropriation Bill, 1919.* 65th Cong., 3rd sess., 1919. Public hearings.

———. *Third Deficiency Appropriation Bill, 1919.* 66th Cong., 1st sess., 1919. Public hearings.

———. *Third Deficiency Appropriation Bill, Fiscal Year 1919.* 65th Cong., 3rd sess., 1919. H. Rep. 1148.

———. *Third Deficiency Appropriation Bill, Fiscal Year 1919.* 66th Cong., 1st sess., 1919. H. Rep. 11.

———. *Treasury and Post Office Departments Appropriation Bill, Fiscal Year 1944.* 78th Cong., 1st sess., 1943. H. Rep. 87.

U.S. House. Committee on Armed Services. *Allegations of Improper Lobbying by Department of Defense Personnel of the C-5B and B-1B Aircraft and Sale to Saudi Arabia of the Airborne Warning and Control System.* 97th Cong., 2nd sess., 1982. Hearing HASC 97-65.

———. *Allegations of Improper Lobbying by Department of Defense Personnel of the C-5B and B-1B Aircraft and Sale to Saudi Arabia of the Airborne Warning and Control System.* 97th Cong., 2nd sess., 1982. Committee Print 24, Report of the Investigations Subcommittee.

U.S. House. Committee on Expenditures in the Agricultural Department. *Expenditures in the Department of Agriculture.* 59th Cong., 2nd sess., 1907. H. Rep. 8147.

U.S. House. Committee on Expenditures in the Executive Departments, Publicity and Propaganda Subcommittee. *Investigation of the Participation of Federal Officials in the Formation and Operation of Health Workshops.* 80th Cong., 1st sess., 1947. H. Rep. 786.

U.S. House. Committee on Expenditures in the Executive Departments, Publicity and Propaganda Subcommittee. *Final Report.* 80th Cong., 2nd sess., 1948. H. Rep. 2474.

———. *Investigation of Agricultural Adjustment Agency and Production and Marketing Administration Publicity and Propaganda in Nebraska.* 80th Cong., 2nd sess., 1948. H. Rep. 1365.

———. *Investigation of Bureau of Reclamation, Department of the Interior.* 80th Cong., 2nd sess., 1948. H. Rep. 2458.

———. *Investigation of Participation of Federal Officials of the Department of the Army in Publicity and Propaganda, as it Relates to Universal Military Training.* 80th Cong., 2nd sess., 1948. H. Rep. 1510.

U.S. House. Committee on Government Operations. *Administration of the Freedom of Information Act; Twenty-First Report.* 92nd Cong., 2nd sess., 1972. H. Rep. 92–1419.

———. *U.S. Government Information Policies and Practices—Administration and Operation of the Freedom of Information Act.* 92nd Cong., 2nd sess., 1972. Public hearings.

U.S. House. Committee on Government Reform and Oversight. *H.R. 3078, Federal Agency Anti-Lobbying Act.* 104th Cong., 2nd sess., 1996. Public hearings.

U.S. House. Committee on Rules. *Department Press Agents.* 62nd Cong., 2nd sess., 1912. Public hearings.

U.S. House. Committee on the Census. *Press Bureau, Bureau of the Census.* 61st Cong., 2nd sess., 1910. H. Rep. 296.

U.S. House. Committee on the District of Columbia. *To Prohibit Raising Funds for Lobbying Purposes.* 62nd Cong., 2nd sess., 1912. H. Rep. 543.

U.S. House. Committee on the Judiciary. *Revision of Title 18, United States Code.* 80th Cong., 1st sess., 1947. H. Rep. 304.

U.S. House. Select Committee on Lobbying Activities. *General Interim Report.* 81st Cong., 2nd sess., 1950. H. Rep. 3138.

———. *Legislative Activities of Executive Agencies,* Part 10. 81st Cong., 2nd sess., 1950. Public hearings.

———. *Report and Recommendations on Federal Lobbying Act.* 81st Cong., 2nd sess., 1951. H. Rep. 3239.

———. *The Role of Lobbying in Representative Self-Government,* Part 1. 81st Cong., 2nd sess., 1950. Public hearings.

U.S. House. Special Committee to Investigate the National Labor Relations Board. *Intermediate Report, Minority Views on the Investigation of the National Labor Relations Board.* 76th Cong., 3rd sess., 1940. H. Rep. 1902, Part 2.

———. *National Labor Relations Act.* 76th Cong., 3rd sess., 1940. H. Rep. 3109, Part 1.

U.S. Senate. *A Statement of the Attendance of Members of the Forest Service at Meetings and Conventions during 1907.* 60th Cong., 1st sess., 1908. S. Doc. 485.

———. *Attendance of Members of Forest Service at Meetings and Conventions during 1907.* 60th Cong., 1st sess., 1908. S. Doc. 449.

U.S. Senate. Committee on Agriculture and Forestry. *Agricultural Appropriation Bill.* 60th Cong., 1st sess., 1908. Public hearings.

U.S. Senate. Committee on Appropriations. *Agricultural Appropriation Bill for 1944.* 78th Cong., 1st sess., 1943. Public hearings.

———. *Agricultural Appropriation Bill, 1944.* 78th Cong., 1st sess., 1943. S. Rep. 287.

———. *Agricultural Appropriation Bill, 1945.* 78th Cong., 2nd sess., 1944. S. Rep. 886.

———. *Agricultural Appropriation Bill, 1948.* 80th Cong., 1st sess., 1947. S. Rep. 474.

———. *Department of Agriculture and Related Agencies Appropriation Bill, 1964.* 88th Cong., 1st sess., 1963. S. Rep. 497.

———. *Department of the Interior and Related Agencies Appropriation Bill, 1978.* 95th Cong., 1st sess., 1977. S. Rep. 95–276.

———. *Departments of Labor and Health, Education, and Welfare and Related Agencies Appropriations for Fiscal Year 1974.* 93rd Cong., 1st sess., 1973. Public hearings.

———. *Departments of Labor and Health, Education, and Welfare, and Related Agencies Appropriation Bill, 1974.* 93rd Cong., 1st sess., 1973. S. Rep. 93–414.

———. *Departments of State, Justice, Commerce, and Labor Appropriation Bill for 1937.* 74th Cong., 2nd sess., 1936. Public hearings.

———. *Departments of State, Justice, and Commerce, the Judiciary, and Related Agencies Appropriation Bill, 1979.* 95th Cong., 2nd sess., 1978. S. Rep. 95–1043.

———. *Independent Offices Appropriation Bill, 1942.* 77th Cong., 1st sess., 1941. S. Rep. 69.

———. *Interior Department Appropriation Bill for 1947.* 79th Cong., 2nd sess., 1946. Public hearings.

———. *Interior Department Appropriation Bill, 1947.* 79th Cong., 2nd sess., 1946. S. Rep. 1434.

———. *Interior Department Appropriation Bill, 1952.* 82nd Cong., 1st sess., 1951. S. Rep. 499.

———. *Interior Department Appropriation Bill, 1954.* 83rd Cong., 1st sess., 1953. S. Rep. 445.

———. *Labor-Federal Security Appropriation Bill, 1952.* 82nd Cong., 1st sess., 1951. S. Rep. 386.

———. *Panama Canal Appropriation.* 59th Cong., 1st sess., 1905. S. Doc. 69. Public hearings.

———. *Second Supplemental Appropriation Bill for 1962.* 87th Cong., 2nd sess., 1962. Public hearings.

———. *Second Supplemental Appropriation Bill, 1962.* 87th Cong., 2nd sess., 1962. S. Rep. 1341.

———. *Supplemental Appropriation Bill, 1952.* 82nd Cong., 1st sess., 1951. S. Rep. 891.

———. *Treasury and Post Office Departments Appropriation Bill, Fiscal Year 1952.* 82nd Cong., 1st sess., 1951. S. Rep. 550.

———, Subcommittee on Senate Resolution 223. *Transfer of Employees, Conserving Office Space, Relief in Housing Conditions, and Promotion of Economy and Efficiency.* 77th Cong., 2nd sess., 1942. S. Rep. 1554.

U.S. Senate. Committee on Banking and Currency, Subcommittee on Housing and Rents. *Propaganda and Publicity in the Office of Rent Control.* 80th Cong., 2nd sess., 1948. Public hearings. Unpublished, CIS (80) SB-T.107.

U.S. Senate. Committee on Finance. *Nominations of James S. Dwight, Jr., William A. Morrill, and Lewis M. Helm.* 93rd Cong., 1st sess., 1973. Public hearings.

U.S. Senate. Committee on Governmental Affairs. *Lack of Accountability in Government Public Information and Publishing Programs.* 96th Cong., 1st sess., 1979. Committee Print.

U.S. Senate. Committee on Military Affairs. *Establishment of Military Justice.* 66th Cong., 1st sess., 1919. Public hearings.

U.S. Senate. Committee on Printing. *The Public Printing.* 52nd Cong., 1st sess., 1892. S. Rep. 18.

U.S. Senate. Committee on Public Lands. *Forest-Reserve Lands.* 58th Cong., 2nd sess., 1904. Public hearings.

U.S. Senate. Select Committee to Investigate the Executive Agencies of the Government. *Investigation of Executive Agencies of the Government: Preliminary Report.* 75th Cong., 1st sess., 1937. S. Rep. 1275.

BOOKS AND ARTICLES

Adams, Katherine H. *Progressive Politics and the Training of America's Persuaders.* Mahwah, N.J.: Lawrence Erlbaum, 1999.

Arnold, R. Douglas. *Congress and the Bureaucracy: A Theory of Influence.* New Haven, Conn.: Yale University Press, 1979.

———. *The Logic of Congressional Action.* New Haven, Conn.: Yale University Press, 1990.

Axelrod, Alan. *Selling the Great War: The Making of American Propaganda.* New York: Palgrave Macmillan, 2009.

Beisner, Robert L. *Dean Acheson: A Life in the Cold War.* New York: Oxford University Press, 2006.

Berman, Daniel M. *In Congress Assembled: The Legislative Process in the National Government.* New York: Macmillan, 1964.

Bernhard, Nancy E. "Clearer Than the Truth: Public Affairs Television and the State Department's Domestic Information Campaigns, 1947–1952." *Diplomatic History* 21, no. 4 (Fall 1997): 545–567.

Berry, Jeffrey M. "Nonprofits and Civic Engagement." *Public Administration Review* 65, no. 5 (September/October 2005): 568–578.

Bertelli, Anthony M., and Lawrence E. Lynn, Jr. *Madison's Managers: Public Administration and the Constitution.* Baltimore: Johns Hopkins University Press, 2006.

Beyle, Herman C. *Governmental Reporting in Chicago.* Chicago: University of Chicago Press, 1928.

Bishop, Joseph Bucklin. *Notes and Anecdotes of Many Years.* 1925; reprint, Freeport, N.Y.: Books for Libraries Press, 1970.

———. *The Panama Gateway.* 1913; reprint, New York: C. Scribner's Sons, 1922.

Bishop, Joseph Bucklin, and Farnham Bishop. *Goethals: Genius of the Panama Canal.* New York: Harper and Row, 1930.

Boot, Max. *The Savage Wars of Peace: Small Wars and the Rise of American Power.* New York: Basic Books, 2002.

Brown, MacAlister. "The Demise of State Department Public Opinion Polls: A Study in Legislative Oversight." *Midwest Journal of Political Science* 5, no. 1 (February 1961): 1–17.

Burns, James McGregor. *Roosevelt: The Fox and the Lion.* New York: Harcourt, Brace and World, 1956.

Burrough, Bryan. *Public Enemies: America's Greatest Crime Wave and the Birth of the FBI, 1933–34.* 2004; reprint, New York: Penguin, 2009.

Caro, Robert A. *Master of the Senate.* Vol. 3 of *The Years of Lyndon Johnson.* New York: Alfred A. Knopf, 2002.

Carpenter, Daniel P. *The Forging of Bureaucratic Autonomy: Reputations, Networks, and Policy Innovation in Executive Agencies, 1862–1928.* Princeton, N.J.: Princeton University Press, 2001.

Catton, Bruce. "Handouts." In *Dateline: Washington. The Story of National Affairs Journalism in the Life and Times of the National Press Club,* edited by Cabell Phillips, 156–170. Garden City, N.Y.: Doubleday, 1949.

———. *The War Lords of Washington.* 1948; reprint, New York: Greenwood, 1969.

Conference on the Press, held at Princeton University, April 23–25, 1931, under the auspices of the School of Public and International Affairs. Washington, D.C.: Printing Corporation of America, 1931.

Cook, Fred J. *The Warfare State.* New York: Macmillan, 1962.

Cook, Rufus George. "A Study of the Political Career of Weldon Brinton Heyburn through His First Term in the United States Senate, 1852–1909." Master's thesis, University of Idaho, 1964.

Croffut, William A. *An American Procession, 1855–1914: A Personal Chronicle of Famous Men.* 1931; reprint, Freeport, N.Y.: Books for Libraries Press, 1968.

Cummings, Grace. "Working with Congress: Building Relationships across the Constitutional Divide." In *The Trusted Leader: Building the Relationships that Make Government Work,* edited by Terry Newell, Grant Reeher, and Peter Ronayne, 213–234. Washington, D.C.: CQ Press, 2008.

Cutlip, Scott M. "The Unseen Power: A Brief History of Public Relations." In *The Handbook of Strategic Public Relations and Integrated Communications,* edited by Clarke L. Caywood, 15–33. New York: McGraw-Hill, 1997.

———. *The Unseen Power: Public Relations. A History.* Hillsdale, N.J.: Lawrence Erlbaum, 1994.

Darrah, William Culp. *Powell of the Colorado*. 1951; reprint, Princeton, N.J.: Princeton University Press, 1969.

Delorme, Denise E., and Fred Fedler. "Journalists' Hostility toward Public Relations: An Historical Analysis." *Public Relations Review* 29, no. 2 (March 2003): 99–124.

DeSanto, Barbara J. "Public Affairs: An American Perspective." *Journal of Public Affairs* 1, no. 1 (January 2001): 38–43.

Drury, Allen. *A Senate Journal, 1943–1945*. 1963; reprint, New York: Da Capo, 1972.

Dyke, Richard W., and Francis X. Gannon. *Chet Holifield: Master Legislator and Nuclear Statesman*. Lanham, Md.: University Press of America, 1996.

Emmerich, Herbert. *Essays on Federal Reorganization*. University [Tuscaloosa]: University of Alabama Press, 1950.

Engstrom, Richard L., and Thomas G. Walker. "Statutory Restraints on Administrative Lobbying—'Legal Fiction.'" *Journal of Public Law* 19, no. 1 (1970): 89–103.

Fenno, Richard F., Jr. *The President's Cabinet: An Analysis in the Period from Wilson to Eisenhower*. Cambridge, Mass.: Harvard University Press, 1959.

Fisher, Louis. *The Politics of Shared Power: Congress and the Executive*. 4th ed. College Station: Texas A&M University Press, 1998.

Fitzpatrick, Dick. "Public Information Activities of Government Agencies." *Public Opinion Quarterly* 11, no. 4 (Winter 1947–1948): 530–539.

Fleming, Thomas. *The New Dealers' War: Franklin D. Roosevelt and the War within World War II*. New York: Basic, 2001.

Freeman, J. Leiper. *The Political Process: Executive Bureau-Legislative Committee Relations*. Rev. ed. New York: Random House, 1965.

Frischknecht, Reed L. "State Extension Services and the Administration of Farm Price and Income Support Programs: A Case Study in Federal-State Relations." *Western Political Quarterly* 10, no. 2 (June 1957): 416–441.

Gaus, John M., and Leon O. Wolcott. *Public Administration and the United States Department of Agriculture*. Chicago: Public Administration Service, 1940.

Goodman, Felice M. "Origins of a Continuing Conflict: Executive vs. Congress over the Public Relations Function in Government, 1900–1913." Master's thesis, University of Wisconsin–Madison, 1967.

Gould, Lewis L. *The Modern American Presidency*. Lawrence: University Press of Kansas, 2003.

Graham, George A. "Trends in Teaching of Public Administration." *Public Administration Review* 10, no. 2 (Spring 1950): 69–77.

Hanson, Elisha. "Official Propaganda and the New Deal." *Annals of the American Academy of Political and Social Science* 179 (May 1935): 176–186.

Harding, T. Swann. "Genesis of One 'Government Propaganda Mill.'" *Public Opinion Quarterly* 11, no. 2 (Summer 1947): 227–235.

———. "Informational Techniques of the Department of Agriculture." *Public Opinion Quarterly* 1, no. 1 (January 1937): 83–96.

Harness, Forest A. "Federal Thought Control: A Study in Government by Propaganda." *American Affairs* 10, no. 2 (April/Spring 1948): Supplement.

Harris, Joseph P. *Congress and the Legislative Process.* 2nd ed. New York: McGraw-Hill, 1972.

Harrison, Robert. *Congress, Progressive Reform, and the New American State.* Cambridge, U.K.: Cambridge University Press, 2004.

Heinemann, Ronald L. *Harry Byrd of Virginia.* Charlottesville: University Press of Virginia, 1996.

Herold, David. "Historical Perspectives on Government Communication." In *Informing the People: A Public Affairs Handbook,* edited by Lewis M. Helm, Ray Eldon Hiebert, Michael R. Naver, and Kenneth Rabin, 14–21. New York: Longman, 1981.

Herring, E. Pendleton. "Official Publicity under the New Deal." *Annals of the American Academy of Political and Social Science* 179 (May 1935): 167–175.

———. *Public Administration and the Public Interest.* 1936; reprint, New York: Russell and Russell, 1967.

———. "Social Forces and the Reorganization of the Federal Bureaucracy." *Southwestern Social Science Quarterly* 15, no. 3 (December 1934): 185–200.

Hilderbrand, Robert C. *Power and the People: Executive Management of Public Opinion in Foreign Affairs, 1897–1921.* Chapel Hill: University of North Carolina Press, 1981.

Holtzman, Abraham. *Legislative Liaison: Executive Leadership in Congress.* Chicago: Rand McNally, 1970.

Horn, Stephen. *Unused Power: The Work of the Senate Committee on Appropriations.* Washington, D.C.: Brookings Institution, 1970.

Houston, David F. *Eight Years with Wilson's Cabinet, 1913 to 1920: With a Personal Estimate of the President.* 1928; reprint, St. Claire Shores, Mich.: Scholarly Press, 1970.

Howard, L. V. "The Agricultural Referendum." *Public Administration Review* 2, no. 1 (Winter 1942): 9–26.

Hutchinson, Wallace I. "Public Relations: What Have We Bought and Where Are We Headed?" *Journal of Forestry* 29, no. 3 (March 1931): 474–483.

John, Richard R. *Spreading the News: The American Postal System from Franklin to Morse.* Cambridge, Mass.: Harvard University Press, 1995.

Kahn, Jonathan. *Budgeting Democracy: State Building and Citizenship in America, 1890–1928.* Ithaca, N.Y.: Cornell University Press, 1997.

Kantrowitz, Stephen. *Ben Tillman and the Reconstruction of White Supremacy.* Chapel Hill: University of North Carolina Press, 2000.

Kaufman, Herbert. *The Forest Ranger: A Study in Administrative Behavior.* 1960; reprint, Washington, D.C.: Resources for the Future, 2006.

Kell, Thomas. "Research and Evaluation: The Wilderness of Government Public Relations." *Journal of Public Communication* 4 (Winter 1978): 1–11.

Kent, Frank R. *Without Grease: Political Behavior, 1934–1936, and a Blueprint for America's Most Vital Presidential Election.* New York: William Morrow, 1936.

Key, V. O., Jr. *Politics, Parties, and Pressure Groups.* 5th ed. New York: Thomas Y. Crowell, 1964.

Kirst, Michael W. *Congress without Passing Laws: Congress' Nonstatutory Techniques for Appropriations Control.* Chapel Hill: University of North Carolina Press, 1969.

Knapp, David C. "Congressional Control of Agricultural Conservation Policy: A Case Study of the Appropriations Process." *Political Science Quarterly* 71, no. 2 (June 1956): 257–281.

Kosar, Kevin R. "The Executive Branch and Propaganda: The Limits of Legal Restrictions." *Presidential Studies Quarterly* 35, no. 4 (December 2005): 784–797.

Larson, Cedric. "How Much Federal Publicity Is There?" *Public Opinion Quarterly* 2, no. 4 (October 1938): 636–644.

Lee, Mordecai. "A Case Study of Congressional Hostility to Agency Public Relations: The Federal Reserve and Senator Heflin, 1922." *Public Relations Review* 35, no. 3 (September 2009): 291–293.

———. "Congressional Controversy over the Federal Prohibition Bureau's Public Relations, 1922." *Public Relations Review* 34, no. 3 (September 2008): 276–78.

———. *The First Presidential Communications Agency: FDR's Office of Government Reports.* Albany: State University of New York Press, 2005.

———, ed. *Government Public Relations: A Reader.* Boca Raton, Fla.: CRC Press/ Taylor and Francis, 2008.

———. "Government Public Relations during Herbert Hoover's Presidency." *Public Relations Review* 36, no. 1 (March 2010): 56–58.

———. "Herman Beyle and James McCamy: Founders of the Study of Public Relations in Public Administration, 1928–1939." *Public Voices* 11, no. 2 (2010): 26–46.

———. "Intersectoral Differences in Public Affairs: The Duty of Public Reporting in Public Administration." *Journal of Public Affairs* 2, no. 2 (May 2002): 33–43.

———. "Origins of the Epithet 'Government by Public Relations': Revisiting Bruce Catton's *War Lords of Washington*, 1948." *Public Relations Review* 35, no. 4 (November 2009): 388–394.

———. "Political-Administrative Relations in State Government: A Legislative Perspective." *International Journal of Public Administration* 29, no. 12 (2006): 1021–1047.

———. "Public Affairs Enters the U.S. President's Subcabinet: Creating the First Assistant Secretary for Public Affairs (1944–1953) and Subsequent Developments." *Journal of Public Affairs* 8, no. 3 (August 2008): 185–194.

———. "A Public Relations Program Even Congress Could Love: Federal Information Centers." *Public Relations Review* 30, no. 1 (March 2004): 61–73.

———. "The Rise and Fall of the Institute for Government Public Information Research, 1978–1981." *Public Relations Review* 32, no. 2 (June 2006): 118–124.

———. "Too Much Bureaucracy or Too Little? Congressional Treatment of Defense Department Legislative Liaison, 1950s–1990s." *Public Administration and Management* 14, no. 2 (2009): 323–361. www.spaef.com/article.php?id= 1116, accessed November 2010.

———. "When Congress Tried to Cut Pentagon Public Relations: A Lesson from History." *Public Relations Review* 26, no. 2 (Summer 2000): 131–154.

Lindsay, Robert. *This High Name: Public Relations and the U.S. Marine Corps.* Madison: University of Wisconsin Press, 1956.

Lippmann, Walter. *Public Opinion.* 1922; reprint, New York: Free Press, 1997.

Liu, Brooke Fisher, and J. Suzanne Horsley. "The Government Communication Decision Wheel: Toward a Public Relations Model for the Public Sector." *Journal of Public Relations Research* 19, no. 4 (2007): 377–393.

Mansfield, Harvey C., and Associates. *A Short History of OPA.* Washington, D.C.: Office of Temporary Controls, Office of Price Administration, 1948.

Marbut, F. B. *News from the Capital: The Story of Washington Reporting.* Carbondale: Southern Illinois University Press, 1971.

Mayhew, David R. *Congress: The Electoral Connection.* 2nd ed. New Haven, Conn.: Yale University Press, 2004.

McCamy, James L. *Government Publicity: Its Practice in Federal Administration.* Chicago: University of Chicago Press, 1939.

———. "Public Relations in Public Administration." In *Current Issues in Library Administration: Papers Presented before the Library Institute of the University of Chicago, August 1–12, 1938,* edited by Carleton B. Joeckel, 301–321. Chicago: University of Chicago Press, 1939.

McCartney, Laton. *The Teapot Dome Scandal: How Big Oil Bought the Harding White House and Tried to Steal the Country.* New York: Random House, 2008.

McCullough, David G. *The Path between the Seas: The Creation of the Panama Canal, 1870–1914.* 1977; reprint, New York: Simon and Schuster, 1999.

McGeary, M. Nelson. *Gifford Pinchot, Forester-Politician.* 1960; reprint, New York: Garland, 1979.

McGerr, Michael. *The Decline of Popular Politics: The American North, 1865–1928.* New York: Oxford University Press, 1986.

———. *A Fierce Discontent: The Rise and Fall of the Progressive Movement in America, 1870–1920.* New York: Free Press, 2003.

Meier, Kenneth J., and Laurence J. O'Toole, Jr. *Bureaucracy in a Democratic State: A Governance Perspective.* Baltimore: Johns Hopkins University Press, 2006.

Merrill, Milton R. *Reed Smoot: Apostle in Politics.* Logan: Utah State University Press, 1990.

Michael, George [pseudo.]. *Handout.* New York: G. P. Putnam's Sons, 1935.

Miller, Char. *Gifford Pinchot and the Making of Modern Environmentalism.* Washington, D.C.: Island Press, 2001.

Murphy, Thomas P., Donald E. Nuechterlein, and Ronald J. Stupak. *Inside the Bureaucracy: The View from the Assistant Secretary's Desk.* Boulder, Colo.: Westview, 1978.

National Committee on Public Reporting. *Public Reporting.* Publication No. 19. New York: Municipal Administration Service, 1931.

O'Reilly, Kenneth. "A New Deal for the FBI: The Roosevelt Administration, Crime Control, and National Security." *Journal of American History* 69, no. 3 (December 1982): 638–658.

Orren, Karen, and Stephen Skowronek. *The Search for American Political Development.* Cambridge, U.K.: Cambridge University Press, 2004.

Parkinson, C. Northcote. *Parkinson's Law and Other Studies in Administration.* New York: Ballantine, 1957.

Patterson, James T. *Congressional Conservatism and the New Deal: The Growth of the Conservative Coalition in Congress, 1933–1939.* 1967; reprint, Westport, Conn.: Greenwood, 1981.

Peters, B. Guy. "The Necessity and Difficulty of Comparison in Public Administration." *Asian Journal of Public Administration* 12, no. 1 (June 1990): 3–28.

Pimlott, J. A. R. *Public Relations and American Democracy.* 1951; reprint, Port Washington, N.Y.: Kennikat, 1972.

Pinchot, Gifford. *Breaking New Ground.* 1947; reprint, Washington, D.C.: Island Press, 1998.

Pinkett, Harold T. *Gifford Pinchot: Private and Public Forester.* Urbana: University of Illinois Press, 1970.

Ponder, Stephen. "Executive Publicity and Congressional Resistance, 1905–1913: Congress and the Roosevelt Administration's PR Men." *Congress and the Presidency* 13, no. 2 (Autumn 1986): 177–186.

———. "Gifford Pinchot, Press Agent for Forestry." *Journal of Forest History* 31, no. 1 (January 1987): 26–35.

———. *Managing the Press: Origins of the Media Presidency, 1897–1933.* New York: St. Martin's, 1999.

———. "Progressive Drive to Shape Public Opinion, 1898–1913." *Public Relations Review* 16, no. 3 (Fall 1990): 94–104.

———. "'Publicity in the Interest of the People': Theodore Roosevelt's Conservation Crusade." *Presidential Studies Quarterly* 20, no. 3 (Summer 1990): 547–555.

Prince, Huberta A., ed. *The Washington Book Mart.* New York: Oceana, 1949.

Proctor, Clarance B. "First Marine Corps Publicity Bureau." *Recruiters' Bulletin* 6, no. 8 (August 1920): 5–6.

Redman, Eric. *The Dance of Legislation.* 1973; reprint, Seattle: University of Washington Press, 2001.

Riggs, Fred W. "Bureaucracy and the Constitution." *Public Administration Review* 54, no. 1 (January/February 1994): 65–72.

Ritchie, Donald A. *Electing FDR: The New Deal Campaign of 1932.* Lawrence: University Press of Kansas, 2007.

———. *Press Gallery: Congress and the Washington Correspondents.* Cambridge, Mass.: Harvard University Press, 1991.

———. *Reporting from Washington: The History of the Washington Press Corps.* New York: Oxford University Press, 2005.

Roberts, Alasdair. *The Collapse of Fortress Bush: The Crisis of Authority in American Government.* New York: New York University Press, 2008.

Rosapepe, Joseph S. "Neither Pinkertons nor Publicity Men." *Public Relations Journal* 27, no. 10 (October 1971): 12–17, 49–50.

Rosten, Leo C. *The Washington Correspondents.* 1937; reprint, New York: Arno, 1974.

Rourke, Francis E. *Bureaucracy, Politics, and Public Policy.* [1st ed.] Boston: Little, Brown, 1969.

———. *Bureaucracy, Politics, and Public Policy.* 3rd ed. Boston: Little, Brown, 1984.

———. *Secrecy and Publicity: Dilemmas of Democracy.* Baltimore: Johns Hopkins Press, 1961.

Runyan, Anne S. "Development of Public Information Laws." In *Informing the People: A Public Affairs Handbook,* edited by Lewis M. Helm, Ray Eldon Hiebert, Michael R. Naver, and Kenneth Rabin, 53–59. New York: Longman, 1981.

Safire, William. *Safire's Political Dictionary.* New York: Oxford University Press, 2008.

Schattschneider, E. E. *The Semi-Sovereign People: A Realist's View of Democracy in America.* 1960; reprint, Fort Worth, Tex.: Harcourt Brace Jovanovich College Publishers, 1988.

Schick, Allen. "Congress and the 'Details' of Administration." *Public Administration Review* 36, no. 5 (September–October 1976): 516–528.

Sheehan, Neil. *A Fiery Peace in a Cold War: Bernard Schriever and the Ultimate Weapon.* New York: Random House, 2009.

Sheingate, Adam D. "'Publicity' and the Progressive-Era Origins of Modern Politics." *Critical Review* 19, nos. 2–3 (January 2007): 461–480.

Shipan, Charles R. "Congress and the Bureaucracy." In *The Legislative Branch,* edited by Paul J. Quirk and Sarah A. Binder, 432–458. New York: Oxford University Press, 2005.

Short, William D. "Effect of the Gillett Amendment of 1913 on the Public Information Activities of Federal Government Communicators." Master's thesis, Memphis State University, 1991.

Simon, Herbert A., Donald W. Smithburg, and Victor A. Thompson. *Public Administration.* 1950; reprint, New Brunswick, N.J.: Transaction, 1991.

Smith, Darrell Hevenor. *The Forest Service: Its History, Activities and Organization.* 1930; reprint, New York: AMS Press, 1974.

Smith, James Allen. *Brookings at Seventy-Five.* Washington, D.C.: Brookings Institution, 1991.

Smith, Lester E. "Old-Time Publicity Bureaus." *Marines Magazine* 1, no. 6 (June 1916): 8.

Spitzer, Carlton E. "Information and Policy." In *The Voice of Government*, edited by Ray Eldon Hiebert and Carlton E. Spitzer, 51–65. New York: John Wiley and Sons, 1968.

Sproule, J. Michael. *Propaganda and Democracy: The American Experience of Media and Mass Persuasion.* Cambridge, U.K.: Cambridge University Press, 1997.

Stedman, Alfred D. "The Development of an Informational Policy." In *Agricultural Adjustment, 1937–38* [Annual Report of the Administrator of the Agricultural Adjustment Administration], 226–243. Washington, D.C.: GPO, 1939.

———. "Public Information and the Preservation of Democracy." In U.S. Department of Agriculture, *The Yearbook of Agriculture, 1940: Farmers in a Changing World.* 1940; reprint, New York: Arno Press, 1976.

Steen, Harold K. *The U.S. Forest Service: A History.* 1976; reprint, Durham, N.C.: Forest History Society in association with University of Washington Press, 2004.

Stegner, Wallace. *Beyond the Hundredth Meridian: John Wesley Powell and the Second Opening of the West.* 1954; reprint, New York: Penguin, 1992.

Stiles, T. J. *The First Tycoon: The Epic Life of Cornelius Vanderbilt.* New York: Alfred A. Knopf, 2009.

Terrell, John Upton. *The Man Who Rediscovered America: A Biography of John Wesley Powell.* New York: Weybright and Talley, 1969.

Wagner, Allen. "Government Public Relations." *Public Relations Journal* 9, no. 1 (January 1953): 19–20, 33.

Walton, Douglas. *Media Argumentation: Dialectic, Persuasion, and Rhetoric.* New York: Cambridge University Press, 2007.

Watson, Robert J. *Into the Missile Age, 1956–1960.* Vol. 4, *History of the Office of the Secretary of Defense.* Washington, D.C.: Historical Office, Office of the Secretary of Defense, Department of Defense, 1997.

Webb, Aileen, and Charles T. Salmon. "United States Government and Public Relations." In *Encyclopedia of Public Relations*, edited by Robert L. Heath, Vol. 2, 877–880. Thousand Oaks, Calif.: Sage, 2005.

White, Helen M. *The Tale of a Comet and Other Stories.* St. Paul: Minnesota Historical Society Press, 1984.

White, Leonard D. *The Republican Era, 1869–1901.* Vol. 4, *A Study in Administrative History.* New York: Macmillan, 1958.

———. *Trends in Public Administration.* New York: McGraw-Hill, 1933.

Yarwood, Dean L., and Ben M. Enis. "Problems in Regulating Federal Executive Branch Publicity and Advertising Programs." *American Review of Public Administration* 18, no. 1 (March 1988): 29–45.

INDEX

Accountability, 9, 222
Advocacy, 11, 163–164, 171, 221. *See also* Lobbying; Propaganda
African Americans, 73
Agency public relations: acceptable vs. unacceptable forms of, 19–20, 161, 180–181, 215–223; action-reaction relationship with Congress, 13–14; and advocacy, 171, 221; by Agricultural Adjustment Agency, 144–146, 163–164; and autonomy, 6, 10, 11, 13, 14, 201, 229; by Bureau of Reclamation, 166–167; by Census Bureau, 68–70, 248n17, 249n29; congressional rationale for opposing, 10–11, 19–26, 98–99, 178; counter-strategies to Congress, 175, 224, 226; by Defense Department, 220, 228, 287–288n12; digital, 228, 232; by FBI, 149; for forestry conservation, 51–54; under Franklin Roosevelt administration, 95, 145–146; goals

and uses of, 8–9, 229; impact on Congress of, 8, 10–11; and information dissemination, 216, 218–219, 221, 223, 227, 230–232; by Interior Department, 152, 171, 223; by Justice Department, 148–149; and lobbying, 11, 101; news media critique of, 25–26; nineteenth-century view of, 136; opaqueness of budgets and titles, 214; by Panama Canal Commission, 3, 46–47; portrayed as manifestation of bureaucracy, 23–24; portrayed as propaganda, 20–22, 159–160; portrayed as waste of tax dollars, 22–23; power of, 7–8, 30, 204; pragmatic uses of, 8–9, 14, 145, 229; and public opinion, 7, 24, 33, 35, 36, 43, 44, 51, 57, 67, 81–82, 178; by State Department, 90, 250n43; as survival tactic, 10, 201; under Taft administration, 67, 68; under Theodore Roosevelt